Mississippi Confederate Grave Registrations

M–Z

Betty Couch Wiltshire

HERITAGE BOOKS
2012

HERITAGE BOOKS
AN IMPRINT OF HERITAGE BOOKS, INC.

Books, CDs, and more—Worldwide

For our listing of thousands of titles see our website
at
www.HeritageBooks.com

Published 2012 by
HERITAGE BOOKS, INC.
Publishing Division
100 Railroad Ave. #104
Westminster, Maryland 21157

Copyright © 1991 Betty Couch Wiltshire

Other Heritage Books by the author:

CD: *Early Mississippi Records*

CD: *Early Mississippi Records: Volume 2*

Holmes County, Mississippi, Pioneers

Marriages and Deaths from Mississippi Newspapers: Volume 2, 1801–1850

Marriages and Deaths from Mississippi Newspapers: Volume 3, 1813–1850

Marriages and Deaths from Mississippi Newspapers: Volume 4, 1850–1861

Mississippi Index of Wills, 1800–1900

International Standard Book Numbers
Paperbound: 978-1-55613-526-2
Clothbound: 978-0-7884-9423-9

TABLE OF CONTENTS

INTRODUCTION

A little known source of Mississippi genealogical information are the confederate grave registrations available on microfilm at the Mississippi Department of Archives and History. These are records of confederate soldiers, many serving in other states during the Civil War, but who died and are buried in Mississippi. Death dates range from Civil War days into the 1930's.

Though some tombstones give only the soldiers name and service unit, the registration card has additional information of interest to genealogical researchers. A sample card follows. As you'll see, I've included only a small part of the information in this book, with the hope that readers will be able to use it as an index and be able to determine whether or not a registration is available for their ancestors. If so, a copy of the card should be ordered from the archives.

I copied the names in the order they will be found on the microfilm. The names are generally listed in alphabetical order, but in some cases are out of place. If they are very far from the correct listing I've included a note referring the reader to where it will be found, but if they are near where they should be I didn't.

Always remember that the information is only as accurate as the source. For example, I'm aware that some of the places of birth are incorrect because the counties that were given didn't exist at the date of birth, but I've copied the information as given on the registration card. Also, there were many cards that were blurred or otherwise difficult to read, so I may have made some errors in copying even though I attempted to be as accurate as humanly possible.

Betty Couch Wiltshire

ABBREVIATIONS

Postal abbreviations are used for states and countries. Other abbreviations are:

Adam	Adams	Lown	Lowndes
Alco	Alcorn	Madi	Madison
Amit	Amite	Mari	Marion
Atta	Attala	Mars	Marshall
Bent	Benton	Monr	Monroe
Calh	Calhoun	Mont	Montgomery
Carr	Carroll	Nesh	Neshoba
Cav	Cavalry	Newt	Newton
Chic	Chickasaw	Noxu	Noxubee
Choc	Choctaw	Okti	Oktibbeha
Clai	Clairborne	Pano	Panola
Clar	Clarke	Pear	Pearl River
Coah	Coahoma	Perr	Perry
Copi	Copiah	Pont	Pontotoc
Covi	Covington	Pren	Prentiss
DeSo	DeSoto	Rank	Rankin
Forr	Forrest	Scot	Scott
Fran	Franklin	Shar	Sharkey
Geor	George	Shrpshtr	Sharpshooter
Gree	Greene	Simp	Simpson
Gren	Grenada	Smit	Smith
Hanc	Hancock	Ston	Stone
Harr	Harrison	Sunf	Sunflower
Hind	Hinds	Swed	Sweden
Holm	Holmes	Tall	Tallahatchie
Inf	Infantry	Tipp	Tippah
Itaw	Itawamba	Tish	Tishomingo
Jack	Jackson	Unio	Union
Jasp	Jasper	Walt	Walthall
JeDa	Jefferson Davis	Wayn	Wayne
Jeff	Jefferson	Warr	Warren
Jone	Jones	Wash	Washington
Kemp	Kemper	Webs	Webster
Lafa	Lafayette	Wilk	Wilkinson
Lama	Lamar	Wins	Winston
Laud	Lauderdale	Yalo	Yalobusha
Lawr	Lawrence	Yazo	Yazoo
Leak	Leake		
Lefl	Leflore		
Linc	Lincoln		

SAMPLE REGISTRATION CARD

Name McAlister, B. F.
Home Address Ripley, MS
Next of Kin W. A. McAlister (s) Address Ripley, MS
Born 4-13-1839   At South Carolina
Date of Death 5-28-1911   Cause Sinus Trouble
Buried _____ At New Hope Cemetary
City 8 mi. South of Ripley, MS County Chickasaw
Grave No. ___ Lot ___ Block ___ Section ____
War Record Co. G. 1st South Carolina Regt. Inf.
Branch of Service Army CSA   Rank Pvt.
Enlisted 3-9-1861 Discharged 4-26-1865
Information Given By Relative
Remarks _____
Headstone _____

MISSISSIPPI CONFEDERATE GRAVE REGISTRATIONS

Name	Service Unit	Year of Birth/ Death	Co. Or State Of Birth	County Where Buried
McADAMS, I. P.	18th MS Cav.	1834-1912		Atta
McAFEE, John H.	Maj. Harper	1815-1890		Tall
McALISTER, B. F.	1st SC Inf.	1839-1911	SC	Tipp
McALISTER, W. A.	31st MS Inf.	1828-1917	Pont	Unio
McALISTER, W. E.	2nd MS Cav.	1847-1910	MS	Bent
McALLISTER, A. G.	7th MS Inf.	1843-1909	Fran	Unio
McALLISTER, A. H.	Ballentines Cav.	1846-1921	MS	Unio
McALLISTER, A. P.	11th MS Inf.	1846-1924	MS	Lee
McALLISTER, Charles G.	4th LA Inf.		Adam	Adam
McALLISTER, J. N.	1st MS Inf.	1838-1862	Monr	Monr
McALLISTER, Joshua	15th MS Inf.	1840-1902		Mont
McALLISTER, Thomas T.	23rd MS Inf.	1839-1914	Pont	Unio
McALLISTER, Thomas W.	48th MS Inf.	____-1872		Rank
McALLISTER, William A.	31st MS Inf.	1831-1924	Pont	Unio
McALPIN, James T.	1st MS Lt. Art.	1834-1923		Hind
McANALLY, B. F.	29th AL Cav.	1826-1898	AL	Tish
McANINCH, E. G.	29th MS Inf.	1843-1915	Tate	Tate
McANULTY, John Williams	23rd MS Inf.	1841-1912	Tish	Alco
McARNS, William	Lays MS Cav.	1845-1874	MS	Jeff
McARTHUR, C. C.	35th MS Inf.	1843-1913	MS	Choc
McARTHUR, Hiram	43rd MS Inf.	1830-1918	Kemp	Kemp
McARTHUR, Lott	3rd MS Inf.	1846-1921	MS	Lama
McARTHUR, Solomon	17th Cav.	1834-1891	MS	Hanc
McARTHUR, W. R.	13th MS Inf.	1842-1903	AL	Laud
McARTHUR, William	3rd MS Inf.	1823-1903		Hind
McBEATH, John C.	5th MS Inf.	1831-1910	MS	Nesh
McBETH, A. W.	5th MS Inf.	1813-1889	MS	Leak
McBETH, J. C.	40th MS Inf.	1832-1915	MS	Leak
McBETH, W. A.	6th MS Inf.	1835-1862	MS	Leak
McBRIDE, A. M.	5th MS Inf.	1845-1906	MS	Nesh
McBRIDE, James A.	57th VA Inf.	1843-____	SC	Copi
McBRIDE, James W. Sr.	24th MS Inf.	1810-1892		Webs
McBRIDE, Jim	24th MS Inf.	1812-1898		Webs
McBRIDE, Jim W. Jr.	24th MS Inf.	1848-1909		Webs
McBRIDE, Marion	5th AL Inf.	1840-1912	AL	Laud

1

McBRIDE, S. J.	16th MS Inf.	1838-1902	Forr
McBRIDE, S. L.	24th SC Inf.	1846-1919 SC	Carr
McBRIDE, William	1st MS Cav.	1810-1873 Madi	Madi
McBRIDE, William	Adams MS Cav.	1848-1924 Madi	Madi
McBRIDE, William H.	24th MS Inf.	1840-1921 SC	Holm
McBROOM, John H.	Adams MS Cav.	1848-1930 MS	Warr
McBROOM, Joseph Alex.	6th TX Cav.	1845-1903 MS	Warr
McBROOM, W. F.	21st MS Inf.	1845-1921	Unio
McBROOM, Wessley	48th MS Inf.	1841-1862 MS	Warr
McBROOME, Thomas L.	21st MS Inf.	1843-1863 MS	Warr
McBRYDE, J. A.	2nd MS Inf.	1838-1908 AL	Tipp
McCAA, Samuel N.	14th Cav.	1834-1909 Fran	Fran
McCAA, W. W.	16th MS Inf.	1841-1916 Adam	Adam
McCABE, Alexander L.	11th AL Cav.	1845-1906 AL	Tish
McCAFFERTY, Charley	2nd MS Cav.	1833-1898 MS	Choc
McCAFFERTY, Isaac	4th MS Inf.	1841-___ Choc	Sunf
McCAFFERTY, J. M.	4th MS Inf.	1836-1898 MS	Choc
McCAFFEHTY, W. M.	2nd MS Cav.	1839-1911 AL	Choc
McCAFFERTY, Yewing	MS Inf.	1838-1881 MS	Choc
McCAIN, Isac L.	29th MS Inf.	1836-1884 SC	Lafa
McCAIN, J. A.	3rd MS Inf.	1835-1901 Newt	Newt
McCAIN, J. R.	2nd MS Cav.	1833-1922 MS	Choc
McCAIN, John	39th MS Inf.	1826-1863 MS	Scot
McCAIN, John	Stanfords Art.	1831-1922 MS	Webs
McCAIN, R. W.	4th MS Inf.	1844-1916 MS	Lafa
McCAIN, William	48th MS Inf.	1835-1910 MS	Okti
McCALEB, F. H. Sr.	3rd MS Inf.	1846-1909 Harr	Harr
McCALEB, J. F.	Jefferson Lt.Art.	1836-1862 Adam	Adam
McCALEB, Jonathan	1st MS Inf.	1844-1918 Adam	Adam
McCALIP, D. A.	State Troops	1847-1916	Copi
McCALL, D. D.	11th MS Cav.	1841-1905 Kemp	Laud
McCALL, Isaac R.	27th LA Inf.	1844-1862 LA	Warr
McCALL, J. C.	37th MS Inf.	1848-1923 Jasp	Jack
McCALL, John M.	21st SC Inf.	1839-1910 SC	Forr
McCALL, T. G.	2nd MS Inf.	1822-1902	Rank
McCALLISTER, George W.	35th MS Inf.	Kemp	Kemp
McCALLUM, Duncan (Dr.)	NC Art.	1832-1917 NC	Simp
McCALLUM, J. E.	12th MS Inf.	1838-1891 NC	Linc
McCALLUM, Duncan	4th MS Cav.	1821-1878	Hind
McCAMPBELL, David Cole	McCulloughs Brig.	1838-1912	Mars
McCAMEY, Milton	1st TN Cav.	1845-1917 TN	Chic
McCANN, E. (Rev.)	40th AL Inf.	1841-1906 AL	Laud
McCANN, Gus W.	40th AL Inf.	1832-1889 AL	Laud
McCANN, J. C.	47th GA Inf.	1833-1899 GA	Leak
McCANN, Robert C. (Dr.)	1st MS Lt. Art.	1831-1891 Yazo	Yazo
McCANN, W. M.	48th MS Inf.	1837-1910	Okti
McCARDLE, William H.	12th MS Inf.	1815-1892	Hind
McCARDLE, William H.	1st MS Cav.	1842-1923	Pear
McCARGO, R. P.	1st MS Inf.	1844-1923	DeSo
McCARGO, W. H.	3rd MS Cav.	1846-1904	DeSo
McCARKLE, J. S.	64th GA Inf.	1844-1901 GA	Leak

2

McCARLEY, Mose	23rd MS Inf.	1829-1882	Pren
McCARLEY, William B.	11th MS Inf.	1835-1904 MS	Carr
McCARTER, C. A.	41st MS Inf.	1831-1907 Pont	Pont
McCARTY, Daniel	21st MS Inf.	1837-1913 MS	Talla
McCARTY, E. F/P.	8th MS Inf.	1838-1923 MS	Clar
McCARTY, Edward	37th MS Inf.	1841-1912 Jasp	Jasp
McCARTY, James	6th MS Cav.	1844-1924 Rank	Smit
McCARTY, James H.	2 & 12 MS Cav.	1838-1911 Choc	Choc
McCARTY, John	7th MS Inf.	1843-1916 Jasp	Jasp
McCARTY, John	3rd MS Inf.	1832-1884 Pear	Pear
McCARTY, Lawrence B.	40th MS Inf.	1835-1929 Clar	Jasp
McCARTY, Simpson	5th MS Inf.	1816-1892 MS	Wayn
McCARVER, Harry S.	2nd MS Inf.	1839-1907 Pont	Pont
McCARVER, J. R.	2nd MS Inf.	1838-1899 Pont	Pont
McCASKILL, A. P.	1st MS Cav.	1832-1915 SC	Noxu
McCASKILL, Hampton	3rd SC Cav.	1830-1927 SC	Carr
McCASKILL, James Lufkin	18th MS Inf.	1837-1908	Rank
McCASKILL, John C.	1st MS Lt. Art.	1843-1862 Carr	Carr
McCASKILL, Kenneth	35th MS Inf.	1834-1896 Kemp	Kemp
McCASKILL, Lawrence A.	39th MS Inf.	1843-1922 Simp	Simp
McCASKILL, Wm. H.	1st MS Lt. Art.	1841-1862 Carr	Carr
McCAUGHAN, George	5th LA Cav.	1839-1910	Harr
McCLAIN, Jim	14th Cav.	1845-1934 Gree	Wayn
McCLAIN, John J.	12th MS Inf.	1828-1905 Jeff	Jeff
McCLAIN, Lewis	34th MS Inf.	1819-1912 AL	Tipp
McCLAIN, Robt. Waite	17th MS Inf.	1841-1878 Mars	Mars
McCLAMROCH, G. W.	4th TN Inf.	1838-1923 TN	Alco
McCLARY, D. R.	43rd MS Inf.	1839-1920 Lown	Lown
McCLARY, S. F.	43rd MS Inf.	1838-1912 Lown	Lown
McCLELLAN, A. D.	1st MS Lt. Art.	1837-1921 MS	Mont
McCLELLAN, Benjamin F.	48th MS Inf.	1840-1883 Warr	Warr
McCLELLAN, F. A.	Forests Cav.	1845-1924 MS	Lafa
McCLELLAN, George D.	28th MS Cav.	1844-1913 Holm	Holm
McCLELLAND, James P.	12th MS Inf.	1833-1902	Okti
McCLELLAND, Thomas	21st MS Inf.	1845-1926	Hind
McCLELAND, William J.	1st MS Lt. Art.	MS	Atta
McCLENDON, Marsh W.	33rd MS Inf.	1841-1924 Amit	Amit
McCLENDON, N. C.	6th MS Inf.	1846-1922 Simp	Simp
McCLEOD, John T.	35th MS Inf.	1843-1925 Wins	Wins
McCLERSKEY, J. P.	41st MS Inf.	1839-1899 Pont	Pont
McCLINTOCK, Samuel H.	11th MS Cav.	1847-1923 GA	Hump
McCLOUD, Henry C.	11th MS Inf.	1831-1897 MS	Coah
McCLUNG, Elias	33rd MS Inf.	1841-1863 Leak	Bent
McCLUNG, J. R.	33rd MS Inf.	1839-1862 Leak	Bent
McCLURE, J. W.	16th MS Inf.	1841-1862 Clai	Clai
McCLURE, John S.	2nd Ohio Inf.	1844-1914 Ohio	Clay
McCLURE, R. C.	1st MS Lt. Art.	1837-1922 MS	Choc
McCLURG, C. M.	1st MS Cav.	1828-1909 Carr	Carr
McCLURG, Yancy Crawford	28th MS Cav.	1828-1914 Carr	Carr
McCLURKY, L. D. L.	8th MS Inf.	1837-1897 MS	Clay
McCLUSKEY, John Daniel	2_nd AL Inf.	1841-1912 AL	Monr
McCLUSKEY, L. D. L.	8th MS Cav.	1837-1897 MS	Clay

3

Name	Unit	Dates		
McCLUSKEY, W. M.	4th MS Inf.		Atta	Atta
McCLUTCHIE, M. A.	Jefferson Art.	1825-1892	Jeff	Adam
McCOA, David Monroe	14th MS Inf.	1845-1922	Clar	Fran
McCOLLOUGH, J. R.	17th MS Inf.	1837-1909	MS	Pont
McCOLLOUGH, Robert M.	17th MS Inf.	1836-1913	Pont	Pont
McCOLLUM, Andrew M.	1st MS Lt. Art.	1843-1930	Jeff	Jeff
McCOLLUM, Duncan	4th MS Cav.	1837-1884	Covi	Covi
McCOLLUM, H. D.	26th MS Inf.	1835-1921	MS	Pren
McCOLLUM, H. S.	12th MS Inf.	1836-1868	Jeff	Jeff
McCOLLUM, J. M.	10th AL Cav.	1827-1915	AL	Okti
McCOLLUM, James M.	1st AL Inf.	1829-1928	AL	Okti
McCOLLUM, Lawrence	4th MS Cav.	1824-1890		Simp
McCOMBS, J. W.	2nd MS Inf.	1848-1929	SC	Lee
McCONN, James H.	1st MS Cav.	1834-1867	MS	Yazo
McCOOL, George C.	6th AL Cav.	1846-1941		Atta
McCOOL, James Francis	28th MS Cav.	1847-1885	Madi	Holm
McCORD, Campbell W.	3rd Cav.	1846-1926	AL	Alco
McCORD, George A.	12th MS Cav.	1845-1901	Jasp	Alco
McCORD, J. D.	2nd MS Inf.	1851-1917	MS	Jasp
McCORD, James Newton	1st MS Inf.	1835-1917	GA	Lee
McCORD, John T.	4th MS Inf.	1844-1898	MS	Calh
McCORD, Simeon	1st MS Inf.	1827-1862	Pont	Pont
McCORKLE, J. M.	9th Inf.	1833-1919		DeSo
McCORKLE, Jesse D.	Adams MS Cav.	1846-1912	Yazo	Yazo
McCORKLE, John E.	11th MS Inf.	1846-1918	Lafa	Lafa
McCORKLE, William W.	20th MS Inf.	1839-1882	Choc	Mont
McCORMACK, Robert J.	3rd MS Inf.	1837-1878	Yazo	Yazo
McCORMICK, J. A.	12th MS Inf.	1831-1931	NC	Linc
McCORMICK, J. L.	4th MS Inf.	1841-1925		Yalo
McCORMICK, James V.	27th MS Inf.	1836-1895	Laud	Laud
McCORMICK, John S.	1st MS Lt. Art.	1831-1904	Jeff	Jeff
McCORMICK, John Wesley	37th MS Inf.	1835-1914	Jasp	Jasp
McCORMICK, Joseph	Bradfords Scouts	1844-1929	Wash	Wash
McCORMICK, P. J. Jr.	Medical	1830-1905	IR	Yazo
McCORMICK, Thomas R.	27th MS Inf.	1841-1919	Laud	Laud
McCOWEL, J. R.	5th MS Inf.	1840-1862	Nesh	Chic
McCOWN, James	17th MS Inf.	1838-1899	TN	Tipp
McCOY, A.	39th MS Inf.	1825-1901	VA	Newt
McCOY, A.	13th MS Inf.	1833-1903	MS	Newt
McCOY, C. C.	15th MS Inf.	1841-1921	Mont	Mont
McCOY, C. W.	26th MS Inf.	1825-1898	TN	Tipp
McCOY, H. B.	39th MS Inf.	1843-1927	VA	Newt
McCOY, J. S. (Dr.)	26th AL Inf.	1834-1862	AL	Monr
McCOY, James	2nd MS Cav.	1840-1911	Tish	Tish
McCOY, James N.	35th MS Inf.	1829-1911	Perr	Perr
McCOY, N. B.	7th MS Inf.	1838-1882	Amit	Amit
McCOY, R.	35th MS Inf.	1832-1908	AL	Kemp
McCOY, S.	4th MS Cav.	1828-1870	Amit	Wilk
McCOY, S. D.	39th MS Inf.	1845-1935		Rank
McCOY, W. C.	23rd MS Inf.	1838-1907	Tipp	Tipp
McCOY, W. H.	2nd MS Cav.	1823-1908	Monr	Pren
McCOY, W. T.	19th MS Inf.			Adam

McCRACKEN, Leonedis	3rd MS Cav.	1846-1919 Yalo	Gren
McCRACKEN, Robert	3rd MS Cav.	1847-1910 Gren	Gren
McCRAINE, Hugh W.	24th MS Cav.	1842-1920 Wilk	Wilk
McCRAINE, John C.	23rd MS Cav.	1848-1890 Wilk	Wilk
McCRAINE, N. W.	38th MS Inf.	1836-1862 Wilk	Wilk
McCRANEY, John T.	16th MS Inf.	1844-1937 MS	Jasp
McCRANEY, Phillip	5th MS Inf.	1833-1930 MS	Lama
McCRARY, Alfred M.	16th MS Inf.	1843-1908 Clai	Lown
McCRAW, John W.	13th MS Inf.	1838-1899 Laud	Kemp
McCRAW, Lawson Newberry	31st MS Inf.	1831-1882 SC	Unio
McCRAW, S. G.	31st MS Inf.	1833-1924 Unio	Unio
McCREARY, A. M. Sr.	26th MS Inf.	1839-1924 MS	Pren
McCREARY, Joseph	1st MS Cav.	1847-1932 MS	Carr
McCREIGHT, Henry A.	14th MS Inf.	1842-1911	Okti
McCREIGHT, James B.	48th MS Inf.	1840-1920 MS	Okti
McCREIGHT, R. C.	14th MS Inf.	1837-1912 Lown	Kemp
McCRORY, Ebb B.	40th MS Inf.	1842-1914 Nesh	Nesh
McCRORY, Jim	43rd MS Inf.	1840-1909 Nesh	Atta
McCRORY, R. P.	6th MS Inf.	1842-1928 Nesh	Atta
McCRORY, R. R.	8th LA Inf.	1845-1862 La	Warr
McCRORY, Robert	43rd MS Inf.	1838-1923 Kemp	Scot
McCROSKY, H. A.	9th MS Inf.	1818-1878 Mars	Mars
McCRUM, J. N.	10th MS Inf.	1842-1895 SC	Tipp
McCULLAN, Henry Clay	Adams MS Cav.	1846-1935	Newt
McCULLAR, A. J.	14th MS Lt. Art.	1841-1906	Pano
McCULLEY, G. H.	9th TN Cav.	1843-1917 TN	Unio
McCULLEY, J. H.	20th MS Inf.	1813-1884 SC	Wins
McCULLLY, J. M.	20th MS Inf.	1837-1901 Leak	Wins
McCULLEY, W. J.	20th MS Inf.	1834-1915 Wins	Wins
McCULLUM, R/H. H.	Blythes Cav.	1842-1863 DeSo	Lafa
McCULLOCH, S. F.	5th MS Inf.	1840-1909 MS	Choc
McCULLOUGH, Eli D.	2nd AL Inf.	1843-1892 SC	Mars
McCULLOUGH, Robert	8th MS Cav.	1837-1913 Tall	Tall
McCULLOUGH, S. D.	Shoemaker	1825-1911 MS	Chic
McCULLOUGH, W. F.	34th MS Regt.	1840-1936 MS	Lafa
McCULLOUGH, William	1st MS Cav.	1843-1928 Nesh	Scot
McCULLOUGH, William J.	38th MS Cav.	1834-1906 Pike	Linc
McCULLY, James Daniel	4th MS Inf.	1824-1911 SC	Lee
McCULLY, J. S.	20th MS Inf.	1839-1921 Leak	Wins
McCULLY, W. W.	20th MS Inf.	1847-1880 Wins	Wins
McCUNE, J. T.	19th MS Inf.	1832-1909 MS	Lown
McCUNE, T. B.	MS Inf.	1829-1900 GA	Newt
McCURDY, Cyrus M.	MS Inf.	1841-1900 Jasp	Jasp
McCURDY, William	37th MS Inf.	1836-1906 Jasp	Jasp
McCUTCHAM, Absolum C.	2nd MO Cav.	1840-1901 MO	Mars
McCUTCHEN, John M.	28th MS Cav.	1841-1884 Wash	Wash
McDADE, G. A.	35th MS Inf.	1847-1915 MS	Kemp
McDADE, John C.	35th MS Inf.	1843-1919 MS	Kemp
McDADE, W. J.	35th MS Inf.	1839-1917 Kemp	Kemp
McDADE, W. T.	Graves MS Cav.	1838-1908	Copi
McDADE, William J. (Dr.)	35th MS Inf.	1848-1900 MS	Kemp
MCDANIALD, Wilbert A.	2nd MS Cav.	1844-1905 Laud	Laud

McDANIEL, A. J.	1st MS Inf.	1842-1931 VA	Smit
McDANIEL, Allen	3rd Regt.	1812-1896 Mari	Mari
McDANIEL, Cyrus C.	7th MS Inf.	1818-1908 Jone	Jone
McDANIEL, Daniel Judson	39th MS Inf.	1838-1908 MS	Walt
McDANIEL, E. C.	19th TN Inf.	1843-1925 TN	Pont
McDANIEL, J. B.	MS Lt. Art.	1846-1927	Scot
McDANIEL, J. K.	1st MS Cav.	1844-1927 MS	Carr
McDANIEL, J. M.	4th MS Cav.	1850-1929 MS	Alco
McDANIEL, James	37th MS Inf.	1843-1927 Newt	Smit
McDANIEL, James	8th MS Inf.	1824-1884 GA	Newt
McDANIEL, James V.	39th MS Inf.	1828-1908 MS	Lawr
McDANIEL, Jeptha	16th MS Inf.	1833-1908	Pike
McDANIEL, John	16th MS Inf.	1829-1909	Pike
McDANIEL, John	16th MS Inf.	1829-1909 Pike	Pike
McDANIEL, John A.	1st MS Cav.	1823-1901 VA	Warr
McDANIEL, Josiah A.	54th AL Inf.	1825-1892 AL	Chic
McDANIEL, M.	33rd MS Inf.	1840-1922 Amit	Pike
McDANIEL, Mathew	18th AL Inf.	1835-1921 AL	Kemp
McDANIEL, Morgan J.	26th AL Inf.	1838-1906 AL	Atta
McDANIEL, Pinkney	39th MS Inf.	1828-1894 Pike	Pike
McDANIEL, Thomas J.	37th MS Inf.	1841-1929 MS	Smit
McDANIEL, W. B.	7th MS Inf.	1844-1923 MS	JEDA
McDANIEL, W. H.	17th MS Cav.	1843-1917 MS	Harr
McDANIEL, Wm.	7th MS Inf.	1842-1923 Jone	Carr
McDANIEL, W. S.	15th MS Inf.	1843-1917 Choc	Harr
McDAVID, J. B.	7th MS Inf.	1840-1906 Linc	Linc
McDAVID, S. P.	41st MS Inf.	1837-1912 MS	Harr
McDAVID, W. C.	16th MS Inf.	1838-1912 Pike	Linc
McDAVITT, Cornevis P.	2nd AL Inf.	1843-1905 Jasp	Jasp
McDERMOTT, Chas.	MS Lt. Art.	1836-1881 IL	Warr
McDERNOTT, Joseph A.	59th TN Inf.	1836-1863 TN	Warr
McDILL, Thomas A.	20th MS Inf.	1824-1909 MS	Newt
McDONAL, W.	40th AL Inf.	1830-1889 AL	Laud
McDONALD, A.	3rd MS Inf.	1842-1926 Newt	Newt
McDONALD, A. J.	15th MS Inf.	1838-1910 Holm	Warr
McDONALD, Alexander W.	28th Cav.	1831-1875 MS	Holm
McDONALD, Archibald	11th MS Inf.	1832-1876 Nesh	Nesh
McDONALD, Benjamin E.	16th MS Inf.	1830-1910 Jone	Jasp
McDONALD, Calvin	7th MS Inf.	1836-1917 Covi	Covi
McDONALD, Claiborne	13 & 21 MS Inf.	1836-1913	Rank
McDONALD, David S.	Adams MS Cav.	1812-1888 MS	Leak
McDONALD, Elijah	4th MS Cav.	1813-1888 Wilk	Wilk
McDONALD, H. W.	5th MS Inf.	1844-1897 Nesh	Nesh
McDONALD, J. F.	1 & 40 Inf.	1843-1913 AL	Laud
McDONALD, J. L.	33rd MS Inf.	1839-1929 MS	Harr
McDONALD, J. L.	33rd MS Inf.	1823-1907 Choc	Lefl
McDONALD, James	18th MS Inf.	1815-1902	Rank
McDONALD, James	Niles Legion	1826-1909 IR	Adam
McDONALD, James	40th AL Inf.	1814-1906 AL	Laud
McDONALD, James D.	7th MS Inf.	1844-1924 Jone	Clar
McDONALD, James D.	7th MS Inf.	1840-1918 NC	Jone
McDONALD, James R.	18th MS Cav.	1848-1928 MS	Wayn

6

McDONALD, John	13th MS Inf.	1833-1878 Laud	Laud
McDONALD, John	47th NC Inf.	1839-1929 NC	Harri
McDONALD, John	State Troops	1827-1883 AL	Gree
McDONALD, John	1st MS Inf.	1827-1907 Tipp	Unio
McDONALD, Richard	2nd MS Inf.	1828-1918	Hump
McDONALD, Richard G.	1st LA Inf.	1844-1913 ST	Amit
McDONALD, Robert V.	1st MS Lt. Art.	1836-1917 Jeff	Jeff
McDONALD, S. D.	4th MS Cav.	1822-1913 Covi	Covi
McDONALD, S. W.	2nd MS Cav.	1838-1865 Tate	Tate
McDONALD, Sam	Army		Covi
McDONALD, Thomas Owens	6 & 15 MS Inf.	1840-1881	Leak
McDONALD, William	36th AL Inf.	1844-___	Monr
McDONNELL, John	1st MS Inf.	1833-1904 IR	Hind
McDOUGAL, J. A.	24th MS Inf.	1835-1902 Itaw	Itaw
McDOUGAL, Thomas	26th MS Inf.	1843-1931 Tish	Tish
McDOUGAL, W. F.	17th MS Inf.	1835-1909 Tish	Tish
McDOUGAL, W. H.	32nd MS Inf.	1841-1889 MS	Alco
McDOUGAL, William C.	26th MS Inf.		Monr
McDOUGALD, N. R.	46th MS Inf.	1835-1921 Nesh	Nesh
McDOUGLE, John Wesley	26th MS Inf.	1840-1916 Tish	Tish
McDOWELL, Alex	12th MO Cav.	1832-1863	DeSo
McDOWELL, Andrew Jack.	43rd MS Inf.	1843-1896 Lown	Lown
McDOWELL, James	2nd MS Inf.	1833-1906 Pont	Pont
McDOWELL, Joel C.	39th MS Inf.	1817-1905 Newt	Newt
McDOWELL, John	Adams MS Cav.	1833-1904	Tuni
McDOWELL, Leroy Davis	11th MS Inf.	1838-1918 Chic	Okti
McDOWELL, N. B.	14th Cav.	1846-1899 Amit	Pike
McDOWELL, Solomon W.	18th MS Inf.	1840-1905	Rank
McDOWELL, T. N.	28th MS Cav.	1834-1918 MS	Pano
McDOWELL, William M. F.	24th MS Inf.	1821-1884 Gree	Amit
McDUFF, R. F.	State Troops	1818-1888	Copi
McDUFF, W. H.	State Troops	1823-1897 Leak	Leak
McDUFF, Webster Daniel	Perrins MS Cav.	1830-1914 MS	Forr
McDUFFIE, W. W.	2nd MS Cav.	1850-1932 SC	Monr
McDUFFIE, J. M.	2nd MS Cav.	1847-1933 GA	Monr
McEACHERN, Alexander L.	31st MS Inf.	1846-1924 AL	Geor
McEARCHERN, A. T.	Ballentines Cav.	1846-1915 Carr	Carr
McEARCHERN, M. A.	Ballentines Cav.	1836-1912 Carr	Carr
McEARCHERN, W. H. (Dr.)	1st MS Lt. Art.	1838-1901 Carr	Carr
McELBANNON, James	7th MS Cav.	1844-1912 Tish	Alco
McELHENNEY, George W.	30th GA Inf.	1832-1900 GA	Newt
McELRATH, Samuel H.	14th MS Cav.	1833-1901 MS	Fran
McELROY, J. A.	6th SC Inf.	1848-1916 SC	Harr
McELROY, J. C.	39th MS Inf.	___-1912	Newt
McELROY, Ransom L.	2nd MS Inf.	1844-1933 MS	Laud
McELROY, W. F.	4th AL Cav.	1837-1914 AL	Wayn
McELVANY, S. M.	20th MS Inf.	1843-1927	Okti
McELWEE, A. A.	5th MS Cav.	1847-1929 MS	Harr
McELWEE, Andrew Blaine	Jeff Davis Cav.	1837-1926 Chic	Amit
McELVEEN, R. H.	18th MS Inf.	1832-1894 MS	Copi
McELVEEN, Sylvester D.	2nd MS Inf.	1844-1926 MS	Pike
McELVEEN, W. E.	33rd MS Inf.	1843-1893 Amit	Amit

Name	Unit	Dates		
McELWAIN, Joe	22nd MS Inf.	1846-1916	Linc	Tipp
McELWAIN, Joseph	22nd MS Inf.	1824-1865	NC	Tipp
McEWEN, John B. (Dr.)	4th MS Cav.	1826-1864		Lafa
McEWIN, Archie	38th MS Cav.	1841-1913	Pike	Pike
McFADDEN, O. P.	26th MS Cav.	1845-1919		Itaw
McFARLAND, Andrew J.	1st MS Lt. Art.	1843-1916	Warr	Copi
McFARLAND, Baxter	41st MS Inf.	1839-1925	NC	Monr
McFARLAND, J. B.	5th MS Inf.	1816-1889	NC	Jasp
McFARLAND, John	44th MS Inf.	1848-1925	MS	Linc
McFARLAND, John P.	14th MS Inf.	1826-1916	Fran	Linc
McFARLAND, Ruston	3rd MO Inf.	1842-1862	MO	Lown
McFARLAND, T. J.	19th MS Cav.	1843-1900	Yalo	Yalo
McFARLAND, Walter M.	38th AL Inf.	1839-1918	AL	Kemp
McFARLIN, C. C.	17th MS Inf.	1823-1920	MS	Unio
McFERRIN, Henry	26th AL Inf.	1828-1885	AL	Tall
McFERRIN, J. Henry	26th AL Inf.	1837-1888		Tall
McFERRIN, Levy	26th AL Inf.	1825-1882		Tall
McGAHEY, Thomas Jon.	35th MS Regt.			Hind
McGAN, Daniel	28th AL Inf.	1840-1862	AL	Chic
McGARR, Leroy J.	33rd MS Inf.	1837-1910		Webs
McGARRITY, B. F.	2nd MS Cav.	1845-1908	Choc	Tall
McGAUGHY, B. A.	154th TN Inf.	1839-1911	Pont	Lee
McGAUGHY, N. R. (Dr.)	17th TN Inf.	1834-1864	MS	Lee
McGEE, Frank D.	15th MS Inf.	1836-1921	MS	Holm
McGEE, George B.	1st MS Lt. Art.	1845-1929	Yazo	Jone
McGEE, J. F.	25th MS Inf.	____-1890	Holm	Atta
McGEE, J. P.	40th MS Inf.	1827-1911	MS	Leak
McGEE, Jacob	38th MS Cav.	1836-1919	Rank	Scot
McGEE, R. H.	36th MS Inf.	1826-1895	Newt	Newt
McGEE, Robbin	38th MS Cav.	1833-1918	Rank	Scot
McGEE, S. F.	24th MS Cav.	1843-1924	MS	Linc
McGEE, Samuel L.	14th MS Inf.	1838-1903		Lown
McGEE, William P.	11th MS Cav.	1834-1899	TN	Wins
McGEEHEE, A. M.	3rd MS Inf.	1847-1916	MS	Wilk
McGEEHEE, Charles G.	Powers MS Cav.	1823-1903	MS	Wilk
McGEHEE, E. D.	45th MS Inf.	1830-1890	Pike	Amit
McGEHEE, Edward John	21st MS Inf.	1843-1908	MS	Wilk
McGEHEE, George A.	22nd MS Inf.	1842-1921	Amit	Amit
McGEHEE, George Thomas	21st MS Inf.	1833-1906	MS	Wilk
McGEHEE, Harry T.	21st MS Inf.	1845-1924	MS	Wilk
McGEHEE, J. _.	14th Cav.	1826-1893	Fran	Fran
McGEHEE, J. R.	8th MS Inf.	1848-1907	Smit	Linc
McGEHEE, James Powell	LA Regt.	1830-1914	LA	JEDA
McGEHEE, John Burruse	3rd LA Cav.	1836-1913	Wilk	Wilk
McGEHEE, Hal Leigh	18th MS Inf.	1837-1905		Hind
McGEHEE, Hansford J.	22nd MS Guards	1837-1901	Amit	Amit
McGEHEE, Lee Hobson	16th MS Cav.	1831-1906		Hind
McGEHEE, Louis	4th MS Cav.	1822-1914	Amit	Amit
McGEHEE, T. L.	4th MS Cav.	1845-1930	Amit	Pike
McGEHEE, T. W.	7th MS Inf.	1841-1925	Fran	Amit
McGEHEE, Theodore Lew	44th MS Inf.	1845-1930	Amit	Pike
McGEHEE, Wood	9th MS Cav.	1837-1898		Pear

8

Name	Unit	Dates		
McGEHEE, Woodford L.	14th MS Cav.	1846-1892	Clar	Amit
McGILBERRY, Murdock	7th MS Inf.	1830-1895	Wayn	Wayn
McGILL, John	41st MS Inf.	1838-1890	IN	Hind
McGILL, Richard F.	18th MS Inf.	1834-1908		Hind
McGILL, Thomas	1st MS Inf.	1835-1882	Pont	Pont
McGILVRAY, Angus	4th MS Cav.	1840-1904	MS	Jone
McGINNIS, A.	Engineer Corp.	1834-1920	IR	Harr
McGINNIS, George W.	9th GA Inf.	1845-1921	GA	Tate
McGLADERY, H.	19th MS Inf.	1829-1912	IR	Harr
McGOUGH, William M.	14th GA Inf.	1842-1915	Rank	Scot
McGLATHERY, James M.	MS & TN Cav.	1845-1918	Alco	Harr
McGOVERN, James	15th MS Inf.	1833-1911	Choc	Choc
McGOWAN, A. B.	4th MS Cav.	1836-1893	Copi	Hind
McGOWAN, James E.	40th MS Inf.	1847-1916	Jasp	Jasp
McGOWAN, James Monroe	3rd MS Inf.	1846-1923	MS	Hind
McGOWAN, John Leslie	9th MS Inf.	1837-1900	Mars	Mars
McGOWAN, Joseph	3rd MS Inf.	1843-1930	Okti	Okti
McGOWAN, Robert	9th MS Inf.	1832-1894	Mars	Mars
McGOWAN, Robert S.	9th MS Inf.	1840-1921	Mars	Mars
McGOWAN, Wm. M.	1st MS Lt. Art.	1841-1911	Hind	Harr
McGowan, William H.	14th MS Inf.	1838-1913	Clar	Jone
McGOWEN, H. L.	12th MS Inf.	1846-1905		Hind
McGOWEN, Hugh	38th MS Inf.	___-1889	Clai	Walt
McGOWEN, Russell R.	1st MS Inf.			Hind
McGOWEN, T. H.	4th MS Cav.	1846-1908	Pike	Pike
McGOWEN, William T.	20th Cav.	1838-1926	Hind	Hind
McGRATH, James	20th MS Regt.	1831-1890		Hind
McGRAW, Ansell	3rd LA Cav.	1836-1918	Wilk	Wilk
McGRAW, E. M.	17th MS Inf.	1822-1916		Harr
McGRAW, Robert A.	3rd LA Cav.	1845-1918	Wilk	Wilk
McGEE, T. J.	11th MS Cav.	1847-1916	Wins	Copi
McGREGOR, W. J.	30th MS Inf.	1808-1893	Carr	Carr
McGREGOR, W. W.	41st MS Inf.	1834-1911	Pont	Pont
McGREGOR, Wiley	18th IL Inf.	1839-1918	IL	Pont
McGREW, J. F.	27th MS Inf.	1833-1906	MS	Lama
McGREW, L. D.	27th MS Inf.	1842-1903	MS	Covi
McGROW, E. H.	35th MS Inf.	1841-1902	Nesh	Nesh
McGRUDER, Henry	18th MS Inf.	1841-1896	Madi	Madi
McGUFFEE, Alfred H.	33rd MS Inf.	1833-1920	Lawr	Lawr
McGUFFEN, M. A.	3rd MS Cav.	1845-1923	MS	Warr
McGUFFIE, D. Z.	33rd MS Inf.	1840-1918	Lawr	Linc
McGUFFIE, J. J.	Hughes MS Cav.	1828-1903		Rank
McGUFFIE, J. J.	4th MS Cav.			Hind
McGUIN, T. F.	1st MS Cav.	1844-1903		Boli
McGUINTY, Hugh	28th MS Cav.		IR	Adam
McGUINTY, John	16th MS Inf.		IR	Adam
McGUIRE, Henry W.	4th MS Inf.	1838-1908	MS	Calh
McGUIRE, Michael	O'Haras Gun Boat	1846-1928	NY	Warr
McGUIRK, John	9th MS Inf.	1827-1871	Mars	Mars
McHAFFEY, A. B.	39th MS Inf.	1848-___	Simp	Simp
McHAFFEY, Isaac Newton	Hams MS Cav.	1842-1897	AL	Pren

9

McHAFFEY, Robert Newell	11th MS Cav.	1838-1909 AL	Pren
McHANN, Hezakah	15th MS Inf.	1839-1863 Okti	Okti
McHATHERY,			
Samuel Jacobs	19th TN Cav.	1844-1894 TN	Lefl
McHUGH, James	17th MS Inf.	1835-1878 Mars	Mars
McILWAIN, James	3rd MS Inf.	1826-1890	Okti
McINNIES, Christopher C.	24th MS Inf.	1804-1879 MS	Gree
McINNIES, John	24th MS Inf.	1816-1899 MS	Gree
McINNIS, Colon L.	24th MS Inf.	1829-1878 MS	Gree
McINNIS, D. B. (Dr.)	4th MS Cav.	1839-1874	Covi
McINNIS, Daniel	37th MS Inf.	1835-1886 Laud	Laud
McINNIS, H. D.	11th MS Cav.	1844-1928 Amit	Amit
McINNIS, Hugh Wiggins	27th MS Inf.	1843-1900 Perr	Forr
McINNIS, John D.	36th AL Inf.	1843-1918 AL	Laud
McINNIS, L. J.	36th AL Inf.	1831-1898 AL	Laud
McINNIS, Murdock	9th MS Cav.	1835-___ MS	Geor
McINNIS, Neil	7th MS Inf.	1818-1893	Linc
McINNIS, Norman	27th MS Inf.	1814-1876	Covi
McINNIS, Randall	24th MS Inf.	1837-1907 MS	Gree
McINNIS, T. J.	27th MS Inf.	1844-1913	Linc
McINTIRE, John	Lays MS Cav.	1820-1919	Fran
McINTOSH, A. J.	McNairs MS Cav.	1836-1865	Copi
McINTOSH, B. F. (Dr.)	Marmadukes		
	Cav.	1840-1906	DeSo
McINTOSH, Daniel	20th MS Inf.	1825-1872 Noxu	Noxu
McINTOSH, Frank	18th NC Inf.	1840-1928 NC	Copi
McINTOSH, J. R.	24th MS Inf.	1837-1904	Laud
McINTOSH, J. R. B.	36th AL Inf.	1819-1901 MD	Gree
McINTOSH, John	36th MS Inf.	___-1913	Hind
McINTOSH, John Alex.	20th MS Inf.	1830-1917	Hind
McINTOSH, John H.	6 & 15 MS Inf.	1824-1885	Copi
McINTOSH, Samuel McCall	27th MS Inf.	1839-1916 AL	Covi
McINTURFF, Willis	23rd MS Inf.	1819-1894 AL	Tipp
McINTYRE, Duncan	33rd MS Inf.	1824-1891	Rank
McINTYRE, J. C.	16 & 20 MS Inf.	1819-1875 NC	Rank
McINTYRE, Patrick	24th MS Inf.	1847-1897 Warr	Warr
McINTYRE, William	McLaurins Co.	1833-1873	Rank
McIVEN, Leonard	Nelsons Art.	1840-1862 TN	Copi
McIVER, John	21st MS Inf.	1842-1869 Warr	Warr
McIVER, Wm.	21st MS Inf.	1840-1878 Warr	Warr
McKAY, B. W.	14th MS Inf.	___-1905	Rank
McKAY, C. C.	15th MS Inf.	1844-1876	Madi
McKAY, _. Daniel A.	46th MS Inf.	1820-1904 Smit	Copi
McKAY, E. J.	15th MS Inf.	1831-1921 Yalo	Leak
McKAY, J. A.	5th MS Inf.	1815-1867 MS	Nesh
McKAY, J. J.	33rd MS Inf.	1839-1913 MS	Leak
McKAY, John	3rd Inf.	1814-1900	Rank
McKAY, John	38th AL Inf.	1820-1904 AL	Wayn
McKAY, John F.	39th MS Inf.	1848-1863	Rank
McKAY, R. H.	5th MS Inf.	1835-1906 Wins	Wins
McKAY, W. F.	10th MS Inf.	1835-1900 Madi	Madi
McKEE, Daniel	VA Inf.	1827-1862 VA	Lafa

10

McKEE, H. K.	36th MS Inf.	1820-1894 Laud	Kemp
McKEE, John	36th MS Inf.	1828-1910 Newt	Nesh
McKEE, John H.	5th KY Cav.	1848-1900 KY	Wilk
McKEE, W. R.	15th MS Inf.	1831-1885 Wayn	Wayn
McKEE, William C.	35th MS Inf.	1830-1910	Webs
McKELLAR, A. L.	35th MS Inf.	1813-1885 Wins	Kemp
McKELLAR, Preston	1st NC Inf.	1848-1922 SC	Tate
McKELVAINE, Robert P.	24th MS Inf.	1838-1868 Kemp	Kemp
McKELVEY, J. W.	4th AL Cav.	1834-1916 AL	Tipp
McKELVY, William R.	4th MS Cav.	1827-1906 AL	Lee
McKENNA, Jerry	12th MS Inf.	1851-1888 IR	Warr
McKENNY, A. J.	8th MS Cav.	1828-1899 Lown	Chic
McKENZIE, Charlie	6 & 46 MS Inf.	1813-1867 MS	Smit
McKENZIE, Daniel B/H.	19th MS Inf.	1842-1883 MS	Bent
McKENZIE, Donald	9th MS Inf.	1839-1896 ST	DeSo
McKENZIE, Duncan A.	Navy Yards	1845-1891 GA	Laud
McKENZIE, Hector A.	9th MS Inf.	____-1875 ST	DeSo
McKENZIE, James	27th MS Inf.	1841-1886 Covi	Covi
McKENZIE, John	Navy Yards	1824-1888 GA	Laud
McKENZIE, John C.	15th MS Inf.	____-1920 Carr	Mont
McKENZIE, M. L.	9th MS Cav.	1846-1926 Perr	Forr
McKEONE, Patrick	28th MS Cav.	1834-1878 IR	Wash
McKEOWN, J. P.	56th AL Regt.	1836-1911 AL	Hind
McKEOWN, James	2nd MS Inf.	Tish	Alco
McKEY, Charles A.	Andersons MS Scouts	1848-1930 Wilk	Wilk
McKIE, Benj. Franklin	19th MS Inf.	1841-1911 MS	Mars
McKIE, John H.	19th MS Inf.	1840-1876 Mars	Lafa
McKIE, Nathan W.	18th MS Inf.	1849-1878 Madi	Madi
McKINLEY, Michael	23rd MS Inf.	1841-____ Tish	Choc
McKINLEY, Seabern	Yergers Cav.	1825-1900	Copi
McKINNEY, Benjamin F.	4th AL Cav.	AL	Chic
McKINNEY, D. B. (Doc.)	16th MS Inf.	1847-1938 MS	Monr
McKINNEY, Eugene V.	11th MS Cav.	1845-1918 Pont	Wash
McKINNEY, J. A.	45th AL Inf.	1847-1914 AL	Laud
McKINNEY, J. W.	43rd MS Inf.	1837-1891 SC	Monr
McKINNEY, James Benj.	27th MS Inf.	1843-1917 MS	Monr
McKINNEY, James Thomas	44th MS Inf.	1836-1889 SC	Mars
McKINNEY, John B.	4th AL Cav	1838-1899 AL	Tish
McKINNEY, S. A.	1st Inf.	1843-1862 Gren	Lafa
McKINNEY, Thomas	11th MS Cav.	1833-1926 AL	Tipp
McKINNEY, W. D.	42nd AL Inf.	1843-1865 AL	Lafa
McKINNEY, William	21st MS Inf.	1838-1899 Wilk	Wilk
McKINNEY, William C. H.	2nd MS Inf.	1842-1938 Smit	Shar
McKINNIE, Michael	18th MS Cav.	1830-1905	DeSo
McKINNON, C. A.	31st MS Inf.	1845-1911 Calh	Alco
McKINNON, D. P.	15th MS Inf.	1842-1913 Choc	Choc
McKINNON, Sink	15th MS Inf.	1841-1920 Atta	Atta
McKINSTRY, John T.	18th MS Inf.	1843-1868 Jasp	Jasp
McKINZIE, Augustus	27th MS Inf.	1837-1912 Covi	Covi
McKINZIE, D. M.	Steeds MS Cav.	1844-1930 Mari	Mari
McKINZIE, E. J.	Steeds MS Cav.	1848-1932	Mari

11

McKINZIE, J. M.	Adams Cav.	1836-1900 SC	Wins
McKNIGHT, F. M.	15th MS Inf.	1836-1903 Choc	Choc
McKNIGHT, Frank S.	4th AL Cav.	1848-1934 AL	Monr
McKNIGHT, Ike	30th MS Inf.	1840-1909 Choc	Choc
McKNIGHT, Jonathan P.	18th MS Inf.	1845-1922 MS	Chic
McKNIGHT, Robert L.	24th MS Cav.	1844-1884 Amit	Amit
McKNIGHT, Robert N.	1st MS Cav.	1839-1901 Pont	Pont
McKNIGHT, T. S.	22nd MS Inf.	1840-1904 Amit	Amit
McKOWN, Thomas R.	Army	1824-1863	Chic
McKOWN, Wm. Mitchell	1st MS Inf.	1830-1862 AL	Monr
McLAIN, A. C.	39th MS Inf.	1827-1906	Rank
McLAIN, Anguish	36th AL Inf.	1844-1907 MS	Gree
McLAIN, Enoch Bateman	4th MS Inf.	1829-1915 Amit	Amit
McLAIN, I. D.	24th MS Inf.	1824-1922 Gree	Amit
McLARITY, A. M.	4th MS Inf.	1848-1931 MS	Lafa
McLARTY, J. M.	2nd NC Inf.	1839-1910 NC	Lafa
McLARTY, J. R.	7th MS Inf.	1845-1921 Mari	Lafa
McLARTY, John C.	8th MS Cav.	1822-1883 MS	Yalo
McLARTY, John R.	4th MS Inf.	1826-1899 MS	Lafa
McLARTY, W. W.	1st MS Inf.	1841-1914 Pont	Lafa
McLAUGHLIN, E. D.	40th AL Inf.	1836-1912 AL	Leak
McLAUGHLIN, William	15th MS Inf.	1837-1876 MS	Mont
McLAURIN, Ansolm Joseph	3rd MS Cav.	1848-1909	Rank
McLAURIN, C. J.	8th MS Inf.	1822-1886 Smit	Smit
McLAURIN, Charles	6th MS Inf.	1849-1905	Rank
McLAURIN, D. L.	Stubbs MS Cav.	1847-1916	Simp
McLAURIN, G. W.	1st State Troops	1837-1923	Boli
McLAURIN, Henry	28th MS Cav.	1841-1879	Rank
McLAURIN, Hugh D.	18th MS Inf.	____-1876	Rank
McLAURIN, Hugh N.	37th MS Inf.	1843-1925 MS	Jone
McLAURIN, James C.	27th MS Inf.	1842-1913 Jasp	Jasp
McLAURIN, John Sr.	Berrys MS Inf.	1821-1891 Clar	Kemp
McLAURIN, John D.	20th MS Inf.	1849-1928	Rank
McLAURIN, John W.	27th MS Inf.	1846-1914 Jasp	Jasp
McLAURIN, L. L.	27th MS Inf.	1839-1863 LA	Warr
McLAURIN, R. D.	4th MS Cav.	1831-1882	Rank
McLAURIN, Robert L.	18th MS Inf.	1842-1880	Rank
McLEAN, F. H.	Stanfords Lt.Art.	1842-1895 Carr	Carr
McLEAN, J. L.	52nd MS Inf.	1830-1906 MS	Alco
McLEAN, James N.	38th MS Cav.	1842-1898 MS	Holm
McLEAN, Thomas S.	38th MS Cav.	1844-1918 Holm	Lefl
McLEAN, William H.	35th MS Inf.	1845-1919 Laud	Laud
McLEAN, William L.	1st MS Sharpshooters	1846-1905 MS	Holm
McLEAN, William Lampkin	18th MS Inf.	1840-1890 GA	Holm
McLEAN, WIllan T.	35th MS Inf.	1846-1878 Laud	Laud
McLEAN, William W.	38th MS Cav.	18 2-1905 MS	Holm
McLEAN, William Wade	15th MS Inf.	1843-1926 Holm	Holm
McLELLAN, Angus	1st FL Cav.	1836-1919 FL	Jasp
McLELLAN, J. H.	38th MS Inf.	1842-1864 Holm	Holm
McLELLAN, J. _.	1_ MS Inf.	1844-1905 MS	Holm
McLELLAN, John	38th MS Cav.	1820-1883 Noxu	Holm

12

McLELLAN, John W.	12th MS Inf.	1840-1926 Holm	Holm
McLELLAN, Richard T.	38th MS Cav.	1847-1922 Holm	Holm
McLELLAN, Sam	29th MS Inf.	1840-1888 Atta	Holm
McLELLAN, Tobe	38th MS Cav.	1844-1911 Carr	Holm
McLELLAN, William S.	12th MS Inf.	1839-1913 Holm	Holm
McLELLAND, Samuel	7th MS Inf.	____-1865 MS	Mari
McLELLAND, Samuel	7th MS Inf.	1832-1864 Mari	Mari
McLEMORE, Amos	37th MS Inf.	1823-1903 MS	Laud
McLEMORE, Maise Amos	27th MS Inf.	1823-1863 MS	Forr
McLEMORE, C. W.	3rd MS Inf.	1825-1904 Yazo	Laud
McLEMORE, Joshua	37th MS Inf.	1839-1918 Laud	Laud
McLEMORE, Leon W.	3rd MS Inf.	____-1883	Hind
McLEMORE, R. S. (Dr.)	1st MS Cav.	1837-1905	Leflo
McLEMORE, Richard	38th MS Cav.	1837-1908 Fran	Fran
McLENDON, E. M.	1st MS Cav.	1842-1909 Wayn	Wayn
McLENDON, H.	_9th MS Inf.	1843-1863 Simp	Lafa
McLENDON, J. M. (Dr.)	14th MS Lt. Art.	1827-1877 MS	Tall
McLENDON, Kenneth	13th MS Inf.	1829-1911 Clar	Forr
McLEOD, A.	46th MS Inf.	1842-1917 MS	Simp
McLEOD, Allen	3rd MS Inf.	1846-1896 MS	Gree
McLEOD, Alix	3rd MS Cav.	1809-1868 TN	Yazo
McLEOD, Calvin H.	Starks Cav.	1845-1917 MO	Sunf
McLEOD, Dan	24th MS Inf.	1838-1919	Gree
McLEOD, Daniel	23rd MS Inf.	1836-1919 MS	Gree
McLEOD, J. M.	35th MS Inf.	1834-1916 Wins	Wins
McLEOD, John	24th MS Inf.	1842-1925 MS	Gree
McLEOD, John	24th MS Inf.	1843-1926	Gree
McLEOD, John	56th AL Cav.	1846-1932 Covi	Covi
McLEOD, John J.	24th MS Inf.	1846-1932 MS	Gree
McLEOD, John Nelson	21st MS Inf.	1837-1911 MS	Tall
McLEOD, Randel	1st MS Cav.	1826-1900 Noxu	Noxu
McLEOD, Sweyn	24th MS Inf.	1832-1908 Gree	Gree
McLEOD, W. W.	35th MS Inf.	1844-1917 Wins	Noxu
McLEOD, William A.	2nd MS Inf.	1845-1914 MS	Covi
McLEOD, William P.	2nd AL Lt. Art.	1843-1862 AL	Lown
McLERAN, Wm. Galbreth	32nd MS Inf.	1839-1912 MS	Pren
McLEROY, Nedham L.	34th MS Inf.	1839-1920 GA	Mars
McMAHAN, James O.	14th SC Inf.	1832-1906 SC	Gren
McMAHAN, W. S.	14th SC Inf.	1829-1863	Gren
McMAHAN, William	48th MS Inf	1843-1911 Warr	Warr
McMAHON, Terry	Englishs MS Art.	Adam	Adam
McMAKIN, James O.	20th MS Inf.	1839-1862 SC	Wins
McMAKIN, P. C.	3rd AR Cav.	1835-1903 AR	Wins
McMAMES, James P.	19th MS Inf.	1834-1909 SC	Okti
McMANUS, S. V.	27th MS Inf.	1839-1911 Jone	Jone
McMANUS, Steven A.	14th Conf. Cav.	1825-1910 Fran	Fran
McMASTER, Alex Uriah	17th MS Inf.	1842-1901 MS	Tish
McMASTER, John	21st MS Inf.	1830-1917 MS	Yazo
McMASTER, Sam	1st MO Inf.	1837-1934 MO	Tate
McMASTER, Thomas E.	1_ MS Cav.	1846-1932 MS	Itaw
McMATH, Joseph H.	22nd MS Inf.	1848-1909 MS	Carr
McMATH, W. A.	15th MS Inf.	1844-1921 Gren	Lefl

13

McMICHAEL, John David	43rd MS Inf.	1847-1937 Lown	Lama
McMILLAN, Alexander	34th MS Inf.	1832-1873 ST	Rank
McMILLAN, D. Wesley	5th MS Inf.	1839-1916 MS	Nesh
McMILLAN, Felix L.	15th MS Inf.	1844-1913 Atta	Atta
McMILLAN, Henderson	4th MS Inf.	1837-1909 Choc	Copi
McMILLAN, Henry C.	Kit Allens Inf.	1847-1911 Leak	Leak
McMILLAN, Hue	40th MS Inf.	1840-1921 MS	Leak
McMILLAN, J. P.	12th MS Inf.	1839-1920 Linc	Linc
McMILLAN, J. Frank	5th MS Cav.	1827-1907 SC	Holm
McMILLAN, John A.	6th MS Inf.	1835-1913 MS	Leak
McMILLAN, John M.	5th MS Inf.	1832-1913 MS	Nesh
McMILLAN, John N.	15th MS Inf.	1826-1908 MS	Atta
McMILLAN, Judge G. S.	12th MS Inf.	1829-1900 NY	Linc
McMILLAN, Lee	28th MS Cav.	1844-1932 Carr	Carr
McMILLAN, Robert C.	31st MS Inf.	1842-1886 Chic	Pren
McMILLAN, Thomas J.	14th Conf. Cav.	1840-1905 Fran	Copi
McMILLAN, William	27 & 29 MS Inf.	1829-1868 ST	Rank
McMILLAN, William A.	27th MS Inf.	1826-1904 MS	Monr
McMILLIN, J. J.	34th MS Inf.	1827-1913 TN	Tipp
McMILLIAN, Archibald	Army	1833-1863	Jeff
McMILLIAN, Calvin E.	7th MS Inf.	1832-1918 Fran	Fran
McMILLIAN, Joseph W.	1st MS Lt. Art.	1816-1882 SC	Shar
McMILLIAN, Samuel	13th MS Inf.	1828-1888 SC	Wins
McMILLIN, A. M.	5th MS Inf.	1839-1916 Nesh	Nesh
McMILLIN, J. F.	35th MS Inf.	1837-1925 MS	Wins
McMILLIN, Leroy D.	13th MS Inf.	1842-1911 MS	Wins
McMINN, A. M.	35th MS Inf.	1844-1920	Okti
McMINN, A. V.	1st MS Cav.	1839-1926 Pano	Pano
McMINN, Berry H.	1st MS Cav.	1822-1898	Pano
McMINN, H. P.	35th MS Inf.	1842-1913 MS	Choc
McMORROUGH, T. J.	5th MS Cav.	1824-1903 NC	Holm
McMULLAN, H. C.	5th MS Inf.	1846-1935 Newt	Newt
McMULLAN, Jesse	5th GA Inf.	1816-1879 GA	Newt
McMULLAN, Patrick	63rd GA Inf.	1820-1896 GA	Newt
McMULLAN, T. J.	39th MS Inf.	1831-1879 GA	Newt
McMULLAN, W. M.	2nd MS Cav.	1843-1864 MS	Newt
McMULLAN, W. M.	3rd MS Inf.	1825-1900 Newt	Newt
McMULLEN, D. M.	2nd AL Cav.	1832-1913 GA	Harr
McMULLEN, J. O.	Stanfords Lt.Art.	1829-1900 Gren	Gren
McMULLEN, John	Warren Lt. Art.	1837-1896 Warr	Warr
McMULLEN, Nathan James	Johnsons Cav.	1839-1902 Tall	Tall
McMULLEN, Robert J.	31st MS Inf.	1827-1908 Okti	Okti
McMURPHY, Cole	Provost Guard	1847-1924 AL	Scot
McMURPHY, James A.	GA Inf.	1844-1919 GA	Ston
McMURRY, D. A.	1st MS Cav.	1841-1926	Pano
McMURRAY, J. W.	12th MS Cav.	1847-1929 MS	Pont
McMURRY, Thomas W.	11th MS Cav.	1837-1913 Leak	Leak
McMURTREY, George R.	1st MS Cav.	1837-1923	Pren
McNAIR, Angus Kelly	1st MS Lt. Art.	1838-1907 NC	Jeff
McNAIR, David R.	3rd MS Inf.	1844-1878	Hind
McNAIR, Evander	8th MS Inf.	1847-1917	Hind
McNAIR, J. H.	28th AL Inf.	1844-1916 AL	Pren

14

Name	Unit	Dates		
McNAIR, James M.	4th MS Cav.	1839-1912 Copi	Covi
McNAIR, John	6th MS Inf.	1830-1907	Rank
McNAIR, John C.	6th MS Inf.	1837-1919 Smit	Smit
McNAIR, M. D.	6th MS Inf.	1819-1907 MS	Nesh
McNAIR, Manlius C.	3 & 6 MS Rifles	1835-1864	Hind
McNAIR, Milton	8th MS Inf.	1839-1931	Simp
McNAIR, Neal	8th MS Inf.	1837-___ Simp	Simp
McNAIR, Reuben	8th MS Inf.	1844-1934	Simp
McNAIR, Richmond	Fenners Batt.	1844-1940 Simp	Simp
McNAIR, Robert A.	3rd MS Inf.	1839-1876	Hind
McNAIR, Thomas C.	12th MS Inf.	1839-1920 Jeff	Linc
McNAIR, W. B.	5th MS Inf.	1841-1918 Carr	Chic
McNAMARA, John H.	15th MS Inf.	1843-1862 MD	Mont
McNEAL, Daniel W.	18th MS Inf.	1838-1906 Yazo	Yazo
McNEASE, A. J.	Stubbs MS Cav.	1846-1921 Lawr	JEDA
McNEASE, J. R.	7th MS Inf.	1840-1913 Covi	JEDA
McNEASE, W. J.	5th MS Inf.	1846-1919	JEDA
McNEAL, Samuel	1st MS Res.	1847-1923 Laud	Laud
McNEELY, John King	10th MS Inf.	1842-1903 Madi	Hind
McNEELY, Joseph A.	6th MS Cav.	1834-1907 Lown	Alco
McNEELY, Murdock D.	7th Q. M. MS	1833-1907 Wilk	Wilk
McNEELEY, R. A.	18th MS Cav.	1843-1899	DeSo
McNEELY, William	Graves MS Cav.	1847-1912 Wilk	Wilk
McNEER, A. H.	38th MS Cav.	1843-1912 Holm	Holm
McNEER, John L.	3_ MS Cav.	1844-1918 AL	Holm
McNEIL, A. J.	7th MS Inf.	1840-1898 Fran	Pont
McNEIL, Adin	8th MS Inf.	1833-1863 MS	Clar
McNEIL, Dan H.	5th MS Inf.	1837-1920 Kemp	Kemp
McNEIL, James D.	5th MS Inf.	1827-1890 Jasp	Jasp
McNEIL, John	2nd MS Inf.	1824-1891 Jasp	Jasp
McNEIL, John Hector	15th MS Inf.	1839-1891 Mont	Mont
McNEIL, Johnnie	14th MS Inf.	1835-1918 IR	Wins
McNEIL, Laughin James	43rd MS Inf.	1831-1890 Kemp	Kemp
McNEIL, Reuben C. Sr.	38th MS Cav.	1840-1905 Wilk	Wilk
McNEIL, Rufus L.	5th MS Inf.	1822-1898 Kemp	Kemp
McNEIL, Wiley	8th MS Inf.	1836-1862 MS	Clar
McNEILL, G. B.	37th MS Inf.	1835-1905 Clar	Harr
McNEILL, John	1st MS Inf.	1816-1881	Hind
McNEILL, Neil	15th MS Inf.	1842-1924	Copi
McNEILL, Thomas Hector	21st MS Inf.	1848-1914 MS	Gren
McNEILL, W. D.	1st AL Inf.	1833-1913 AL	Jone
McNEILY, John Seymour	21st MS Inf.	1841-1924 Wilk	Wash
McNEMAR, H. B.	1 & 6 MS Inf.	1845-___	Simp
McNICE, Lewis	4th MS Inf.	1840-1920 MS	Itaw
McNIEL, C. W.	17th MS Inf.	1819-1899 NC	Lee
McNIEL, Robert B.	2nd MS Inf.	1848-1938 MS	Lee
McNUR, Daniel Martin	MS Inf.	1845-1884 Holm	Holm
McNURE, G. W.	8th MS Inf.	1842-1909 MS	Harr
McNUTT, Henry J.	17th MS Inf.	1839-1909 MS	Unio
McNUTT, S. D.	31st MS Inf.	1841-1911 MS	Unio
McNUTT, T. B.	2nd MS Inf.	1843-1926 Unio	Unio
McNUTT, Thomas L. Sr.	7th AL Cav.	1826-1888 AL	Tish

15

McPEAKE, V.	Blythes MS Cav.	1827-1905	DeSo	DeSo
McPHAIL, A. M.	38th MS Cav.	1845-1922		JEDA
McPHAIL, David D.	4th MS Inf.		MS	Calh
McPHAIL, J. A.	5th MS Inf.	1846-1886	Nesh	Leak
McPHAIL, J. D.	5th MS Inf.	1832-1893	Monr	Leak
McPHAIL, Joseph	46th MS Inf.	1843-1924		JEDA
McPHEARSON, John T.	37th MS Inf.	1842-1917	Wayn	Wayn
McPHEARSON, William W.	8th MS Inf.	1827-1909	SC	Jasp
McPHEETERS, Gabraiel P.	LA Inf.	1831-1862	LA	Adam
McPHEETERS, Wm. A.	Jeff Davis Legion	1840-1896	Adam	Adam
McPHERESON, J. V.	12th MS Inf.	1839-1904	MS	Clai
McPHERSON, A. A.	13th MS Inf.	1835-1926	Carr	Carr
McPHERSON, J. E. (Dr.)	9th MS Inf.	1839-1919	Mars	Mars
McPHERSON, Joseph N. (Dr)	1st MS Lt. Art.	1836-1892		Jeff
McPHERSON, Thomas	20th MS Inf.			Rank
McPHERSON, W. R.	22nd MS Regt.	1837-1873		Hind
McQUAIDE, John J.	1st MS Lt. Art.	1842-1903	LA	Warr
McQUEEN, Robert L.	11th MS Cav.	1845-1870	MS	Wins
McQUIEN, Henry (Rev.)	11th MS Cav.	1820-1880	GA	Laud
McQUIN, Angus D.	14th NC Regt.	1842-1921	NC	Fran
McQUIRTER, J. W.	13th MS Inf.	1835-1918	Wins	Wins
McQUISTON, Thomas J.	Saunders Scouts	1841-1898	Monr	Monr
McQUISTON, William D.	5th MS Inf.	1848-1886	Wayn	Jack
McQUOWN, J. M.	1_ MS Inf.	1842-1910	MS	Lown
McRAE, Allen W.	21st MS Inf.	1839-1867	Warr	Warr
McRAE, Daniel M.	13th MS Inf.	1829-1907	MS	Wayn
McRAE, James A.	35th MS Inf.	1837-1917	Kemp	Kemp
McRAE, James B.	3rd MS Inf.			Jack
McRAE, James B.	24th MS Cav.	1827-1906	Wayn	Wayn
McRAE, M. L.	13th MS Inf.	1840-1915	Gree	Gree
McRAE, R. D.	28th MS Cav.	1844-1922		Rank
McRAE, S. P.	28th MS Cav.	1843-1922		Rank
McRAE, William A.	1st AL Inf.	1841-1908	AL	Tish
McRANEY, Cornelius	12th MS Cav.	1844-1922	MS	Covi
McRANEY, D. C.	1st MS Cav.	1842-1912	Covi	Covi
McRANEY, G. W.	7th MS Inf.	1829-1916	Covi	Covi
McRANEY, John C. Jr.	1st MS Cav.	1848-1917	Covi	Covi
McRANEY, John C. Sr.	1st MS Cav.	1818-1875	Covi	Covi
McRANEY, John M.	46th MS Inf.	1838-1907	Covi	Covi
McRANEY, W. G.	7th MS Inf.	1849-1889	Lawr	Covi
McRAVEN, D. J.	48th MS Inf.	1842-1905	Warr	Warr
McRAVEN, John Wilson	3rd MS Cav.	1828-1914		Hind
McREE, Davis	12th MS Inf.	1814-1894	Copi	Linc
McREE, F. M.	Seven Star Art.	1843-1905	Copi	Linc
McREE, S. P.	Seven Star Art.	1843-1894	Copi	Linc
McVEY, Oliver M.	30th MS Inf.	1837-1902	Okti	Okti
McVEY, Virgil Smith	Adams MS Cav.	1834-1877		Okti
McSWAIN, J. L.	26th NC Inf.	1845-1925		Pano
McSWAIN, M. W.	9th MS Cav.	1844-1930	Gree	Gree
McSWAIN, Jonathan	4th MS Inf.	____-1891	Yalo	Calh
McWHORTER, B. F.	21st MS Inf.	1827-1889	Unio	Unio
McWHORTER, Ezekiel	6th MS Inf.	1829-1911	Smit	Scot

16

McWHORTER, J. H.	31st MS Inf.	1846-1921 MS	Choc
McWHORTER, John M.	31st MS Inf.	1841-1935 MS	Pont
McWHORTER, M. D. (Dr.)	31st MS Inf.	1835-1911 Choc	Unio
McWILLIAMS, D. E. Jr.	2nd MS Inf.	1847-1907 Noxu	Kemp
McWILLIAMS, David E. Sr.	2nd MS Inf.	1818-1906 Noxu	Kemp
McWILLIAMS, George W.	6th MS Inf.	1840-1905 LA	Rank
McWILLIAMS, James M.	24th MS Inf.	1841-1916 Kemp	Kemp
McWILLIAMS, J. Mancah	24th MS Inf.	1816-1932 Kemp	Kemp
McWILLIAMS, Robert A.	2nd KY Cav.	1842-1921 KY	Mars
McWILLIE, James (Dr.)	1st MS Cav.	1847-1890	Hind
McWILLIE, William	18th MS Inf.	1795-1869 Madi	Madi
McWILLIE, William Jr.	18th MS Inf.	1842-1922 SC	Hind
MABRAY, Phillip	4th MS Inf.	1828-1906 Carr	Carr
MABRY, Benjamin H.	4th MS Inf.	1845-1929 MS	Atta
MABRY, E. B.	11 & 41 MS Inf.	1840-1914 Lee	Lee
MABRY, G. W.	Hospital Batt.	1846-1924 GA	Newt
MABRY, J. T.	48th MS Inf.	1839-1906 MS	Harr
MABRY, Levi	MS Cav.	1843-1923 Madi	Madi
MABRY, Levi W.	2nd MS Inf.	1846-1891 Okti	Atta
MABRY, William G.	15th MS Inf.	1839-1862 Atta	Chic
MACKEY, L. W.	52nd TN Inf.	1844-1931 TN	Yalo
MACKEY, Samuel H.	12th LA Inf.	1846-1910 Warr	Warr
MACKLIN, A. H.	15th MS Inf.	1837-1913 SC	Choc
MACKLIN, John A.	15th MS Inf.	1805-1881 Choc	Choc
MADDEN, E. J.	1st MS Inf.	1832-1912 MS	Newt
MADDEN, J. L.	32nd MS Inf.	1829-1897 Alco	Alco
MADDEN, J. W.	40th MS Inf.	1825-1909 MS	Leak
MADDOX, Benjamin F.	11th MS Cav.	1843-1910 Tall	Atta
MADDOX, Cicero H.	42nd MS Inf.	1830-1877 MS	Tate
MADDOX, J. A.	Tenn. Art.	1840-1908 TN	Laud
MADDOX, James H.	33rd AL Inf.	1842-1929 Simp	Simp
MADDOX, Joseph B.	4th TN Inf.	1846-1932 Tipp	Tipp
MADEN, Waldus	GA Art.	1838-1913 GA	Lama
MADISON, John W.	43rd MS Inf.	1837-1921 Nesh	Nesh
MAER, William E.	14th MS Inf.		Lown
MAFF, J. B.	3rd LA Inf.	1837-1863 LA	Warr
MAGANOS, Joseph L.	22nd LA Cav.	1825-1899 MD	Warr
MAGEE, A. B.	1st MS Inf.	1816-1894	Hind
MAGEE, Alva A.	7th MS Inf.	1841-1884 Fran	Fran
MAGEE, B. P.	4th MS Cav.	1832-1892 MS	JEDA
MAGEE, C. S.	4th MS Cav.	1845-1919 MS	Harr
MAGEE, Calvin C.	33rd MS Inf.	1845-1914 Pike	Walt
MAGEE, Eland	4th MS Cav.	1841-1881 MS	Walt
MAGEE, Fleet Cooper	38th MS Cav.	1825-1879 Pike	Walt
MAGEE, Frank D.	15th MS Inf.	1835-1921 MS	Holm
MAGEE, George W.	21st MS Inf.	1838-1905 MS	JEDA
MAGEE, Hardy H.	7th MS Inf.	1838-1933 Fran	Fran
MAGEE, Hiram	4th MS Cav.	1845-1914 MS	JEDA
MAGEE, Hosie L. (Dr.)	9th LA Cav.	1846-1912 LA	Amit
MAGEE, Hugh R.	38th MS Cav.	1833-1900 Covi	JEDA
MAGEE, Jackson G.	6 & 46 MS Inf.	1831-1905 Covi	JEDA
MAGEE, James Irving	33rd MS Inf.	1825-1905 Lawr	Linc

MAGEE, Japhet Lee	Powers MS Cav.	1831-1929 Copi	Fran
MAGEE, John	7th MS Inf.	1837-1916 Mari	Lama
MAGEE, Laurin R.	4th MS Cav.	1825-1905 Covi	Covi
MAGEE, Lewis L.	7th MS Inf.	1842-1910 Fran	Fran
MAGEE, Marion	1st MS Cav.	1841-1909 Pano	Pano
MAGEE, Needham W.	7th MS Inf.	1820-1873 Fran	Fran
MAGEE, R. L.	4th MS Cav.	1847-___	Copi
MAGEE, Thomas	7th MS Inf.	1822-1891 Fran	Fran
MAGEE, Thomas C.	36th MS Inf.	1836-1862	Copi
MAGEE, W. J.	46th MS Inf.	1839-1887	Simp
MAGEE, W. J.	48th MS Inf.	1839-1887	Rank
MAGEE, W. F.	1st MS Lt. Art.	1847-1914 MS	Linc
MAGEE, W. H.	22nd MS Inf.	1833-1915 Lawr	Copi
MAGEE, William Luke	16th MS Inf.	1833-1861 MS	Walt
MAGEE, William W.	33rd MS Inf.	1842-1913 MS	Walt
MAGNON, James Felix	22nd LA Inf.	1838-1889 LA	Warr
MAGRUDER, I. D.	4th MS Cav.	1845-1933 Clai	Clai
MAGRUDER, Joseph Moore	12th MS Inf.	1829-1863 MS	Clai
MAGRUDER, L. W.	18th MS Inf.	1842-1905 Yazo	Warr
MAGRUDER, Levin W. (Dr.)	LA Cav.	1840-1900 LA	Wilk
MAGRUDER, Samuel	1st MS Inf.	1818-1897 GA	Copi
MAGRUDER, Thomas Samuel	24th MS Inf.	1843-1863 Madi	Madi
MAGRUDER, Wm. Howard	29th Inf.	1837-1918 MS	Holm
MAHAFFEY, J. J.	32nd MS Inf.	1844-1924 Jack	Simp
MAHAFFEY, William M.	6th MS Inf.	1838-1920 Smit	Scot
MAHAN, A. J.	1st AR Art.	1823-1909 IR	Coah
MAHER, Thomas	LA Inf.	1846-___ LA	Jeff
MAHON, Andrew Jackson	36th MS Inf.	1836-1881 MS	Copi
MAHONEY, Florence	22nd MS Inf.		Hind
MAHONEY, R. H.	18th AL Regt.	1843-1923 AL	Pont
MAJOR, Duplane	LA Art.	1842-1863 LA	Lafa
MAJOR, O. P.	41st MS Inf.	1828-1899 Pont	Unio
MAJORS, Henry C.	40th MS Inf.	1845-1923	Hind
MAJORS, John N.	15th LA Cav.	1838-1874 LA	Jeff
MAJURE, Dan	40th MS Inf.	1832-___ MS	Leak
MAKANSON, C. R.	11th AL Inf.	1838-1909 AL	Clay
MAKAMSON, Charles	11th MS Cav.	1847-1919 Okti	Okti
MALLET, Richard J.	1st MS Lt. Art.	___-1901 Hind	
MALLETT, Clemmer	36th AL Inf.	1836-1913 Geor	Geor
MALLETT, D. R.	12th MS Inf.	1840-1923	Harr
MALLETT, James Jeff.	15th MS Inf.	1840-1925 Atta	Atta
MALLETT, Robert W.	1st MS Lt. Art.	1826-1917 Hind	Hind
MALLETT, W. E.	27th MS Inf.	1838-1885	Hind
MALLETTE, James	4th MS Inf.	1846-1888 Jack	Geor
MALLETTE, William	27th MS Inf.	1838-1865 Jack	Geor
MALLORY, Jas. David Sr.	14th MS Inf.	1840-1899 Choc	Okti
MALONE, Geo. Washington	31st MS Inf.	1843-1920 Unio	Unio
MALONE, J. B.	11th MS Inf.	1843-___ Wins	Okti
MALONE, J. D.	42nd MS Inf.	1840-1912	Pano
MALONE, James	44th MS Inf.	1845-1882 Clay	Clay
MALONE, Miles W.	5th MS Inf.	1845-___ Choc	Atta

Name	Unit	Dates	
MALONE, Samuel B.	43rd MS Inf.		Monr
MALONE, Thomas M.	20th MS Inf.	1834-1891 Monr	Monr
MALONE, W. H.	7th MS Inf.	1832-1920 Clar	Forr
MALONE, W. M.	5th MS Cav.	1819-1896 Holm	Holm
MALONE, W. P.	35th MS Inf.	1813-1901 MS	Clay
MALONE, Wm. Milton	12th MS Inf.	1845-1921 Holm	Holm
MALPUS, Sam I.	2nd MS Inf.	1847-1924 Itaw	Harr
MANDEVILLE, Theodore	1st MS Inf.	1830-1863 Adam	Adam
MANGOLD, Andrew	Brookhaven		
	Lt. Art.	1842-1903 Copi	Copi
MONTGOMERY, J. C.	2nd MS Inf.	1842-1923 Tish	Tish
MANGRUM, J. R.	10th AL Inf.	1843-1931 AL	Monr
MANGUM, Arthur W.	6th MS Inf.	1844-1920 Simp	Simp
MANGUM, Henry L.	6th MS Inf.	1840-1911 Simp	Simp
MANGUM, James	6th MS Inf.	1835-1907 Simp	Simp
MANGUM, John C.	6th MS Inf.	1842-1915 Simp	Simp
MANGUM, Robert	16th MS Inf.	1843-1916 Simp	Simp
MANGUM, S. H.	1st MS	1837-___	Hind
MANGUM, Samuel	6th MS Inf.	18_-1911 Simp	Simp
MANGUM, Wm. Edward	39th MS Inf.	18 -1918Scot	Scot
MANLOVE, T. B.	48th MS Inf.	1842-1880 Warr	Warr
MANLY, James S.	AL Inf.	1842-1921 VA	Mont
MANN, Battle	15th MS Inf.	____-1873	Madi
MANN, C. _.	24th MS Inf.	1839-192_ SC	Mont
MANN, Croford	1st MS Lt. Art.	1840-1935 MS	Choc
MANN, James P.	17th MS Inf.	1844-1916 Mars	Mars
MANN, John Gideon	7th MS Cav.	1834-1899	Hind
MANN, W. E.	19th AL Inf.	1837-1920 AL	Tish
MANN, Wm. Marshall	1st MS Lt. Art.	1845-1926 Madi	Shar
MANNING, A. _.	40th MS Inf.	1833-1924 TN	Wins
MANNING, A. J.	1st MS Inf.	1842-___ Itaw	Lafa
MANNING, John W.	38th MS Cav.	1829-1900 Pike	Walt
MANNING, Napoleon B.	2nd MS Cav.	1846-1930 Scot	Covi
MANNING, Peyton Thomas	11th MS Inf.	1837-1868 TN	Monr
MANNING, Richard E.	36th MS Inf.	1830-1916	Copi
MANNING, Thomas M.	11th MS Inf.	1840-1867 TN	Monr
MANNING, W. L.	39th MS Inf.	1840-1928 Rank	Simp
MANNING, Woodard	23rd MS Cav.	1847-1889 MS	Copi
MANNS, Charlie D.	41st MS Inf.	1839-1923 AL	Carr
MANOR, John Thomas	1st MS Lt. Art.	1831-1924 EN	Shar
MANSFIELD, Gideon	12th GA Rangers	1835-1914 GA	Pano
MANSFIELD, J. L.	12th MS Cav.	1826-1877 Jasp	Tipp
MANSHIP, C. H.	1st MS Cav.		Hind
MANSHP, D. D.	1st MS Cav.	1845-1907	Hind
MAPLES, Abner C.	Smiths Lt. Art.	1837-___ Clar	Gree
MAPLES, Jesse	10th MS Inf.	1842-___	Hind
MAPLES, Thomas	MS Lt. Art.	1838-1915 Gree	Gree
MAPP, James A.	8th MS Inf.	1835-1907 GA	Newt
MAPP, Samuel O.	3rd MS Inf.	1824-1882 AL	Newt
MARON, John D.	22nd MS Inf.	1839-1913 Hind	Yazo
MARDIS, Abner	Jeff Davis Legion	Adam	Adam
MARETT, Elias J.	3rd MS Inf.	1834-1917 Bent	Mars

19

Name	Unit	Dates		
MARGAN, John P.	23rd MS Inf.	18_2-1935	Calh	Calh
MARIOLE, William	32nd MS Inf.	1842-1926	Tish	Alco
MARIGNY, Amadee	LA Inf.	1824-1873	LA	Adam
MARION, F. T.	8th MS Cav.	1846-1914	Lown	Chic
MARION, R. B.	11th MS Inf.	1837-1918	Chic	Chic
MARION, Robert	11th MS Inf.	1840-1917	Chic	Chic
MARION, William	11th MS Inf.	1834-1903	Chic	Chic
MARK, John Patrick	8th MS Cav.	1847-1887	TN	Laud
MARK, W__	10th AL Inf.	1831-1912	AL	Itaw
MARK, William	10th AL Inf.	1834-1875	AL	Itaw
MARKHAM, Wm. F.	10th MS Inf.	1843-1864	Yazo	Warr
MARKS, Alexander	3 & 15 LA Inf.	1841-1886	LA	Adam
MARKS, Isaac	38th MS Cav.	1831-1909	Holm	Holm
MARKS, Sleigh	TN Inf.	1827-1911	TN	Laud
MARLER, J. A.	Lt. Art.	1835-1919		Webs
MARLAR, Joseph	26th MS Inf.	1838-1909	Tish	Tish
MARLAR, Thomas	7th AL Cav.	1817-1909	Tish	Tish
MARLER, B/H. D.	6th MS Inf.	1838-1905	Smit	Scot
MARLOW, _. W.	30th MS Inf.	1843-1862	Wins	Lown
MARLOW, William D.	30th MS Inf.	___-1892	Holm	Copi
MARONY, Dempsey	1st MS Inf.	1828-1906	Leak	Leak
MARRON, John F/P.	12th MS Inf.	1835-1891	Adam	Adam
MARS, George W.	35th MS Inf.	1837-1908	Nesh	Nesh
MARS, James H.	35th MS Inf.	1828-1904	Nesh	Nesh
MARSALIS, Elisha	39th MS Inf.	1842-1862	Pike	Amit
MARSALIS, James	24th MS Inf.	1821-1882	Gree	Amit
MARSALIS, P. L.	22nd MS Inf.	1845-1927	Amit	Pike
MARSALIS, William	22nd MS Inf.	1809-1877	Amit	Amit
MARSH, G__	12th MS Inf.	1832-1870	Adam	Adam
MARSH, Cyrus Jr.	12th MS Inf.	1839-1869	Adam	Adam
MARSH, James I. (Dr.)	12th MS Inf.	1843-1871	Adam	Adam
MARSH, William E.	28th MS Cav.	1837-1876	Warr	Warr
MARSHALL, Caleb B.	1st MS Lt. Art.	1839-1874	Adam	Adam
MARSHALL, Calvin Y.	5th MS Cav.	1842-1920	Choc	Webs
MARSHALL, Chancey C.	21st MS Inf.	1847-1884		Copi
MARSHALL, G. M.	10th MS Inf.	1830-1899	Adam	Adam
MARSHALL, G. W.	22nd AL Inf.	1835-1917	AL	Wayn
MARSHALL, George	1st MS Lt. Art.	1828-1905	KY	Warr
MARSHALL, H. T.	18th MS Cav.	1846-1913	Pont	Unio
MARSHALL, Henry C.	3rd MS Inf.	1842-1915	Jack	Hind
MARSHALL, J. A.	14th MS Inf.	1843-1913		Jone
MARSHALL, James	4th MS Inf.	1838-1886	Carr	Carr
MARSHALL, John Sr.	3rd MS Inf.	1822-1902	Warr	Linc
MARSHALL, John Rodney	17th MS Inf.	1847-1864	MS	Webs
MARSHALL, John R.	11th MS Inf.	1837-1934	Nesh	Kemp
MARSHALL, John S.	1st MS Lt. Art.	1845-1887	Adam	Adam
MARSHALL, John W.	4th MS Inf.	1841-1871	Carr	Carr
MARSHALL, Julian	Adams MS Cav.		Leak	Atta
MARSHALL, Martin		1846-1895	Warr	Warr
MARSHALL, R. _.	Seven Star Art.	1838-1916		Copi
MARSHALL, Robert	Warren Lt. Art.	1833-1905	ST	Warr
MARSHALL, W. D.	43rd MS Inf.	1821-1879	Itaw	Monr

20

MARSHALL, W. _.	12 & 16 MS Cav.	1823-1900 Monr	Monr
MARSHALL, W. M.	42nd SC Inf.	1843-1916 NC	Harr
MARSHALL, William B.	11th MS Inf.	1831-1910 KY	Carr
MARSHALL, William Ball	1st MS Cav.	1836-1909 VA	Tall
MARTIN, A. D.	2nd MS Inf.	1836-1913 MS	Itaw
MARTIN, A. E.	3rd MS Cav.	1828-1869	Rank
MARTIN, A. G. B.	6th MS Inf.	1841-1908	Copi
MARTIN, A. J.	5th MS Inf.	1838-1915	Copi
MARTIN, A. J.	32nd MS Inf.	1831-1906 Tish	Alco
MARTIN, A. P.	10th MS Inf.	1835-1909 EN	Adam
MARTIN, Ambros	25th MS Inf.	1838-1922 Tish	Tish
MARTIN, A. Monroe	12th MS Inf.	1844-1921	Copi
MARTIN, Angus	28th MS Cav.	1832-1909 Carr	Carr
MARTIN, C. R.	21st MS Inf.	1844-1925 Unio	Unio
MARTIN, E. W.	2nd GA Inf.	1825-1902 GA	Unio
MARTIN, Edward C/O.	11th MS Inf.	1836-1900 PA	Holm
MARTIN, F. M.	17th MS Inf.	1846-1939	Nesh
MARTIN, F. M.	49th AL Inf.	1827-1904 AL	Jone
MARTIN, Felix A.	15th MS Inf.	1830-1919 TN	Gren
MARTIN, Francis M. Sr.	24th MS Cav.	1825-1895	Rank
MARTIN, G. M.	8th MS Inf.	1846-1924 Smit	Smit
MARTIN, G. W.	Lays MS Cav.	1826-1924 Hanc	Lama
MARTIN, Gideon Lee	16th MS Inf.	1839-1907 Smit	Smit
MARTIN, Henry C.	29th MS Inf.	1836-1914 Pano	Tall
MARTIN, I. W.	29th MS Inf.	1841-1931 Yazo	Yazo
MARTIN, J. A.	Stanfords Lt.Art.	1831-1918 Gren	Gren
MARTIN, J. B.	8th MS Inf.	1814-1904 MS	Harr
MARTIN, J. C.	9th MS Inf.	1826-1888 Tish	Alco
MARTIN, J. C.	Jeff Davis Cav.	1846-1926	Noxu
MARTIN, J. F.	4th MS Cav.	1826-1877 Amit	Amit
MARTIN, J. N.	6th MS Inf.	1839-1903 Smit	Smit
MARTIN, J. S.	7th GA Cav.	1837-1916 GA	Mars
MARTIN, Jackson W.	9th MS Cav.	1840-1925 Chic	Chic
MARTIN, James	13th MS Inf.	1834-1865 Laud	Laud
MARTIN, James	3rd MS Inf.	1817-1896	Rank
MARTIN, James B.	3rd MS Inf.	1836-1921 Harr	Pike
MARTIN, James E.	4th & 48th Inf.	1834-1862 TN	Clai
MARTIN, James P.	11th MS Inf.	1846-1931 Nesh	Nesh
MARTIN, James W.	Adams Cav.	1839-1922 Yazo	Yazo
MARTIN, James W.	4th MS Cav.	1828-1900 Clai	Jeff
MARTIN, Jim M. (Dr.)	Medical Corps	1827-1900 AL	Linc
MARTIN, John	3rd MS Inf.	1823-1874 AL	Monr
MARTIN, John	40th MS Inf.	1830-___ AL	Clay
MARTIN, John	46th MS Inf.	1844-1924 Wayn	Wayn
MARTIN, John Bennett	18th MS Inf.	1842-1913 MS	Madi
MARTIN, John E. A.	5th LA Cav.	1848-1924 MS	Smit
MARTIN, John P.	17th MS Inf.	1838-1903 Calh	Calh
MARTIN, John Walter	2nd MS Cav.	1846-1890 Kemp	Alco
MARTIN, Joseph	2nd MS Inf.	1824-1928 MS	Tipp
MARTIN, Joseph	2nd MS Inf.	1832-1928 MS	Unio
MARTIN, Joseph T.	2nd MS Inf.	1836-1900 KY	Tipp
MARTIN, Joseph Wyatt	35th MS Inf.	1838-1917 AL	Okti

MARTIN, Louis	Adams MS Cav.	1827-1905 Oktl	Oktl
MARTIN, M. H.	18th LA Cav.	1845-1925 LA	Amit
MARTIN, Oliver	1st MS Lt. Art.	1818-1895 Yazo	Yazo
MARTIN, P. O.	37th MS Inf.	1836-1923 Laud	Laud
MARTIN, R. H.	2nd MS Cav.	1842-1913 Kemp	Alco
MARTIN, R. R.	18th MS Cav.	1845-1905 Tall	Tall
MARTIN, Robert M.	23rd MS Inf.	1838-1906 Alco	Alco
MARTIN, Robert Pearson	4th MS Cav.	1834-1923 Pike	Pike
MARTIN, S. G.	34th MS Inf.	1829-1895 Mars	Mars
MARTIN, Samuel P.	34th MS Inf.	1839-1909	Pano
MARTIN, Simeon Robert	46th MS Inf.	1843-1917 Newt	Warr
MARTIN, Thomas E.	26th MS Inf.	1824-1894 Tish	Tish
MARTIN, W. H.	2nd MS Cav.	1821-1907 Newt	Newt
MARTIN, W. M.	46th MS Inf.	1847-1920 Wayn	Wayn
MARTIN, Wm. W.	LA Inf.	1842-1863 LA	Warr
MARTIN, Wid L.	2nd MS Cav.	1844-1936 Pike	Pike
MARTIN, Wiley	35th MS Inf.	1839-1864 Choc	Choc
MARTIN, Wiley	4th MS Cav.	1831-1886 GA	Walt
MARTIN, Wiley James	18 & 36 MS Inf.	1834-1917	Copi
MARTIN, William	Lt. Art.	1838-1930 EN	Jack
MARTIN, William	6th MS Cav.	1840-1929 Laud	Laud
MARTIN, William C.	12th MS Cav.	1828-1901 Tish	Alco
MARTIN, William H.	9 & 10 MS Inf.	1826-1906	Rank
MARTIN, William L.	16th MS Inf.	1846-1936 Pike	Pike
MARTIN, William M.	12th MS Inf.	1832-1864 Linc	Clai
MARTIN, William M.	46th MS Inf.	1835-1900 Wayn	Wayn
MARTIN, William T.	Adams MS Cav.	1845-1928 Tate	Tate
MARTIN, Wm. Thompson	Jeff Davis Cav.	1823-1910 KY	Adam
MARTINDALE, Wm. Jesse	2nd MS Inf.	1834-1907 Alco	Alco
MARTZ, John	1st MS Lt. Art.	1828-1889 GE	Hind
MARZE, James	28th LA Inf.	1839-1863 LA	Warr
MASER, J. A.	7th AL Cav.	1846-1936 AL	Tish
MASON, Allen	36th AL Inf.	1846-1921 AL	Gree
MASON, Armstead Thompson	34th MS Inf.	1828-1895 Tipp	Bent
MASON, Emery	36th MS Inf.	1845-1923	Lee
MASON, Hucled E.	33rd MS Inf.	1844-1926 Linc	Linc
MASON, John	33rd MS Inf.	1827-1904 Lawr	Linc
MASON, Morris	24th MS Inf.	1834-1923 Gree	Forr
MASON, Powell	36th AL Inf.	1826-1909 Gree	Gree
MASON, Presley	23rd NC Inf.	1841-1928 NC	Jone
MASON, Ruben Hall	2nd MS Inf.	1847-1907 NC	Pren
MASON, Solomon M.	33rd MS Inf.	1824-1898 Nesh	Nesh
MASON, W. A.	4th SC Inf.	1849-1917 SC	Lown
MASON, W. C.	33rd MS Inf.	1842-1930 Linc	Linc
MASS, Van Buren	Washingtons Art.	1835-1926 MD	Harr
MASSENGALE, E. S.	2nd MS Cav.	1833-1902 Newt	Newt
MASSENGALE, J. A.	1st MS Inf.	1837-1906 Clar	Jasp
MASSENGILL, S. F.	18th MS Inf.	1842-1924 TN	Linc
MASSEY, Anderson	42nd MS Inf.	MS	Calh
MASSEY, Benjamin P.	40th MS Inf.	1843-1910 Atta	Atta
MASSEY, J. T.	40th MS Inf.	1830-1909 MS	Leak

22

MASSEY, J. W.	16th MS Inf.	1838-1909	Copi
MASSEY, James	8th MS Inf.	1840-1934 AL	Jasp
MASSEY, Levi	8th MS Inf.	1844-1926 AL	Jasp
MASSEY, Thomas	33rd MS Inf.	1830-1902 Pano	Pike
MASSEY, Warren	6th MS Inf.	1824-1866 MS	Copi
MASSEY, William	40th MS Inf.	1814-1907 TN	Jasp
MASSIE, J. W.	16th MS Inf.	1838-1909	Copi
MASSINGALE, C. B.	8th MS Inf.	1832-1911 NC	Jasp
MASTERSON, James	22nd MS Inf.		Hind
MATHENEY, _. J.	2nd MS Cav.	1842-1911 Laud	Laud
MATHENY, J. M.	AL Art.		Monr
MATHENY, Joseph Allen	1st MS Cav.	1848-1899	Copi
MATHEWES, William M.	11th MS Inf.	1846-1938 Lafa	Pont
MATHEWS, Arthur	6th MS Inf.	1837-1898	Copi
MATHEWS, Fred H.	41st MS Inf.	____-1925	Lee
MATHEWS, Hines B.	20th MS Inf.	1842-1913 Carr	Carr
MATHEWS, J. M.	19th MS Inf.	1831-1864 Lafa	Lafa
MATHEWS, John E.	2nd MS Cav.	1835-1885 Tate	Tate
MATHEWS, Peter M.	19th MS Inf.	1838-1877 Lafa	Lafa
MATHEWS, T. H. (Dr.)	30th MS Inf.	1839-1911 Carr	Carr
MATHEWS, William Sidney	36th MS Inf.	1832-1905	Scot
MATHIS, E. D.	Baxters MS Cav.	1829-1878 Gren	Alco
MATHIS, J. H.	5th MS Inf.	1841-1929 Wins	Lafa
MATHIS, John C.	32nd MS Inf.	1827-1905	Tipp
MATHIS, John	48th MS Inf.	1833-1912	Copi
MATLOCK, G. S.	3rd MS Inf.	1820-1893 Tipp	Bent
MATTHEWS, A. G.	6th MS Inf.	1845-1932	Copi
MATTHEWS, E/F.	3rd MS Inf.	1834-1894	Hind
MATTHEWS, George N.	16th MS Inf.	1832-1867 Pike	Pike
MATTHEWS, James	20th MS Inf.	Carr	Carr
MATTHEWS, John	17th NC Inf.	1838-1896 NC	Wilk
MATTHEWS, John C.	43rd MS Inf.	1846-1934	Hind
MATTHEWS, John M.	1st Conf. Cav.	1845-1916 TN	Monr
MATTHEWS, Lycurgus C.	Powers MS Cav.	1847-1928 LA	Linc
MATTHEWS, Mirt	4th MS Cav.	1839-1909 Mars	Mars
MATTHEWS, Publeus	2nd KY Cav.	1838-1893 KY	Mars
MATTHEWS, S. A.	16th MS Inf.	1822-1901 Pike	Pike
MATTHEWS, Samuel P.	Stubbs Cav.	1838-1874	Hind
MATTHEWS, Seaborn J.	21st MS Inf.	1795-1866 Tall	Tall
MATTHEWS, T. F.	19th MS Inf.	1840-1862 Lafa	Lafa
MATTHEWS, Ulysses	4th MS Cav.	1848-1935 Mars	Mars
MATTHEWS, W. D.	1st MS Inf.	1842-1931 Mars	Harr
MATTHIS, J. C.	10th MS Inf.	1842-1929 Tipp	Tipp
MATTINGLY, J. B.	Adams Cav.	1844-1875 Warr	Warr
MATTINGLY, J. B.	Adams MS Cav.	1843-1931 Warr	Yazo
MATTINGLY, A. D.	Cheathams Div.	1809-1889 KY	Warr
MATTOX, Charles C. (Dr.)	1st MS Cav.	1838-1900 Carr	Carr
MATTOX, G. W.	24th MS Inf.	1844-1919 Itaw	Itaw
MAUFFRAY, J. C.	5th AL Inf.	1841-1919 MS	Hanc
MAULDEN, James	14th MS Inf.	1846-1918 Okti	Okti
MAULDIN, C.	28th MS Cav.	1810-1883 MS	Monr
MAULDIN, Hugh	23rd MS Inf.	1835-1925 Alco	Bent

Name	Unit	Years		
MAULDIN, J. A.	7th SC Cav.	1845-___	SC	Atta
MAULDIN, J. H.	23rd MS Inf.	1830-1925	GA	Tipp
MAULDIN, J. H.	3rd MS Inf.	1843-1887	Chic	Pont
MAULDIN, Jessie	1st MS Cav.	1845-1895	Noxu	Noxu
MAULDIN, John L.	5th MS Cav.	1845-1901	Yalo	Yalo
MAULDIN, W. P.	1st MS Cav.	1845-1928	Wayn	Wayn
MAULDIN, William Joab	11th MS Inf.	1841-___	Yalo	Yalo
M___, James W.	6th & 15th MS Inf.			Rank
MAUNEY, M. C.	NC Inf.	1843-___	NC	Tipp
MAUNEY, Michael C.	7th MS Cav.	1829-1873	NC	Tipp
MAURY, James F.	21st MS Inf.	1842-1875	Clai	Clai
MAUS, Henry	4th LA Inf.	1838-1909	GE	Harr
MAXEY, Napoleon	18th MS Inf.	1841-1875	Rank	Rank
MAXEY, Robert S.	39th MS Inf.	1843-1923		Rank
MAXEY, V. B.	7th AL Cav.	1846-1922	Itaw	Itaw
MAXEY, W. J.	5th MS Inf.	1832-1907	MS	Noxu
MAXEY, William L.	18th MS Inf.	___-1923		Rank
MAXWELL, A. E.	Brookhaven Lt. Art.	1825-1898	Copi	Linc
MAXWELL, Franklin C.	33rd MS Inf.	1831-1906	MS	Amit
MAXWELL, Henry Jackson	Brookhaven Lt. Art.	1840-1912	Lawr	Lawr
MAXWELL, Jesse M.	33rd MS Inf.	1842-1891	Lawr	Lawr
MAXWELL, Jesse W.	12th MS Inf.	1841-1902	MS	Linc
MAXWELL, John Wilson	Poagues Art.	1837-1917	Madi	Madi
MAXWELL, I. C.	33rd MS Inf.	1837-1902	Linc	Linc
MAXWELL, L. W.	33rd MS Inf.	1843-1863	Hanc	Lafa
MAXWELL, Simeon	33rd MS Inf.	1826-1914	Lawr	Lawr
MAXWELL, Thomas B.	18th Regt.	1845-1930	Madi	Madi
MAXWELL, _. L.	18th MS Inf.	1838-1906	Madi	Madi
MAY, Andrew J.	22nd MS Inf.	1828-1877		Hind
MAY, E. A.	18th MS Cav.	1835-1925		Harr
MAY, Eliha	7th MS Inf.	1838-1913	Linc	Linc
MAY, G. _.	39th MS Inf.	1834-1908		Simp
MAY, J. A.	1st MS Cav.	1844-1913		Hind
MAY, J. M.	33rd MS Inf.	1834-1915	Lawr	Linc
MAY, J. P.	28th MS Cav.	1846-1919	Quit	Clar
MAY, J. W.	33rd MS Inf.	1842-1928	Pike	Harr
MAY, J. W.	1st MS Inf.	1847-1918		Rank
MAY, James	4th MS Cav.	1822-1889		Rank
MAY, James P.	Brookhaven Lt. Art.	1845-1890	Lawr	Linc
MAY, Jared B.	16th MS Regt.	1828-1907		JEDA
MAY, Joda	33rd MS Inf.	1820-1884	Lawr	Lawr
MAY, John D.	14th MS Cav.	1831-1907	Lawr	Lawr
MAY, John E.	36th MS Inf.	1825-1900	SC	Newt
MAY, John W.	33rd MS Inf.	1840-1928	MS	Harr
MAY, John W.	36th MS Inf.	1845-1928	Scot	Scot
MAY, Jonathan	39th MS Inf.	1835-1913		Rank
MAY, Joseph	16th MS Inf.	1840-1917	Simp	Simp
MAY, Joseph	12th & 16th MS Cav.	1834-___		Monr

Name	Unit	Dates	State	County
MAY, Richard	33rd MS Inf.	1842-1899 MS	Walt	
MAY, Robert	22nd MS Inf.	1830-1914 MS	Linc	
MAY, Thomas	40th MS Inf.	1822-1888 Nesh	Nesh	
MAY, W. B.	Stanfords MS Art.	1828-1878 Gren	Gren	
MAY, W. M.	36th MS Inf.	1848-1928 MS	Newt	
MAY, William	16th MS Inf.	1826-___ Pike	Walt	
MAY, William G.	39th MS Inf.	1814-1901 Simp	Simp	
MAY, Willoughby T.	6th MS Inf.	1826-1910 Simp	Simp	
MAYBIN, J. W. (Dr.)	12th MS Inf.	1823-1908 Adam	Hanc	
MAYER, David	10th MS Inf.	1836-1908 GE	Warr	
MAYER, John	9th MS Inf.	1838-1906 Mars	Mars	
MAYER, Simon	10th MS Inf.	1837-1903 Adam	Adam	
MAYERHOFF, Charles J.	1st Cav. Res.	1846-1908 Laud	Laud	
MAYERHOFF, Frank M.	14th MS Inf.	1844-1909 Clar	Laud	
MAYERS, Pizaro Kemp	9th MS Cav.	1833-1914 MS	Jack	
MAYES, Edward	4th MS Cav.	1846-1917	Hind	
MAYES, Joseph	32nd MS Inf.	1829-1865 KY	Hind	
MAYES, William	28th MS Cav.	1825-1872 MS	Yalo	
MAYFIELD, H. R.	5th GA Inf.	1840-1924 GA	Atta	
MAYFIELD, H. V.	27th MS Inf.	1838-1864 MS	Monr	
MAYFIELD, J. M.	12th MS Cav.	1841-1930 Holm	Lee	
MAYFIELD, J. W.	1st MS Inf.	1827-1914 Smit	Smit	
MAYFIELD, James M.	16th Conf. Cav.	1843-1930 SC	Monr	
MAYFIELD, John T.	Miles LA Legion	1837-1862 LA	Clai	
MAYFIELD, P. J.	1st MS Cav.	1847-1927 Carr	Atta	
MAYFIELD, Stevens Wm.	37th MS Inf.	1834-1924 MS	Smit	
MAYFIELD, William W.	12th MS Inf.	1841-1916 Itaw	Holm	
MAYHALL, A. D.	44th MS Inf.	1825-1898 Amit	Amit	
MAYNARD, George W.	2nd AR Cav.	1839-1911 LA	Hanc	
MAYNARD, T. J.	23rd AL Inf.	1836-1910 AL	Wins	
MAYNOR, Welborn Marshall	46th MS Inf.	1838-1919 Smit	Hind	
MAYO, Anderson T.	26th MS Inf.	1841-1901 MS	Pren	
MAYO, D. C.	4th MS Inf.	1840-1888 Atta	Atta	
MAYO, Hardy P.	33rd MS Inf.	1835-1928 Leak	Leak	
MAYO, W. C.	6th MS Cav.	1818-1909 Atta	Atta	
MAYO, W. J. D.	26th MS Inf.	1818-1900 Tish	Tish	
MAYS, Joe	12th MS Cav.	1824-1909 AL	Monr	
MAYS, Llewellyn M.	28th MS Cav.	1831-1899 SC	Gren	
MAYS, W. M.	29th MS Inf.	1826-1875 TN	Holm	
MAYSON, J. R.	Lomax's Art.	1820-1895 Madi	Madi	
MAYSON, James H.	7th MS Inf.	1833-1869	Hind	
MAZA, John	1st MS Cav.	1806-1885 Calh	Calh	
MEADER, B. F.	7th MS Inf.	1836-1918 Pike	Newt	
MEADERS, J. H.	11th GA Cav.	1846-1912 GA	Harr	
MEADOR, Benjamin	2nd MS Inf.	1815-1878 NC	Wayn	
MEADOR, D. T.	21st MS Inf.	1832-1904 Unio	Unio	
MEADOR, L. P.	36th MS Inf.	1835-1905 Forr	Forr	
MEADOW, A. F.	Blythes Cav.	1828-1916	Harr	
MEADOWS, James J.	Brandons Inf.	1847-1929 Smit	Smit	
MEADOWS, Jim M.	5th MS Inf.	1827-1892 SC	Itaw	
MEAGHER, Patrick F.	18th MS Inf.	1823-1902 IR	Yazo	

Name	Unit	Dates		
MEANS, J. C.	5th MS Inf.	1821-1887		Rank
MEANS, T. A.	25th GA Inf.	1834-1903	GA	Laud
MEANS, T. B.	1st SC Rifles	1829-1895	SC	Lee
MEARES, E. J.	17th MS Inf.	1837-1933	Itaw	Itaw
MEARS, James A.	26th MS Inf.	1837-1928	Lee	Lee
MEASELS, J. D.	48th MS Inf.	1833-1896		Rank
MEAUT, Henry Joseph	1st LA Inf.	1842-1936	LA	Harr
MEAUT, Justin	3rd MS Inf.	1847-1923	Harr	Harr
MECKLIN, G W.	15th MS Inf.	1837-1862		Mont
MEDERS, E. A.	19th MS Inf.	1843-1919	Lafa	Gren
MEDFORD, Isom M.	11th MS Cav.	1848-1930	Tipp	Tipp
MEDFORD, James S.	TN Regt.	1848-1926	TN	Pren
MEDLEY, Benjamin B.	26th MS Inf.	1852-1937	Tish	Tish
MEDLIN, B/E. F.	8th MS Cav.	1845-1897	Chic	Chic
MEDLIN, Eleozer	4th MS Inf.	1843-1862	Chic	Chic
MEDLIN, H. Levi	4th NC Inf.	1841-1928		DeSo
MEECE, John W.	24th MS Inf.	1848-1928		Webs
MEEK, George W.	15th MS Inf.	1837-1915	Atta	Holm
MEEK, J. B. W. (Dr.)	4th & 6th MS Cav.			Lown
MEEK, J. T.	9th MS Inf.	____-1888		Madi
MEEK, James	18th MS Cav.	1822-1871		Bent
MEEK, John H.	18th MS Cav.	18_4-1927	Monr	Monr
MEEK, Robert Drayton	4th MS Inf.	1833-1904	SC	Holm
MEEK, William T.	1st MS Cav.	1838-1909	MS	Tate
MEEKS, L. A.	2nd MS Inf.	1835-1910	Tall	Alco
MEEKS, L. C.	1st MS Cav.	1837-1927	Yazo	Alco
MEEKS, L. F.	12th MS Inf.	1835-1927	Lawr	Alco
MEEKS, Thomas	7th MS Inf.	1829-1899	Fran	Alco
MEEKS, W. C.	32nd MS Inf.	1834-1916	Tall	Alco
MEEKS, W. T.	8th MS Inf.	1843-1925	Smit	Jone
MEEKS, William	32nd MS Inf.	1839-1908	Tipp	Tipp
MEEKS, William M.	2nd MS Inf.	1847-1924	MS	Holm
MEGEE, John T.	4th MS Inf.	1836-1879	MS	Holm
MEHARY, Eli	Blythes Cav.	1821-1891		DeSo
MELLARD, A. _.	5th AL Inf.	1845-1892	Kemp	Laud
MELLEN, Granville	12th MS Inf.		Warr	Adam
MELLON, Thomas A.	3rd MS Inf.	1826-1873	MS	Hind
MELTON, Abram J.	Jefferson Art.	1830-1924	AL	Adam
MELTON, Isham W.	5th MS Cav.	1839-1927	Holm	Holm
MELTON, J. A.	8th MS Inf.	1844-1918	Scot	Scot
MELTON, J. H.	13th MS Inf.	1841-1921	Clar	Clar
MELTON, J. M.	3rd MS Inf.	1832-1915	GA	Newt
MELTON, Lamuel C.	2nd MS Inf.	1845-1928		Bent
MELTON, William H.	29th MS Inf.	1837-1923	Holm	Holm
MELVIN, J. S.	39th MS Inf.	1839-1899		Rank
MELVIN, James	32nd MS Inf.	1832-1906	Alco	Alco
MELVINE, Willis C.	59th GA Inf.	1846-1918	GA	Lama
MENASCO, Andrew J.	17th MS Cav.	1823-1900		Jone
M____ , John W.	41st MS Inf.	1845-1938	Noxu	Harr
MERCER, F. _.	5th MS Cav.	1813-1898	Holm	Holm
MERCER, George	2nd MS Cav.	1826-1898	Newt	Newt
MERCHANT, Ellis	7th AL Inf.	1847-1936	AL	Wayn

26

MERCHANT, W. M.	9th LA Inf.	1808-1918 LA	Amit
MEREDETH, D. E.	35th MS Inf.	1832-1918 AL	Hind
MERIDETH, D. E.	35th MS Inf.	1832-___ AL	Choc
MERIWEATHER, Charles S.	2nd MS Cav.	1804-1871 GA	DeSo
MERIWEATHER, Henry W.	29th MS Inf.	1840-1884	DeSo
MERIWEATHER, James O.	Armstrongs Cav.	1831-1915 GA	Tate
MERRIWEATHER, Thomas N.	22nd MS Inf.	1838-___ Carr	Carr
MERIWEATHER, Valentine	29th MS Inf.	1828-1884	DeSo
MERIWEATHER, John W.	30th MS Inf.	1844-1932 Holm	Holm
MERRELL, Green R.	37th MS Inf.	1835-1862 Jasp	Jasp
MERRELL, Nelson C.	1st MS Inf.	1846-1881 Jasp	Jasp
MERRIL, Edward	4th AL Cav.	1839-1912 Tish	Tish
MERRITT, L. F.	3rd MS Inf.	1839-1893 Hanc	JEDA
MERRITT, S. A.	3rd MS Inf.	1842-1924	Harr
MERRITT, T. M.	4th MS Inf.	___-1887 Holm	Holm
MERRITT, Thomas	4th MS Inf.	1842-1917	Hind
MERRITT, William	2nd MS Cav.	1823-1900 Clar	Gren
MERRITTE, Anguish L.	Home Guards	1846-1921 Gree	Gree
MERVIN, T. A.		1838-1925 TX	Laud
MESTER, W. F.	15th MS Inf.	184_-1924 Harr	Harr
METCALF, Henry C.	Jeff Davis Legion	1829-1912 Adam	Adam
METCALF, Napoleon	21st MS Inf.	1843-1862 Tall	Tall
METCALFE, George W.	10th AL Inf.	1839-1896 AL	Lee
METCALFE, W. R.	2nd MS Cav.	1828-1904 AL	Lee
METIER, R. H.	1st MS Lt. Art.	1835-1915 Jeff	Jeff
METTS, George Y.	11th MS Cav.	1844-1905 SC	Wins
METTS, _. W.	1st MS Inf.	1836-1936 AL	Lafa
MICHAEL, M. L.	23rd MS Inf.	1833-1925 NC	Pren
MICHIE, Mathew R.	1st MS Cav.	1848-1932 Carr	Carr
METTS, M. A.	11th MS Cav.	1825-1899 SC	Wins
MICKLE, Helton	9th MS Inf.	1828-1906 Mars	Mars
MIDDLEBROOK, Joseph	8th MS Cav.	1846-1917 MS	Chic
MIDDLEBROOKS, _. T.	Bells AL Inf.	1826-1895 AL	Atta
MIDDLEBROOKS, Thomas	8th MS Cav.	1840-1875 Chic	Chic
MIDDLETON, Edward L.	7th MS Inf.	1843-1905 Fran	Adam
MIDDLETON, H. A. Sr.	4th MS Cav.	1836-1915	Fran
MIDDLETON, John B.	4th MS Cav.	1830-1899	Copi
MIDDLETON, M. C.	3rd MS Inf.	1816-1886 VA	Monr
MIDDLETON, R. M.	1st MS Lt. Art.	1839-1922 Yazo	
MIDDLETON, Thomas (Rev)	31st MS Inf.	1839-1919	Webs
MIDDLETON, Thomas James	14th MS Inf.	1846-1924 Lawr	Fran
MIFEY, H. C.	23rd MS Inf.	1841-1862 MS	Chic
MIKELL, George W.	38th MS Cav.	1841-1903 Lawr	JEDA
MIKELL, John J.	38th MS Cav.	1829-1881 Lawr	JEDA
MILAM, John W.	2nd MS Cav.	1830-1924 Pont	Pont
MILAM, Martin V. (Dr.)	Adams MS Cav.	1837-1873 Mars	Tate
MILES, Abe	2nd MS Cav.	1834-1899 MS	Scot
MILES, _.	26th MS Inf	1844-1934 Wins	Atta
MILES, Elzie B.	5th MS Inf.	1833-1900 Wins	Wins
MILES, James Hamilton	39th MS Inf.	1835-1893	Scot

MILES, John P.	1st MS Inf.	1832-1886 GA	Scot
MILES, Robert Paul	2nd MS Cav.	1837-1885 MS	Scot
MILES, Thomas	3rd MS Inf.	1841-1918 Jack	Ston
MILES, W. B. P.	26th MS Inf.	1844-1920 Nesh	Wins
MILES, W. J.	41st MS Inf.	1840-1916 Pont	Laud
MILEY, D. G.	6th MS Inf.	1834-1890 Smit	Smit
MILEY, D. _.	6th MS Inf.	1845-1917 Smit	Smit
MILEY, _. _.	6th MS Inf.	1840-1927	Smit
MILEY, Henry	6th MS Inf.	1835-1886 Smit	Smit
MILEY, John J.	6th MS Inf.	1837-1905 Smit	Smit
MILEY, W. M.	Ballentines Cav.	1829-1911 Carr	Carr
MILFORD, George M.	26th MS Inf.	1835-1910 Tish	Tish
MILFORD, James H.	26th MS Inf.	1842-1911 Tish	Tish
MILFORD, _. W.	26th MS Inf.	1839-1923 Tish	Tish
MILLER, A. J.	2nd MS Cav.	1816-1877	Unio
MILLER, A. P.	5th MS Cav.	1833-1908 MS	Choc
MILLER, A. S.	46th MS Inf.	1840-1914 MS	Lama
MILLER, Andrew	5th MS Inf.	1801-1864 Pont	Pont
MILLER, B. F.	12th TN Cav.	1829-1906 TN	Atta
MILLER, B. J.	51st VA Inf.	1826-1891 VA	Laud
MILLER, Benjamin F.	18th MS Inf.	1836-1923	Copi
MILLER, C. R.	61st VA Inf.	1846-1921 VA	Harr
MILLER, Charles	3rd MS Inf.	1848-1930	Harr
MILLER, Charles J.	7th MS Inf.	1839-1903 Pike	Pike
MILLER, D. M.	1st MS Cav.	1844-1918 Sunf	Sunf
MILLER, David Drake	25th LA Inf.	1841-1918 LA	Adam
MILLER, E. E.	3rd MS Cav.	1823-1893 Mars	Mars
MILLER, E. M.	9th MS Cav.	1841-1911 MS	Gree
MILLER, Earl	1st MS Lt. Art.	1844-1910 Hind	
MILLER, Edward	46th MS Inf.	1846-1903	Hind
MILLER, Edward G.	1st MS Cav.	1842-1863 Pont	Pont
MILLER, Edward T.	14th Conf. Cav.	1842-1863 Pont	Pont
MILLER, Edwin A.	13th MS Inf.	1827-1869 Wayn	Wayn
MILLER, Finis W.	18th MS Inf.	1846-1918 Smit	Tate
MILLER, George J.	12th MS Inf.	1842-1876	Copi
MILLER, George W.	Seven Star Art.	1839-1905 MS	Copi
MILLER, George W.	42nd MS Inf.	Calh	Calh
MILLER, G. Wash.	12th MS Inf.	1847-1917 AL	Pren
MILLER, Henry E.	1st MS Lt. Art.	1829-1885 Euro	Yazo
MILLER,__ Reid	42nd MS Inf.	1811-1863 Pont	Monr
MILLER, I. N.	39th MS Inf.	1848-1929	Simp
MILLER, Irvin (Rev.)	20th MS Inf.	1836-1906 Leak	Leak
MILLER, Israel T.	2nd MS Cav.	1832-1902 Pont	Pont
MILLER, J. A.	4th GA Inf.	1850-1916 GA	Tate
MILLER, J. D.	2nd MS Cav.	1835-1908 Laud	Laud
MILLER, J. _.	9th MS Inf.	1831-1914 SC	Tipp
MILLER, J. H.	21st MS Inf.	1839-1890 MS	Lawr
MILLER, J. W.	2nd MS Cav.	1829-1903 Choc	Choc
MILLER, J. W.	52nd NC Inf.	1839-1863 NC	Lafa
MILLER, J. W. (Dr.)	1st MS Regt.	1830-1907 NC	Lee
MILLER, J. W.	9th LA Inf.	1840-1904 LA	JEDA
MILLER, James J.	40th MS Inf.	1842-1913 Atta	Atta

28

MILLER, James Jeff.	12th MS Cav.	1844-1933 AL	Pren
MILLLER, James S.	34th MS Inf.	1826-1863 Tipp	Unio
MILLER, James T.	7th MS Inf.	18_-1909 Pren	Pren-
MILLER, Jeremiah	3rd MS Inf.	____-1909	Hanc
MILLER, John Cheves	17th MS Inf.	1836-1915 Chic	Chic
MILLER, John H.	7th AL Cav.	1831-1899	Tish
MILLER, John H.	41st MS Inf.	1826-1884	Pont
MILLER, John H.	7th MS Cav.	1831-1912 MS	Pren-
MILLER, John H.	48th MS Inf.	1845-1905 Smit	Covi
MILLER, John Henry	16th MS Inf.	1847-1928 Jasp	Harr
MILLER, John L.	4th MS Cav.	1827-1897 Pont	Pont
MILLER, John M.	24th MS Inf.	1840-1920 Gree	Gree
MILLER, John P.	2nd MS Cav.	1840-1905	Hind
MILLER, John R.	1st MS Inf.	1824-1864	Hind
MILLER, John T.	36th MS Cav.		Copi
MILLER, Joseph E.	32nd MS Inf.	1831-1894 AL	Pren
MILLER, Joseph H.	1st MS Cav.	1842-1880 Choc	Copi
MILLER, Joseph H.	11th LA Inf.	1824-1874 LA	Pike
MILLER, Joseph H.	7th MS Inf.	1841-1874 Pike	Pike
MILLER, Joseph S.	24th MS Inf.	1839-1862 Monr	Chic
MILLER, J. Preston	16th MS Inf.	1843-1921 Wilk	Wilk
MILLER, L. S.	55th AL Inf.	1846-1906 AL	Wins
MILLER, Landon H.	3rd MS Cav.	1847-1926 Mars	Mars
MILLER, M. Abram	4th MS Cav.	1802-1870 MS	Choc
MILLER, Martin	1st LA Art.	1834-___ LA	Adam
MILLER, Micah	19th LA Inf.	1834-1862 LA	Lee
MILLER, Napoleon N.	6th SC Inf.	1826-1892	Okti
MILLER, Nicholas	22nd MS Inf.	1845-1918 GE	Adam
MILLER, P. W.	17th MS Inf.	1831-1897 Pano	Pano
MILLER, Phillip McK.	15th MS Inf.	1840-1905	Gren
MILLER, R. W.	44th MS Inf.	1828-1908 Adam	Chic
MILLER, Reuben	1st MS Lt. Art.	1833-1906 Clar	Laud
MILLER, Robert Andrew	24th MS Inf.	1830-1911 Atta	Clay
MILLER, S. A.	18th MS Cav.	1839-1921 Tate	Tate
MILLER, S. G.	5th MS Inf.	1835-1913 Wins	Choc
MILLER, S. K.	7th MS Inf.	184_-1919 MS	JEDA
MILLER, Samuel C.	5th MS Inf.	1838-18_3 Choc	Choc
MILLER, Samon	35th GA Inf.	1843-1917	Tate
MILLER, Shipman	36th MS Inf.	1847-1937 Linc	Linc
MILLER, Thomas S.	32nd MS Inf.	1841-1907 AL	Pren
MILLER, Wm. B.	7th MS Inf.	1839-1919 AL	Harr
MILLER, W. J.	28th MS Inf.	1840-1914 MS	Fran
MILLER, W. S.	2nd MS Cav.	1836-1903 SC	Choc
MILLER, William	5th GA Inf.	1846-1921	Tate
MILLER, William H.	26th GA Inf.	1846-1924	Hind
MILLER, William Howard	1st MS Cav.	1845-1930 Chic	Chic
MILLER, William M.	26th MS Inf.	1832-1878 AL	Pren
MILLER, William P.	32nd MS Inf.	1821-1909 MS	Pren
MILLER, William	3rd MS Inf.	1830-1909 MS	Hanc
MILLETTE, Samuel Morgan	Jeff Davis Legion	1836-1918 GA	Adam
MILLICAN, (No first name)	26th MS Inf.	1846-1928 MS	Tish
MILLIGAN, Jaynes Taylor	18th MS Inf.	1848-1927 Hind	Hind

MILLIGAN, Jessie H.	43rd MS Inf.	1838-1918 Monr	Monr
MILLIGAN, William M.	TN Inf.	1841-1903 MS	
MILLEY, D.	Stockdales Cav.	1845-1924 Covi	JEDA
MILLS, A. P.	15th MS Inf.	1833-1908 Nesh	Choc
MILLS, Charles	1st AL Art.	1834-1910 AL	Leak
MILLS, David R.	56th AL Cav.	1833-1913 AL	Wayn
MILLS, Fed	27th MS Regt.	1827-1917	JEDA
MILLS, George W.	30th VA Inf.	1837-1917 VA	Mars
MILLS, George W.	Cooks AL Art.	1837-1926 AL	Wayn
MILLS, George W.	4th MS Inf.	1839-1924	Leak
MILLS, Henry	7th MS Inf.	1836-1863 Pike	Wins
MILLS, Henry G.	24th MS Inf.	1820-1904 Gree	Gree
MILLS, Henry Gardner	4th MS Cav.	1846-1926 Simp	Harr
MILLS, J. F.	4th AL Inf.	1845-1931 AL	Harr
MILLS, James	23rd MS Inf.	1836-1923 Tish	Wins
MILLS, James B.	24th MS Inf.	1833-1920 Leak	Leak
MILLS, James __	Poagues Art.	1834-1895 Madi	Madi
MILLS, James W.	53rd AL Inf.	1838-1896 AL	Leak
MILLS, Jim M.	30th MS Inf.	1840-1917 Yazo	Yazo
MILLS, John Henry	7th MS Inf.	1843-1904 Pike	Pike
MILLS, Pleasant S.	37th MS Inf.	1848-1927 Wayn	Gree
MILLS, T. A.	24th MS Cav.	1842-1916 MS	Wayn
MILLS, Thomas	46th MS Inf.	1832-1880 Wayn	Alco
MILLS, W. B.	41st MS Inf.	1824-1900 MS	Pont
MILLS, W. W.	Hams MS Cav.	1822-1891 MS	Alco
MILLS, Washington W.	24th MS Inf.	1841-1908 Gree	Gree
MILLS, William W.	24th MS Inf.	1848-1908 MS	Gree
MILLSAPS, Edmund J.	32nd MS Inf.	1824-1901 MS	Tish
MILLSAPS, Horace G.	23rd MS Cav.	1842-1905 Jeff	Jeff
MILLSAPS, Jerry M.	26th MS Inf.	1834-1903 Tish	Tish
MILLSAPS, R. W.	12th MS Inf.	1829-1913	Copi
MILLSAPS, Reuben W.	12th MS Inf.	1837-1931	Copi
MILLSAPS, T. E.	36th MS Inf.	1834-1909	Copi
MILLSAPS, T. J.	36th MS Inf.	1832-1910	Copi
MILLSAPS, Uriah	McLaurins Cav.	1828-1897 MS	Copi
MILLSTEAD, William	30th AL Inf.	1824-1899 AL	Monr
MILLSTEAD, Z. M.	34th TN Inf.	1827-1913 TN	Tipp
MILNER, Mathew D.	40th MS Inf.	1821-1906 Leak	Leak
MILTON, J. A.	5th AR Inf.	1840-1862 AR	Chic
MILTON, Samuel N.	Adams Cav.	1825-1902 Madi	Madi
MILTON, W. H.	24th MS Inf.	1821-1902 SC	Linc
MIMMS, E. Baldwin	6th MS Cav.		Hind
MIMS, G. A.	4th AL Inf.	1843-1905 AL	Monr
MIMS, H. B.	Brookhaven Lt. Art.	1827-1901 Lawr	Lama
MIMS, Jacob S.	40th MS Inf.	1815-1880 Leak	Nesh
MIMS, Robert Burr	Lays MS Cav.	1846-1919 MS	Hind
MIMS, William D. (Dr.)	17th MS Inf.	1840-1907	DeSo
MINCEY, J. M.	9th MS Inf.	1841-1925 Alco	Alco
MINCY, J. M.	9th MS Inf.	1837-1925 DeSo	Alco
MING, Christopher	2nd MS Cav.	1823-1875 Monr	Monr
MING, James P.	35th MS Inf.	1848-1932	Pano

30

MINIECE, Walter R.	12th MS Cav.		Kemp
MINOR, Duncan	1st MS Inf.	1844-1862 Adam	Adam
MINOR, Henry A.	11th MS Inf.	1835-1920 Noxu	Noxu
MINOR, W. P.	9th AL Inf.	1845-1920 AL	Noxu
MINSHEW, Richard	1st State Troops	1814-1900 Leak	Leak
MINTER, Asa C.	1st MS Lt. Art.	1842-1930 MS	Madi
MINTER, J. J.		1834-1906 Monr	Monr
MINTER, _. J.	3rd MS Inf.	1842-186_ Hind	
MINTER, William D.	18th MS Inf.	1839-1864	Copi
MINYARD, J. F/P.	1st MS Cav.	1847-1895 Carr	Carr
MISKELLY, Samuel	23rd MS Inf.	1833-1891 TN	Tipp
MISKELLY, W. _.	34th MS Inf.	1838-1923 Tipp	Carr
MISSO, Rocco	1st MS Cav.	1841-1906 Sicily	Noxu
MISTER, M. K.	Stanfords Lt.Art.	1834-1892 Gren	Gren
MITCHAL, George T.	21st MS Inf.	____-1898 Madi	Madi
MITCHELL, A. H.	15th MS Inf.	1841-1926 Choc	Webs
MITCHELL, A. L.	41st MS Inf.	1839-1862 MS	Lafa
MITCHELL, Benjamin T.	21st MS Inf.	1842-1911 Madi	Atta
MITCHELL, Charles B.	21st MS Inf.	1843-1892	Pont
MITCHELL, Daniel Edmund	31st MS Inf.	1827-1913 Tish	Unio
MITCHELL, David T.	4th KY Cav.	1840-1918 KY	Lefl
MITCHELL, George B.	6th MS Cav.	1841-1866 Alco	Alco
MITCHELL, George F.	30th MS Inf.	1835-1909 Atta	Atta
MITCHELL, George T.	1st MS Inf.	1821-1915 Kemp	Kemp
MITCHELL, George W.	Ballentines MS Cav.	1844-1924 Pano	Pano
MITCHELL, George W.	4th MS Inf.	1843-1863 Holm	Warr
MITCHELL, Henry P/B.	2nd MS Inf.	1846-1936 AL	Gren
MITCHELL, Houston	23rd MS Inf.	1824-1877 Tish	Alco
MITCHELL, I. J.	20th MS Inf.	1832-1888 Wins	Wins
MITCHELL, J. B.	18th MS Cav.	1847-1921 Tate	Pano
MITCHELL, J. D.	21st MS Inf.	1839-1911 FR	Warr
MITCHELL, J. W.	11th MS Cav.	1815-1877	Pren
MITCHELL, James	41st MS Inf.	1845-1927 Tipp	Unio
MITCHELL, James H.	20th MS Inf.	1845-1922 NC	Wins
MITCHELL, John	15th MS Inf.	1845-1936	Harr
MITCHELL, John A.	10th MS Inf.	Hind	Calh
MITCHELL, John W.	1st MS Inf.	1838-1898 Itaw	Itaw
MITCHELL, L. A.	11th MS Cav.	1841-1926	Lee
MITCHELL, L. B.	42nd MS Inf.	1830-1909 MS	Alco
MITCHELL, Lafayette	14th MS Inf.		Monr
MITCHELL, Phillips B.	1st TN Inf.	1843-1912 TN	Pren
MITCHELL, Orlando A.	7th MS Inf.	1830-1922	Pear
MITCHELL, R. P.	Saunders MS Cav.	1836-1907 Monr	Monr
MITCHELL, Robert	2nd MS Inf.	1844-1920 Tipp	Tipp
MITCHELL, Robert M.	18th MS Inf.		Hind
MITCHELL, S. V.	36th MS Inf.	1838-1893 Copi	Jone
MITCHELL, Samual Frank.	10th TN Cav.	1841-1924 TN	Calh
MITCHELL, S. Calvin	3rd MS Inf.	1830-1921 Hanc	Pear
MITCHELL, Thomas A.	44th MS Inf.	1820-1884	Tall
MITCHELL, Thomas J. (Dr)	3rd MS Inf.	1839-1911	Hind

MITCHELL, Thomas J.	3rd MS Inf.	1836-1917 MS	Pear
MITCHELL, W. F.	26th MS Inf.	1845-1936 Pont	Pont
MITCHELL, William F.	3rd MS Inf.	1833-1914	Pear
MITCHELL, William G.	2nd MS Inf.	1847-1927	Tipp
MITCHELL, William H.	32nd MS Inf.	1838-1915 MS	Mars
MITCHELL, William H.	7th MS Inf.	1835-1918 Lefl	Mont
MIXON, Abner J.	33rd MS Inf.	1844-1926 Amit	Pike
MIXON, Cornelius L.	3rd MS Cav.	1847-1908	Perr
MIXON, Edwin B/H.	33rd MS Inf.	1826-1909 Amit	Amit
MIXON, Ichabod	24th MS Inf.	1829-1910 Chic	Chic
MIXON, John	7th MS Inf.	1827-1914 Pike	Forr
MIXON, Joseph	14th MS Cav.	1843-1928 LA	Pike
MIXON, Joseph L.	12th MS Cav.	1834-1913 Chic	Chic
MIXON, W. P.	33rd MS Inf.	1842-1932 Amit	Pike
MIZE, Henry C.	12th MS Cav.	1846-1898	Rank
MIZE, _. A.	AL Co.	1845-1900	Rank
MIZE, J. E.	42nd AL Inf.	1844-1921 AL	Pren
MIZE, R. H.	8th MS Cav.	1841-1913 AL	Monr
MIZE, W. B.	9th MS Cav.	1845-1879 Yalo	Yalo
MIZE, W. J. F.	AL Arsenal	1847-1876 AL	Lee
MIZE, W. W.	26th AL Inf.	1842-1902 AL	Monr
MIZELL, David S.	19th MS Inf.	1835-1913 Jack	Geor
MIZELLE, Auguston	48th MS Inf.	1818-1892 NC	Hind
MOAK, A. A.	24th MS Cav.	1846-1919 Amit	Amit
MOAK, Jacob S.	7th MS Inf.	1845-___ Pike	Harr
MOAK, Joel	7th MS Inf.	1833-1903 Pike	Pike
MOACK, T. A.	7th MS Inf.	1839-1882 Pike	Linc
MOAK, William H.	7th MS Inf.	1841-1910 Fran	Fran
MOBLEY, B. F.	22nd MS Inf.	1833-1918 Copi	JEDA
MOBLEY, I. _.	7th MS Inf.	1844-1928 LA	Harr
MOBLEY, Fayan G.	5th MS Inf.		Hind
MOBLEY, W. W.	4th MS Cav.	1845-1903 Lawr	JEDA
MOCK, J. F.	7th AL Cav.	1827-1897 Tish	Tish
MOFFETT, Curtis Alex.	11th MS Inf.	1846-1936 Chic	Chic
MOFFETT, Silas L.	2nd MS Inf.	1843-1939 Pont	Pont
MOFFETT, Woodson Worth	37th MS Inf.	1846-1937 Clar	Jone
MOFFITT, John	7th MS Cav.	1822-1902 SC	Tipp
MOHEAD, William	5th MS Inf.	1826-1907 Carr	Carr
MOHON, Andrew Jackson	36th MS Inf.	1836-1881 MS	Copi
MOLAISON, Jules	26th LA Inf.	1839-1862 LA	Warr
MOLP_S, W. W.	23rd AR Inf.	1845-1915 AR	Laud
MOLPUS, Charles N.	2nd MS Cav.	1838-1916 Laud	Laud
MOLPUS, J. W.	2nd MS Cav.	1841-1915 Laud	Laud
MOLPUS, R. E.	2nd MS Cav.	1831-1898 Laud	Laud
MON, Edmond	3rd MS Inf.	1843-1920 Jack	Jack
MONAGAN, Leroy	32nd MS Inf.	1829-1928 Monr	Monr
MONAGHAN, James Alex.	10th MS Cav.	1829-1877 AL	Lee
MONAHAN, James D.	16th MS Regt.	1844-1896	Hind
MONETTE, A. C.	10th MS Inf.	1843-1899 Adam	Jeff
MONEY, Hernando DeSoto	11th MS Inf.	1839-1912 Carr	Carr
MONK, J. L.	13th MS Inf.	1824-1895 AL	Newt
MONROE, Albert M.	1st MS Inf.	1848-1931 Newt	Newt

32

Name	Unit	Dates/Location	
MONROE, H. C.	3rd TX Rangers	1835-1862 TX	Mars
MONROE, James M.	2nd MS Inf.	1835-1890 Tish	Alco
MONROE, James V.	36th MS Inf.	1829-1896 MS	Newt
MONTGOMERY, Abner	43rd MS Inf.		Monr
MONTGOMERY, C. T.	39th MS Inf.	1847-1918 Linc	Linc
MONTGOMERY, C. W.	5th MS Cav.	1839-1924 Madi	Adam
MONTGOMERY, Christopher	15th MS Inf.	1833-1902 Yalo	Yalo
MONTGOMERY, Daniel	1st MS Inf.	1835-1898 Fran	Wash
MONDGOMERY, F. A.	1st MS Cav.	1830-1903 Boli	Boli
MONTGOMERY, F. T.	5th MS Inf.	1844-1900 MS	Laud
MONTGOMERY, G. A.	41st MS Inf.	1831-1913 Pont	Pont
MONTGOMERY, G. H.	32nd MS Inf.	1844-1896 MS	Tish
MONTGOMERY, J. G.	43rd MS Inf.	1833-1908 Monr	Monr
MONTGOMERY, J. J.	10th MS Inf.	1839-1923 Tish	Tish
MONTGOMERY, J. T.	8th MS Cav.	1838-1894 Jasp	Jone
MONTGOMERY, J. T.	48th MS Inf.	1842-1917	Okti
MONTGOMERY, J. W.	4th AL Brig.	1844-1916 Wins	Wins
MONTGOMERY, James H.	2nd MS Cav.	1818-1892 Monr	Monr
MONTGOMERY, James Mal.	1st MS Inf.	1841-1910 Wash	Wash
MONTGOMERY, J. Minor	Adams MS Cav.	1844-1934 MS	Okti
MONTGOMERY, John	4th MS Inf.	1836-1908 Calh	Linc
MONTGOMERY, John G.	MS Cav.	1835-1928 Carolina	
			Holm
MONTGOMERY, John Gill.	43rd MS Inf.	1842-1887	Pano
MONTGOMERY, John Milton	1st MS Cav.	1844-1939 Okti	Okti
MONTGOMERY, John T.	48th MS Inf.	1821-1883 Okti	Okti
MONTGOMERY, Jonathan A.	1st MS Cav.	1846-1908 Mont	Mont
MONTGOMERY, Julian	Adams MS Cav.	1840-1869 Madi	Madi
MONTGOMERY, Lafayette J.	Adams MS Cav.	1843-1863 Madi	Warr
MONTGOMERY, Robert	6th MS Inf.	1847-1924 Simp	Simp
MONTGOMERY, Robert	Brookhaven Lt. Art.	1798-1873 TN	Linc
MONTGOMERY, Robert M.	31st MS Inf.	1822-1886	Pano
MONTGOMERY, S. _.	MS	1840-19__ Holm	Holm
MONTGOMERY, Samuel Mc.	1st LA Inf.	1837-1866 LA	Harr
MONTGOMERY, W. A.	2nd MS Regt.	1844-1925 Wins	Hind
MONTGOMERY, Thomas G.	1st MS Lt. Art.	1834-1892 Pont	Pont
MONTGOMERY, W. _.	15th MS Inf.	1829-1904 Okti	Okti
MONTGOMERY, W. D.	48th MS Inf.	1840-1918 MS	Okti
MONTGOMERY, W. H.	22nd MS Inf.	1844-1898 Tish	Amit
MONTGOMERY, Wiley H.	16th MS Inf.	1835-1927 Amit	Pike
MONTGOMERY, William	39th MS Inf.	1833-1918 MS	Fran
MONTGOMERY, William B.	15th MS Inf.	1807-1891 SC	Choc
MONTGOMERY, William D.	15th & 48th MS Inf.	1841-____ Lown	Clay
MONTGOMERY, Wm. Davis	15th MS Inf.	1840-1918 Lown	Okti
MONTGOMERY, Wm. Eugene	2nd MS Cav.	1833-1903 Fran	Adam
MONTJOY, Gid Sr.	Warren Lt. Art.	1844-1920 MS	Lefl
MONTROY, Henry Clay	11th MS Inf.	1842-1907 MS	Coah
MONTS, Isaac	1st MS Inf.	1833-1924	Lee

MONTS, John A.	MS Cav.	1847-1921		Okti
MOODY, C. B.	44th MS Inf.	1844-1924	Ston	Ston
MOODY, Curtis	1st MS Cav.	1847-1920	Wayn	Wayn
MOODY, Daniel N.	21st MS Inf.	1837-1912	Warr	Warr
MOODY, George Wash.	24th MS Inf.	1840-1913	AL	Jack
MOODY, Isom R.	24th MS Inf.	1844-1921	Clar	Laud
MOODY, J.	37th MS Inf.	1823-1895	Wayn	Wayn
MOODY, J. W.	34th MS Inf.	1832-1911		Webs
MOODY, James A.	37th MS Inf.	1831-1922	Wayn	Wayn
MOODY, James Jr.	32nd NC Inf.	1829-1890	VA	Lown
MOODY, Martin V.	Steeds MS Cav.	1846-1906	MS	Gree
MOODY, Merritt	37th MS Inf.	1845-1914	Alco	Alco
MOODY, Robert	15th MS Inf.	1828-1915	MS	Holm
MOODY, William F.	17th MS Cav.	1842-1907	Jack	Geor
MOODY, William H.	2nd MS Inf.	1836-1862	Tish	Tish
MOODY, William M.	46th MS Inf.	1831-1920	MS	Geor
MOON, Acker	24th MS Inf.	1849-1935	Monr	Monr
MOON, Ely	24th MS Inf.	1854-___		Monr
MOON, James Bell	1st MS Cav.	1843-1928	Carr	Pano
MOON, Joel Adair	24th MS Cav.	1849-1935	Monr	Monr
MOON, Nathan	5th MS Inf.	1832-1903	Monr	Monr
MOON, Thomas J.	24th MS Inf.			Monr
MOONEY, A. Q.	3rd MS Cav.	1848-1922	MS	Leak
MOONEY, G. W.	4th MS Inf.	1829-1918	Leak	Leak
MOONEY, J. _.	2_ MS Inf.	1846-1911	MS	Leak
MOONEY, R. M.	33rd MS Inf.	1831-1905	Leak	Scot
MOONEY, Rubin M.	33rd MS Inf.	1846-1911		Leak
MOONEY, S. _.	59th AL Inf.	1842-1912	AL	Leak
MOONEY, Thomas G.	15th MS Inf.	1835-1901	SC	Pont
MOONEYHAM, B/R. O.	29th MS Inf.	1836-1911	Chic	Unio
MOORE, A. J.	3rd MS Inf.	1848-1915		Okti
MOORE, A. J.	12th MS Inf.	1838-1905	MS	Jeff
MOORE, A. J.	40th MS Inf.	1844-1935	Atta	Atta
MOORE, A. _.	44th MS Inf.	1839-1913	Yalo	Yalo
MOORE, A. M.	40th AL Inf.	1830-1897	AL	Kemp
MOORE, Alexander	SC Inf.	1829-1862	SC	Choc
MOORE, Alfred G.	25th MS Inf.	1843-1904		Hind
MOORE, Alexander Fox	17th MS Inf.	1843-1878	Mars	Mars
MOORE,	11th MS Inf.	1845-1862	SC	Holm
MOORE, Benjamin	12th MS Inf.	1829-1878	Holm	Holm
MOORE, C. A.	12th MS Inf.	1826-1914	MS	Tish
MOORE, C. C/G.	14th Conf. Cav.	184_-19_		Chic
MOORE, C. M.	18th MS Inf.	1846-1927	Yazo	Yazo
MOORE, Calvin A.	12th MS Inf.	1848-1921	Tish	Tish
MOORE, Charlie Henry	28th MS Cav.	1848-1937	MS	Scot
MOORE, E. H/R.	4th MS Cav.	1832-1904	Clai	Clai
MOORE, Edwin Thomas	41st MS Inf.	1846-1909	MS	Lown
MOORE, Eli	63rd TN Inf.	1847-1916	TN	Tate
MOORE, Ezekiel Alex.	2nd MS Inf.	1826-1891	Amit	Yazo
MOORE, F. B.	1st MS State Troops	1842-1886		Lown
MOORE, G. W.	3rd MS Inf.	1847-1902	MS	Leak

MOORE, G. W.	3rd MS Cav.	1848-1917	Jone
MOORE, Garry	42nd MS Inf.	1831-1912 Calh	Calh
MOORE, George E.	8th MS Inf.	1841-1932 Linc	Linc
MOORE, George W.	26th MS Inf.	1841-1911 Tish	Tish
MOORE, George W.	28th MS Cav.	1831-1875 AL	Scot
MOORE, George W.	7th AL Cav.	1830-1922 AL	Tish
MOORE, George W.	24th MS Inf.	1847-1939	Rank
MOORE, _. W.	3rd MS Inf.	1843-1929 Harr	Ston
MOORE, ____	41st MS Inf.	1833-1901 Noxu	Noxu
MOORE, H. B.	15th MS Inf.		Copi
MOORE, Hance Hamilton	28th MS Cav.	1825-18_8 AL	Scot
MOORE, Harrison	18th MS Inf.	1841-1920 Yazo	Yazo
MOORE, Harry H.	10th MS Inf.	1846-1885 Warr	Warr
MOORE, Henry F.	15th MS Inf.	1844-1906 Gren	Gren
MOORE, Henry H.	7th MS Cav.	1845-1938 Wayn	Wayn
MOORE, Henry H.	26th MS Inf.	1835-1903 MS	Pren
MOORE, J. A.	3rd MS Cav.	1833-1923 MS	Jone
MOORE, J. C.	1st MS Lt. Art.	1842-1918 IR	Warr
MOORE, J. E.	8th GA Inf.	1837-1909 GA	Leak
MOORE, J. F.	89th AL Art.	1830-1909	Harr
MOORE, J. H.	1st MS Inf.	1839-1900 MS	Webs
MOORE, J. H.	1st MS Cav.	1839-1879 Choc	Webs
MOORE, J. H.	24th AL Inf.	1838-1925 AL	Lefl
MOORE, J. L.	25th LA Inf.	1839-1862 LA	Chic
MOORE, J. L. F.	Adams MS Cav.	1835-1923	Madi
MOORE, J. M.	8th MS Inf.	1831-1891 MS	Smit
MOORE, J. M.	2nd MS Inf.	1819-1905	Rank
MOORE, J. N.	23rd MS Inf.	1844-1910 MS	Pren
MOORE, J. S.	18th MS Cav.	1846-1911 Choc	Leak
MOORE, J. S. (Dr.)	12th MS Inf.	1839-1878 Adam	Adam
MOORE, J. T.	16th MS Inf.	1828-1904 Clai	Clai
MOORE, J. T.	12th MS Inf.	1840-1911 Holm	Holm
MOORE, J. W.	6th MS Cav.	1836-1925	Harr
MOORE, J. W.	2nd MS Inf.	1847-1924 Itaw	Itaw
MOORE, J. W.	1st MS Inf .	1830-1870 Pont	Pont
MOORE, Jacob	46th MS Inf.	1831-1907 Nesh	Nesh
MOORE, James	3rd MS Cav.	1839-1924 Yalo	Yalo
MOORE, James	18th MS Inf.	1806-1881 Hind	Holm
MOORE, James Jr.	11th MS Inf.		Monr
MOORE, James	2nd MS Inf.	1812-1876 Itaw	Itaw
MOORE, James Bestor	11th MS Inf.	1844-1917	Lown
MOORE, James H.	9th TX Cav.	1839-1930 TX	Carr
MOORE, James J.	7th AL Cav.	1840-1929 AL	Tish
MOORE, James L.	13th MS Inf.	1832-1883 Laud	Laud
MOORE, James M.	6th MS Inf.		Rank
MOORE, James S.	22nd AL Inf.	1846-____ AL	Calh
MOORE, James S.	42nd MS Inf.	1840-1913 Tate	Tate
MOORE, James Williams	17th MS Inf.	1838-1903 Mars	Mars
MOORE, Jameison H.	11th MS Regt.	1838-1863	Chic
MOORE, Jesse	43rd MS Inf.	1839-1917 Monr	Monr
MOORE, J. Foster	1st MS Lt. Art.	1839-1896 Hind	Hind
MOORE, John	28th MS Cav.	1800-1880	Scot

MOORE, John	1st MS Cav.	1846-1931 Covi	Covi
MOORE, John	2nd MS Cav.	1820-1902 Tish	Tish
MOORE, John	40th MS Inf.	1841-1915 Nesh	Nesh
MOORE, John	14th Conf. Cav.	1844-1923 Fran	Fran
MOORE, John A.	11th MS Cav.	1844-1925 Leak	Carr
MOORE, John Hinley	28th MS Cav.	1838-1925 AL	Lefl
MOORE, John James	20th MS Inf.	1842-1913 Noxu	Pear
MOORE, John Jay	32nd MS Inf.	1835-1924	Tish
MOORE, John M.	1st MS Cav.	1846-1932 IR	Covi
MOORE, John N.	14th MS Inf.	1845-1917	Leak
MOORE, John R.	32nd MS Inf.	1834-1895 NC	Pren
MOORE, John R.	28th MS Cav.	1845-1916 Scot	Scot
MOORE, John T.	Stanfords Lt.Art.	1838-1899 Yalo	Gren
MOORE, John T.	15th MS Inf.	1841-1920 Chic	Choc
MOORE, John T.	30th MS Inf.	1835-1879 AL	Mont
MOORE, John W.	15th MS Inf.	1830-1904 TN	Mont
MOORE, John W.	5th & 20th MS Inf.	1844-1933 Choc	Choc
MOORE, John W.	26th MS Inf.	1840-1899 Tish	Alco
MOORE, John Wesley	6th MS Inf.	1839-1918	Rank
MOORE, John William	5th & 6th MS Inf.	1849-1887 KY	Hind
MOORE, Jonathan	42nd MS Inf.	1847-1922	Tate
MOORE, Joseph	36th MS Inf.	1817-1881 Lawr	Lawr
MOORE, Joseph	12th MS Inf.	1840-1903 Holm	Holm
MOORE, Joseph G.	18th MS Inf.	1843-1930	Hind
MOORE, Joseph M. D.	GA Batt.	1840-1905 IR	Adam
MOORE, Josephus	12th MS Inf.	1845-1925 Holm	Holm
MOORE, Joshua L.	13th & 40th MS Inf.	1836-1926 Jone	
MOORE, L. B.	20th MS Inf.	1842-1925 MS	Harr
MOORE, L._.	MS Reg.	1842-1925 MS	Laud
MOORE, L. C.	48th MS Inf.	____-1933	Hind
MOORE, L. K.	4th MS Inf.	1835-1918 TN	Mont
MOORE, Larkin _eby	20th MS Inf.	1825-1899 Laud	Laud
MOORE, Lemuel C.	48th MS Inf.	1828-1889	Hind
MOORE, Lewis	11th MS Inf.	1802-1866 MS	Chic
MOORE, Lodwick Robert	20th MS Inf.	1833-1894 AL	Scot
MOORE, ___ A.	7th GA Cav.	1821-1889 GA	Laud
MOORE, Lucien B.	11th MS Inf.		Monr
MOORE, Lucien L.	Withers Art.	1840-1888	Hind
MOORE, M.	1st MS Cav.	18_-18_ Pont	Pont
MOORE, M. W.	7th MS Cav.	1839-1920 Tish	Alco
MOORE, Mark L.	44th MS Inf.	1839-1912 Calh	Calh
MOORE, Maurice Paul	18th MS Cav.	1847-1936 TN	Tate
MOORE, Milton M.	32nd MS Inf.	1848-1902 Tish	Alco
MOORE, Mitchael Lee	1st GA Cav.	1848-1933 GA	Lee
MOORE, Moore	Stanfords Lt.Art.	1848-1917 Gren	Gren
MOORE, Nathan	40th MS Inf.	1832-1891 MS	Leak
MOORE, Needham	40th AL Inf.	1845-1910 AL	Kemp
MOORE, Noah	6th MS Inf.	1838-1925 Scot	Scot
MOORE, O___	40th MS Inf.	1844-1916 Nesh	Nesh

MOORE, Pleasant Lane	4th MS Inf.	1838-1881 MS	Lafa
MOORE, R.	33rd MS Inf.	1822-1906 Leak	Leak
MOORE, R. J.	25th MS Inf.	1837-1908 MS	Pren
MOORE, R. M.	33rd MS Inf.	1839-1919 Covi	Covi
MOORE, R. W.	6th MS Inf.	1824-1905	Rank
MOORE, Richard	14th MS Inf.	1844-1932 AL	Okti
MOORE, Richard E.	8th Regt. Cav.		Lown
MOORE, Robert	40th AL Inf.	1842-1921 AL	Kemp
MOORE, Robert Anderson	17th MS Inf.	1818-1898 Mars	Mars
MOORE, S. B.	7th MS Inf.	1835-1864 Amit	Amit
MOORE, S. B.	7th MS Inf.	1834-1922 Amit	Amit
MOORE, S. R. Sr.	4th MS Cav.	1826-1895 Holm	Holm
MOORE, S. W.	44th MS Inf.	1831-1917 Yalo	Pano
MOORE, Sam R. Jr.	4th MS Cav.	1846-1932 Holm	Holm
MOORE, Samuel _.	Jeff Davis MS Cav.	1830-1869 Chic	Chic
MOORE, Samuel W.	44th MS Inf.	1831-1917 NC	Pano
MOORE, Samuel W.	12th MS Inf.	1814-1889 Holm	Holm
MOORE, Stephen	11th MS Cav.	1834-1910 MS	Tish
MOORE, Steve	11th MS Cav.	1834-1910 Tish	Tish
MOORE, T. G.	1st State Troops	1827-1888 Leak	Leak
MOORE, T. H.	3rd MS Cav.	1845-1913 Gren	Gren
MOORE, T. J.	2nd MS Cav.	____-1899 Laud	Laud
MOORE, T. J.	7th GA Inf.	1843-1894 GA	Laud
MOORE, Underhill H.	9th LA Inf.	1844-1929 LA	Walt
MOORE, W. B.	39th MS Inf.	1841-1901 Newt	Newt
MOORE, William	35th MS Inf.	1836-1891 Fran	Fran
MOORE, W. F.	18th MS Cav.	1826-1919	Alco
MOORE, W. J.	2nd MS Inf.	1831-1918 Tish	Tish
MOORE, W. N.	6th MS Inf.	1848-1913 Pano	Simp
MOORE, W. W.	7th MS Inf.	1839-1912 Amit	Pike
MOORE, William	42nd MS Inf.	1834-1889 MS	Calh
MOORE, William	Berrys MS Cav.	1848-1916 MS	Laud
MOORE, William	36th MS Inf.	1850-1936	Scot
MOORE, William	40th AL Inf.	1820-1892 IR	Kemp
MOORE, William B.	2nd MS Inf.	1832-1878 Mari	Linc
MOORE, William Gray	45th MS Inf.	1823-1881 Adam	Warr
MOORE, William H.	8th MS Inf.	1829-1902 MS	Smit
MOORE, William H.	43rd MS Inf.	1829-1862 Monr	Monr
MOORE, William H.	12th & 21st MS Inf.	____-1878 MS	Clai
MOORE, William L.	46th MS Inf.	1838-1896 Covi	Covi
MOORE, William M.	28th LA Inf.	1832-1909 LA	Clay
MOORE, William T.	2nd MS Inf.	1837-1909 Tipp	Bent
MOOREHEAD, C. J.	35th MS Inf.	1844-1872 Wins	Wins
MOORELAND, J. _.	58th AL Inf.	1831-1920 Unio	Unio
MOORELAND, James	14th MS Inf.	1833-1909	Okti
MOORMAN, B.	1st MS Inf.	1808-1890 Carr	Gren
MOORMAN, C. H.	Stanfords Lt.Art.	1842-1900 Carr	Gren
MORAN, C. W.	18th MS Cav.	1839-1921	Bent
MORAN, John B.	Gun Boat Morgan	1837-1924 AL	Harr

MORAN, H. _.	3rd MS Inf.	1836-1887 MS	Copi
MORAN, Peter	3rd MS Inf.	1837-1921 Hanc	Harr
MORAN, Victor	38th MS Cav.	1841-1907	Hanc
MOREE, Josh	2nd MS Inf.	1848-1931 MS	Mari
MOREHEAD, Cortez	1st MS Lt. Art.	1826-1911 SC	Mont
MOREHEAD, Joseph J.	5th AL Inf.	1840-1919 AL	Lown
MOREHEAD, William T.	Hughes MS Cav.	1843-1886	Copi
MOREHOUSE, Charles	3rd MS Inf.	1841-1916 Sunf	Sunf
MOREHOUSE, Charles	3rd MS Inf.	1842-1923 Sunf	Harr
MORELAND, H. H.	47th AL Inf.	1837-1920 AL	Unio
MORELAND, J. P.	33rd MS Inf.	1826-1899 Calh	Calh
MORELAND, Robert	32nd MS Inf.	1840-1926 AL	Pren
MORELAND, Thomas	17th MS Inf.	1844-1916 MS	Alco
MORELAND, W. B.	6th MS Inf.	1843-1917 AL	Monr
MORETON, Alfred Elliot	4th MS Inf.	1835-1925 Carr	Linc
MORGAN, Andrew Green	35th MS Inf.	1845-1900	Webs
MORGAN, B. C.	2nd MS Inf.	1832-1895 DeSo	Bent
MORGAN, Ben F.	14th MS Cav.	1840-1914 Lawr	Lawr
MORGAN, Charles	8th MS Cav.	1845-1902	Hind
MORGAN, Charles	2nd GA Regt.	1846-1935 GA	Rank
MORGAN, Charles G.	42nd MS Inf.	1837-1864 Calh	Calh
MORGAN, Constantine	1st MS Cav.	18_4-1929 MS	Copi
MORGAN, David	45th MS Inf.	1833-1895 Unio	Unio
MORGAN, E. J.	11th LA Inf.	1836-1929 LA	Harr
MORGAN, F. A.	12th MS Cav.	____-1910	Monr
MORGAN, F. B.	14th Conf. Cav.	1839-1929 MS	Amit
MORGAN, F. M.	15th MS Cav.	1844-1921	Rank
MORGAN, Frank M.	11th MS Cav.	1845-1898 Noxu	Noxu
MORGAN, G. D.	1st MS Cav.	1824-1911 MS	Okti
MORGAN, G. W.	11th AR Inf.	1848-1933 AR	Amit
MORGAN, Hiram	33rd MS Inf.	1824-1863 Amit	Amit
MORGAN, J. A.	7th MS Inf.	1822-1927 Mari	Mari
MORGAN, J. B/E.	23rd MS Inf.	1818-1899 AL	Tipp
MORGAN, J. H.	61st TN Inf.	1833-1908 TN	Pano
MORGAN, J. P.	1st MS Lt. Art.	1845-1922	Mont
MORGAN, J. P.	45th MS Inf.	1842-1933 SC	Lee
MORGAN, J. W.	56th AL Rangers	1841-1919 Laud	Laud
MORGAN, J. W.	24th MS Inf.	1828-1915 Chic	Chic
MORGAN, James Sr.	43rd MS Inf.	1825-1904 Monr	Monr
MORGAN, James	36th MS Inf.		Hind
MORGAN, James Henson	26th MS Inf.	1843-1930 NC	Pren
MORGAN, James P.	9th LA Inf.	1838-1884 MD	Warr
MORGAN, James T.	19th MS Cav.	1840-1923 Lafa	Calh
MORGAN, James W.	Perrins Cav.	1847-1864 Wins	Wins
MORGAN, Jeff	7th MS Inf.	1831-1905 Mari	Mari
MORGAN, John	8th MS Inf.	1810-1882 Calh	Calh
MORGAN, John D.	27th MS Inf.	1835-1919 Jasp	Jasp
MORGAN, John H.	17th MS Inf.	1838-1862	DeSo
MORGAN, John T.	11th MS Inf.	1845-1920 SC	Noxu
MORGAN, Joseph	21st MS Inf.	1847-1932 Madi	Harr
MORGAN, Levi	7th MS Inf.	1829-1909 MS	Fran
MORGAN, Newton W.	4th MS Cav.	1842-1926	Covi

38

MORGAN, Ruben D.	45th MS Inf.	1843-1909		Lee
MORGAN, S. G.	14th MS Inf.	1840-1927 Itaw		Itaw
MORGAN, S. P.	15th Conf. Inf.	1847-1932 AL		Harr
MORGAN, S. P.	15th Conf. Inf.	1849-1921 AL		Sunf
MORGAN, Samuel D.	18th TN Inf.	1842-1929 TN		Yalo
MORGAN, Steven B.	31st MS Inf.		Calh	Calh
MORGAN, Thomas J.	1st MS Inf.	1837-1864 MS		Chic
MORGAN, Thomas M.	3rd MS Inf.	1829-1888 MS		Newt
MORGAN, W. A.	1st MS Lt. Art.	1841-1929 GA		Atta
MORGAN, W. H.	3rd MS Inf.	1835-1905 Carr		Carr
MORGAN, _. _.(Dr.)	20th MS Inf.	1845-1900 MS		Leak
MORGAN, William D.	1st MS Lt. Art.		Carr	Carr
MORGAN, William Mitchell	16th MS Cav.	1845-1927 Monr		Monr
MORIARITY, Thomas	12th MS Inf.	1820-1903 IR		Adam
MORIARITY, Patrick J.	22nd LA Inf.	1829-1888 LA		Warr
MORRAH, John R.	6th MS Inf.	1836-1863 Rank		Rank
MORRIS, Albert F.	39th MS Inf.	1832-1906 Simp		Lawr
MORRIS, Benjamin F.	43rd MS Inf.	1836-1891		Copi
MORRIS, _____ L.	6th MS Inf.	1842-1903 MS		Copi
MORRIS, Charles Enoch	24th MS Inf.	1843-1912 Lown		Lown
MORRIS, E. G.	14th MS Inf.	1824-1910 Clar		Clar
MORRIS, E. W.	5th MS Cav.	1848-1932 AL		Tish
MORRIS, Frederick B.	39th MS Inf.	1844-1926		Lefl
MORRIS, J. C.	7th AL Cav.	1843-1923 Tish		Tish
MORRIS, J. S.	7th GA Inf.	1836-1916 GA		Unio
MORRIS, James C.	21st MS Inf.	1841-1880 Wilk		Wilk
MORRIS, Jessie	31st MS Inf.	1833-1901 MS		Chic
MORRIS, J. Frank	32nd MS Inf.	1846-1918 Pren		Pren
MORRIS, John W.	Warren Lt. Art.	1845-1916 Warr		Pano
MORRIS, Joseph Henry	5th MS Reg.	1845-1926		Hind
MORRIS, Monroe	4th MS Cav.	1834-1897 LA		Wilk
MORRIS, Offie	38th MS Cav.	1844-1929 MS		Walt
MORRIS, Peter	7th LA Inf.	1841-1928 Pike		Walt
MORRIS, Q. E.	7th MS Inf.	1842-1864 Fran		Lafa
MORRIS, R. A.	35th MS Inf.	1820-1887 Wins		Nesh
MORRIS, R. J.	Brookhaven			
	Lt. Art.	1835-1907 Lawr		Linc
MORRIS, S. _.	3rd MS Inf.	1827-1905 Noxu		Noxu
MORRIS, Sam	19th MS Inf.	____-1907 Noxu		Chic
MORRIS, Samuel	41st TN Inf.	1844-1928 TN		Rank
MORRIS, Seaborn	3rd Alcorns Brig.	1818-1914 Mari		Mari
MORRIS, Tom Jess	22nd MS Inf.	1842-1939 Lafa		Unio
MORRIS, Thomas C.	10th MS Inf.	1834-1915 KY		Warr
MORRIS, W. A.	12th MS Cav.	1844-1893 Itaw		Lee
MORRIS, W. B.	16th MS Inf.	1837-1916 MS		Jasp
MORRIS, W. G.	2nd MS Cav.	1843-1929 Itaw		Itaw
MORRIS, W. H.	1st MS Inf.	184_-1922 Clar		Clar
MORRIS, W. J.	4th Art. Batt.	1811-1875 SC		Holm
MORRIS, W . M.	41st MS Inf.	1843-1929		Lee
MORRIS, W. T.	38th MS Cav.	1827-1875 Clai		Mari
MORRIS, William A.	7th AL Cav.	1836-1919 Tish		Tish
MORRIS, William James	4th MS Inf.	1839-1927 GA		Holm

MORRIS, William L.	6th KY Cav.	1843-1914 KY	Jone
MORRIS, William Powel	22nd Inf.	1842-1866	Hind
MORRIS, Winston	46th MS Inf.	1822-1862 Covi	Mari
MORRISON, Daniel	10th MS Inf.	____-1886	Hind
MORRISON, George	1st MS Inf.	1825-1898 IR	Copi
MORRISON, J. T.	43rd AL Inf.	1843-1908 AL	Copi
MORRISON, James Robert	5th MS Cav.	1837-___ Lafa	Lafa
MORRISON, John E.	30th LA Inf.	1838-1911 LA	Harr
MORRISON, John T.	4th MS Cav.	1832-1909	Lafa
MORRISON, L. S.	2nd MS Inf.	1817-1882 TN	Jasp
MORRISON, Madison	41st MS Inf.	1843-1911 Pont	Pont
MORRISON, P.	Pointe Coupee Art.	1842-1863 LA	Lafa
MORRISON, Robert	26th MS Inf.	1822-1880 Tish	Alco
MORRISON, Robert F.	26th MS Inf.	1845-1928 Tish	Alco
MORRISON, Robert Hardey	34th MS Inf.	1846-1892 Lafa	Lafa
MORRISON, Stephen	9th MS Cav.	1832-1922 Pear	Pear
MORRISON, William S.	22nd MS Inf.	1829-1876	Hind
MORRISON, William T.	15th MS Inf.	1836-1864 Yalo	Yalo
MORROW, A. J. W.	5th MS Inf.	1844-1869 Nesh	Nesh
MORROW, David	41st MS Inf.	1839-1916 Laud	Laud
MORROW, David W.	5th MS Cav.	1847-1924 MS	Lama
MORROW, Francis	1st MS Inf.	1834-1862 Monr	Monr
MORROW, J. L.	43rd MS Inf.	1839-1918 Monr	Monr
MORROW,____	5th MS Inf.	1829-1894 Nesh	Leak
MORROW, John	28th MS Cav.	1823-1900 MS	Itaw
MORROW, John _.	19th MS Inf.	1846-1864	Holm
MORROW, Joseph	5th MS Inf.	1833-1868 Nesh	Nesh
MORROW, Joseph W.	MS Inf.	1832-1900 Leak	Leak
MORROW, W. A. J.	5th MS Inf.	1838-1912 Nesh	Harr
MORSE, Allen	35th MS Inf.	1836-1910 Lown	Laud
MORSE, John W.	1st MS Inf.	1833-1930 Mars	Itaw
MORSE, William	1st MS Inf.	1835-1924 Itaw	Itaw
MORSON, Arthur A.	3rd MS Regt.	1846-1914	Hind
MORTIMER, Chesterfield	Deesons MS Cav.	1847-1928 Carr	Mont
MORTIMER, Edward	2nd MS Cav.	1842-1876 Carr	Mont
MORTIMER, George J.	1st MS Cav.	1828-1912 PA	Copi
MORTIMER, James P.	1st MS Cav.	1845-1936 Carr	Mont
MORTON, David Samuel	26th MS Inf.	1847-1872 Tish	Alco
MORTON, ___ W.	7th MS Cav.	1837-___ Tipp	Tipp
MORTON, J. D.	34th MS Inf.	1832-1911 Tipp	Bent
MORTON, Thomas	37th MS Inf.	1815-1895 Laud	Laud
MORTON, Terry Y.	7th MS Cav.	1832-1911 TN	Tipp
MORTON, W. H.	14th NC Inf.	1833-1915 NC	Unio
MORTON, Whitfield	15th MS Inf.	1834-1862 Yalo	Lown
MORTON, William J.	11th MS Cav.	1847-1931 Lown	Lown
MORTON, Wilson M.	32nd MS Inf.	1845-1909 MS	Alco
MOSAL, Mathews	1st MS Regt.	1825-1906	Hind
MOSBY, James L.	41st MS Inf.		Monr
MOSBY, John	5th MS Inf.	1844-1908 AL	Laud
MOSBY, Robert Overton	44th MS Inf.	1841-1929 TN	Tate
MOSBY, William F.	13th MS Inf.	1833-1890 Laud	Laud

40

MOSBY, William J.	9th MS Inf.	1834-1907 Madi	Madi
MOSELEY, George Madison	1st MS Inf.	1836-1863 Mars	Mars
MOSELEY, Wass	3rd AL Cav.	1831-1891 SC	Jasp
MOSELEY, William	40th AL Inf.	1836-1909 AL	Clar
MOSELY, Leroy	37th AL Inf.	1845-1928	Hind
MOSELY, Thaddous Mort.	14th AL Inf.	1846-1931 AL	Clay
MOSER, G. _.	AL Cav.	1824-1912 AL	Pren
MOSER, R. K.	6th MS Inf.	1829-1897 Tish	Tish
MOSES, Monroe C.	23rd MS Inf.	1843-1909 MS	Alco
MOSES, William Newton	28th AL Inf.	1836-1920 AL	Sunf
MOSER, J. P.	2nd Inf.	1818-1872	Tall
MOSIER, J. E.	27th MS Inf.	1847-1920 MS	Harr
MOSIER, T. _.	Forrests Cav.	1847-1920 Tall	Harr
MOSLEY, Elijah	24th MS Inf.	1845-1891 Kemp	Nesh
MOSLEY, J. B.	7th AL Cav.	1839-1923 Laud	Laud
MOSLEY, John Townes	1st MS Cav.	1823-1923 Laud	Laud
MOSLEY, Marion	4th AL Inf.	1844-1908 AL	Lee
MOSLEY, R. J.	24th MS Inf.	1834-1892 Kemp	Kemp
MOSLEY, Robert J.	35th MS Inf.	1832-1878 Wins	Laud
MOSLEY, R. W.	35th MS Inf.	1842-1927 Wins	Laud
MOSLEY, T___	35th MS Inf.	1840-1930 Wins	Laud
MOSLEY, Willis	6th MS Cav.	1827-1902 Chic	Chic
MOSS, Benjamin Franklin	8th MS Inf.	1834-1917 Jasp	Jasp
MOSS, Christopher C.	2nd MS Cav.	1848-1922	Hind
MOSS, D. C.	2nd MS Cav.	1843-1919 Choc	Choc
MOSS, Dock C.	4th MS Cav.	1847-1927 MS	Choc
MOSS, H. B.	15th MS Inf.	1843-1919 Choc	Choc
MOSS, J. W.	15th MS Inf.	1841-1910 Choc	Choc
MOSS, James	2nd MS Cav.	1833-1923 AL	Choc
MOSS, John Owen	3rd MS Cav.	____-1884	Smit
MOSS, Robert	11th MS Cav.	1831-1910	Hind
MOSS, W. A.	2nd MS Cav.	1838-1927 Choc	Choc
MOSS, Wm. R.	6th MS Inf.	1847-1918	Hind
MOSS, Wiley J.	Adams MS Cav.	1817-1878	Okti
MOSS, Wiley J.	Adams MS Cav.	1845-1895 Okti	Holm
MOSS, William	5th MS Inf.	1833-1902 MS	Monr
MOTES, K. C.	25th AL Inf.	1829-1920 AL	Unio
MOTLEY, R. A.	12th TN Cav.	1847-1936 MS	Lee
MOTT, Christopher H.	19th MS Inf.	1826-1862 Mars	Mars
MOTT, James Jefferson	13th MS Inf.	1841-1924 Laud	Kemp
MOTTOX, Thomas J.	24th MS Inf.	1842-1912 Itaw	Itaw
MOULDS, George W.	8th MS Inf.	1839-1901 Jasp	Jasp
MOULDS, Jefferson	1st MS Cav.	1847-1921 Jasp	Jasp
MOULDS, William M.	40th MS Inf.	1839-1898 NC	Jasp
MOUNCE, M. L.	2nd MS Cav.	1838-1927 Pont	Pont
MOUNCE, Robert T.	2nd MS Inf.	1830-1914 Tipp	Unio
MOUNGER, William H.	27th MS Inf.	1843-1901 Jasp	Jasp
MOW, W. E.	7th TN Cav.	1842-1862 TN	Lafa
MOYER, Wm. F.	15th GA Inf.	1838-1907 GA	Adam
MOZINGO, George J.	1st MS Cav.	1818-1889	Wayn
MOZINGO, William P.	1st MS Cav.	1843-19__ AL	Wayn
MUCKELRATH, Wm. Jasper	MS Inf.	1844-1928 MS	Lama

41

MUH, Geo. Sr.	Capt. Halls Co.	1815-1890	Hind
MUIRHEAD, Gusham S.	1st MS Lt. Art.	1838-1879 Clai	Holm
MULCANY, James Charles	22nd MS Inf.	1839-1914 Mars	Mars
MULDROW, Henry Lowndes	14th MS Inf.	1837-1905 Okti	Okti
MULHOLLAND, Joseph	12th MS Inf.	1830-1869 IR	Laud
MULLEN, D.	Hendersons Scouts	1823-1891 MS	Adam
MULLEN, E. P.	36th MS Inf.	1844-1935 Copi	Harr
MULLEN, J. H.	12th MS Inf.	1830-1877	Tall
MULLEN, Joseph Hooper	12th MS Inf.	1839-1900 Hind	Warr
MULLEN, Merritt M.	30th MS Inf.	1846-1933 Carr	Tall
MULLEN, Nicholas Reuben	30th MS Inf.	1848-1909 Carr	Gren
MULLEN, W. _.	4th MS Inf.	1841-1885 Carr	Carr
MULLENS, Andy	7th MS Inf.	1841-1913 Alco	Alco
MULLEN, Elisha L.	3rd MS Art.	1818-1879 Carr	Carr
MULLENS, L. Malone	31st MS Inf.	1834-1913 Okti	Okti
MULLER, Frederick W.	3rd MS Inf.	1847-1862	Hind
MULLER, Henry	38th MS Cav.	1821-1884 GE	Hind
MULLIN, Edward Sims	44th MS Inf.	1843-1918 Tall	Tall
MULLINS, H. M.	12th MS Inf.	1845-1929 Copi	Pike
MULLINS, J. M.	22nd MS Inf.	1845-1911 MS	Lawr
MULLINS, James R.	42nd MS Inf.	1818-1885 IR	Gren
MULLINS, M.	48th MS Inf.	1825-1867	Choc
MULLINS, Marion M.	2nd MS Inf.	1836-1925 NC	Lee
MULLINS, Martin N.	7th MS Inf.	1837-1908	Alco
MULLINS, W. L.	14th MS Inf.	1845-1923 Monr	Fran
MULLINS, William	33rd MS Inf.	1835-1915 MS	Fran
MULLINS, William E.	14th MS Cav.	1847-1923 Fran	Fran
MULLINS, William Yancy	10th MS Cav.	1840-1910 SC	Pren
MUNCE, Henry	12th MS Inf.	Warr	Adam
MUNGER, John F.	14th MS Inf.	1838-1876 Lown	Lown
MUNN, John Sr.	36th MS Inf.	1821-1884 Newt	Newt
MUNSON, C. W. (Dr.)	8th MS Inf.	1839-1917 Clar	Monr
MUNSON, W. V.	6th MS Cav.		Lown
MURCH, Robert J.	28th MS Cav.	1836-1915 Wilk	Warr
MURDAUGH, John T.	9th MS Inf.	1836-1889 MS	Alco
MURDOCK, B. N.	39th GA Regt.	1835-	Pear
MURDOCK, William Bristol	La. Comm.	1843-1903 LA	Clai
MURFF, Connell A.	24th MS Inf.	1837-1906 Monr	Monr
MURFF, George W.	42nd MS Inf.	1830-1910 Calh	Calh
MURFF, James R.	24th MS Inf.	1845-1904 Monr	Monr
MURFF, W. R.	1st MS Inf.	1842-1917 AL	Forr
MURFF, Wiley	2nd MS Inf.	1809-1891 Monr	Monr
MURLEY, James D.	26th MS Inf.	Tish	Alco
MURLEY, Jefferson K.	32nd MS Inf.	1825-1907 NC	Tipp
MURPHREE, James K.	1st MS Cav.	Carr	Calh
MURPHREE, T. M.	4th MS Inf.	1844-1905 Calh	Calh
MUHPHREE, W. A.	8th MS Cav.	1839-1918 Yalo	Chic
MUHPHREE, William P.	8th MS Cav.	1847-1916 Yalo	Pano
MURPHY, A. J.	48th MS Inf.	1832-1919 Yalo	Choc
MURPHY, Charles	4th MS Inf.	1813-1889 SC	Holm
MURPHY, Daniel	3rd MS Cav.	1843-1912	Laud

42

MURPHY, E. H.	16th MS Inf.	1836-1861	KY	Pike
MURPHY, J. _.	18th MS Cav.	1832-1924		Tate
MURPHY, J. D.	43rd MS Inf.	1840-1920	Lown	Lown
MURPHY, J. E.	8th MS Inf.	1844-1927	MS	Leak
MURPHY, J. F.	31st MS Inf.	1832-1888	Pont	Pren
MURPHY, J. H.	5th MS Cav.	1846-1924	Tate	Tate
MURPHY, James	30th MS Inf.	1832-1918	MS	Harr
MURPHY, James K. Poke	7th AL Inf.	1839-1911	AL	Tish
MURPHY, James M.	19th MS Inf.	1842-1904	Pano	Pano
MURPHY, James R.	9th MS Inf.	1847-1911	MS	Alco
MURPHY, John	Surgeon	1831-1888	SC	Holm
MURPHY, John	Englishs MS Art.	1828-1863	IR	Adam
MURPHY, John	Seven Star Art.	1842-1929	Copi	Harr
MURPHY, John	24th MS Inf.	1835-1915	Warr	Warr
MURPHY, John S.	10th MS Inf.	1836-1908	Yazo	Yazo
MURPHY, Harrison H.	4th AL Inf.	1841-1925	AL	Itaw
MURPHY, Louis	18th MS Cav.	1827-1921		Tate
MURPHY, M. A.	1st MS Inf.	1815-1905	Atta	Atta
MURPHY, Patrick	12th MS Inf.	1829-1885	IR	Adam
MURPHY, R. J. (Dr.)	14th MS Inf.	1838-1923	VA	Lown
MURPHY, Robert H.	18th MS Inf.	18_-1904	IR	Hind
MURPHY, Robert M.	12th MS Inf.	1834-1882	SC	Holm
MURPHY, V. L.	41st MS Inf.	1822-1890	MS	Laud
MURPHY, Victor M. (Dr.)	5th MS Inf.	1805-1862	NC	Noxu
MURPHY, W. A.	19th MS Inf.	1846-1932		Carr
MURPHY, W. A.	7th AL Cav.	1842-1926	AL	Tish
MURPHY, William	Woods MS Cav.	1840-1909	Yazo	Yazo
MURPHY, William B.	2nd MS Cav.	1833-1900	TN	Mont
MURPHY, William D.	1st MS Lt. Art.	1839-1875		Hind
MURRAH, A. T.	53rd AL Cav.	1834-1929	AL	Geor
MURRAH, J. _.	4th MS Inf.	1843-1914	Holm	Lown
MURRAH, John M.	9th MS Inf.	1847-1932	MS	Webs
MURRAH, Morgan Henry	2nd GA Inf.	1843-1918	GA	Alco
MURRAY, Church	36th AL Cav.	1824-1884	NC	Gree
MURRAY, J. F.	39th MS Inf.	1835-1916	Simp	Lama
MURRAY, John Young	23rd MS Inf.	1829-1915	TN	Tipp
MURRAY, L. W.	6th MS Cav.	1833-1885	MS	Simp
MURRAY, Thomas B.	6th MS Cav.	1836-1917		Simp
MURREL, W. J.	1st MS Lt. Art.	1833-1914	LA	Pike
MURRY, Eli	5th MS Cav.	1823-1910	Yalo	Yalo
MURRY, James K.	7th MS Cav.	1832-1909	Tipp	Tipp
MURRY, John E.	8th MS Inf.	1823-1894	MS	Jasp
MURRY, John M.	1st AR Inf.	1844-1913	Tipp	Tipp
MURRY, Pat	12th MS Inf.	1843-1905	IR	Adam
MURRY, W. B.	2nd MS Inf.	1846-1925		DeSo
MUSE, Benjamin F.	18th MS Inf.	1841-1897		Madi
MUSE, J. S.	39th MS Inf.	1844-1892		Rank
MUSE, Jesse W.	47th TN Inf.	1837-1909	TN	Pren
MUSE, Joseph Harrison	Adams MS Cav.	1837-1896		Madi
MUSE, Joseph Newton	2nd MS Inf.	1847-1925	TN	Pren
MUSE, Vigil Lee	22nd MS Inf.	1845-1868	Lawr	Lawr
MUSGROVE, John	40th MS Inf.	1836-1909	Jasp	Jasp

MYATT, Joseph C.	46th MS Inf.	1842-1912 Kemp	Kemp
MYERS, Alvin	6th MS Inf.	1827-1902 Covi	Covi
MYERS, A. L.	56th AL Inf.	1839-1907 AL	
MYERS, A. W.	36th MS Inf.	1828-1902	Copi
MYERS, D. L.	39th MS Inf.	1839-1907	Rank
MYERS, D. M.	6th MS Inf.	1845-1885 Smit	Smit
MYERS, David L.	39th MS Inf.	1822-1910	Rank
MYERS, David Ransom	36th MS Inf.	1829-1912	Copi
MYERS, E. D.	12th MS Cav.	1847-1925	Rank
MYERS, E. G.	3rd MS Regt.	1845-1902	Rank
MYERS, Ephraim	10th MS Inf.	1838-1905 Rank	Scot
MYERS, Felden Frederick	Adams MS Cav.	1840-1926 Madi	Perr
MYERS, Frank W.	22nd MS Inf.	1842-1907 Amit	Amit
MYERS, G. W.	23rd MS Inf.	1840-1918 MS	Alco
MYERS, H.	12th MS Inf.	1819-1875 OH	Warr
MYERS, Isham	39th MS Inf.	1831-___	Simp
MYERS, J. W.	Army	___-1909	Adam
MYERS, J. W.	1st MS State Troops	1832-1906	Leak
MYERS, James H.	6th MO Inf.	1841-1861 MO	Clai
MYERS, James Mathew	3rd MS Inf.	1848-1917 NC	Newt
MYERS, John David	3rd SC Inf.	1840-1921 SC	Pano
MYERS, Lee	8th MS Inf.	1846-1924 MS	Lawr
MYERS, Malcolm S.	22nd MS Inf.	1845-1924 Amit	Pike
MYERS, Marcus	7th MS Inf.	1833-1880 MS	Scot
MYERS, Preston	39th MS Inf.	1839-1921 MS	Copi
MYERS, S. C.	39th MS Inf.	1839-1901	Rank
MYERS, S. H.	11th MS Cav.	1838-1911 Tall	Alco
MYERS, Simon	31st MS Inf.	1821-1878 Chic	Chic
MYES, W. A.	6th NC Inf.	1843-1909 VA	Forr
MYERS, W. L.	Yergers Cav.	1845-1936	Rank
MYRICK, Augustus B.	GA Regt.	1846-1935	Lown
MYRICK, Ely M.	27th MS Inf.	1844-1924 Perr	Forr
MYRICK, George H.	1st MS Cav.	1832-1889 Leak	Leak
MYRICK, George H.	Leake Rangers	___-1889	Atta
MYERS, J. S.	13th MS Cav.	1847-1925 Nesh	Nesh
MYRICK, R. A.	MS Inf.	1822-1906	Hind
MYRICK, Willis W.	37th MS Inf.	1841-1924 Jasp	Jasp
NABERS, James I.	14th MS Inf.	1844-1877 Monr	Monr
NABERS, Frank M.	12th MS Cav.	1839-1914 AL	Monr
NABERS, John Alfred	14th MS Inf.	1841-1911 AL	Monr
NABERS, Lewis	2nd MS Cav.	1808-1865 MS	Monr
NABERS, Sam R.	23rd MS Inf.	1838-1907 Tipp	Tipp
NABERS, William B.	2nd MS Cav.	1848-1864 MS	Monr
NABORS, George R.	38th MS Cav.	1846-1919 Holm	Holm
NABORS, J. M.	4th MS Inf.	1830-1899 Carr	Carr
NABORS, Jacob J.	41st AL Inf.	1839-1862 AL	Chic
NABORS, Joshua W.	5th MS Cav.	1821-1901 Carr	Carr
NABORS, W. M. Sr.	4th MS Inf.	1838-1918	Mont
NABORS, William F.	38th MS Cav.	1812-1885 Holm	Holm
NAIL, John S.	Ballentines Cav.	1832-1873 Carr	Carr

44

NAIL, W. F.	6th SC Inf.	1836-1920 SC	Lafa
NALES, James N.	2nd AR Inf.	1841-1862 AR	Lafa
NALL, Merrill	37th AL Inf.	1841-1863 AL	Lafa
NALTY, John	Miles LA Legion	Adam	
NANCE, A. (Gus) H.	23rd MS Inf.	1847-1934	Tipp
NANCE, Augustus Polk	23rd MS Inf.	1837-1923 Tipp	Tipp
NANCE, George C.	12th MS Cav.	1845-1922 Lown	Lown
NANCE, H. E. W.	5th MS Cav.	1834-1917 SC	Webs
NANCE, J. H.	40th MS Inf.	1835-1902 Nesh	Kemp
NANCE, James H.	34th MS Inf.	1833-1914 Tipp	Tipp
NANCE, James Harvey	34th MS Inf.	1809-1886 Tipp	Tipp
NANCE, John M.	32nd MS Inf.	1831-1907 Alco	Tipp
NANCE, John Morgan	34th MS Inf.	1832-1907	Tipp
NANCE, John O.	2nd MS Inf.	1843-1915 Tipp	Bent
NANCE, Richard D.	40th MS Inf.	1845-1821 Kemp	Wins
NANCE, Ruffen Brown	2nd MS Inf.	1846-1833 Tipp	Tipp
NANCE, Thomas	2nd MS Inf.	1837-1863 Tipp	Tipp
NANCE, Wesley B.	4th MS Cav.	1820-1877 NC	Holm
NANCE, William W.	32nd MS Inf.	1829-1904 Tipp	Tipp
NANNEY, Uriah P.	2nd MS Cav.	1836-1897 MS	Itaw
NARON, Benjamin F.	24th MS Inf.	1838-1929 Chic	Calh
NARON, G. W.	31st MS Inf.	1828-1911 GA	Webs
NARON, J. M.	24th MS Inf.	1835-1916 Chic	Chic
NARON, Thomas J.	MS Inf.	1831-1927 Chic	Chic
NARON, Thomas J.	31st MS Inf.	____-1917 Choc	Calh
NASH, Albert Newton (Dr)	MS Inf.	____-1862 Okti	Okti
NASH, Daniel	26th MS Inf.	1840-1906 Tish	Alco
NASH, E. W.	26th MS Inf.	1845-1917 Tish	Alco
NASH, Edmon	27th MS Inf.		Monr
NASH, Ira P.	2nd MS Cav.		Monr
NASH, J. J.	2nd MS Cav.	1818-1899 Kemp	Monr
NASH, John Jasper N.	5th MS Inf.	1829-1911	Nesh
NASH, Jonas	26th MS Inf.	1835-1877 Tish	Alco
NASH, Joshua M.	26th MS Inf.	1834-1878 Tish	Alco
NASH, N. E.	43rd MS Inf.	1837-1920 Monr	Monr
NASH, Peter W.	11th MS Inf.	1838-1915	Pren
NASH, T. Wilson	28th MS Cav.	1838-1919 Monr	Monr
NASH, Wiley N.	Adams MS Cav.	1846-1906 Noxu	Okti
NASH, William M.	27th MS Inf.	1840-___ MS	Monr
NASON, John A.	26th MS Inf.	1843-1911 Tish	Choc
NASON, Richard J.	Stanfords MS Art.	1817-1894 Yalo	Gren
NATIONS, Abraham	33rd MS Inf.	1834-1911 Lawr	Linc
NATIONS, Andrew J.	24th MS Cav.	1843-1907 Lawr	Copi
NATIONS, E.	33rd MS Inf.	1848-1927 Lawr	Linc
NATIONS, J. O.	2nd State Troops	____-1864 Lawr	Linc
NATIONS, James C.	2nd MS Cav.	1825-1902 MS	Calh
NATIONS, W. W.	15th MS Inf.	1842-1915 Choc	Mont
NATIONS, William	3rd MS Cav.	1846-1922 Linc	Linc
NAUL, C. J.	33rd MS Inf.	1827-1877 Amit	Amit
NAUL, J. W. (Dr.)	16th LA Inf.	1833-1909 LA	Pike
NAYLOR, J. C.	3rd TX Cav.	1824-1870 KY	Kemp

45

NAYLOR, M. L.	3rd TX Cav.	1846-1927 TX	Kemp
NEAL, Christopher Col.	36th MS Inf.	1842-1881 MS	Kemp
NEAL, C. G.	17th MS Inf.	1841-1931 Chic	Chic
NEAL, G. _.	8th MS Cav.	1846-1882 Chic	Chic
NEAL, George W.	20th MS Inf.	1833-1906 Scot	Scot
NEAL, J. J.	5th MS Inf.	1813-1894 Calh	Unio
NEAL, Jeremiah	7th MS Inf.	1839-1910 Fran	Linc
NEAL, John	31st MS Inf.	1847-1929 Chic	Chic
NEAL, John M.	31st MS Inf.	1847-1929 Chic	Chic
NEAL, Pinkney George	24th MS Inf.	Choc	Choc
NEAL, Sam	3rd MS Cav.		Carr
NEAL, __	14th MS Cav.	1845-192_ Lawr	Lawr
NEAL, Stephen S.	7th MS Inf.	1833-1878 MS	Lafa
NEARS, Ervin J.	17th MS Inf.	1837-1933 Itaw	Itaw
NEATHERLAND, William	33rd MS Inf.	1833-1884 Lawr	Lawr
NECAISE, Charles	3rd MS Inf.	1839-___ MS	Hanc
NEEDHAM, Thomas Lumkin	4th MS Cav.	1835-1915 Jeff	Pano
NEEL, B. S.	31st MS Inf.	1799-1880 Chic	Chic
NEEL, J. W.	1st MS Inf.	1830-1913	Hind
NEEL, William	36th AL Inf.	1830-1908 AL	Gree
NEELAND, John	41st MS Inf.	1833-___	Monr
NEELY, Alexander S.	2nd MS Inf.	1839-1905 Tipp	Tipp
NEELY, Austin	39th MS Inf.	1831-1917	Warr
NEELY, Isiah	12th SC Inf.	1836-1915 SC	Okti
NEELY, John	18th Cav.	1847-1934 Mars	Mars
NEELY, John T.	21st MS Inf.	1844-1913 Tall	Tall
NEELY, Joseph	Lays MS Cav.		Rank
NEELY, S. L.	1st MS Cav.	1839-1884 Pont	Unio
NEELY, Sam C/G.	1st MS Lt. Art.	1832-1890 Warr	Warr
NEELY, Thomas	Mechanic	1832-1868 TN	Tipp
NEELY, William N.	2nd MS Inf.	1843-1910 TN	Tipp
NEESE, Harry	60th AL Inf.	1825-1902 AL	Nesh
NEIGHBORS, Thomas J.	41st AL Inf.	1826-1899 AL	Chic
NEILSON, Captain William	6th TN Inf.	1837-1924 Lafa	Lafa
NEILSON, C. P.	44th MS Inf.	1836-1894 Amit	Wilk
NEILSON, Charles Bowen	11th MS Inf.	1847-1917 Lafa	Lafa
NEILSON, David W.	7th MS Inf.	1844-1862 Amit	Amit
NEILSON, John A.	14th MS Inf.	1834-1922 Lown	Lown
NEILSON, William	14th MS Inf.	1843-1911 Lown	Lown
NELMS, A. M.	28th MS Cav.	1837-1870 Carr	Carr
NELMS, Charles G.	22nd MS Inf.	1839-1862 DeSo	Mars
NELMS, Eben	9th MS Inf.	1817-1902	DeSo
NELMS, Henry F.	41st AL Inf.	1843-1927 AL	Bent
NELMS, John J.	8th MS Cav.	1844-1921 AL	Calh
NELMS, Joseph Horace	8th MS Cav.	1848-1916 Wash	Wash
NELMS, Matthias M.	2nd MS Inf.	Pont	Alco
NELMS, Nathaniel	29th MS Inf.	Yalo	Calh
NELSON, A. J.	15th MS Inf.	1829-1900 MS	Yalo
NELSON, Charles O.	22nd MS Inf.	1842-1925 Hind	Harr
NELSON, G. W.	54th AL Inf.	1840-1916 AL	DeSo
NELSON, George W.	39th MS Inf.	1831-1910 Newt	Jone
NELSON, H. _.	28th MS Cav.	1826-1907	JEDA

46

NELSON, J. M.	5th MS Inf.	1849-1930 Nesh	Harr
NELSON, J. N.	15th MS Inf.	1844-1914 Yalo	Jack
NELSON, J. O.	37th MS Inf.	1838-1917 Jasp	Harr
NELSON, James Oliver	10th MS Cav.	1848-1905 Unio	Pren
NELSON, John	29th MS Inf.	1828-1900 Nesh	Scot
NELSON, L. D.	36th MS Inf.	1828-1875 GA	Newt
NELSON, S. H.	Adams MS Cav.	1829-1911 DeSo	Pano
NELSON, S. J.	36th MS Inf.	1824-1887 GA	Newt
NELSON, Theodore F.	2nd MS Inf.	Carr	Carr
NEREAUX, Joseph Adolph	27th LA Inf.	1833-1862 LA	Warr
NESBIT, John M.	23rd MS Inf.	1848-1922 Pont	Pont
NESBITT, Edward S.	29th MS Inf.	1830-1915	DeSo
NESBITT, T. McKinney	11th MS Regt.	1840-1864	DeSo
NESTER, J. N.	37th MS Inf.	1827-1908 Clar	Newt
NESTLR, John M.	5th MS Inf.	1839-1926 Kemp	Kemp
NETTERVILLE, J. T.	4th MS Cav.	1824-1899 Wilk	Wilk
NETTERVILLE, Jesse N.	4th MS Cav.	1835-1921 Wilk	Wilk
NETTERVILLE, T. J.	14th MS Inf.	1843-1917 Oktl	Harr
NETTERVILLE, Thomas D.	4th MS Cav.	1845-1928 Wilk	Wilk
NETTLES, E. W.	7th MS Inf.	1819-1897 Fran	Fran
NETTLES, William Jeff.	14th MS Inf.	1848-1936 Monr	Fran
NETTO, Frank	3rd MS Inf.	1831-1911 Harr	Harr
NEVELS, M. S.	4th MS Inf.	1841-1930 MS	Jeff
NEVELS, ___ W.	1st MS Lt. Art.	1838-1911 Jeff	Linco
NEVELS, Robert Payton	1st MS Sharpshooters	1841-1926 Holm	Holm
NEVELS, William	Adams Co. Inf.	1808-1883 VA	Holm
NEVILL, Ellison Rogers	27th MS Inf.	1847-1927 SC	Jone
NEVILLE, William Jr.	20th MS Inf.	1839-1903	Kemp
NEW, L. M.	26th MS Inf.	1830-1889 Tish	Alco
NEWELL, Edward Henry	3rd LA Cav.	1845-1916 LA	Adam
NEWELL, James B.	1st MS Inf.	1825-1894 Kemp	Laud
NEWELL, John S.	3rd MS Inf.	1844-1907 Linc	Linc
NEWELL, John T.	Adams MS Cav.	1842-1925 Perr	Perr
NEWELL, John T.	35th MS Inf.	1842-1895 Kemp	Kemp
NEWELL, S. L.	41st MS Inf.	1834-1885 Pont	Pont
NEWELL, William	Brookhaven Lt. Art.	1839-1889 Linc	Linc
NEWELL, William	17th MS Inf.	1847-1922 Mars	Mars
NEWELL, William J.	41st MS Inf.	1845-1927 NC	Pont
NEWELL, William J.	AL Inf.	1842-___	Monr
NEWER, Edward Eugene	30th LA Inf.	1841-1910 LA	Lefl
NEWMAN, George R.	Army	___-1907	Adam
NEWMAN, James A.	1st MS Lt. Art.	1845-1905 Warr	Warr
NEWMAN, J. P. (Tom)	14th MS Cav.	1848-1920 Pike	Linc
NEWMAN, John T.	33rd MS Inf.	1842-1923 Amit	Amit
NEWMAN, M. V. B.	22nd MS Inf.	1839-1920 Amit	Harr
NEWMON, Press C.	11th MS Inf.	1840-1891 Lown	Tall
NEWMAN, Rudolph Session	14th MS Cav.	1846-1916 Pike	Linc
NEWMAN, T. M.	33rd MS Inf.	1845-1917 MS	Amit
NEWMAN, Thomas H.	16th MS Inf.	1844-1904 Pike	Pike
NEWMAN, W. S.	6th MS Inf.	1837-1895	Copi

47

NEWSOM, J. B.	4th MS Cav.	1845-1914 Wayn	Wayn
NEWSOM, Joel Robert		1843-1917 MS	Holm
NEWSOM, John B.	Yeagers Regt.	1847-1935 Lawr	Lawr
NEWSOM, Joseph D.	38th MS Inf.	1828-1919 Laud	Laud
NEWSOME, Lewis J.	7th MS Inf.	1837-1897 Mari	Mari
NEWSOM, _. L.	16th MS Inf.	1843-1917 Lawr	Lawr
NEWSOM, J. _. B.	30th MS Inf.	1836-1907 Lawr	Lawr
NEWSOM, R. E.	41st MS Inf.	1842-1928 Pont	Harr
NEWSOM, W. A.	33rd MS Inf.	1831-1912 Leak	Leak
NEWTON, Adam B.	3rd MS Cav.	1843-1925 Copi	Linc
NEWTON, I. W.	MS Cav.	1846-1918 Copi	Linc
NEWTON, James	1st MS Inf.	1827-1897 MS	Laud
NEWTON, James M.	6th MS Inf.	1835-1925 Copi	Linc
NEWTON, James Marius	1st MS Lt. Art.	1838-1895 Hind	Copi
NEWTON, L. Emmett	4th LA Inf.	1842-1907 LA	Adam
NEWTON, Oscar	1st MS Cav.	1830-1913 MS	Copi
NEWTON, Owen G.	7th MS Inf.	1838-1862 JEDA	JEDA
NEWTON, Wiley A.	9th MS Inf.	1842-1877	Tate
NEYLAND, Robert H.	24th MS Cav.	1824-1920 Wilk	Wilk
NIBLETTE, T. J.	2nd MS Inf.	1843-1921 MS	Lee
NICAISE, Edmond	3rd MS Inf.	1837-1899 Hanc	Hanc
NICHLES, Larmarsuis D.	Pettus MS Art.	1839-192_	Pano
NICHOLAS, Elijah	14th MS Inf.	1839-1915 Laud	Laud
NICHOLAS, J. A.	Lt. Lacy	1845-1927	Itaw
NICHOLAS, T. _.	13th MS Inf.	1842-191_ Chic	Chic
NICHOLLS, William C.	12th MS Cav.	1832-1908 AL	Jeff
NICHOLS, Augustus N.	16th MS Inf.	1846-1914 Monr	Monr
NICHOLS, D. R.	25th MS Inf.	1827-1911	Perr
NICHOLS, David E.	7th & 14th MS Inf.	1848-1927 Pike	Jone
NICHOLS, F. M.	11th MS Inf.	1849-1911	Monr
NICHOLS, J. _.	8th MS Inf.	1815-1900 MS	Smit
NICHOLS, J. W.	22nd MS Inf.	____-1922 DeSo	DeSo
NICHOLS, Jimmie R.	26th MS Inf.	1824-1902 SC	Pren
NICHOLS, John W.	15th MS Inf.	1832-1915	Perr
NICHOLS, Needham	7th MS Inf.	1822-1900 Mari	Lama
NICHOLS, _. W.	3rd MS Cav.	1825-1890 Madi	Madi
NICHOLS, Thaddeus Lee	39th MS Inf.	1847-1940 MS	Harr
NICHOLSON, Asbery M.	36th MS Inf.	1842-1909 Copi	Nesh
NICHOLSON, A. B.(Rev.)	4th MS Cav.	1826-1900	Copi
NICHOLSON, Asberry	35th MS Inf.	1842-19__ Nesh	Nesh
NICHOLSON, C. T.	48th MS Inf.	1847-1910 Laud	Laud
NICHOLSON, Daniel	40th MS Inf.	1840-___	Newt
NICHOLSON, James M.	1st MS Inf.	1839-1894 Mars	Lafa
NICHOLSON, Henry J.	35th MS Inf.	1816-1892 Nesh	Nesh
NICHOLSON, Thomas J.	2nd MS Inf.	1843-1935 VA	Pren
NICHOLSON, Wm. H.	10th MS Inf.	1844-1913 Hind	Warr
NICHOLSON, Wm. Hartwell	10th MS Inf	____-1918	Rank
NICKELS, R. F.	43rd MS Inf.	1843-1896 Okti	Okti
NICKLE, J. T.	28th MS Cav.	1845-1919	Tall
NICKLES, Chasper W.	28th MS Cav.	1830-1885 Carr	Pano
NICKOLS, D. J.	20th MS Inf.	1830-1903	Lefl

Name	Unit	Dates	State/County
NICKOLS, William F.	56th AL Inf.	1830-1895 AL	Itaw
NIMMO, Thomas G.	11th MS Cav.	1838-1914	Okti
NIX, Austin	41st MS Inf.	1839-1862 Monr	Monr
NIX, D. Clinton	3rd MS Cav.	1845-1919	Copi
NIX, Green	5th MS Inf.	1838-1915 Monr	Monr
NIX, John S.	41st MS Inf.	1841-1889 Monr	Monr
NIX, Pleasant	27th AL Inf.	1835-1917 AL	Calh
NIXON, George D.	12th MS Inf.	1842-1897	Hind
NIXON, J. T.	1st MS Inf.	1839-1907 MS	Holm
NIXON, Nimrod Porter	Forrests Cav.	1846-19_ MS	Tish
NIXON, Oliver Woodson	MO Med. Dir.	1829-1905 MO	Harr
NIXON, Thomas L.	26th MS Inf.	1826-1899 MS	Pren
NIXON, W. W.	23rd AL Inf.	1824-1902 AL	Pano
NIXON, William _.	26th MS Inf.	1835-1899 Tish	Tish
NOAH, A. G.	15th MS Inf.	1827-1897 Atta	Atta
NOAH, William R.	2nd MS Inf.	1847-1923	Monr
NOBEL, John	1st MS Cav.	1851-1916 Boli	Harr
NOBLE, John E. (M.D.)	1st MS Inf.	1847-1920	Rank
NOBLE, Patrick H.	45th MS Inf.	1831-1908	Hind
NOBLE, Robert P.	3rd AR Inf.	1840-1925 AL	Jone
NOBLES, Elder G.	7th MS Inf.	1823-1903	Lama
NOBLES, W. T.	3rd MS Inf.		Rank
NOBLES, William Henry	4th MS Cav.	1805-1876 MA	Wilk
NOBLIN, Crawford	6th & 15th MS Inf.	1831-1905	Hind
NOBLIN, G. H.	16th MS Inf.	1837-1897	Hind
NOBLIN, H. A.	24th MS Inf.	1837-1913 NC	Clay
NOBLIN, R. H.	1st MS State Troops	1841-1897	Hind
NOBLIN, Robert H.	16th MS Inf.	1816-1883 MS	Smit
NOBLIN, Thomas Richard	12th MS Cav.	1845-1908	Webs
NOEL, George	36th MS Inf.	1841-1913 Scot	Scot
NOEL, William L.	29th MS Inf.	1827-1887 VA	Holm
NOELL, Robert G.	20th MS Inf.	1823-____ Harr	Scot
NOLAND, H. P.	1st MS Lt. Art.	1841-____ Warr	Warr
NOLAND, H. W.	42nd AL Inf.		Rank
NOLAND, R. M.	5th AL Inf.	1841-1921 AL	Lown
NOLAND, T. V.	1st MS Lt. Art.	1843-____ Warr	Warr
NOLAND, Thomas Vaughn	21st MS Inf.	1834-1908 Harr	Harr
NOLEN, John M.	2nd MS Inf.	1844-1888 Tipp	Bent
NOLEN, _. L.	17th MS Inf.	1827-1904 Choc	Yalo
NOLEN, James Baxter	23rd AR Inf.	1831-1862 AR	Chic
NOLLEY, Alexander Young	MS Cav.	1835-1883	Warr
NORDAN, William T.	39th AL Inf.	1836-1920 AL	Scot
NORFLEET, Thomas M.	20th AR Inf.	1837-1910 AR	Tate
NORMAN, B. F.	39th MS Inf.	1836-1919 Newt	Newt
NORMAN, Christopher R.	10th MS Inf.	1828-1910	Hind
NORMAN, Harvey G.	12th MS Cav.	1829-1898	Yazo
NORMAN, J. F.	6th MS Inf.	1830-1910 MS	Holm
NORMAN, James	2nd MS Cav.	1843-1920 Mars	Mars
NORMAN, James Montgomery	4th MS Cav.	1833-1906 Copi	Copi

49

NORMAN, John D.	3rd MS Cav.	1845-1918 Lee	Lee
NORMAN, Thomas J.	VA Cav.	____-1904	Copi
NORRELL, Albert G.	28th MS Cav.	1845-1918 Rank	Rank
NORRIS, J. A.	4th AR Inf.	1848-1934 Unio	Yalo
NORRIS, J. A.	8th MS Cav.	1846-1913 Lown	Alco
NORRIS, J. L.	63rd AL Inf.	1843-1924 Tipp	Unio
NORRIS, Luke	37th MS Inf.	1831-1885 Covi	Covi
NORRIS, Thomas S.	27th GA Inf.	1845-____	Mont
NORTH, John H.	3rd MS Cav.	1822-1890	Yazo
NORTON, _. J.	24th MS Inf.	1823-1905 Monr	Linc
NORTON, J. T.	1st MS Lt. Art.	1838-1903 Hind	Warr
NORTON, James J.	2nd MS Cav.	1832-1912 TN	Monr
NORTON, John F.	2nd MS Cav.	1840-1920 Tipp	Tipp
NORTON, W. C.	2nd MS Inf.	____-1924 Tipp	Yazo
NORVEL, J. O.	6th KY Inf.	1839-1862 KY	Lown
NORVELL, James M.	2nd MS Inf.	1838-1897 Noxu	Unio
NORVELL, Samuel Houston	7th MS Inf.	1840-1926 Mars	Unio
NOWELL, Gideon P.	14th MS Inf.	1845-1928 MS	Nesh
NORWOOD, J. C.	6th MS Inf.	1839-1874	Rank
NORWOOD, Jesse P.	3rd MS Cav.	1819-1886	Hind
NORWOOD, Pickens C.	Harveys Scouts	1842-1937 Lown	Noxu
NOWELL, J. S.	14th MS Inf.	1842-1914 Wins	Wins
NOWELL, John P.	Stanfords Lt.Art.	1830-1909 Gren	Gren
NUGENT, William Lewis	28th MS Cav.	1823-1897	Hind
NULL, D. W.	2nd MS Cav.	1836-1905	Laud
NUNLEY, William	11th AL Cav.	1833-1909 AL	Tish
NUNNALLEE, James M.	2nd MS Inf.	1844-1926 AL	Lee
NUNNERY, David	7th MS Inf.	1839-1906 Amit	Amit
NUNNERY, George	14th Cav.	1847-1914 MS	Amit
NUNNERY, Henry	7th MS Inf.	1825-1900 Amit	Amit
NUNNERY, John	41st MS Inf.	1824-1880 MS	Laud
NUNNERY, Reubin	7th MS Inf.	1837-1910 Amit	Amit
NUNNERY, Samuel	7th MS Inf.	1839-1916 MS	Amit
NUNNERY, William Robert	41st MS Inf.	1844-1922 Laud	Laud
NUNNLEY, John J.	38th TN Inf.	1840-1929 AL	Pren
NUSOM, G. A.	20th MS Inf.	1845-1907 Monr	Linc
NUTT, G. W.	37th MS Inf.	1834-1887	Clar
NUTT, J. A.	6th & 15th MS Inf.	1842-1915 MS	Scot
NUTT, Thomas J.	40th MS Inf.	1845-1916 GA	Leak
NUTT, W. C.	1st Cav.	1847-1904 GA	Leak
OAKES, John T.	30th Ms. Inf.	1842-1906 Yazo	Tall
OAKS, Felix	Graves MS Cav.	1842-1906 Wilk	Wilk
OAKS, J. W.	Ballentines Cav.	1827-1903 MS	Unio
OAKS, James F.	26th MS Inf.	1826-1911 Tish	Tish
OATES, William E.	21st MS Inf.	1845-1907 Warr	Warr
O'BANNON, B. W.	3rd MS Inf.	1845-1901 Leak	Leak
O'BANNON, W. C.	20th MS Inf.	1828-1907 Okti	Okti
O'BRANTE, Dalis	20th MS Inf.	1842-1901	Atta
O'BRANTE, Woodson	20th MS Inf.	1807-1885	Atta
O'BRIAN, J. W.	9th KY Inf.	1843-1907 KY	Newt

50

O'BRIAN, John	13th MS Inf.	1838-1866 MS	Oktl
O'BRIEN, R. E.	Montgomerys Scouts	1848-1878	Hind
O'BRYANT, Dallas	20th MS Inf.	1845-1935 Atta	Atta
O'BRYANT, W. J.	35th AL Inf.	1840-1931 AL	Harr
O'CAIN, Charles G.	Adams MS Cav.	1843-1919 Madi	Madi
O'CAIN, Frank J.	1st MS Cav.		Copi
O'CALLAHAM, James P.	Hams Cav.	1827-1882 MS	Unio
ODOM, I. C.	36th AL Inf.	1828-1907 AL	Gree
ODEN, Elias M.	35th MS Inf.	1844-1921 Jone	Jone
ODEN, George W.	35th MS Inf.	1828-1894 MS	Kemp
ODEN, Leander G.	14th MS Inf.		Lown
ODENEAL, John Hayward	10th MS Inf.	1839-1902	Hind
ODGEN, G. W. W.	6th MS Inf.		Rank
ODOM, Alson	16th MS Inf.	1837-1909 Jasp	Forr
ODOM, Asa Benjamin	13th MS Inf.	1843-1910	Rank
ODOM, C. D.	Woods MS Cav.	1824-1905 MS	Simp
ODOM, C. F/P.	3rd MS Inf.	1842-1916 Leak	Leak
ODOM, Charles J.	44th MS Vols.	1840-1864 TN	DeSo
ODOM, D. S.	28th MS Cav.	1845-191_ Scot	Scot
ODOM, E.	13th MS Cav.	1844-1916 MS	Harr
ODOM, George W.	38th MS Cav.	1837-1892 Holm	Holm
ODOM, Jack	9th MS Cav.	1828-1903 Perr	Gree
ODOM, James H/R.	17th MS Cav.	1848-1931 MS	Pear
ODOM, John	4th MS Cav.	1840-1900 Oktl	Oktl
ODOM, John W.	29th MS Inf.	1842-1906	DeSo
ODOM, Sam	2nd MS Inf.	1836-1899 MS	Leak
ODOM, William	13th MS Inf.	1834-1902 Wayn	Wayn
O'DOM, Willis	7th MS Inf.	1838-1906 Perr	Wayn
O'DONELL, J.	27th MS Inf.	1843-1900 Wayn	Wayn
O'DONNELL, Abe	24th MS Inf.	1838-1913 Leak	Jone
O'DONNELL, Ed	24th MS Inf.	1840-1900 Madi	Jone
O'DONNELL, T. J.	65th TN Inf.	1846-1924 ST	DeSo
OFFICER, A.	25th TN Inf.	1837-1862 TN	Lown
O'FLYNN, Dan	2nd MS Inf.	1847-1925 MS	Jasp
O'FLYNN, Timothy	16th MS Inf.	1845-1910 MS	Laud
OGLESBY, G. S.	3rd GA Inf.	1836-1925 GA	Madi
OGLESBY, Richard H.	24th AL Inf.	18_7-1922 AL	Webs
OGLETREE, A. C.	5th MS Cav.	1815-1895 Carr	Holm
OHLEYER, John	3rd MS Regt.	1820-1890 FR	Rank
O'KEEFE, John Jr.	5th MS Cav.	1846-1898 Carr	Carr
O'KEEFE, John Sr.	5th MS Cav.	1817-1863 Carr	Carr
O'KEEFE, Michael	22nd MS Inf.	1842-1914 Carr	Mont
O'KELLY, J. B.	1st MS Lt. Art.	1824-1867 Adam	Adam
OLDHAM, L. N.	6th MO Inf.	1835-1863	Hind
OLDHAM, Leondias	6th MO Inf.	1841-1863 MO	Clai
OLDHAM, Lucius B.	48th MS Inf.	1839-1861 Atta	Carr
OLDHAM, Zera	1st MS Cav.	1812-1897 Carr	Carr
O'LEARY, Ignacius S.	18th MS Inf.	1836-1915 GA	Warr
O'LEARY, J. P. (Dr.)	18th MS Inf.	1802-1878 Madi	Madi
O'LEARY, Richard	18th MS Inf.	1833-1916 GA	Warr
OLIN, Caleb	38th MS Cav.	1814-1866	Hind

OLINGER, J. D.	31st MS Inf.	1845-1926 Yalo	Yalo
OLIPHANT, James M.	13th TN Inf.	1834-1893 TN	Bent
OLIPHANT, Thomas A.	63rd GA Inf.	1841-1913 GA	Monr
OLIPHANT, Wilford	1st TX Inf.	1842-1911 TX	Leak
OLIVAR, Dan Jones	34th MS Inf.	1847-1878	Mars
OLIVE, James Lazarus	9th AL Inf.	1848-1935 TN	Pren
OLIVER, C. L.	24th MS Cav.	____-1913	Adam
OLIVER, David T.	22nd MS Inf.	DeSo	DeSo
OLIVER, Francis D.	35th MS Inf.	1822-1902	Kemp
OLIVER, G. M.	33rd TN Inf.	1844-1863 TN	Lafa
OLIVER, H. C. Sr.	16th MS Inf.	1846-1924 Adam	Unio
OLIVER, Jim	AL Inf.	____-1899	Monr
OLIVER, John C.	40th MS Inf.	1837-1901 Nesh	Nesh
OLIVER, Morris S.	40th MS Inf.	1834-1913	Nesh
OLIVER, Peter M.	40th MS Inf.	1831-1862	Nesh
OLIVER, S. P.	24th MS Inf.	1850-1924 Monr	Linc
OLIVER, Simeon	18th MS Cav.	1796-1865	DeSo
OLIVER, Stephen D.	21st SC Inf.	1829-1906 SC	Clar
OLIVER, Thomas J.	24th MS Inf.	1837-1918 Carr	Mont
OLIVER, W. F.	8th TN Inf.	1837-1912 TN	Chic
OLIVER, W. K.	33rd MS Inf.	1837-1909	Pano
OLIVER, William	1st MS Lt. Art.	1841-____ Carr	Mont
OLIVER, William	1st MS Lt. Art.	1829-1891 AL	Copi
OLIVER, William H.	40th MS Inf.	1841-1901 MS	Nesh
OLLETT, F. P.	26th LA Inf.	1843-1862 LA	Warr
OLLIPHANT, Samuel R.	Surgeon	1840-1890 Newt	Newt
OLTENBURG, Cass	19th MS Inf.	1823-1908 OH	Holm
O'MALLEY, Patrick	43rd MS Inf.		Lown
O'MARA, Michael	Poagues MS Art.	1822-1907 IR	Madi
O'NEAL, A. W.	1st MS Lt. Art.	1838-1924 Clar	Harr
O'NEAL, Asae E.	15th MS Inf.	1836-1864 Carr	Carr
O'NEAL, H. S.	36th MS Inf.	1839-____ Newt	Carr
O'NEAL, Hansfred	1st MS Sharpshooters	1841-1862 Carr	Carr
O'NEAL, Hillard	40th AL Inf.	1845-1926 AL	Harr
O'NEAL, J.	25th AL Inf.	1831-1920 AL	Harr
O'NEAL, J. W.	Peytons MS Cav.	1845-1915 Hind	
O'NEAL, Judson J.	15th MS Inf.	1843-1929 Holm	Carr
O'NEAL, Joseph	13th MS Inf.	1849-1929 Clar	Harr
O'NEAL, Major J.	3rd MS Inf.	1842-1937 Ston	Ston
O'NEAL, R. H.	15th MS Inf.	1846-1909	Mont
O'NEAL, W.	11th AL Inf.	1840-1915 AL	Harr
O'NEILL, James	Miles Legion	1812-1888 IR	Adam
O'NEILL, John	12th MS Inf.	1832-1904	Covi
O'NEILL, Numa Pompilius	23rd AL Inf.	1842-1923 AL	Lown
O'QUINN, John	1st MS Lt. Art.	1826-1875 Jeff	Jeffer
O'QUINN, Thomas Jeff.	1st MS Lt. Art.	1830-1899 Jeff	Jeff
O'REILY, John H/R. Y.	1st MS Lt. Art.	1832-1905 IR	Warr
ORR, H. C. (M.D.)	31st MS Inf.	1826-1891 Pont	Pont
ORR, Ira Baxter	11th MS Inf.	1840-1922 Lafa	Lafa
ORR, J. A.	31st MS Inf.	1828-1921 SC	Lown
ORR, John A.	31st MS Inf.	1820-1891 MS	Jeff

Name	Unit	Dates	Col1	Col2
ORR, Samuel	1st & 10th MS Inf.		Adam	Adam
ORR, William	10th MS Inf.		Adam	Adam
ORR, William Henry	36th GA Inf.	1845-1924	GA	Leak
ORREN, C. Remulus	38th MS Cav.	1827-1888	Clai	Mari
OSBORN, Andrew Jackson	41st MS Inf.	1847-1913	Itaw	Lee
OSBORN, David	41st AL Inf.	1831-1899	AL	Tish
OSBORN, John S.	3rd MS Inf.	1843-1921		Hind
OSBORN, Wm.	Powers Cav.	1845-1909		Hind
OSBORNE, J. S.	4th MS Cav.	1843-1921	Hind	Hind
OSBORNE, Hampden (Dr.)	53rd NC Inf.	1845-1926	VA	Lown
OSTEEN, J. J.	33rd MS Inf.	1841-1914	MS	Linc
O'SULLIVAN, Jerry F.	10th MS Inf.			Hind
OSWALD, John B.	3rd MS Cav.	1845-1915		DeSo
OSWALT, M. Benton	27th MS Inf.	1846-1917		Okti
OTEY, William Smith	15th & 23rd AR Inf.	1838-___	AR	Adam
OTIS, John A.	3rd MS Cav.	1845-1928	SC	Noxu
OTT, John Aaron	9th LA Inf.	1829-1904	LA	Linc
OTT, Frank M.	45th MS Inf.	___-1905	Yazo	Pike
OTTS, W. M.	43rd AL Inf.	1830-1910	AL	Lafa
OURY, Tandy H. Sr.	11th MS Inf.	1836-1900	Carr	Carr
OUSLEY, Rufus N.	21st MS Inf.	1845-1911	Madi	Atta
OUSLEY, Thomas J.	Montgomerys Scouts	1846-1904		Atta
OUTLAW, Dossey W.	35th MS Inf.	1843-1918		Okti
OUTLAW, Drew A.	12th TN Inf.	1832-1898		Lefl
OVERBY, G. F.	MS Inf.	1846-1924	Sunf	Smit
OVERBY, J. A.	42nd MS Inf.	1841-1933	Pano	Calh
OVERBY, J. L.	39th MS Inf.	1846-1921	Simp	Smit
OVERBY, James L.	39th MS Inf.	___-1862		Simp
OVERBY, James W.	39th MS Inf.	1837-1862	Simp	Simp
OVERBY, James W.	39th MS Inf.	1843-1863	Simp	Lafa
OVERBY, Jefferson	42nd MS Inf.	1833-1919	Calh	Calh
OVERBY, N. W.	41st MS Inf.	1827-1864	Pont	Pont
OVERBY, R. Y.	Woods MS Cav.	1844-1924	Simp	Simp
OVERSTREET, Bowen	8th MS Inf.	1840-1909	Jone	Harr
OVERSTREET, John H.	13th MS Inf.	1842-1912	Kemp	Wins
OVERSTREET, Oliver H.	31st AR Inf.	1829-1911	AR	Nesh
OVERSTREET, S. M.	36th MS Inf.	1838-1929	Newt	Newt
OVERSTREET, Samuel	56th AL Rangers	1831-1920	AL	Wayn
OVERSTREET, W. B.	1st MS Lt. Art.	1839-1900	Mont	Mont
OVERSTREET, W. J.	43rd MS Inf.	1844-1908	Kemp	Kemp
OVERSTREET, W. J.	46th MS Inf.	1839-1921	Wayn	Jone
OWEN, A. _.	31st MS Inf.	1840-1913	Calh	Pano
OWEN, D. M.	6th MS Inf.	1824-1863	Tipp	Unio
OWEN, Henry	24th MS Inf.	1844-1895	MS	Chic
OWEN, Irvin	22nd AL Inf.	1825-1914	AL	
OWEN, J. P.	1st MS Lt. Art.	1843-1920	Pont	Pont
OWEN, Joe P.	Conf. Art.	1843-1920	Pont	Pont
OWEN, Thomas J.	17th MS Inf.	1836-1864		DeSo
OWEN, William A.	43rd MS Inf.	1845-1865	MS	Monr
OWENS, Andrew T.	19th MS Inf.	1837-1897	Lafa	Lafa

OWENS, Benson H.	11th MS Cav.	1833-1900	Atta
OWENS, Dave T.	Stanfords Lt.Art.	1836-1915 Gren	Gren
OWENS, Durant	Commissary	1836-1906 NC	Noxu
OWENS, E. W.	1st MS Cav.	1815-1869	Hind
OWENS, Edward T.	21st MS Inf.	1840-1864 PA	Warr
OWEN, G.	1st MS Inf.	184_-1900 Pont	Pont
OWENS, Andrew Franklin	TN Lt. Art.	1845-1925 AL	Pren
OWENS, Andrew J.	10th MS Inf.	1827-1906 MS	Bent
OWENS, David	1st AL Inf.	1838-1920 AL	Kemp
OWENS, G. W.	39th MS Regt.	1839-___	Simp
OWENS, J. H.	46th MS Inf.	1844-1931	Copi
OWENS, J. H.	14th MS Inf.	1833-1920 Okti	Harr
OWENS, James E/F.	14th MS Inf.	1844-1907 Fran	Fran
OWENS, James M.	1st MS Cav.	1849-1898	DeSo
OWENS, John R.	2nd MS Cav.	1835-1910 Scot	Scot
OWENS, R. A.	12th MS Inf.	1841-1910 Lawr	Clai
OWENS, R. W.	3rd TN Inf.	1843-1911 TN	Tuni
OWENS, Robert Jessie	34th MS Inf.	1840-1907 Tipp	Bent
OWENS, S. B.	24th MS Cav.	___-1930 LA	Adam
OWENS, Russell A.	6th MS Regt.	1845-1923	Scot
OWENS, Thomas G.	40th AL Inf.	1842-1918 Kemp	Kemp
OWENS, Thomas Y.	2nd MS Cav.	1835-1924 AL	Monr
OWENS, Washington	38th MS Cav.	1834-1880 Wilk	Wilk
OWENS, William	5th TX Inf.	1831-1915 TX	Leak
OWINGS, ___ C.	8th AL Inf.	1843-1908 AL	Monr
PACE, A. C.	8th MS Inf.	1832-1897 Laud	Laud
PACE, A. T.	8th MS Inf.	1825-1879 Laud	Laud
PACE, Albert G.	2nd MS Cav.	1847-1905 Tish	Tish
PACE, Bennett R.	8th MS Inf.	1819-1895 TN	Laud
PACE, Dow L.	9th MS Regt.	1839-1862 Madi	Madi
PACE, Edwin J.	41st MS Inf.	1842-1900 MS	Kemp
PACE, J. G.	8th MS Inf.	1836-1921 Laud	Lama
PACE, James R.	39th MS Inf.	1832-1895 Newt	Newt
PACE, Leb	8th MS Inf.	1838-1892 Laud	Lama
PACE, N. M.	41st MS Inf.	1837-1911 MS	Kemp
PACE, Napoleon L.	41st MS Inf.	1838-1930 Kemp	Kemp
PACE, R. B.	8th MS Inf.	1839-1899 GA	Newt
PACE, Thomas Dredzell	10th MS Inf.	1831-1914 GA	Hind
PACK, Dalles B.	1st MS Cav.	1846-1921 Noxu	Tate
PACK, E. E.	2nd MS Cav.		Laud
PACK, Jesse A.	13th MS Inf.	1834-1917 AL	Jone
PACK, W. J. Sr.	32nd AL Inf.	1838-1928 AL	Forr
PACKER, John C.	14th MS Lt. Art.	1842-1881 MS	Pano
PACKWOOD, Samuel E.	13th MS Inf.	1837-1907 AL	Walt
PADELFORD, Caleb Edward	1st MS State Troops	1848-1911 Hind	
PADELFORD, William B.	1st MS Inf.	1845-1873	Hind
PADEN, R. W. Sr.	7th AL Cav.	1835-1922 AL	Tish
PADEN, T. G. (Dr.)	32nd MS Inf.	1844-1910 Tish	Tish
PADEN, William A.	7th AL Cav.	1825-1897 AL	Tish
PAGAN, George B.	6th MS Cav.	1816-1901 PA	Wins

PAGE, A. J.	1st MS Cav.	1849-1910	Copi
PAGE, Alphonso	35th MS Inf.	1844-1905 Oktl	Oktl
PAGE, C. W.	2nd MS Cav.	1846-1914 Laud	Laud
PAGE, F. H.	10th MS Inf.	1844-1925 Warr	Harr
PAGE, George M.	37th MS Inf.	1839-1908 Clar	Pike
PAGE, H. G.	2nd MS Cav.	1843-1904 Laud	Lama
PAGE, Harrison	35th MS Inf.	1843-1924 Lown	Alco
PAGE, Henry W.	24th MS Inf.	1839-1862 Kemp	Kemp
PAGE, J. T.	42nd NC Inf.	1839-1918 Tish	Tish
PAGE, Joseph R.	2nd MS Cav.	1816-1883 Laud	Laud
PAGE, Robert B.	23rd MS Inf.	1844-1864	Coah
PAGE, T. H.	16th MS Inf.	1843-1925	Harr
PAGE, W. C.	3rd MS Inf.	1820-1899 Nesh	Monr
PAGE, W. R. Sr.	1st MS Cav.	1822-1908 Leak	Leak
PAGE, W. W. (Rev.)	18th AL Inf.	1846-1925 Tish	Tish
PAINE, Charles	28th MS Cav.	1823-1895 Warr	Warr
PAINE, Thos.	12th MS Inf.	1841-1896 Adam	Warr
PAINTER, Ira	61st TN Inf.	1837-1863 TN	Warr
PALLARD, A. J.	41st MS Inf.	1837-1919 MS	Harr
PALM, Gustavus Adolphus	9th MS Inf.	1839-1917 Mars	Mars
PALMER, Alexander	Gamblins MS Cav.	1846-1932 MS	Kemp
PALMER, Charley P.	Jeff Davis Legion	1839-1912 Kemp	Kemp
PALMER, David Z.	3rd MS Inf.	1817-1887 MS	Monr
PALMER, E. A.	2nd MS Cav.	1831-1924 Itaw	Itaw
PALMER, J. G.	15th TX Legion	1840-1862 TX	Alco
PALMER, James	Gamblins MS Cav.	1834-1898 MS	Kemp
PALMER, James	32nd MS Inf.	1837-1894	Wayn
PALMER, James L.	54th AL Inf.	1829-1909 AL	Scot
PALMER, James Monroe		1843-1899	Rank
PALMER, Joe S.	24th MS Inf.	1837-1923 Perr	Perr
PALMER, John D.	36th MS Inf.	18_4-___ NC	Tipp
PALMER, Luke	36th AL Inf.	1843-1915 AL	Copi
PALMER, M. C.	39th MS Inf.	1845-191_ Pike	Pike
PALMER, Thomas B.	5th MS Inf.	1842-1912 Monr	Monr
PANINAN, J. F.	1st AR Inf.	1839-1862 AR	Chic
PANKEY, S. S.	2nd MS Cav.	1849-1884	Bent
PANKEY, Stephen	16th MS Cav.	1845-1867 AL	Noxu
PANNELL, B. F.	7th Cav.	1842-1919 Unio	Tipp
PANNELL, J. L.	33rd MS Inf.	1843-1927 MS	Unio
PANNELL, Joseph C.	1st MS Lt. Art.	____-1909 Copi	
PANNELL, P. H.	17th MS Inf.	1830-1885 Unio	Unio
PANNELL, W. B.	45th MS Inf.	1840-1924 Pont	Unio
PANNELL, W. E.	31st MS Inf.	1833-1917 Pont	Pont
PANNELL, Walter Minor	23rd SC Inf.	1821-1892 SC	Pren
PANNELL, William P.	45th MS Inf.	1844-1916 Pont	Unio
PARAMORE, W. R.	35th MS Inf.	1837-1912 Clay	Clay
PARCHMAN, James M.	43rd MS Inf.	1844-1913 Monr	Monr
PARDUE, John	20th AL Inf.	1836-1914 AL	Pren
PARHAM, Gabe J.	43rd MS Inf.	1830-1891	Monr
PARHAM, George W.	43rd MS Inf.	1845-1921 Monr	Monr

PARHAM, Isham	43rd MS Inf.	1836-1862 Monr	Monr
PARHAM, John W.	43rd MS Inf.	1830-1904 Monr	Monr
PARHAM, M. C.	43rd MS Inf.	1832-1911 Monr	Monr
PARISH, Edward	Withers Art.	1821-___	Hind
PARISH, John R.	7th MS Inf.	1838-1922 Covi	Covi
PARISH, R. P.	18th MS Inf.	1843-1882 ME	Lefl
PARKER, A. N.	18th MS Inf.	1842-1918 Madi	Madi
PARKER, Abraham	19th MS Inf.	1827-1896 Noxu	Kemp
PARKER, Acquella	42nd MS Inf.	MS	Calh
PARKER, Alfred	1st MS State Troops	1814-1890 Leak	Leak
PARKER, Ambrous	45th MS Inf.	1837-1928 Pont	Unio
PARKER, Benjamin	10th MS Inf.	1828-1909	Copi
PARKER, Benjamin	2nd MS Inf.	1817-1900 AL	Unio
PARKER, D. G.	1st MS Inf.	1836-1895 Adam	Adam
PARKER, David R.	13th MS Inf.	1843-1893	Copi
PARKER, E. F.	2nd MS Inf.	1844-1904 Noxu	Kemp
PARKER, Elijah B.	15th MS Inf.	1843-1922 Atta	Atta
PARKER, Elisha	5th MS Inf.	1830-1893 Nesh	Leak
PARKER, F. L.	6th MS Inf.	1838-1894 Leak	Leak
PARKER, G. W.	46th Inf.	1845-1927 Smit	Smit
PARKER, George	19th MS Cav.	1819-1904 MS	Calh
PARKER, Harrison	5th MS Inf.	1842-1931 Nesh	Nesh
PARKER, Henry	37th MS Reg.	1832-1907 Jasp	Jasp
PARKER, Henry C/G.	11th MS Cav.	1830-1909 TN	Pren
PARKER, Henry P.	AL Inf.	AL	Calh
PARKER, Hubbard	27th MS Inf.	1843-1929 MS	Geor
PARKER, Hugh	5th MS Inf.	18__-191_ MS	Nesh
PARKER, I. N.	Seven Star Art.	1811-1901	Copi
PARKER, J. A.	22nd TN Inf.	1841-1897 TN	Lafa
PARKER, J. C.	20th MS Inf.	1833-1909 Scot	Scot
PARKER, J. E.	37th Inf.	1842-1912 Jone	Jone
PARKER, J. H.	6th MS Inf.	1841-1914 Leak	Leak
PARKER, J. N.	7th MS Art.	1811-1901	Copi
PARKER, J. S.(Dr.)	36th MS Inf.	1822-1893 GA	Newt
PARKER, J. T.	13th MS Inf.	1839-1917	Copi
PARKER, J. T.	29th MS Inf.	1822-1876 Tall	Tall
PARKER, James D.	1st MS Cav.	184_-1917 Jasp	Jasp
PARKER, James H.	5th MS Cav.	1839-1910 Choc	Webs
PARKER, James H.	6th MS Inf.	1840-1911 Leak	Leak
PARKER, James Henderson	7th MS Inf.	1844-1927 Fran	Fran
PARKER, James Porter	21st MS Inf.	1842-1909 Clai	Clai
PARKER, James R.	17th MS Inf.	1834-1897 Chic	Chic
PARKER, Jefferson F.	31st LA Inf.	1841-1863 LA	Warr
PARKER, Jeptha	37th MS Inf.	1843-1917	Pike
PARKER, Jessie	1st MS Cav.	1846-1926 Jack	Geor
PARKER, Jim	27th MS Inf.	1845-1907 MS	Jack
PARKER, Joe James (Dr.)	Machine Shop	1844-1925 MS	JEDA
PARKER, John	35th MS Inf.	1833-1862 MS	
PARKER, John	15th MS Inf.	1844-1922 Jack	Geor
PARKER, John A.	5th MS Inf.	1846-1918 Laud	Linc
PARKER, John R.	24th MS Inf.	1827-1901 Perr	Perr

Name	Unit	Dates	Loc1	Loc2
PARKER, John Thomas	30th MS Inf.	1839-1901 Gren	Gren	
PARKER, John W.	14th MS Inf.	1830-1887 Okti	Okti	
PARKER, Joseph Warren	10th MS Inf.	1839-1908 Carr	Warr	
PARKER, L. J.	17th MS Inf.	1833-1882 Chic	Chic	
PARKER, L. W.	15th MS Inf.	Atta	Atta	
PARKER, Lewis	Abbotts Cav.	1848-1925	Unio	
PARKER, M. L.	7th MS Inf.	1840-1922 Jasp	Jasp	
PARKER, M. Dallas	37th MS Inf.	1844-1926 Jasp	Jasp	
PARKER, O. _.	37th MS Inf.	1821-1907 Jasp	Lama	
PARKER, Oliver C.	15th MS Inf.	1842-1898 Yalo	Atta	
PARKER, P. S.	17th MS Inf.	1832-1904 MS	Chic	
PARKER, R. A.	1st MS Cav.	1847-1925 Holm	Harr	
PARKER, Rufus B.	17th MS Cav.	1845-1900 MS	Geor	
PARKER, S. E.	44th MS Inf.	1844-1926 Chic	Chic	
PARKER, S. E.	5th MS Inf.	1842-1931 MS	Nesh	
PARKER, Samuel	37th MS Inf.	1820-1906 Jasp	Clar	
PARKER, T. C.	7th MS Inf.	1842-1910 Fran	Amit	
PARKER W. G.	15th AL Cav.	1834-1912 AL	Wayn	
PARKER, W. J.	6th MS Cav.	1846-1924 AL	Pont	
PARKER, W. M.	6th MS Cav.	1849-1911 Nesh	Sunf	
PARKER, W. W.	41st MS Inf.	1837-1904 Itaw	Itaw	
PARKER, William	38th MS Cav.	1835-1929 Pike	Walt	
PARKER, William	42nd AL Inf.	1832-1910 AL	Calh	
PARKER, William Jasper	5/45 MS Cav.	1845-1919 Gren	Gren	
PARKER, William W.	40th MS Inf.	1833-1891 Leak	Leak	
PARKER, Willis J.	7th MS Inf.	1841-1921	Kemp	
PARKER, Young A.	44th MS Inf.	1841-1867 MS	Calh	
PARKES, George	5th MS Inf.	1841-1894 Wins	Wins	
PARKES, J. F.	5th MS Inf.	1844-1911 Wins	Wins	
PARKHILL, J. F.	3rd MS Inf.	1842-___	Newt	
PARKINSON, Ebenezer	1st MS Lt. Art.	1837-1906 SC	Holm	
PARKMAN, D. _.	11th AR Cav.	1850-1914 Linc	Harri	
PARKMAN, E. B.	MS Cav.	1844-1922 Lawr	JEDA	
PARKMAN, James	3rd MS Cav.	1818-1887	Hind	
PARKMAN, John R.	33rd MS Inf.	1845-1930 Lawr	Lawr	
PARKMAN, John Robert	11th MS Inf.	1845-1930 Lawr	Linc	
PARKMAN, Sanders	38th MS Cav.	1832-1913	JEDA	
PARKER, Tyrene	7th MS Inf.	1842-1923 JeDa	JEDA	
PARKS, D. O.	3rd SC Cav.	1846-1917 MS	Harr	
PARKS, E. H.	46th MS Inf.	1845-1911 Covi	Yalo	
PARKS, Franklin C.	22nd MS Inf.	1829-1878 Lafa	Lafa	
PARKS, G. J.	37th MS Inf.	1837-1928 Clar	Wins	
PARKS, George W.	6th MO Inf.	1839-1863 MO	Clai	
PARKS, John Allen (Dr.)	Ship Doctor	1829-1882 AL	Scot	
PARKS, John D.	32nd MS Inf.	1835-1919 Tall	Alco	
PARKS, J. P.	8th MS Inf.	___-1894	Scot	
PARKS, S. G.	1st MS Lt. Art.	1828-1899 Warr	Warr	
PARKS, Samuel B.	AL Inf.	1842-1914 AL	Scot	
PARKS, Thomas	39th MS Inf.	1830-1865 Newt	Newt	
PARKS, W. C.	35th MS Inf.	1840-1907 Wins	Wins	
PARKS, William F.	17th MS Inf.	1818-1901 Mars	Mars	
PARMER, J. L.	29th AL Inf.	1832-1912 AL	Kemp	

PARMER, Joseph Calvin	Saunders Scouts	1827-1863 SC	Tuni
PARMER, W. _.	29th MS Inf.	1835-1908 TN	Pano
PARNELL, J. W.	33rd MS Inf.	1838-1886 Lawr	Linc
PARNELL, Levi	38th MS Cav.	1828-1906 Marl	Harr
PARR, Joseph	1st Conf. Inf.	1837-1862 MS	Lafa
PARR, Milton T.	17th MS Inf.	1839-1904 Tipp	Unio
PARRETTT, William	10th MS Inf.	1844-1922	Copi
PARRISH, Benjamin James	35th MS Inf.	1837-1897 Okti	Okti
PARRISH, Benjamin Perry	49th AL Inf.	1837-1910 SC	Pren
PARRISH, William	43rd MS Inf.	1827-1864 TN	Monr
PARSLEY, Edward	7th AL Cav.	1847-1915 AL	Jack
PARSON, Eugene	MS Cav.	Adam	Adam
PARSONS, David W. E.	Adams MS Cav.	1846-1904 Pike	Madi
PARSONS, Evan E.	Keiglers MS Co.	1849-1933 MS	Walt
PARSONS, L. G.	8th AL Inf.	1841-1908 AL	Lown
PARTEE, Charles W.	12th MS Inf.	1844-1929 TN	Coah
PARTEE, Charles Watkins	12th MS Inf.	1844-1929 TN	Quit
PARTEE, William Locker	1st MS Cav.	1844-1939 Lafa	Pano
PARTIN, C. P. (Dr.)	36th MS Inf.	1825-1893 MS	Newt
PARTIN, E. W.	36th MS Inf.	184_-1906 Newt	Newt
PARTIN, Orren	38th MS Cav.	1837-1890 Wilk	Wilk
PARTIN, Patrick	Berrys MS Inf.	1839-1921 MS	Laud
PARTLOW, Albert M.	32nd & 45th MS Inf.	1837-1915 AL	Lee
PARTLOW, J. C.	45th MS Inf.	1834-1897 Itaw	Lee
PARTRIDGE, J. B.	34th AL Inf.	1847-1929 AL	Mont
PARTRIDGE, J. H.	36th MS Inf.	1836-1913	Nash
PASCHAL, L. P.	22nd GA Inf.	1836-1908 GA	Alco
PASS, M. T.	1st Partisan Cav.	1830-1896 Pont	Unio
PASS, W. D.	29th MS Inf.	18_7-1911 Yalo	Yalo
PASS, W. N.	MS Lt. Art.	1836-1897 Gren	Gren
PASSURE, Eli F.	37th NC Inf.	1843-1914 NC	Harr
PATE, C. L.	6th MS Cav.	1847-1911 Tish	Tish
PATE, J. M.	17th AL Inf.	1847-1925 AL	Monr
PATE, James L.	14th Conf. Cav.	1835-1924 Amit	Amit
PATE, Joseph Henderson	22nd MS Inf.	1842-1862 Carr	Carr
PATE, Thomas M.	3rd MS Inf.	1839-1862 Hanc	Chic
PATE, W. S.	24th MS Inf.	1823-1911 AL	Chic
PATRIC, E__	Inf.	1841-1932 Carr	Holm
PATRICK, A. B. C. Sr.	Seven Star Art.	1820-1880	Copi
PATRICK, George Wilson	2nd MS Inf.	1837-1908 MS	Pren
PATRICK, J. M.	6th MS Inf.	1846-1923	Rank
PATRICK, James J.	1st MS Inf.	1816-1872 SC	Rank
PATRICK, James Macon	1st MS Inf.	1839-1886	Copi
PATRICK, John G.	1st MS Lt. Art.	1844-1908 Hind	Warr
PATRICK, John W.	1st MS Inf.	1820-1898	Pren
PATRICK, Joseph	1st MS Inf.	1818-1904	Rank
PATRICK, Henry V.	24th SC Inf.	1847-1912 SC	Jasp
PATRICK, Luke P.	6th MS Inf.	1812-1896 MS	Wayn
PATRICK, Nathan C.	Mormons Batt.	1848-1924	Copi
PATRICK, Robert A.	1st MS Lt. Art.	1816-1884	Hind
PATRICK, T. M.	18th MS Inf.	1840-1923 Madi	Scot

Name	Unit	Dates		
PATRICK, Wm. Luke	6th MS Inf.	1847-1902		Rank
PATTERSON, C. R.	1st MS Inf.	1831-1891	Pont	Tall
PATTERSON, D. G.	4th MS Cav.	1826-1899		Copi
PATTERSON, F. L.	Forrests Cav.	1843-1864	Carr	Lafa
PATTERSON, Frank	1st MS Cav.	1831-1925	Tall	Yalo
PATTERSON, Greenberry	SC Lt. Art.	1820-1912	SC	Itaw
PATTERSON, J. S.	3rd MS Cav.	1812-1869	Gren	Gren
PATTERSON, J. T.	48th MS Inf.	1847-1936	Mars	Laud
PATTERSON, J. W.	7th AL Cav.	1839-1914	AL	Tish
PATTERSON, J. W.	9th LA Inf.	1847-1924		Copi
PATTERSON, J. W. H.	1st MS Lt. Art.	1839-1898	Adam	Adam
PATTERSON, Jas. A.	21st MS Inf.	____-1887		Hind
PATTERSON, Jasper M.	23rd MS Regt.	1839-1915	Tipp	Unio
PATTERSON, John	1st MS Lt. Art.	1837-1910	Jeff	Jeff
PATTERSON, John E.	1st MS Cav.	____-1889		Hind
PATTERSON, John H.	26th MS Inf.	1829-1903	MS	Pren
PATTERSON, John M.	Stanfords MS Art.	1840-1923	Yalo	Calh
PATTERSON, N. G.	11th MS Cav.	1822-1911	Noxu	Pont
PATTERSON, R. I.	6th MS Inf.	1836-1907	Simp	Simp
PATTERSON, Robert J.	12th MS Inf.	1840-1882	Hind	Clai
PATTERSON, S. A.	6th MS Inf.	1837-1898	Newt	Okti
PATTERSON, Sammie J.	42nd MS Inf.	1841-1884	MS	Calh
PATTERSON, Sanford	11th MS Cav.	18_3-1910	MS	Chic
PATTERSON, Thomas J.	24th MS Inf.	1845-1861	Monr	Monr
PATTERSON, Thomas J.	22nd MS Inf.	1839-1910	Lawr	Lawr
PATTERSON, W. A. (Dr.)	46th MS Inf.	1827-1874		Hind
PATTERSON, W. H.	1st MS Lt. Art.	1827-1898	Yazo	Yazo
PATTERSON, W. J.	30th MS Inf.	1840-1919	Choc	Wins
PATTERSON, P. W.	5th AL Cav.	1846-1913	AL	Tish
PATTERSON, W. P. (Dr.)	1st MS Lt. Art.	1838-1920		Copi
PATTERSON, William A.	35th MS Inf.	1842-1880	Noxu	Noxu
PATTERSON, William A.	35th MS Inf.	1839-1903	Wins	Wins
PATTERSON, William J.	6th MS Inf.	1846-1935	GA	Calh
PATTERSON, William J.	6th MS Inf.	1841-1916	Scot	Calh
PATTISON, Alexander	29th MS Inf.	1821-1879	Tall	Tall
PATTON, A. D.	7th MS Inf.	1845-1929	MS	Lafa
PATTON, A. T.	16th AL Inf.	1842-1925	AL	Alco
PATTON, Alford	4th MS Cav.	1820-1885		Hind
PATTON, Byron Young	1st MS Cav.	1848-1898		Copi
PATTON, Edward D.	3rd MS Cav.	1833-1909	CA	Hind
PATTON, George W.	23rd AL Inf.	1841-1899	AL	Clar
PATTON, George W.	23rd AL Inf.	____-1899		Wayn
PATTON, Harry	15th MS Inf.	1840-1867	Yalo	Yalo
PATTON, John C.	28th MS Cav.	1807-1864	Wayn	Wayn
PATTON, Mathew F.	22nd MS Inf.	1842-1922	Lafa	Lafa
PATTON, W. M.	48th MS Regt.			Hind
PATTON, William Lee	14th MS Inf.	1822-1913	VA	Hind
PATTON, Wm. S.	1st MS Inf.	1813-1889	Laud	Laud
PATTRICK, T. A.	10th MS Inf.	1845-1920	Lown	Harr
PATTY, Robert Calhoun	Perrins MS Cav.	1844-1890	Wins	Noxu
PATTY, T. J.	13th MS Inf.	1812-1912	Wins	Noxu

PAULETTE, Robert	40th MS Inf.		Atta
PAXTON, R. E.	10th MS Inf.	1844-1908 Warr	Warr
PAYNE, Albert F.	30th AL Inf.	1832-1928 GA	Copi
PAYNE, Americus E.	22nd MS Inf.	1835-1868	DeSo
PAYNE, Andrew S.	14th MS Inf.	1830-1918 Lown	Lown
PAYNE, C. C.	41st MS Inf.	1842-1924	Lee
PAYNE, D. C.	32nd GA Inf.	1833-1895 GA	Newt
PAYNE, Francis Marion	26th MS Inf.	1838-1903 Lee	Lee
PAYNE, J. P.	35th MS Inf.	1842-1863 MS	Lafa
PAYNE, J. T.	10th MS Inf.	1828-1878 Hind	Chic
PAYNE, John C/G.	8th MS Inf.	1841-1875 NC	Newt
PAYNE, Jordan A.	42nd MS Inf.	1842-1893	DeSo
PAYNE, Joseph D.	3rd MS Inf.	1847-1924 Newt	Leak
PAYNE, Linton	Jefferson Art.	1841-___ Jeff	Jeff
PAYNE, Louis J.	13th LA Inf.	1845-1929 MS	Walt
PAYNE, Luther R.	4th MS Cav.	1842-1879 Tish	Tish
PAYNE, N. R.	38th MS Cav.	1822-___ MS	Walt
PAYNE, T. D.	41st MS Inf.	1824-1887 Lafa	Chic
PAYNE, T. L.	13th MS Inf.	1836-19_ Kemp	Kemp
PAYNE, Thomas J.	Bufords Escort	___-1862 VA	Lee
PAYNE, Thomas Owen	Adams MS Cav.	1839-1906 MS	Warr
PAYNE, Whit	2nd MS Inf.	1845-1899 Tish	Alco
PAYNE, William D. (Dr.)	66th AL Rangers	1835-1875 AL	Gree
PAYNE, William H.	2nd MS Cav.	1842-1923 Gren	Gren
PEACOCK, Daniel	16th MS Inf.	1838-1911 MS	Simp
PEACOCK, J. C.	24th MS Inf.	1843-1905 Choc	Choc
PEACOCK, Lovic Pierce	Stanfords Lt. Art.	1842-1909	Mont
PEACOCK, Wesley Parks	15th & 44th MS Inf.	1839-1918 NC	Coah
PEACOCK, William L.	6th MS Inf.	1840-1889 Simp	Simp
PEARCE, Andrew J.	24th MS Inf.	1833-1913 Itaw	Itaw
PEARCE, Alfred	3rd MS Cav.		Perr
PEARCE, David R.	24th MS Inf.	1839-1896 Itaw	Itaw
PEARCE, James	9th MS Inf.	1833-1883 Covi	Covi
PEARCE, James L.	24th MS Inf.	1834-1876 Itaw	Itaw
PEARCE, Jeremiah	5th MS Inf.	1840-1932 Monr	Monr
PEARCE, John	43rd MS Inf.	1809-1906 Monr	Monr
PEARCE, John C.	9th MS Inf.	1843-1909 Perr	Perr
PEARCE, Joseph	34th MS Inf.	1836-1908 TN	Tipp
PEARCE, R. S. (Dr.)	2nd MS Inf.	1847-1935 Tipp	Tipp
PEARCEFIELD, P. M.	Jefferson Art.	1844-1918	Boli
PEARCEFIELD, P. M.	Jefferson Art.	1844-1918 MS	Jeff
PEARSALL, Madison	31st MS Inf.	1841-1917 Pont	Chic
PEARSELL, L. M.	3rd MS Cav.	1845-1909 Chic	Chic
PEARSON, Christopher C.	Roddys MS Cav.	1837-1881 Laud	Itaw
PEARSON, George W.	24th MS Inf.	1848-1912 Choc	Quit
PEARSON, J. T.	38th MS Cav.	1833-1924 MS	Copi
PEARSON, John H.	15th MS Inf.	1821-1891 AL	Mont
PEARSON, John W.	6th MS Inf.	1840-1883	Rank
PEARSON, N. L.	23rd AL Inf.	1837-1915 GA	Jone
PEARSON, R. A.	4th MS Cav.	1843-1896 Choc	Choc

Name	Unit	Dates		Location
PEARSON, Richard V.	15th MS Inf.	1836-1924	MS	Yalo
PEARSON, Thomas	23rd MS Inf.	1844-1921	Wins	Wins
PEARSON, W. J. Jr.	4th MS Inf.	1845-1901	Choc	Choc
PEARSON, W. J. Sr.	17th MS Inf.	1817-1883	Choc	Choc
PEARSON, W. W.	36th MS Inf.	1844-1889	Leak	Scot
PEARSON, William Laf.	9th MS Inf.	___-1933		Boli
PEASE, John B. (M.D.)	2nd MS Inf.	1839-1917	Boli	Boli
PEASTER, Lim C.	21st MS Inf.	1840-1910	Gree	Gree
PEAVEY, C. C.	3rd MS Cav.			Lown
PEAVY, C. W.	21st AL Inf.		AL	Newt
PEAVY, Levi D.	8th MS Inf.	1826-1897	FL	Newt
PEAY, Austin	11th MS Cav.	1846-1886		Okti
PECK, J. W.	27th MS Inf.	1831-1908	VA	Monr
PEDEN, James A.	1st MS Inf.	1846-1907	Pont	Kemp
PEDEN, James D.	5th MS Inf.	1825-1887	Kemp	Kemp
PEDEN, John B.	18th MS Inf.	1845-1922	Hind	Chic
PEDEN, Rufus	41st MS Inf.	1827-1862	Chic	Chic
PEDEN, Thomas J.	40th MS Inf.	1813-1870	Kemp	Kemp
PEEBLES, Joseph J.	4th MS Inf.	1829-1900	Nesh	Nesh
PEEBLES, T. M.	1st MS Lt. Art.	1845-1932	Hind	Harr
PEEK, G. F.	14th MS Inf.	1836-1901	NC	Jasp
PEEK, Wm. R.	3rd AL Inf.	1842-1912	AL	Jasp
PEEK, W. W.	2nd MS Inf.	1843-1927	GA	Pren
PEEL, David Lawson	13th MS Inf.	1839-1911	Atta	Lefl
PEEL, R. H.	19th MS Inf.	1832-1903	MS	Mars
PEELER, James F.	4th MS Inf.	1832-1895	Atta	Atta
PEELER, Jesse B.	23rd MS Inf.	1810-1887	SC	Tipp
PEELER, Richmond	Warren Lt. Art.	1816-1890	Warr	Warr
PEELER, Samuel G.	5th MS Inf.	1820-1898	Wins	Atta
PEEPLES, Allen	5th MS Cav.	1839-1903		Webs
PEEPLES, J. M.	1st MS Lt. Art.	1845-1932	Hind	Harr
PEEPLES, J. F.	31st MS Inf.	1839-1903		Webs
PEEPLES, J. S.	30th MS Inf.	1842-1914	Choc	Webs
PEEPLES, William A.	5th MS Cav.	1845-1927		Webs
PEETE, T. F.	8th AR Inf.	1834-1912	AL	Harr
PEETS, Delos Tully	36th MS Inf.	1843-1915		Copi
PEETS, George H. (Dr.)	21st MS Inf.	1834-1911	Wilk	Wilk
PEGRAM, G. G.	1st MS Lt. Art.	1840-1893	Warr	Warr
PEGRAM, J. W.	17th MS Inf.	1845-1918	SC	Tipp
PEGRAM, Thomas F.	7th MS Cav.	1843-___		Carr
PEGRAM, W. G.	34th MS Inf.	1828-1887	Tipp	Bent
PEGUES, Malchi	13th MS Inf.	1847-1900	Lafa	Lafa
PEGUES, S. B.	41st MS Inf.	1837-1864	Pont	Pont
PELL, George P. W.	3rd MS Cav.	1842-1925		Copi
PELL, William Franklin	3rd MS Cav.			Copi
PENDER, D. D.	1st MS Cav.	1813-1894	Noxu	Atta
PENDER, George W.	5th MS Inf.	1844-1921	Wins	Atta
PENN, James A.	6th MS Inf.			Rank
PENN, John A.	7th LA Inf.	1847-1922	LA	Linc
PENN, Thomas J.	Hughes MS Cav.	1830-1906		Copi
PENN, W. D. (Dr.)	18th MS Inf.	1840-1922	Yazo	Harr
PENN, William H.	5th MO Inf.	1842-1929	MO	Linc

61

PENNEBAKER, S. W.	2nd MS Inf.	1848-1927	Tipp	Harr
PENNELL, L. J.	1st State Troops	1818-1891	Leak	Leak
PENNINGTON, Abner	2nd MS Cav.	1835-1929	Newt	Lama
PENNINGTON, E. M.	5th MS Inf.	1836-1910	GA	Newt
PENNINGTON, J. H.	3rd MS Inf.	1840-1899	MS	Newt
PENNINGTON, N. G.(Dr.)	43rd MS Inf.	1830-1895	AL	Monr
PENNY, F. _.	39th GA Regt.	1832-1910	GA	Kemp
PENTECOST, George Wash.	28th MS Cav.	1831-1899	Carr	Carr
PENTECOST, Nathan West	15th MS Inf.	1829-1906	NC	Mont
PENTECOST, Robert T.	5th MS Cav.	1823-1899	Carr	Carr
PENTON, Alfred	38th MS Cav.	1841-1863	Hanc	Warr
PENTON, Emanuel	38th MS Cav.	1838-1918	Hanc	Pear
PEOPLES, J. C.	16th MS Inf.	1847-1934	Clai	Harr
PEPPER, A. F.	1st MS Lt. Art.	1840-1889	MS	Yazo
PEPPER, Charles W	8th MS Inf.	1845-1884	Choc	Webs
PEPPER, Daniel Gilbert	39th MS Inf.	1835-1918	SC	Holm
PEPPER, Elisha	1st MS Lt. Art.	1820-1885	Yazo	Yazo
PEPPER, J. Horton	1st MS Lt. Art.	1837-1905	Yazo	Yazo
PEPPER, R. B.	1st MS Lt. Art.	1839-1917	Yazo	Yazo
PERKINS, C. A.	16th MS Cav.	1843-1929	Itaw	Itaw
PERKINS, J. H.	35th MS Inf.	1836-1902	Wins	Noxu
PERKINS, J. H.	35th MS Inf.	1836-1902	SC	Wins
PERKINS, John	18th MS Cav.	1824-1901	Smit	Ston
PERKINS, John C.	10th MS Inf.	1840-1928	AL	Tipp
PERKINS, John C.	10th MS Inf.	1840-1906	Yazo	Tipp
PERKINS, John Randolph	12th MS Inf.	1823-1895	Pike	Linc
PERKINS, Joseph Bolivar	14th MS Inf.	1829-1899		Okti
PERKINS, Lender B.	3rd AR Inf.	1844-1913		Forr
PERKINS, P. H.	19th MS Inf.	1838-1909	Pren	Pren
PERKINS, Pinkard M.	48th MS Inf.	____-1886		Clai
PERKINS, William J.	48th MS Inf.	1842-1907	Warr	Lown
PERKINS, William Wright	14th MS Inf.	1833-1913	Laud	Pano
PERMENTER, Thomas D.	Jeff Davis Cav.	1834-1926	Noxu	Kemp
PERMENTER, W.	Jeff Davis Cav.	1837-1926	Noxu	Kemp
PERMINTER, James S.	41st MS Inf.	1845-1926	NC	Noxu
PERNELL, J. M.	3rd MS Inf.	1836-1910	AL	Tipp
PERRAULT, Edward J.	16th MS Inf.		Adam	Adam
PERRAULT, Sam J.	16th MS Inf.	1838-1914	Adam	Adam
PERRETT, Henry	10th MS Inf.			Copi
PERRETT, W. N.	10th MS Inf.	1841-1924	Copi	Harr
PERRETTE, F. J.	36th MS Inf.	1843-1919		Copi
PERRIGIN, William	38th TN Inf.	____-1913	TN	Choc
PERRIN, T. _.	Jeff Davis Cav.	1832-1887	SC	Kemp
PERRIN, William	Jeff Davis Cav.	1831-1901	Kemp	Kemp
PERRY, A. G.	29th MS Inf.	18_4-1924		DeSo
PERRY, A. G.	29th MS Inf.	1845-1923	AL	Laud
PERRY, A. _.	1st MS Inf.	1828-19__	Pont	Pont
PERRY, B. F.	3rd MS Inf.	1827-1914	Yazo	Yazo
PERRY, Horatio J.	43rd MS Inf.	1845-1865	Monr	Monr
PERRY, James	22nd MS Inf.	1818-1871	Lafa	Lafa
PERRY, James M.	5th MS Inf.	1834-1913	Leak	Leak
PERRY, Josiah	11th MS Inf.	1843-1920	Nesh	Leak

Name	Unit	Dates	County
PERRY, N. C.	1st MS Cav.	1835-1891	Hind
PERRY, O. H.	Lundis Art.	1839-1863 GA	Lafa
PERRY, O. H.	28th MS Cav.	1822-1882 Warr	Warr
PERRY, R. W.	2nd MS Inf.	1846-1925 PA	Sunf
PERRY, Reuben R.	15th MS Inf.	1834-1890 SC	Gren
PERRY, Samuel P.	9th KY Cav.	1821-1912 KY	Chic
PERRY, Silas	38th MS Inf.	1829-1864	Lee
PERRY, Sims	1st MS Cav.	1846-1930 AL	Yazo
PERSONS, John W.	1st MS Vol.	1847-1921	Hind
PERSONS, Thomas T.	15th Inf.	1836-1886	Hind
PERSONS, Will T.	11th MS Inf.	1849-1921 AL	Hind
PETERS, Arnold	28th MS Cav.	18_2-1862	Holm
PETERS, J. L.	15th MS Inf.	1826-1890 Choc	Mont
PETERS, John W.	14th MS Inf.	1818-1869 Wins	Wins
PETERS, Reason L.	42nd MS Inf.	1836-1919 GA	Tall
PETERS, Thomas H.	6th & 19th MS Cav.	1846-1905	Lown
PETERS, William L.	2nd MS Cav.	1842-1907 Tate	Tate
PETERSON, Henton James	27th MS Inf.	1838-1901 MS	Tall
PETERSON, J. S.	14th MS Lt. Art.	1844-1909	Pano
PETERSON, John	Forrests Cav.	1831-1912 GE	Harr
PETRIE, David H.	33rd NC Inf.	1838-1897 NC	Sunf
PETRIE, Henry Frederick	18th MS Inf.	____-1861	Hind
PETTERS, William C.	14th MS Inf.	1841-1929	Hind
PETTEY, H. W.	28th MS Cav.	1849-1918 Lefl	Lefl
PETTIGREW, J. L. (Rev.)	4th & 30th MS Inf.	1834-1905	Hind
PETTIGREW, James T.	40th MS Inf.		Copi
PETTIGREW, John Newton	15th MS Inf.	1837-1928 MS	Scot
PETTIGREW, John Newton	40th MS Inf.	1837-1928 Leak	Scot
PETTIGREW, Robert	3rd MS Cav.	1847-1924 Carr	Carr
PETTIT, J. C.	Warren Lt. Art.	1843-1883 Warr	Warr
PETTIT, John J.	Adams MS Cav.	1826-1899 Warr	Wash
PETTUS, J. T.	14th MS Inf.	1829-1920 Holm	Holm
PETTWAY, John Robert	1st MS Lt. Art.	1837-1920 VA	Warr
PETTY, A.	17th MS Inf.	1832-1895	Oktl
PETTY, Green	26th MS Inf.	1833-1908 Tish	Alco
PETTY, John	26th MS Inf.	Tish	Alco
PEUGH, William E.	1st MS Inf.	1837-1896 NC	Monr
PEYTON, E. A.	3rd MS Inf.	1823-1906 TN	Wash
PEYTON, Frank L.	12th MS Inf.	1843-1861 Hind	Hind
PEVEY, Edwin	33rd MS Inf.	1836-1870 Lawr	Lawr
PEYTON, Harry	3rd MS Inf.	1830-1864 Hind	Hind
PEYTON, John W.	22nd MS Inf.	1828-1907	Hind
PEYTON, Murray	3rd MS Inf.	1837-1916 TN	Wash
PEYTON, W. H/R.(Dr.)	4th MS Regt.	1822-1864	Hind
PHARES, Wilbur F.	21st MS Inf.	1840-1911 Wilk	Wilk
PHARR, Holland J.	6th MS Cav.	1845-1924 MS	Tish
PHARRIS, J. W.	13th TX Cav.	1843-____ TX	Sunf
PHELPS, J. B/E.	9th MS Inf.	1843-1912 Laud	Pano
PHELPS, W. H.	17th MS Inf.	1840-191_ Tish	Tish
PHELPS, W. J.	41st MS Inf.	1827-1906 Noxu	Noxu

PHELPS, William A.	24th MS Inf.	1834-1889 Choc	Choc
PHEVOATT, Wm. Jackson	1st MS Inf.	1839-1921 Atta	Harr
PHILIPS, William M.	5th MS Cav.	1838-1901 Nesh	Nesh
PHILLIPS, Lemuel J.	8th MS Cav.	1821-1879	Lafa
PHILLIPPS, T. E.	1st MS Lt. Art.	1843-1916 Adam	Adam
PHILLIPS, Aron A.	40th MS Inf.	1832-1903	Nesh
PHILLIPS, D. M.	43rd MS Inf.	1828-1908 Monr	Monr
PHILLIPS, Elias	6th MS Inf.	1841-1904 Leak	Atta
PHILLIPS, Elias E.	13th MS Inf.	1841-1918 TN	Jone
PHILLIPS, Erasmus Porter	11th MS Cav.	1844-1919 Kemp	Alco
PHILLIPS, F. M.	33rd MS Inf.	1827-1864 Nesh	Nesh
PHILLIPS, Fielding T.	1st AR Inf.	1842-1862 AR	Lafa
PHILLIPS, George C. (Dr)	22nd MS Inf.	1833-1927 Carr	Holm
PHILLIPS, George W.	2nd MS Cav.	1829-1899 NY	Laud
PHILLIPS, Henry Clay	27th TN Cav.	1845-1930 TN	Mars
PHILLIPS, Hill G.	6th MS Cav.	1824-1886 MS	Alco
PHILLIPS, J. H.	2nd MS Cav.	1847-1891 Pano	Alco
PHILLIPS, J. T.	9th MS Cav.	1847-1904	Laud
PHILLIPS, J. W.	12th MS Inf.	1839-1864 MS	Clal
PHILLIPS, James J.	39th MS Inf.	1834-___	Newt
PHILLIPS, James K.	6th MS Inf.	1845-1932 Leak	Leak
PHILLIPS, James W.	5th MS Inf.	1845-1932	Nesh
PHILLIPS, Joe M.	2nd MS Inf.	1840-1894 Tish	Alco
PHILLIPS, John A.	8th MS Inf.	1846-1911 Simp	Pont
PHILLIPS, John B.	1st LA Art.	1837-1863 LA	Warr
PHILLIPS, John L.	11th MS Cav.	1822-1909 Tall	Leak
PHILLIPS, John Richard	40th AL Inf.	1818-1901 VA	Laud
PHILLIPS, John W.	39th MS Inf.	1837-___	Newt
PHILLIPS, Joseph P.	1st MS Cav.	1832-1912 Lafa	Tate
PHILLIPS, L. N.	2nd MS Inf.	1823-1869 Alco	Alco
PHILLIPS, L. W.	7th MS Inf.	1843-1930	Pont
PHILLIPS, Levi	2nd MS Cav.	1820-1875 Gren	Gren
PHILLIPS, Levi W.	1st MS Cav.	1843-1930	Pont
PHILLIPS, Mose	40th MS Inf.	1836-1914 Nesh	Nesh
PHILLIPS, Moses Newton	29th MS Inf.	1822-1879 Pano	Pano
PHILLIPS, N. _.	Turners Lt. Art.	1846-1925	Hind
PHILLIPS, O. L.	7th AL Cav.	1844-1929 AL	Tish
PHILLIPS, Peter	Deasons MS Cav.	1821-1894	Lefl
PHILLIPS, R. S.	13th TN Inf.	18_-1926 GA	Jone
PHILLIPS, Robert	4th MS Inf.	1830-1904	Laud
PHILLIPS, Samuel Alfred	7th NC Inf.	1829-1909 NC	Lafa
PHILLIPS, S. Mose	10th MS Inf.	____-1861	Hind
PHILLIPS, T. J.	2nd MS Cav.	1833-1907 Monr	Monr
PHILLIPS, W. D.	43rd MS Inf.	1848-1910 Monr	Monr
PHILLIPS, W. H.	1st MS Inf.	1843-1920	Okti
PHILLIPS, W. H.	1st MS Cav.	Calh	Calh
PHILLIPS, W. L.	19th TN Inf.	1845-1908 Nesh	Harr
PHILLIPS, W. R.	8th TN Cav.	1844-1931 NC	Tish
PHILLIPS, William E.	30th MS Inf.	1845-1914 Yazo	Yazo
PHILLIPS, William H.	41st MS Inf.	1839-1911 Monr	Monr
PHILLIPS, William J.	17th MS Inf.	1828-1888 AL	Jasp

64

Name	Unit	Dates		
PHILLIPS, William W.	5th or 6th MS Inf.	1833-1906	Covi	Covi
PHILPOT, Thomas	2nd MS Inf.	1830-1915	Tipp	Calh
PHIPPS, Frank M.	38th MS Cav.	1844-1928	Wilk	Wilk
PHIPPS, James W.	1st MS Lt. Art.	1822-1863	Wilk	Adam
PHIPPS, Richard B.	4th MS Cav.	1848-1912	Wilk	Wash
PIAZZA, Frank A.	Shoemaker	1835-1907	Ital	Warr
PICKARD, Henry A. (Rev.)	Berry Inf.	1847-1933	Laud	Laud
PICKARD, Henry Asberry	1st MS Cav.	184_-1933	MS	Covi
PICKARD, William Craig	Berrys Cav.	1845-1916	Laud	Laud
PICKEL, Frank B.	37th MS Inf.	1834-1908	Laud	Laud
PICKENS, E. M.	19th MS Inf.	1843-1923	Lafa	Pont
PICKENS, Ike B. (Isaac)	29th MS Inf.	1836-1876	Holm	Holm
PICKENS, Israll A.	2nd MS Inf.	1808-1898	AL	Tipp
PICKENS, James Jackson	4th Inf.	1833-1876	Holm	Holm
PICKENS, John C.	12th MS Cav.	1847-1925	Holm	Holm
PICKENS, Joseph S.	2nd MS Inf.	1834-1862	AL	Tipp
PICKENS, W. A.	17th MS Inf.	1848-1932	Tish	Tish
PICKENS, William A.	1st MS Inf.	1847-1932	Tish	Tish
PICKERING, James T.	48th MS Inf.	1813-1884	Covi	Covi
PICKERING, John	7th MS Inf.	1835-1902	Covi	Covi
PICKERING, Thomas A.	24th MS Cav.	1844-1911		Copi
PICKET, Henry W.	Jeff Davis Legion	1845-1926	Kemp	Kemp
PICKETT, Johnie	14th MS Art.	1834-1908	Pano	Pano
PICKETT, John William	Jeff Davis Legion	1836-1923	Kemp	Kemp
PICKETT, Perry L.	14th MS Inf.	1839-1903	Laud	Laud
PICKETT, Robert	14th MS Inf.	1836-1905	Laud	Laud
PICKETT, W. R.	36th MS Inf.	1824-1906		Hind
PICKINS, I. A.	2nd MS Inf.	1838-1882	AL	Tipp
PICKLE, Alfred	5th MS Inf.	1829-1900	Monr	Monr
PICKLE, Elijah	2nd MS Cav.	1828-1902	Clar	Monr
PICKLE, Henry K.	2nd MS Cav.			Monr
PICKLE, J. H.	2nd MS Cav.			Monr
PICKLE, J. M.	Wards Lt. Art.	1846-1922	Pano	Harr
PICKLE, William R.	24th MS Inf.	1843-1922	MS	Monr
PIERCE, A. G.	3rd MS Cav.	1849-1934		Copi
PIERCE, Aaron	12th MS Inf.	1846-1932	Hind	Newt
PIERCE, Edward	38th MS Cav.	1838-1916	MS	Walt
PIERCE, Francis Marion	6th MS Inf.	1843-1909	MS	Lawr
PIERCE, J. C.	17th MS Cav.	____-1911		Adam
PIERCE, James L.	3rd MS Regt.	1830-1872		Hind
PIERCE, Jeremiah	5th MS Inf.	1846-1932	Monr	Monr
PIERCE, John C.	1st MS Lt. Art.	1832-1913	Holm	Holm
PIERCE, John Calhoun	3rd MS Inf.	1848-1864	Tipp	Linc
PIERCE, Levi	6th TN Cav.	1823-1903	NC	Pren
PIERCE, Robert N.	3rd MS Inf.	1833-1916	Yazo	Yazo
PIERCE, Simeon	48th MS Inf.	1827-1910	Okti	Okti
PIERCE, Thomas	2nd MS Cav.			Rank
PIERCE, Thomas Jeff.	Seven Star Art.	1842-1934	Copi	Copi
PIERCE, T. W.	Artillery	1837-1915	Copi	Hind
PIERCE, Wiley	1st MS Inf.			Rank
PIERCE, William D.	3rd MS Cav.	1845-1904		Rank

65

PIERCE, William S.	15th MS Inf.	1844-1927 MS	Holm
PIGFORD, Jacob W.	13th MS Inf.	1844-1862 Laud	Laud
PIGFORD, T. D.	13th MS Inf.	1839-1908 Laud	Laud
PIGFORD, T. S.	13th MS Inf.	1824-1899 Laud	Laud
PIGFORD, Wright	1st MS Inf.	1812-1881 Laud	Laud
PIGG, Augustus S.	27th AL Inf.	1831-1899	Leak
PIGG, Charles L.	11th MS Inf.	1834-1907 MS	Nesh
PIGG, W. C.	Hughes AL Inf.	1846-1921 AL	Leak
PIGOTT, John	7th MS Inf.	1831-1891 Mari	Walt
PIGOTT, William	38th MS Cav.	1838-1899 MS	Walt
PIKE, R. A.	KY Cav.	1844-1916 KY	Wash
PILCHER, J. D.	41st MS Inf.	1838-1901 Pont	Unio
PILCHER, John T.	5th MS Inf.	1844-___ MS	Atta
PILCHER, William	5th MS Inf.	1845-1925 MS	Atta
PILGHER, Stephen	43rd MS Inf.	1834-1911 Pont	Pont
PILGREEN, K. T.	44th MS Inf.	1833-1915 Calh	Chic
PILGREEN, Silas	4th MS Inf.	1821-1879 Calh	Calh
PILLOW, Walter	7th TN Inf.	1844-1920 TN	Lefl
PIZER, W. J.	46th NC Inf.	1847-1927 NC	Mari
PINER, W. J.	46th NC Inf.	1842-1910 NC	Forr
PINKARD, John J.	2nd TN Inf.	1842-1924 TN	Atta
PINKERTON, Sam D.	38th MS Cav.	1830-1906 MS	Walt
PINKSTON, W. A.	37th MS Inf.	1816-1916 Smit	Laud
PINNIX, T. A.	5th MS Inf.	1846-1873	Choc
PINSON, J. W.	1st MS Lt. Art.	1848-1914 AL	Choc
PINSON, W. M.	36th MS Inf.	1843-___	Newt
PIPKINS, Absolom	24th MS Inf.	1842-1924 Gree	Geor
PIPKINS, Charlie	3rd MS Inf.	1847-1930 MS	Geor
PIKINS, James	24th MS Inf.	1840-1887 Gree	Gree
PIKINS, George M. D.	24th MS Inf.	1845-1918 Gree	Gree
PIPPEN, William M.	13th MS Cav.	1845-1920 Clar	Wayn
PIPPIN, Berry	2nd MS Inf.	1820-1899 MS	Jasp
PISTOLE, L. A.	24th AL Inf.	1843-1912 AL	Laud
PITCHFORD, Augustus	18th MS Inf.	1847-1924 Holm	Holm
PITCHFORD, John C.	Poagues MS Art.	1834-1926	Madi
PITMAN, Calvin G.	1st MS Inf.		
PITMAN, John D.	3rd MS Inf.		Hind
PITTMAN, Calvin	7th MS Inf.	1830-1920	Mari
PITTMAN, E. E. (Dr.)	15th MS Inf.	1839-1907 Choc	Tall
PITTMAN, Geo. W.	11th MS Cav.	1844-1877 MS	Alco
PITTMAN, J. W.	13th MS Inf.	1840-1862 Wayn	Wayn
PITTMAN, James B.	36th AL Inf.	1824-1900 AL	Wayn
PITTMAN, James O.	2nd MS Inf.	1822-1875	Hind
PITTMAN, John A.	7th MS Cav.	1845-1917 MS	JEDA
PITTMAN, John G. D.	11th GA Inf.	1837-1918 GA	JEDA
PITTMAN, Joseph M.	15th MS Inf.	1838-1917	Webs
PITTMAN, Nuit Jr.	30th MS Inf.	1832-1862 NC	Mont
PITTMAN, R. J.	4th MS Inf.	1841-1917 Carr	Rank
PITTMAN, Stephen D.	7th MS Inf.	1835-1917 Mari	Mari
PITTMAN, T. J.	32nd GA Inf.	1843-1921 GA	Forr
PITTMAN, Warren Wesley	8th MS Inf.	1835-1922 Smit	Smit
PITTMAN, William J.	8th MS Inf.	1847-1917 Smit	Harr

PITNER, Wm. J.	7th MS Cav.	1839-1903 Tipp	Tipp
PITTS, D. T.	2nd MS Cav.	1841-1865 MS	Pont
PITTS, Dan T.	2nd MS Cav.	1841-1924 Pont	Pont
PITTS, Hillary	1st MS Inf.	1831-1900 Pont	Pont
PITTS, I.	41st MS Inf.	1847-1873 Pont	Pont
PITTS, J. T.	2nd MS Cav.	1825-1895 Pont	Pont
PITTS, N.	8th MS Inf.	1846-1926 MS	Jone
PITTS, R. L.	2nd MS Cav.	1845-1930 MS	Pont
PITTS, R. S.	41st MS Inf.	1841-1886 Pont	Pont
PITTS, Richard B.	2nd MS Cav.	1843-1930	Pont
PITTS, Robert B.	2nd MS Inf.	1819-1892 Pont	Pont
PITTS, W. C.	28th MS Inf.	1826-1919 MS	Tish
PITTS, W. P.	2nd MS Inf.	1844-1925 MS	Pont
PITTS, William C.	2nd MS Inf.	1828-1906 Pont	Pont
(PIZER located after PILLOW)			
PLANT, S. H.	22nd MS Inf.	1823-1915 Lafa	Lafa
PLATT, J. E.	38th AL Inf.	1837-1908 AL	Laud
PLAXICO, G. W.	32nd MS Inf.	1834-1907 MS	Pren
PLEASANT, S. W.	4th MS Cav.	1846-1921	Hind
PLEASANTS, Frank P.	30th MS Inf.	1822-1877 Carr	Lefl
PLITT, Louis	21st MS Inf.	1834-1889 GE	Wilk
PLUMMER, I. L.	15th MS Cav.	1835-1920 AL	Wayn
PLUNKETT, John D.	37th MS Inf.	1842-1863 Jasp	Jasp
POAG, Joe W.	9th MS Inf.	1846-1911 Tate	Tate
POE, A. P.	1st MS	1846-1919	Tate
POE, J. H.	9th MS Inf.	1836-1897 Mars	Unio
POGUE, T. K.	31st MS Inf.	1838-1923 Choc	Webs
POINDEXTER, W. G.	3rd MS Inf.	1842-1893 Sunf	Lefl
POINTER, Monroe	1st MS Cav.	1838-1890	Pano
POINTER, Phil	1st MS Inf.	1836-1893 Pano	Pano
POLK, Elias	7th MS Inf.	1844-1921 JEDA	JEDA
POLK, Frank M.	46th MS Inf.		Rank
POLK, Franklin M.	7th MS Inf.	1844-1903 MS	JEDA
POLK, Franklin M.	7th MS Inf.	1820-1909 Covi	JEDA
POLK, H. G.	42nd MS Inf.	1844-1906 Yalo	Webs
POLK, James K.	4th MS Cav.	1845-1922 MS	JEDA
POLK, John	38th MS Inf.	1832-1914	JEDA
POLK, John L.	4th MS Cav.	1825-1904 MS	JEDA
POLK, Lewis G.	21st MS Inf.	1845-1891 Tall	Tall
POLK, T. J.	24th MS Inf.	1839-1911 MS	Lown
POLK, W. W.	38th MS Cav.	1834-1914 Lawr	JEDA
POLKINGHORNE, H. G.	12th MS Inf.	Adam	Adam
POLLAN, John W.	29th MS Inf.	1834-1916 Carr	Gren
POLLARD, Austin	41st MS Inf.		Monr
POLLARD, H. L.	19th MS Inf.	1844-1912 Pano	Pano
POLLARD, Robert	Shipbuilder	1835-1892 VA	Holm
POLLARD, W. B.	41st AL Inf.	1843-1922 AL	Pren
POLLOCK, L. B.	35th MS Inf.	1838-1926 Kemp	Kemp
POLLAND, E. H. (Dr.)	16th MS Inf.	1835-1904 Clai	Clai
POLSON, Thomas J.	5th MS Cav.	1843-___	Mont
POND, H. S.	18th MS Regt.	1840-1922 VA	Hind
POND, Thomas Edward	1st MS Art.	1847-1889 MS	Hind

67

POND, Walter C.	3rd MS Inf.	1838-1871 MS	Hind
PONDER, Finis W.	63rd AL Inf.	1846-1908 AL	Clay
PONDER, J. M.	4th MS Cav.	1826-1913	Rank
POOL, D. R. (Dr.)	4th MS Inf.	1842-1910 Clar	Jone
POOL, Elijah J.	7th MS Inf.	1844-1936 Mari	Mari
POOL, H. H.	24th MS Inf.	1841-1910 Kemp	Kemp
POOL, James B.	38th MS Cav.	1841-1862 Wilk	Lown
POOL, John C.	6th MS Cav.	1847-1930 MS	Leak
POOLE, Isaac	36th MS Inf.	1837-1904 GA	Newt
POOLE, William H.	4th MS Inf.	1844-1911 Atta	Atta
POORE, W. B.	16th MS Inf.	1848-1913 Jasp	Jasp
POPE, Dickerson R.	7th MS Inf.	1828-1899 MS	Walt
POPE, Everett	38th MS Cav.	1831-1907 Clai	Mari
POPE, Henry	7th MS Inf.	1834-1899	Mari
POPE, Horace K.	9th MS Inf.	1839-1872	DeSo
POPE, J. B.	1st MS Inf.	1823-1911 Leak	Leak
POPE, Jacob H.	2nd MS Inf.	1832-1885 Mari	Mari
POPE, John W.	39th MS Inf.	1836-1878	Rank
POPE, John T.	40th MS Inf.	1832-1894 Nesh	Kemp
POPE, S. H.	6th MS Cav.	1836-1910 Scot	Lown
POPE, Thomas	38th MS Cav.	1828-1928 Covi	Covi
POPE, Thomas Wesley	20th MS Inf.	1836-1920 Monr	Monr
POPE, W. W.	2nd MS Cav.	1846-1908 Monr	Monr
POPE, Wilbert	15th MS Inf.	1826-1908 MS	Leak
POPE, Wilbert	15th MS Inf.	1825-1903 MS	Atta
POPE, William Allen	12th MS Cav.	1826-1861 AL	Holm
POPE, William Ellzy	6th MS Inf.	1834-1922 Scot	Lown
POPE, William F.	5th MS Inf.	1820-1912 NC	Wins
POPHAM, Isaac A.	43rd MS Inf.	1841-1862 Monr	Chic
POPKINS, C. H.	Englishs Batt.	1839-1863 Adam	Adam
POPP, H. C.	Nelsons MS Cav.	1837-1885 MS	Adam
PORCH, Henry	64th GA Inf.	1837-1918 GA	Yazo
PORCH, J. J.	GA Comm.	1847-1930 GA	Rank
PORTER, A. A.	Holmes Co. Inf.	1816-1886 SC	Holm
PORTER, A. Texas	2nd MS Cav.	1841-1862 Lafa	Lafa
PORTER, Baxter R.	11th MS Cav.	1839-1864 Lafa	Lafa
PORTER, Benj. Franklin	16th MS Regt.	1847-1932 Holm	Hind
PORTER, C. C.	24th MS Inf.	1841-1914 Chic	Chic
PORTER, C. E.	4th MS Cav.	____-1907	Clai
PORTER, Damascus Fishe	5th MS Inf.	1838-1894	Leak
PORTER, Daniel P.	3rd MS Cav.	1835-1899 TN	Hind
PORTER, Elias R.	28th MS Cav.	1837-1863 Lafa	Lafa
PORTER, Henry Estell	11th MS Cav.	1846-1915 TN	Lee
PORTER, J. C.	1st MS Inf.	1816-1908 Laud	Laud
PORTER, J. D.	2nd MS Cav.	1835-1866 Pont	Pont
PORTER, J. R.	11th MS Cav.	1843-1904 Tall	Alco
PORTER, James	3rd MS Inf.	1839-1894 MS	Bent
PORTER, James F.	4th MS Cav.	1833-1913 Fran	Fran
PORTER, James M.	GA Troops	1847-1939 GA	Jone
PORTER, Joe	22nd MS Inf.		Hind
PORTER, John A.	2nd MS Cav.	1840-1881 Lee	Lee
PORTER, John F.	4th MS Cav.	1837-1927 Fran	Fran

PORTER, John L.	35th MS Inf.	1840-1916 Wins	Wins
PORTER, Oliver A.	12th TN Inf.	1843-1936 TN	Tipp
PORTER, Richard B.	17th MS Inf.	1830-1894 MS	Yalo
PORTER, Robert Gilderoy	10th MS Inf.	1839-1908 Okti	Okti
PORTER, Thomas A.	5th MS Inf.	1828-1895 Kemp	Kemp
PORTER, Samuel D.	7th MS Inf.	1836-1909 MS	Fran
PORTER, W. E.(Rev.)	2nd MS Inf.	1846-1888 Pont	Bent
PORTERFIELD, John	9th MS Inf.	1820-187_ IR	Warr
PORTEVENT, Adolph	15th AL Inf.	1845-1922 AL	Laud
PORTIS, C. D.	39th MS Inf.	1824-1904 TN	Newt
PORTIS, John C.	8th MS Inf.	1837-1909 GA	Newt
PORTWOOD, T. J.	20th MS Inf.	1839-1922 Atta	Atta
POSEY, A. A.	5th MS Inf.	1843-1902 MS	Monr
POSEY, Farr	6th MS Cav.	1844-1917 Monr	Monr
POSEY, Jeff	16th MS Inf.	1843-1880 Wilk	Yazo
POSEY, I. H.	40th MS Inf.	1825-1888	Nesh
POSEY, Richard W.	40th MS Inf.	1830-1916 Newt	Smit
POSEY, Stanhope	16th MS Inf.	1832-1893 Wilk	Yazo
POSTELL, Elijah	24th MS Inf.	1824-1894 SC	Madi
POSTELWATE, W. D.	15th MS Inf.	1846-1926 LA	Harr
POTEET, R. W.	5th MS Cav.	1824-1907 Carr	Carr
POTTER, C. O.	23rd MS Inf.	1835-1897 MS	Unio
POTTER, George L.	Adams Regt.	1812-1877	Hind
POTTS, Elisha	33rd AL Inf.	1838-1909 AL	Alco
POTTS, J. F.	23rd MS Inf.	1831-1880 MS	Alco
POTTS, Jas. R.	17th MS Inf.	1838-1875 Mars	Mars
POTTS, William	1st MS Cav.	1821-1900	Alco
POTTS, William	1st MS Cav.	1839-1862 Carr	Lafa
POU, James Francis	24th MS Cav.	1846-1927 Wayn	Wayn
POUND, Daniel H.	38th MS Cav.	1832-1904 Pike	Pike
POUND, G. H. G.	13th MS Inf.	1826-1908 Newt	Pont
POUNDS, B. W.	22nd MS Inf.	1844-1926 Hind	Webs
POUNDS, W. A.	10th MS Cav.	1838-1878 MS	Pren
POVALL, J. P.	5th MS Cav.	1820-1888	Pren
POWE, George W.	2nd MS Inf.	1852-___	Newt
POWE, Samuel Henry	13th MS Inf.	1818-1896 Wayn	Wayn
POWEL, L. L.	8th MS Inf.	1839-1892 Leak	Leak
POWELL, A. _.	29th GA Cav.	1847-1916 GA	Harr
POWELL, A. J.	7th MS Inf.	1844-1904 Mari	Lawr
POWELL, Allen M.	15th MS Inf.	1843-1887	Mont
POWELL, Charles A.	43rd MS Inf.	1838-1911 Lown	Monr
POWELL, Chas. W.	1st MS Lt. Art.	1839-1862 Warr	Warr
POWELL, E. J.	30th MS Inf.	1834-1862 GA	Mont
POWELL, Edward	1st MS Inf.	1824-1868	Hind
POWELL, George W.	9th MS Inf.	1841-1863 Mars	Mars
POWELL, George Wash.	6th MS Inf.	1834-1910 Hind	Shar
POWELL, H. C.	9th MS Inf.	1841-1928 DeSo	Alco
POWELL, H. J.	4th LA Inf.	1847-1920 LA	Shar
POWELL, Henry	32nd MS Inf.		Rank
POWELL, Hiram W.	7th MS Inf.	1830-1885 Jone	Jone
POWELL, J. H.	1st MS Inf.	1849-1912	Hind
POWELL, J. J.	4th MS Cav.	1844-1895 Jeff	Yalo

69

POWELL, James	45th MS Inf.	1843-1907 Pike	Amit
POWELL, James H.	8th MS Inf.	1847-1925 Laud	Calh
POWELL, James W.	15th SC Inf.	1834-1905 SC	Tipp
POWELL, James W.	38th MS Inf.	1831-1915 Clai	Mari
POWELL, John	6th MS Inf.	1838-1897 MS	Scot
POWELL, John S.	4th MS Cav.	1844-1903 Covi	Covi
POWELL, John T.	20th VA Art.	1839-1922 VA	Lafa
POWELL, John W.	15th MS Inf.	1828-1919 NC	Mont
POWELL, John W.	42nd MS Inf.	1825-1893 VA	Gren
POWELL, John W.	12th MS Regt.	1830-1902 VA	Warr
POWELL, Joseph H.	5th AL Cav.	1832-1924 AL	Itaw
POWELL, L. L.	MS Inf.	1832-1892 Leak	Leak
POWELL, L. M.	4th LA Inf.	1840-1916 MS	Warr
POWELL, Lenard L.	36th MS Inf.	1827-1892 MS	Clar
POWELL, Lewis	3rd MS Inf.		
POWELL, M. A. (Dr.)	44th MS Inf.	1830-1922 MS	Calh
POWELL, Michael Amos	32nd MS Inf.	1841-1927 Tish	Alco
POWELL, Riley	36th AL Inf.	1821-1885 AL	Gree
POWELL, Robert	33rd MS Inf.	1827-1915 Pont	Pont
POWELL, S. T.	4th SC Inf.	1846-1933 SC	Tipp
POWELL, Sanford D.	31st MS Inf.	1841-1900 Linc	Linc
POWELL, T. J.	15th SC Inf.	1837-1911 SC	Tipp
POWELL, Thomas	7th MS Inf.	1831-1895 Mari	Mari
POWELL, Thomas	41st MS Inf.	1830-1898 Noxu	Noxu
POWELL, Thomas	3rd MS Cav.	1825-1878 Gren	Gren
POWELL, Tobe	1st MS Lt. Art.	1831-1918 Warr	Warr
POWELL, W. C.	2nd TN Cav.	1837-1898 TN	Alco
POWELL, W. F/P.	11th MS Cav.	1844-1922 Alco	Alco
POWELL, William A.	21st AR Inf.	1842-___ AR	Rank
POWELL, William H.	15th MS Inf.	1821-1904 SC	Gren
POWER, J. L.	15th MS Inf.	1817-1862 SC	Atta
POWER, H. A.	8th MS Inf.	1846-1922	Covi
POWER, Stephen Francis	GA Q. M. Dept.	1828-1900 IR	Adam
POWERS, W. H.	15th MS Inf.	1843-1913 Choc	Choc
POWERS, James D.	22nd VA Cav.	1824-1897 VA	Holm
POWERS, John Logan	1st MS Lt. Art.	1834-1901	Hind
POWERS, Lucius S.	47th MS Inf.	18_7-1906 VA	Holm
POWERS, Pat	4th LA Inf.	Adam	Adam
POWERS, S. C.	42nd MS Inf.	1832-1876 Gren	DeSo
POWERS, Spencer Bird	VA Art.	1840-1928 VA	Shar
POYTHRESS, A. E.	15th AL Inf.	1844-1918 AL	Laud
P'Pool, Elbert Stephen	4th TN Cav.	1837-1922 TN	Hind
PRATHER, Josiah	11th MS Inf.	1836-1908 Carr	Unio
PRATT, W. H.	19th MS Inf.	1844-1920 Monr	Monr
PRAY, Washington D.	Miles LA Reg.	1847-1930 LA	Amit
PRENTISS, James	3rd MS Inf.	1844-1879 Gree	Gree
PRENTISS, Seargent Smith	Woods MS Cav.	1847-1907 MS	Adam
PRESCOTT, Franklin	39th MS Inf.	1825-1902 Pike	Amit
PRESCOTT, Thomas Darling	17th MS Inf.	1843-1922 Choc	Jone
PRESLY, A. J.	33rd MS Inf.	1845-___ Leak	Scot
PRESLEY, E. H.	2nd AR Inf.	1841-1911 AR	Leak
PRESLEY, James T.	44th MS Inf.	1834-1920 SC	Tate

70

Name	Unit	Dates	Place
PRESLEY, John S.	10th SC Cav.	1827-1905 SC	Tate
PRESLEY, Thomas Henry	10th SC Cav.	1841-1905	Tate
PRESTAGE, George	6th MS Inf.	1825-1909 MS	Simp
PRESLEY, W. A.	1st Minute Men	1820-1894 SC	Leak
PRESSLEY, R. C.	39th MS Inf.	1847-1937 Hind	Harr
PRESTAGE, Z. B.	7th MS Inf.	1831-1918 Pike	Warr
PRESTON, John Archibald	Adams MS Cav.	1837-1912 Madi	Madi
PRESTON, Thomas Wilson	VA	1846-1935 VA	Warr
PRESTRIDGE, A.		1835-1906 MS	Itaw
PRESTRIDGE, Robert E.	18th MS Inf.	1846-1929 Hind	Amit
PRESTRIDGE, S. C.	22nd MS Inf.	1836-1864 Lawr	Lawr
PRESTRIDGE, Thomas J.	1st MS Lt. Art.	1838-1908 Yazo	Yazo
PRESTRIDGE, W. A.	14th Cav.	1846-1889 MS	Adam
PRESTRIDGE, W. P.	7th MS Inf.	1842-1930 MS	Linc
PREWETT, Harrison	39th MS Inf.	1841-1892 Pike	Pike
PREWETT, J. S.	39th MS Inf.	1843-1884 Pike	Pike
PREWITT, Dudley	15th MS Inf.	1829-1898 AL	Choc
PREWITT, F. M.	7th AL Cav.	1843-1913 Tish	Tish
PREWITT, Russell G.	15th MS Inf.	1830-1884 Choc	Choc
PREWITT, R. K.	4th MS Inf.	1844-1919 Choc	Choc
PRICE, A. J.	5th MS Inf.	1843-1921 MS	Monr
PRICE, Alex	13th MS Inf.	1843-1909 Newt	Newt
PRICE, Alexander	33rd MS Inf.	1841-1905 NC	Rank
PRICE, Andrew Jackson	19th TN Cav.	1828-1900 TN	Pren
PRICE, Andrew Jackson	38th MS Cav.	1834-1880 Lawr	Lawr
PRICE, Armond	11th MS Inf.	1840-1880 Lafa	Lafa
PRICE, Bazzel	1st MS Inf.	1830-1906 NC	Coah
PRICE, Benjamin	37th MS Inf.	1832-1923 Laud	Laud
PRICE, C. W.	20th MS Inf.	1846-1906	Hind
PRICE, Chaner	38th MS Inf.	1831-1913	Copi
PRICE, Clarkey	15th MS Inf.	1815-1882	Rank
PRICE, Daniel Reeci	7th MS Sharpshooters	1836-1897 Adam	Adam
PRICE, Daniel Thomas	26th MS Inf.	1839-1928 Pren	Pren
PRICE, Francis Marion	12th MS Inf.	____-1890 Clai	Warr
PRICE, G. F.	5th MS Inf.	1840-1919 MS	Monr
PRICE, G. W.	13th MS Inf.	1828-1904 Laud	Laud
PRICE, G. W.	1st MS Lt.Art.	1831-1912 Carr	Atta
PRICE, G. W.	17th MS Inf.	1842-1921 MS	Yalo
PRICE, Henry N.	7th MS Inf.	1839-1913 NC	Hind
PRICE, Huldric	11th MS Inf.	1839-1903 Lafa	Lafa
PRICE, J. A.	33rd MS Inf.	1830-1905 Lawr	Lawr
PRICE, J. _.	8th MS Cav.	1839-1924	Hind
PRICE, J. W.	39th MS Inf.	1846-1934 Rank	Jone
PRICE, James A.	35th AL Inf.	1839-1928 Lown	Alco
PRICE, Joe Sr.	22nd MS Inf.	1837-1914 MS	Lawr
PRICE, John A. (Rev.)	20th MS Inf.	1837-1923 Scot	Pear
PRICE, John W.	37th MS Inf.	1826-1884 Smit	Acot
PRICE, Joseph	33rd MS Inf.	1822-1892 Fran	Fran
PRICE, Joseph	Powers MS Cav.	1828-1879	Copi
PRICE, Joseph	22nd MS Inf.	1842-1911 Lawr	Walt
PRICE, Joseph R.	46th MS Inf.	1847-1903 MS	Chic

Name	Unit	Dates	Col1	Col2
PRICE, M. A.	11th AR Inf.	1845-1927 Wilk	Wilk	
PRICE, M. L.	8th AL Inf.	1845-1911 MS	Laud	
PRICE, Meredith M.	8th AL Cav.	1845-1911 AL	Laud	
PRICE, Moses	14th MS Inf.	1818-___ MS	Scot	
PRICE, Nat S.	10th MS Inf.	___-1867	Hind	
PRICE, P. G.	34th MS Inf.	1842-1909 Tipp	Tipp	
PRICE, Robert	4th MS Cav.	1830-1906	Covi	
PRICE, Solomon	1st MS Inf.	1812-1893	Hind	
PRICE, T. J.	22nd MS Inf.	1843-1900	Hind	
PRICE, Thomas S.	3rd MS Inf.	1825-1886 Chic	Chic	
PRICE, Thomas W.	3rd MS Inf.	1838-1917 MS	Hind	
PRICE, W. B. (Rev.)	5th MS Cav.	1840-1920 Carr	Lefl	
PRICE, W. J.	7th MS Inf.	1833-1897 Pike	Linc	
PRICE, W. M.	2nd MS Inf.	1837-1924 MS	Linc	
PRICE, William	7th MS Inf.	1828-1910 Pike	Pike	
PRICE, William	7th MS Inf.	1839-1898 Noxu	Wins	
PRICE, William	57th AL Inf.	1842-1920	Harr	
PRICE, William Ben	34th MS Inf.	1837-1865 Lafa	Lafa	
PRICE, William Epps	26th MS Inf.	1845-1919 NC	Pren	
PRICE, William Theo.	9th KY Inf.	1843-1927 KY	Harr	
PRICE, Williamson T.	9th KY Inf.	1843-1927 KY	Harr	
PRICE, Wm.	AL Reserves	1847-1915 AL	Warr	
PRICHARD, Britian L.	Adams MS Cav.	1810-1867 Madi	Madi	
PRICHARD. J. Foster	9th MS Inf.	1846-1910	Madi	
PRICHARD, John H.		1843-1901	Adam	
PRICHARD, L. M.	1st AL Cav.	1845-1922 AL	Okti	
(PRIDDY located after PULLEN, George W.)				
PRIDGEN, D. D.	37th MS Inf.	1824-1909 Clar	Covi	
PRIDGEN, Eli C.	37th MS Inf.	1840-1929 Covi	Covi	
PRIEST, Archie H.	38th NC Inf.	1840-1922 NC	Fran	
PRIEST, J. _.	41st MS Inf.	1836-1920 MS	Pont	
PRIEST, T.	3rd Conf. Inf.	1838-1915 Hanc	Harr	
PRIESTLEY, H. D.	MS Cav.	1848-1900	Madi	
PRIESTLEY, James	2nd MS Inf.	1843-1897 Madi	Madi	
PRIESTLEY, John	10th MS Inf.	1840-1893	Madi	
PRIMROSE, John Wm. (Dr.)	1st NC Cav.	1838-1907 NC	Wash	
PRINCE, Francis Marion	11th MS Inf.	1835-1892 Yalo	Kemp	
PRINCE, J. H.	2nd AL Inf.	1838-1910 AL	Unio	
PRINCE, John R.	11th MS Inf.	1837-1910 MS	Noxu	
PRINCE, Levi	7th MS Inf.	1830-1909 Lawr	Jone	
PRINCE, Robert C.	38th MS Cav.	1829-1900	Copi	
PRINCE, W. Berry	5th MS Cav.	1826-1893 Carr	Carr	
PRINE, Linnie	17th MS Cav.	1838-1905 Clar	Gree	
PRINE, Robert W.	17th MS Cav.	1835-1903 Clar	Gree	
PRINE, W. H.	27th MS Inf.	1835-1906 Jone	Simp	
PRISOCK, (blank)	35th MS Inf.	___-1900	Rank	
PRISOCK, Isiah David	41st MS Inf.	1832-1897 SC	Wins	
PRITCHARD, Allen	2nd MS Inf.	1834-1878 Tipp	Tall	
PRITCHARD, Allen	14th MS Lt.Art.	1834-1878	Tall	
PRITCHARD, Benjamin F.	22nd MS Inf.	1839-1928	Tate	
PRITCHARD, C. A.	14th MS Cav.	1847-1931 Fran	Fran	
PRITCHARD, James A.	3rd MO Inf.	1816-1862 Carr	Yalo	

72

PRITCHARD, R. A.	1st MS Lt. Art.	1834-1906 Jeff	Jeff
PRITCHARD, T. J.	2nd & 3rd MS Inf.	1843-1928 MS	Jeff
PRITCHARD, Willis Andrew	6th MS Cav.	1848-1937 Hump	Hump
PROCTOR, D. R.	5th MS Cav.		Atta
PROCTOR, James M.	28th MS Cav.	1845-1868 VA	Holm
PROCTOR, T. A.	1st MS Inf.	1835-1912	DeSo
PROPHET, William R.	13th NC Inf.	1846-1912 NC	Lefl
PROVINE, Flem J.	12th MS Cav.	1836-1910 Tish	Tish
PROVINE, R. N.	29th MS Inf.	1840-1929 MS	Calh
PROWELL, William D.	35th MS Inf.	1844-1912 Lown	Lown
PRUDE,Jesse W.	1st MS Cav.	1833-1917 MS	Pont
PRUDE, Joseph	9th MS Inf.	1830-1908 Tish	Pont
PRUETT, Wiley B.	Hills AL Cav.	1847-1922 AL	Monr
PRUIT, William H.	2nd GA Cav.	1832-1917 GA	Tish
PRUITT, Andrew J.	15th MS Inf.	1841-1900 Simp	Simp
PRUITT, Benjamin	5th MS Inf.	1843-1862 Kemp	Kemp
PRUITT, H. C.	4th MS Cav.	1847-1889 Jeff	Chic
PRUITT, W. B.	Hills AL Cav.	1847-1922 Monr	Monr
PRYOR, Barnett	7th MS Inf.	1846-1898 Jone	Jone
PUCKETT, Allen C.	27th MS Inf.	1840-1909 MS	Monr
PUCKETT, A. L.	19th Cav.	1843-1904 MS	Copi
PUCKETT, Allen N.	3rd MS Inf.	1825-1882 Monr	Monr
PUCKETT, Benjamin	43rd MS Inf.	1833-1916 Tish	Tish
PUCKETT, Charles Miller	6th AL Inf.	1844-1929 AL	Newt
PUCKETT, John	1st MS Inf.	1840-1910 VA	Monr
PUCKETT, Nathan T.	1st MS Inf.	1841-1900 Monr	Monr
PUCKETT, Thomas	1st & 20th MS Inf.	1837-1898 Monr	Monr
PUGH, J. A.	53rd AL Cav.	1848-1925 AL	Clar
PUGH, James S.	2nd MS Inf.	1848-1930 Jasp	Jasp
PUGH, William F.	1st GA Inf.	1830-1899 GA	Itaw
PULLEN, Carter G.	15th MS Inf.	1838-1924 GA	Mont
PULLEN, George W.	22nd MS Inf.	1830-1903 Lawr	Lawr
PRIDDY, Thomas	24th MS Inf.	1841-1909 Itaw	Itaw
PULLEN, Joseph L.	15th MS Inf.	1828-1896 GA	Mont
PULLEN, L. G.	2nd MS Cav.	1846-1910 Monr	Monr
PULLEN, Nathan F.	5th MS Inf.		Monr
PULLEN, W. R.	28th MS Cav.	1835-1887 Carr	Carr
PULLIAM, Andrew Jackson	17th MS Inf.	1836-1910 Fran	
PULLIAM, Joseph Lumpkin	17th MS Inf.	1833-1915 Fran	Chic
PULLIAM, Vachnel W.	22nd MS Inf.	1826-1912 Tipp	Tipp
PULLIN, J. T.	18th MS Cav.	1822-1899	DeSo
PULLINS, Samuel D.	10th AL Inf.	1842-190_ AL	Copi
PUNCHARD, L. H.		____-1902	Adam
PURCELL, George Whit.	5th MS Cav.	1846-1924 Carr	Carr
PURNELL, J. C.	28th MS Cav.	1847-1921 Carr	Mont
PURNELL, M. T.	28th MS Cav.	1843-1862 Carr	Carr
PURNELL, Martin A.	11th MS Inf.	1842-1866 Carr	Carr
PURNELL, William	Adams MS Cav.	1834-1899	Warr
PURSER, Henry	Seven Star Art.	1840-1929	Copi
PURSER, J. M. L.	24th MS Cav.	1846-1914	Copi

PURSER, W. H. H.	Pettus Art.	1840-1864	Copi
PURSER, William	6th MS Inf.	1820-___ Simp	Simp
PURSER, William Henry	24th MS Cav.	1841-1929 Copi	Copi
PURSIS, John	30th MS Inf.	1841-1910 Atta	Atta
PURVIANCE, A.	18th MS Inf.	1841-1924 Madi	Madi
PURVIANCE, Henry S.	Adams Cav.	1845-___	Madi
PURVINE, D. S.	1st MS Inf.	1835-1911 Itaw	Pont
PURVIS, James M.	6th MS Inf.	1841-1880	Rank
PURVIS, James	6th MS Inf.	1830-1909	Smit
PURVIS, James M.	6th MS Inf.	1830-1909 Smit	Smit
PURVIS, John Mitchell	6th MS Inf.	1828-1912	Smit
PURVIS, W. M.	12th MS Inf.	1831-1916 AL	Lafa
PURVIS, William	12th MS Inf.	1831-1916 AL	Lafa
PURVIS, Walden L.	40th MS Inf.	1835-1909 Jasp	Jone
PURYEAR, Achilles	Adams MS Cav.	1835-1909	Hind
PURYEAR, George B.	19th MS Inf.	1842-1923 Mars	Tate
PURYEAR, John Royal	Adams MS Cav.	1836-1926 VA	Tate
PUTNAM, Albert G.	2nd MS Cav.	____-1895	Scot
PUTMAN, E. R.	4th MS Inf.	1824-1865 MS	Calh
PUTMAN, J. E.	36th MS Inf.	1846-1935 MS	Scot
PUTMAN, M. F. Sr.	36th MS Inf.	1849-1937	Scot
PUTNAM, Sam	Warrens Lt. Art.	1831-1917 KY	Warr
PUTT, G. W.	31st MS Inf.	1835-1920 GA	Lee
PYLANT, G. Minor	AL Inf.	1845-1922 AL	Wayn
PYLE, William L.	18th AL Inf.	1842-1924 AL	Pont
PYRON, Albert	4th MS Inf.	1826-1890	Mont
PYRON, A. J.	3rd & 4th MS Inf.	1834-1909	Mont
PYRON, James Allen	4th MS Inf.	1833-1906 Mont	Mont
PYRON, M. B.	43rd MS Inf.	182_-191_ Lown	Chic
QUARTERMAN, E. G.	28th MS Cav.	1846-1921 Adam	Harr
QUARTERMAN, T. R.	16th MS Inf.	1831-1903 EN	Adam
QUATTLEBAUM, S. F.	13th MS Inf.	1838-1864 SC	Newt
QUATTLEBAUM, John F.	20th MS Inf.	183_-1913 Newt	Newt
QUICK, J. E.	5th MS Cav.	184_-1913 Covi	Covi
QUICK, John W.	3rd MS Inf.	1846-1912 Jone	Jone
QUIN, Frank M.	39th MS Inf.	1829-1886 MS	Walt
QUIN, John H.	45th MS Inf.	1839-1915 MS	Pike
QUIN, Josephus R.	14th Cav.	1826-1864 Pike	Pike
QUINE, Lemuel F.	20th MS Inf.	1832-1925 Wilk	Warr
QUINN, A. S.	19th VA Inf.	1842-1906 VA	Yalo
QUINN, H. H.	34th MS Inf.	1831-1894 Tipp	Unio
QUINN, Henry G.	33rd MS Inf.	1830-1890 Amit	Amit
QUINN, Houston	11th MS Inf.	1840-1915 Okti	Choc
QUINN, J. P.	35th MS Inf.	1831-1910 Nesh	Nesh
QUINN, Jim H.	1st MS Cav.	1849-1936 Rank	Wins
QUINN, John F.	7th MS Cav.	1827-1908 Tipp	Tipp
QUINN, John W.	39th MS Inf.	1832-1916 MS	Simp
QUINN, Lucius M.	33rd MS Inf.	1844-1909 Pike	Pike
QUINN, Sherrod R.	4th MS Cav.	1844-1928 Pike	Pike
QUINN, W. B.	35th MS Inf.	1829-1905 Wins	Wins

Name	Unit	Dates	State	County
QUINN, William S.	6th MS Cav.	1820-1902 Clay		Clay
QUINLEY, James Lafayette	16th Cav.	1845-1917 MS		Smit
RABB, Alonzo T.	21st MS Inf.	1844-1920 Wilk		Wilk
RABORN, J. E.	14th MS Cav.	1843-1922 Amit		Amit
RABY, J. M.	Orleans Lt. Art.	1833-1909 AL		Harr
RAE, John R.	5th MS Inf.	1837-1918 Nesh		Kemp
RAFFIELD, John A.	3rd MS Cav.	1846-1926 NC		Mars
RAGAN, W. Y.	2nd MS Inf.	1846-1919 GA		Tipp
RAGLAND, Andrew J.	11th MS Inf.	1834-1862 Lafa		Lafa
RAGLAND, William Alfred	30th AL Inf.	1833-1932 AL		Calh
RAGON, Newton J.	18th MS Inf.	1838-1907 Rank		Choc
RAGON, Samuel D.	5th MS Inf.	1834-1909		Mont
RAGSDALE, H. D.	6th MS Inf.	1840-1923		Hind
RAGSDALE, J. O.	14th MS Inf.	1816-1865 MS		Monr
RAGSDALE, Lewis Andrew	5th MS Inf.	1818-1885		Laud
RAIFORD, William B.	33rd MS Inf.	1829-1898 MS		Amit
RAINES, Samuel L.	18th MS Cav.	1847-1878		DeSo
RAINES, W. G.	28th MS Cav.	1823-1898		Hind
RAINES, William	2nd MS Cav.	1821-1892 Newt		Newt
RAINEY, Beckum S.	Jeff Davis Cav.	1832-1917 Kemp		Wayn
RAINEY, John A.	24th MS Inf.	1833-1904 Madi		Atta
RAINEY, John W.	9th MS Cav.	1846-1932 Jone		Jone
RAINEY, T. H.	37th MS Inf.	1844-1905 Clar		Kemp
RAINWATER, Richard	3rd MS Cav.	1825-1904 Atta		Atta
RALEY, Abraham J.	37th MS Inf.	1844-1915 Clar		Clar
RALEY, Ander Jefferson	7th MS Inf.	1832-1913 Clar		Laud
RALEY, Jempsey David	32nd AL Inf.	1847-1915 AL		Harr
RALSTON, George	1st MS Lt. Art.	1823-1891 PA		Adam
RAMAGE, J. T. H.	1st MS Inf.	1832-1907 Itaw		Lee
RAMAGE, Josiah L.	1st MS Cav.	1803-1872		Atta
RAMAY, Miles	2nd MO Inf.	1839-1920 MO		Pano
RAMBERT, Francis M.	3rd MS Cav.	1823-1914		Copi
RAMSAY, Andrew Jeff.	3rd MS Inf.	1840-1917 MS		Harr
RAMSAY, E. N.	3rd MS Inf.	1832-1916 MS		Jack
RAMSEY, Alfred H.	4th MS Cav.	____-1862 Gree		Gree
RAMSEY, Augustus M.	19th MS Cav.	1835-1910 Calh		Calh
RAMEY, Beckum S.	Jeff Davis Cav.	1832-1917 Kemp		Wayn
RAMSEY, Daniel	3rd MS Inf.	1814-1867 MS		Jack
RAMSEY, Edward	5th AL Inf.	1841-1912 AL		Laud
RAMSEY, Frank	Rices TN Art.	1832-1897 TN		Okti
RAMSEY, J. M.	5th LA Cav.	1824-1891 AL		Laud
RAMSEY, James D.	4th AL Cav.	1838-1911 AL		
RAMSEY, James P.	3rd MS Inf.	1845-1911 MS		Harr
RAMSEY, Josh A.	4th AL Cav.	1840-1911 Fran		Tish
RAMSEY, Siemon Dearing	12th MS Inf.	1823-1897 Copi		Copi
RAMSEY, T. Y.	7th AL Cav.	181_-1891 AL		Holm
RAMSEY, Thomas J.	12th MS Inf .	1819-1899		Copi
RAMSEY, W. L.	4th MS Inf.	1847-1916		Mont
RAMSEY, W. W.	17th MS Cav.	1845-1924 Jack		JEDA
RAND, John Curtis	41st MS Inf.	1840-1906 AL		Okti
RANDALL, James B.	39th MS Inf.	1831-1904 Newt		Newt

RANDALL, John A.	39th MS Inf.	1842-1923 Lawr	Lawr
RANDALL, John B.	8th MS Inf.	1836-1913 Laud	Jone
RANDALL, Putnam P.	17th MS Cav.	1841-1890	Hanc
RANDALL, R. C.	37th MS Inf.	1840-1921 Laud	Jone
RANDLE, Albert G.	45th MS Inf.	1830-1906 Tipp	Unio
RANDLE, J. M.	3rd MS Inf.	1842-1902	Okti
RANDLE, J. M.	39th MS Inf.	1833-1902 Hind	Madi
RANDLE, James T.	4th MS Cav.	1848-1913	Hind
RANDLL. John D.	3rd MS Inf.	1840-1889	Okti
RANDLE, William P.	2nd MS Cav.	18_7-1929 Carr	Mont
RANDOLPH, Joseph Buyce	28th MS Inf.	1826-1900 GA	Pren
RANDOLPH, P. C.	16th MS Cav.	1832-1893 MS	Unio
RANDOLPH, W. Lee O.	11th GA Inf.	1835-1924 GA	Mars
RANEY, Preston	43rd MS Inf.	1840-1892 MS	Coah
RANEY, Samuel	1st MS Lt. Art.	1845-1881 Warr	Warr
RANKIN, C. R.	6th MS Inf.	1844-1_9	Simp
RANKIN, Daniel	13th TN Cav.	184_-1929 TN	Rank
RANKIN, George W.	7th MS Inf.	1830-1895 Mari	Mari
RANKIN, Hiram A.	41st MS Inf.	1848-1920 MS	Harr
RANKIN, J. T.	7th MS Inf.	1837-1862 Mari	Mari
RANKIN, John	6th MS Inf.	1840-1885 MS	Lawr
RANKIN, John W.	7th MS Inf.	1828-1867	Mari
RANKIN, P. H.	29th MS Inf.	18_7-1921 Lafa	Lafa
RANKIN, Robert E.	5th MS Cav.	1837-1864 Tate	Tate
RANKIN, S. E.	7th MS Inf.	1839-1912 Mari	Mari
RANKIN, William A.	9th MS Inf.	1834-1862 Tate	Tate
RANKIN, William J.	7th MS Inf.	1822-1862 Mari	Mari
RANNAGE, James H.	1st MS Cav.	Carr	Calh
RANSOM, Albon J.	Stanfords MS Art.	1830-1902 GA	Gren
RANSOM, Ambrose F.	1st MS Inf.	1826-1879 Tish	Monr
RANSOM, George M.	10th MS Inf.	1832-1881 Carr	Carr
RAPE, C. D.	38th MS Inf.	1835-1911	Scot
RASBERRY, M. Richard	15th MS Inf.	Choc	Calh
RASPBERRY, J. W.		1837-1862	Monr
RAST, J. T.	26th MS Inf.	1834-1861 Tish	Tish
RAST, James D.	7th AL Cav.	1847-1935 Tish	Tish
RAST, W. J.	7th AL Cav.	1844-1887 AL	Tish
RATCLIFF, A. B.	27th MS Inf.	1846-1909 Lawr	Lawr
RATCLIFF, A. _.	38th MS Cav.	1842-1929 LA	Adam
RATCLIFF, H. B.	33rd MS Inf.	1845-1925 Linc	Linc
RATCLIFF, Hamilton	41st MS Inf.	1836-1909 MS	Laud
RATCLIFF, Holloway Huff	7th MS Inf.	1835-1917 Amit	Amit
RATCLIFF, J. D.	24th MS Cav.	1818-1899 Pike	Linc
RATCLIFF, Peter	22nd MS Inf.	1820-1875 VA	Amit
RATCLIFF, T. W.	1st MS Lt. Art.	1848-1914 Clai	Harr
RATCLIFF, Virgil B.	41st MS Inf.	1836-1924 Laud	Laud
RATCLIFF, W. E.	24th MS Cav.	1843-1934 Fran	Fran
RATCLIFF, William R.	7th MS Inf.	1825-1876	Hind
RATCLIFF, William T.	1st MS Lt. Art.	1835-1918 Hind	Hind
RATHELL, J. A.	38th MS Cav.	1832-1924 Holm	Holm
RATLIFF, Benjamin	28th MS Cav.	1820-1908 Leak	Leak

RATLIFF, J. W.	Withers Art.	1834-1909	Hind
RATLIFF, Richard	15th MS Inf.	1836-1932 NC	Mont
RATLIFF, Rufus M.	18th MS Inf.	1843-1879 MS	Scot
RATLIFF, Samuel	15th MS Inf.	1839-1886	Mont
RATLIFF, Thomas J.	18th MS Inf.	1834-1912 VA	Scot
RATLIFF, William	18th MS Inf.	____-1905 Rank	Rank
RAUCH, John Melville	8th MS	1845-1905	Hind
RAULISS, William Thaddus	4th MS Cav.	1846-1929 MS	Fran
RAVENCRAFT, Lafayette	3rd LA Cav.	1843-1919 Pike	Amit
RAWLE, John	GA Art.	1837-1916 GA	Adam
RAWLES, Felix S.	14th MS Inf.	1842-1908 Newt	Covi
RAWLES, G. W.	14th MS Inf.	1820-1881 Newt	Covi
RAWLINGS, George W.	3rd MS Inf.	1839-1912 Hind	Laud
RAWLINGS, James M.	5th MS Inf.	1824-1891	Hind
RAWLS, B. F.	14th MS Inf.	1828-1910 Newt	Lama
RAWLS, James H.	47th AL Inf.	1834-1906 AL	Atta
RAWLS, John	Miles LA Cav.	1837-1916 LA	Pear
RAWLS, R. A.	7th MS Inf.	1841-1928 Fran	Fran
RAWSON, C. L.	41st MS Inf.	1840-1920 Laud	Laud
RAWSON, William	4th MS Inf.	1841-1923 Atta	Leak
RAY, A. J.	9th AL Inf.	1840-1926 AL	Jone
RAY, B. F.	4th MS Inf.	1842-1921 Atta	Atta
RAY, Charlie J.	3rd MS Inf.	1845-1920	Nesh
RAY, D. A.	35th MS Inf.	1840-1918 Laud	Laud
RAY, D. E.	18th MS Inf.	1843-1927 Choc	Choc
RAY, Elijah	3rd MS Inf.	1821-1899	Okti
RAY, Hosea Halcomb	3rd SC Inf.	1843-1912 SC	Alco
RAY, J. F.	2nd MS Inf.	1846-1918 SC	Tipp
RAY, J. H.	15th SC Inf.	1841-1901 SC	Tipp
RAY, J. M.	30th MS Inf.	1833-1915 Atta	Atta
RAY, J. T.	34th MS Inf.	1845-1912 Tipp	Bent
RAY, J. T.	1st MS Inf.	1836-1904 MS	Monr
RAY. J. U.	5th MS Inf.	1805-1873 SC	Choc
RAY. J. W.	2nd MS Inf.	1844-1913 MS	Bent
RAY, James	33rd MS Inf.	1826-1912 Nesh	Nesh
RAY, Jasper N.	42nd AL Inf.	1841-1915 MS	Monr
RAY, Jesse	15th SC Inf.	1821-1864 SC	Tipp
RAY, Jesse J.	30th MS Inf.	1843-190_	Copi
RAY, J. Miles	10th MS Inf.	1845-1916 Copi	Linc
RAY, John	8th MS Cav.	1826-____ Lown	Chic
RAY, John H.	15th SC Vol.	1832-1900 Tipp	Tipp
RAY, John H. Z.	2nd MS Inf.	1834-1886 SC	Tipp
RAY, Joseph	Gun Shop	1830-1919 Mars	Carr
RAY, J. Scott	30th MS Inf.	1831-1899 Atta	Atta
RAY, Robert A. Sr.	31st MS Inf.	1832-1918 Unio	Unio
RAY, Robert F.	2nd MS Cav.	1846-1892 AL	Monr
RAY, Russell	4th MS Inf.	1844-1911 Atta	Atta
RAY, S. _.	2nd MS Cav.	1839-1862 Choc	Choc
RAY, S. O.	41st MS Inf.	1841-1911 Pont	Unio
RAY, W. F.	10th MS Inf.	1837-1911	Madi
RAY, W. F.	1st MS Lt. Art.	1804-1881 Yazo	Yazo
RAY, W. J.	23rd MS Inf.	1845-1919 Tipp	Harr

RAY, W. S.	1st MS Lt. Art.	1832-1894 Choc	Choc
RAY, Wm.	1st MS Lt. Art.	1841-1893 Adam	Adam
RAY, William	30th MS Inf.	1825-1909 Carr	Carr
RAY, William Henry	28th MS Cav.	1838-1872 Gren	Holm
RAY, Wilson	30th MS Inf.	1837-1893 Carr	Sunf
RAYBORN, James L.	39th MS Inf.	1841-1868 Pike	Pike
RAYBORN, Joseph Jackson	39th MS Inf.	1842-1916 MS	Pike
RAYBORN, William	38th MS Cav.	1844-1913 Pike	Pike
RAYBORN, William	1st MS Sharpshooters	1827-1892 Choc	Lama
RAYBURN, H. N.	34th MS Inf.	1828-1905 Lafa	Lafa
RAYBURN, John D.	3rd MS Cav.	1828-1907 Yalo	Yalo
RAYBURN, Samuel H.	9th MS Inf.	1836-1861 MS	Lafa
RAYBURN, W. O. R.	22nd MS Inf.	1837-1879 Lafa	Lafa
RAYBURN, William Andrew	1st MS Sharpshooters	1830-1872 Choc	Gren
RAYFIELD, Benjamin F.	10th AL Inf.		Monr
RAYNER, Ben S.	38th MS Cav.	1844-1904 Holm	Holm
RAYNES, Angus	Woods MS Cav.	1838-1930 AL	JEDA
REA, A. M.	2nd MS Inf.	1837-1905 Itaw	Itaw
REA, Charles	23rd MS Cav.	1832-1911 Linc	Linc
REA, George W	36th MS Inf.	1840-1865	Copi
REA, J. H.	35th MS Inf.	1823-1905 Wins	Kemp
REA, John R.	5th MS Regt.	1837-1918 Nesh	Kemp
REA, Robert Wiley (Dr.)	36th MS Inf.	1844-1923	Copi
REA, Samuel R.	3rd MS Cav.	1847-1889	Kemp
REA, Thomas Meredith	12th MS Inf.	1842-1917	Clai
REA, William A.	8th MS Cav.	1847-1921 Lown	Pont
REA, William J.	6th MS Inf.	1837-1905	Copi
READ, Charles W.	AR	1842-1890 Yazo	Laud
READ, John C.	20th MS Inf.	1838-1910 Scot	Scot
READ, J. H/R. (Dr.)	2nd MS Inf.	1844-1919 Hind	Hind
READY, John	14th MS Cav.	1835-1913 Lawr	Lawr
READY, John J.	42nd MS Inf.	1835-1917 IR	Laud
REAGAN, T. B. E.	44th MS Inf.	____-1880	Calh
REAVES, R. C.	7th MS Cav.	1843-	Unio
REBER, E. H.	6th MS Inf.	1842-1920	Hind
RECORD, George H.	21st MS Inf.	1843-1879 Warr	Warr
RED, E.	8th MS Inf.	1826-1899 GA	Newt
RED, W. C.	4th MS Inf.	1828-1863 Holm	Holm
REDD, C. A	41st AL Inf.	1840-1920 AL	Harr
REDD, J. T. (Dr.)	1st MS Inf.	1834-1868 Adam	Adam
REDD, Thomas S.	12th MS Inf.	1839-1915 KY	Wash
REDDING, J. W.	16th MS Inf.	1829-1890 GA	Lafa
REDDITT, Robert W.	5th MS Cav.	1822-1876 Carr	Carr
REDDITT, Thomas H.	18th MS Inf.	1824-1866 Yazo	Yazo
REDDOCK, C. M.	7th MS Inf.	1842-1909 Covi	Jone
REDDOCK, James O.	7th MS Inf.	1834-1910	Covi
REDDOCK, John A.	1st MS Cav.	1812-1876	Covi
REDDY, Thomas	1st MS Lt. Art.	1819-1882 Adam	Adam
REDELL, John Thomas	14th MS Inf.	1831-1895 Clar	Fran
REDUS, E. X.	1st MS Inf.	1825-1886	Okti

Name	Unit	Dates		
REDMAN, F. M.	9th MS Inf.	1837-1909 Tish	Lawr
REDMOND, F. M.	11th MS Inf.	1839-1922	Pike
REDMON, Henry H.	1st MS Cav.	1847-1928 MS	Covi
REDMOND, Lewis J.	8th MS Inf.	1834-1904 Covi	Covi
REDMOND, Oliver M.	2nd MS Cav.	1825-1891 Kemp	Monr
REDUS, John C.	1st MS Inf.	1820-1903	Copi
REDUS, W. J.	1st MS Inf.	1835-1910 Lee	Lee
REDWINE, P. L.	1st MS Inf.	1835-1890 Lafa	Lafa
REECE, J. C.	26th MS Inf.	1843-1926 Tish	Harr
REECE, Ruben P.	8th AL Cav.	1846-1927 AL	Pren
REED, Allen	23rd MS Inf.	1840-1911 TN	Tipp
REED, Charles	7th MS Cav.	1843-1930 TN	Tipp
REED, Charles A.	23rd MS Inf.	1843-1919	Hind
REED, E.	18th MS Cav.	1834-1889	Hind
REED, Henry	10th MS Inf.	1846-1908 DeSo	Linc
REED, Henry C.	15th MS Inf.	1844-1861 MS	Laud
REED, Henry T.	11th MS Cav.	1819-1910 Okti	Okti
REED, J. B.	36th MS Inf.	1835-1914 Copi	Linc
REED, J. D.	28th MS Cav.	1831-1881 Holm	Holm
REED, J. W.	6th MS Inf.	1846-1926 MS	Simp
REED, James	2nd MS Inf.	1832-1894 AL	Tipp
REED, James	2nd MS Cav.	1819-1878 Choc	Choc
REED, Jasper	6th MS Inf.	1841-1920 Simp	Simp
REED, John F.	11th MS Cav.	1847-1922 MS	Unio
REED, John Henry	Forrests Cav.	1845-1907 Choc	Copi
REED, John L.	5th MS Inf.	1844-1924 MS	Noxu
REED, Joseph	16th AL Inf.	1848-1907 Warr	Harr
REED, Joseph L.	6th MS Inf.	1839-___ Simp	Simp
REED, Joshua	6th MS Inf.	1837-1910	Rank
REED, Leroy	30th MS Inf.	1823-1891 Wins	Wins
REED, Mike	34th MS Inf.	1836-1914 Tipp	Tipp
REED, N. T.	2nd MS Cav.	1840-1933 Choc	Linc
REED, Rasmus J.	1st MS Cav.	1826-1865 Pont	Pont
REED, Robert T.	10th MS Inf.	1844-1908 Adam	Adam
REED, T. J.	13th MS Inf.	1841-192_ Kemp	Harr
REED, Thomas	Jefferson Art.	1817-1891 MS	Adam
REED, Thomas D. (Dr.)	13th MS Inf.	1840-1921 Laud	Harr
REED, Thomas H.	2nd MS Cav.	___-1885 Choc	Choc
REED, Thomas R.	1st MS Lt. Art.	___-1886	Hind
REED, W. N.	11th MS Cav.	1840-1896	Okti
REED, W. V.	35th MS Inf.	1843-1912 Laud	Laud
REED, William M.	23rd MS Inf.	1831-1892 AL	Tipp
REEDY, Sam	4th MS Inf.	1845-1902 Monr	Monr
REEDER, David	Jeff Davis Cav.	1837-1909 Chic	Chic
REEDS, W. W.	9th MS Sharpshooters	1844-1931 MS	Itaw
REES, Joseph V.	MS Inf.	1846-1934 Tipp	Bent
REES, W. H.	32nd MS Inf.	1847-1925	Hind
REESE, E. D.	27th AL Inf.	1836-1898 AL	Leak
REESE, J. C.	28th MS Inf.	1843-1926 Tish	Harr
REESE, Ransome C.	4th MS Inf.	1845-1933 Lefl	Lefl
REESE, Rance C.	1st MS Lt. Art.	1843-1931	Lefl

REEVES, A.	30th MS Inf.	1831-1907 Carr	Linc
REEVES, A. G.	38th MS Cav.	1838-1912 Holm	Holm
REEVES, Andrew J.	32nd MS Inf.	1832-1906 Itaw	Itaw
REEVES, Benjamin	9th MS Cav.	1810-1890 Geor	Geor
REEVES, _. Lafayette	33rd MS Inf.	184_-193_ MS	Walt
REEVES, George C.	11th MS Inf.	1839-1915 Carr	Carr
REEVES, George W.	7th MS Cav.	1841-___	Monr
REEVES, H. W.	33rd MS Inf.	1822-190_ Lawr	Linc
REEVES, J. B.	7th MS Inf.	1844-1913 Covi	Covi
REEVES, J. M.	20th MS Inf.	1846-1920 Carr	Mont
REEVES, J. P.	8th MS Inf.	1833-1906	Leak
REEVES, James	Maxeys Inf.	1830-192_ Jack	Geor
REEVES, John Sr.	9th MS Cav.	1828-1919 Jack	Geor
REEVES, T. S.	2nd & 4th		
	MS Cav.	1840-1925 Newt	Newt
REEVES, Thomas	27th MS Inf.	182_-1862 MS	Covi
REEVES, W. J.	4th MS Cav.	___-1901	Pike
REEVES, W. M.	41st GA Inf.	1834-___ GA	Choc
REEVES, William P.	43rd MS Inf.	1829-1899 Itaw	Itaw
REGAN, Rufus	7th MS Inf.	1825-1892 Mari	Mari
REGAN, T. G.	16th MS Inf.	1842-1909 Pike	Walt
REGAN, W. L.	39th MS Inf.	1842-1862	Rank
REGAN, William S.	38th MS Cav.	1832-1890 Clai	Mari
REGISTER, John W.	3rd LA Cav.	1842-1901 AR	Adam
REICH, J. C.	AR Lt. Art.	1839-1924 AR	Itaw
REID, A. I.	37th MS Inf.	1818-1870 Jasp	Jasp
REID, C. H.	9th MS Inf.	1846-1921	Mars
REID, Enoch S.	22nd MS Inf.	1841-1913 MS	Lawr
REID, Hugh James	22nd MS Inf.	1827-1905 Wilk	Holm
REID, J. B.	1st MS Lt. Art.	1836-___	Warr
REID, J. F.	11th MS Inf.	1845-1922 Chic	Unio
REID, James R.	33rd MS Inf.	1848-1906 MS	Walt
REID, John	14th MS Cav.	___-1898 Lawr	Lawr
REID, John S.	Poagues Art.	1847-1879	Madi
REID, Joseph	3rd MS Inf.	1824-1922 MS	Chic
REID, Samuel	11th MS Inf.	1832-1921 Chic	Chic
REID, Thomas L.	24th MS Inf.	1842-___ AL	Clay
REID, W. T.	42nd AL Inf.	1841-1863 AL	Lafa
REID, Warren D.	11th MS Inf.	1841-1924 Chic	Chic
REID, William N.	2nd MS Cav.	1834-1904 Calh	Calh
REID, William S.	38th MS Cav.	1830-1910 Lawr	Lawr
REINACH, D.	1st MS Cav.	1841-1923	Boli
REMBERT, Edwin B.	4th MS Cav.	1849-1865	Rank
REMBERT, J. A.	Seven Star Art.	1830-1910 Lawr	Lawr
RENFRO, Thomas A.	28th MS Cav.	1837-1911 AL	Monr
RENFROE, John J.	33rd MS Inf.	1830-1899 Lawr	Lawr
RENFROW, M. J.	23rd MS Inf.	1834-1912 TN	Tipp
RENFROW, William	21st MS Inf.	1840-1907 Linc	Copi
RENISK, A. J.	2nd MS Cav.	1845-1923 Bent	Bent
RENNO, Louis	36th MS Inf.	1836-1909	Copi
RENNO, Samuel	16th MS Inf.	1839-1921 Copi	Simp

Name	Unit	Dates	
RENO, S.	6th & 15th MS Inf.	1819-1908	Copi
RENSHAW, James P.	29th MS Inf.	1835-1915 TN	Holm
RESPESS, M. L.	14th AL Inf.	1843-1916 AL	Tall
RESTER, L.	22nd MS Inf.	1835-1923 Lawr	Harr
RESTER, William	38th MS Cav.	1842-1916 Hanc	Pear
REW, ___	23rd AL Inf.	1815-1915 NC	Laud
REW, Edward Young	23rd AL Inf.	1846-1878 AL	Laud
REYNOLDS, A. H.	19th AR Inf.	1845-1928 Okti	Okti
REYNOLDS, Dan F.	32nd MS Inf.	1834-1915 NC	Tipp
REYNOLDS, David	5th MS Cav.	1835-1909 Lown	Alco
REYNOLDS, G. O.	29th MS Inf.	1832-1883 Lafa	Pano
REYNOLDS, George K.	28th MS Cav.	1827-1862	Rank
REYNOLDS, George W.	2nd MS Inf.	1844-1906 Tish	Alco
REYNOLDS, Guilford G.	2nd MS Inf.	1836-1914 Alco	Alco
REYNOLDS, Hiram G.	7th MS Inf.	1839-1862 Fran	Amit
REYNOLDS, J. M.	Seven Star Art.	1837-1899 Copi	
REYNOLDS, J. T.	28th MS Cav.	1845-1920 Jasp	Jasp
REYNOLDS, James H.	8th MS Inf.	183_-1903 Jone	Jone
REYNOLDS, James S.	37th MS Inf.	1841-1861 MS	Laud
REYNOLDS, James S.	11th & 17th AR Cav.	1848-1927 AR	Amit
REYNOLDS, John M.	6th AL Cav.	1813-1883 AL	Fran
REYNOLDS, L. P.	2nd MS Inf.	1834-1911 MS	Pren
REYNOLDS, Leander P.	2nd MS Inf.	1845-1934 Tish	Alco
REYNOLDS, Martin	24th MS Inf.	1841-1915 AL	Gree
REYNOLDS, Plesh	26th AL Inf.	1840-1907 AL	Tish
REYNOLDS, R. J.	36th MS Inf.	1841-1868 Newt	Newt
REYNOLDS, Reuben O.	11th MS Inf.	1829-1887 GA	Monr
REYNOLDS, Seaborn	33rd MS Inf.	1827-1918 Amit	Amit
REYNOLDS, Thomas	1st GA Cav.	1830-1909 GA	Unio
REYNOLDS, Thomas J.	3rd MS Inf.	1837-1934 Newt	Newt
REYNOLDS, W. H.	40th MS Inf.	1841-1917 Atta	Atta
REYNOLDS, W. J.	39th MS Inf.	1830-1912 Newt	Newt
REYNOLDS, W. P.	32nd MS Inf.	1840-1907 Tish	Tish
REYNOLDS, William Henry	6th AR Inf.	1842-1917 GA	Okti
RHEA, Pat	Miles LA	1834-1905 LA	Adam
RHEA, Sam M.	17th MS Cav.	1830-1893 NC	Mars
RHEW, John	3rd MS Cav.	1818-1892 GA	Mars
RHODES, E. W.	6th MS Cav.	1844-1923	Rank
RHODES, J. A. (Dr.)	24th MS Cav.	1846-19_3 AL	Laud
RHODES, J. A.	24th MS Cav.	1846-1922 AL	Laud
RHODES, J. H.	36th MS Inf.	1847-1896 AL	Newt
RHODES, James A.	17th AL Inf.	1837-1907 AL	Covi
RHODES, John F.	18th SC Inf.	1839-1912 SC	Unio
RHODES, L. J.	Forrests Scouts	1832-1901 SC	Lee
RHODES, O. A.	6th MS Inf.	1836-1917	Rank
RHODES, R. A.	33rd MS Inf.	1842-1907 Fran	Adam
RHODES, S. Frank	3rd MS Cav.	1845-1927 Nesh	Nesh
RHODES, Thomas S.	30th MS Inf.	1843-1930 Atta	Atta
RHODSE, R. A.	33rd MS Inf.	1842-1911 Fran	Fran
RHYMES, L. J.	1st MS Inf.	1821-1899	Copi

RHYNE, Drury Willouby	1st MS Sharpshooters	1846-1926	Holm	Holm
RHYNE, James T.	4th MS Inf.	1841-1910	NC	Holm
RHYNE, John S.	15th MS Inf.	1820-1894	Holm	Holm
RIALS, John A.	7th MS Inf.	1842-___	Fran	Copi
RIALS, J. M.	7th MS Inf.	1844-1931	Linc	Linc
RICE, Greek P.	TX Art.	1835-1894	TX	Tall
RICE, Henry M.	11th MS Inf.	1841-1861	MS	Copi
RICE, Jesse W.	3rd MS Inf.	1841-1905	MS	Jack
RICE, Joe D.	27th MS Inf.	1843-1922	Linc	Tall
RICE, John H/R.	Adams MS Cav.	1838-1921	Pano	Pano
RICE, Robert Henry	4th MS Cav.	1848-1911	MS	Copi
RICE, S. C.	4th AL Inf.	1837-___	AL	Clay
RICE, Thomas	40th MS Inf.	1833-1913	Laud	Nesh
RICH, Jacob M.	2nd MS Inf.	1840-1929		Pear
RICH, Stephen C.	9th MS Cav.	1836-1904	MS	Perr
RICHARD, C. E.		1844-1922		Adam
RICHARD, Josh B.	9th MS Inf.	1832-1923	Madi	Madi
RICHARDS, Daniel Marion	25th AL Inf.	1831-1916	AL	Lown
RICHARDS, Edward P.	10th MS Inf.	1840-1896	Lown	Lown
RICHARDS, John	6th MS Inf.	1831-1909		Smit
RICHARDS, John Charles	1st LA Inf.	1842-1895	LA	Adam
RICHARDS, Joshua J.	10th MS Inf.	1839-1923	Madi	Madi
RICHARDS, George S.	Adams MS Cav.	1844-1873	Warr	Warr
RICHARDS, Littleton B.	31st MS Inf.	1831-1898	SC	Noxu
RICHARDS, Mose V.	20th MS Inf.	1836-1909		Harr
RICHARDS, T. W.	10th MS Inf.	1839-1866	Yazo	Yazo
RICHARDS, W. B.	39th MS Inf.	1836-1925	Scot	Harr
RICHARDS, William	Pogues Art.	1825-1910	Madi	Madi
RICHARDS, William C.	9th & 10th MS Inf.	1828-1916	Lown	Lown
RICHARDSON, A. J.	11th MS Cav.	1845-1917	Nesh	Nesh
RICHARDSON, Bonner	Woods MS Cav.	1843-1898	Yazo	Yazo
RICHARDSON, Cabell	Jefferson Flying Art.	1840-1914	Jeff	Adam
RICHARDSON, D. I.	43rd MS Inf.	1847-1916	Monr	Monr
RICHARDSON, David Rich.	44th GA Inf.	1835-1918	GA	Tish
RICHARDSON, E. J.	32nd MS Inf.	1840-1912	AL	Tipp
RICHARDSON, E. L.	20th MS Inf.	1833-1912	Wins	Wins
RICHARDSON, Edward	20th MS Inf.	1828-1917	MS	Harr
RICHARDSON, F. H.	20th MS Inf.	1840-1907	SC	Wins
RICHARDSON, G. W.	1st AR Cav.	1837-1904	AR	Atta
RICHARDSON, H. B.	43rd MS Inf.	1825-1891	Monr	Kemp
RICHARDSON, Isaac Baker	Machinist	1820-1892	GA	Tipp
RICHARDSON, J. D.	2nd MS Cav.	1832-1909	Tipp	Tipp
RICHARDSON, J. H.	1st & 23rd MS Inf.	1846-1900		Hind
RICHARDSON, J. _.	2nd MS Cav.	1844-1920	WV	Newt
RICHARDSON, J. D.	4th & 28th LA Inf.	1836-1926	Wilk	Wilk
RICHARDSON, J. L.	26th MS Inf.	1841-1919	Alco	Alco
RICHARDSON, James	43rd MS Inf.			Monr

Name	Unit	Dates		
RICHARDSON, James S.	30th MS Inf.	1849-1898		Hind
RICHARDSON, John	3rd & 45th MS Inf.	1833-1918	Simp	Simp
RICHARDSON, John H.	32nd MS Inf.	1830-1902	AL	Tipp
RICHARDSON, John Samuel	1st AR Cav.	1843-1926	LA	Warr
RICHARDSON, L. E/H.	11th MS Cav.	1835-1863	Chic	Chic
RICHARDSON, Lumsford	39th MS Inf.	1834-1917	Rank	Laud
RICHARDSON, O. R.	23rd MS Inf.	1838-1914	Tipp	Tipp
RICHARDSON, R. R.	20th MS Inf.	1839-1910	NC	Wins
RICHARDSON, Richard	12th MS Inf.	1822-1877	EN	Warr
RICHARDSON, Thomas Clark	1st MS Lt. Art.	1836-1904	Yazo	Warr
RICHARDSON, Thomas R.	34th TN Inf.	1846-1938	TN	Tipp
RICHARDSON, W.	26th MS Inf.	1842-1911	Tish	Alco
RICHARDSON, W. H.	14th MS Inf.	1838-1918	SC	Wins
RICHARDSON, W. M.	26th MS Inf.	1841-1925	Tish	Alco
RICHARDSON, W. M.	43rd GA Inf.	1846-1925	GA	Harr
RICHARDSON, W. R.	43rd MS Inf.	1841-1908	Monr	Monr
RICHARDSON, W. R.	19th TN Cav.	1827-1906	TN	Alco
RICHARDSON, William B.	43rd MS Inf.	1822-1891	Monr	Kemp
RICHARDSON, William B.	2nd KY Inf.	1843-1936	KY	Newt
RICHARDSON, William W.	42nd AL Inf.	1842-1905	AL	Nesh
RICHEY, Albert	8th MS Cav.	183_-1869	MS	Pont
RICHHEY, David	33rd MS Inf.	1819-1875	GA	Newt
RICHEY, George H.	10th MS Inf.	1840-1901	Lown	Monr
RICHEY, William James	48th MS Inf.	1838-1897	Okti	Okti
RICHIE, Albert W.	8th MS Cav.	1837-1869	Calh	Pont
RICHIE, John Robert	12th MS Inf.	1840-1908	Warr	Warr
RICHMON, J. W.	6th MS Inf.	1839-1900	Leak	Leak
RICHMOND, I. G.	33rd MS Inf.	1835-1894	Amit	Amit
RICHMOND, J. W.	48th MS Inf.	1840-1864	Warr	Clai
RICHMOND, Mathew	42nd MS Inf.	1828-1882	Carr	Carr
RICHMOND, Thomas D.	33rd MS Inf.	1845-1889	Pike	Walt
RICKETTS, J. S.	48th MS Inf.	1841-1920	Lafa	Harr
RICKETTS, Robert S.	2nd LA Inf.	1843-1918		Hind
RICKETTS, W. L.	40th MS Inf.	1844-1868	Atta	Atta
RICKITTS, D. P.	1st MS Lt. Art.	1840-1909	Carr	Carr
RICKS, Benj. Sherrod	28th MS Cav.	1843-1899	Warr	Yazo
RIDDDELL, Isaac A.	33rd MS Inf.	1833-1919	Leak	Leak
RIDDICK, W. B.	2nd MS Cav.	1835-1907	Yalo	Yalo
RIDDLE, Jesse	4th MS Inf.	1836-1905	Carr	Carr
RIDDLE, T. J.	4th AL Inf.			Rank
RIDDLE, W. F.	35th MS Inf.	1840-1918	MS	Harr
RIDDLE, William A.	Cooks TN Inf.	1844-1935	TN	Pont
RIDDLE, William A.	32nd TN Inf.	1842-1935	TN	Pont
RIDLESPERGER, S. V.	Davis 1st Bat.	1836-1903	Tipp	Unio
RIDER, John M.	2nd TN Cav.	1844-1903	TN	Jeff
RIDINGS, J. L.	2nd MS Cav.	1846-1864	Monr	Monr
RIDINGS, T. H.	44th MS Inf.			Monr
RIETTI, David C.	10th MS Inf.	1844-1912	NJ	Hind
RIETTI, John C.	10th MS Inf.	1842-1896		Hind

RIFE, W. E.	35th MS Inf.	1843-1924 Clay	Clay
RIGBY, William P.	15th MS Inf.	1846-1929 MS	Atta
RIGDON, E. A.	29th AL Inf.	1845-1894 GA	Kemp
RIGDON, John T.	29th AL Inf.	1840-1917 GA	Kemp
RIGDORN, J. J.	29th AL Inf.	1839-1922 AL	Harr
RIGGAN, J. W.	3rd MS Inf.	1824-1897 Itaw	Monr
RIGGAN, James Jackson	8th MS Cav.	1849-1936	Hind
RIGGAN, Jeremiah L.	2nd & 43rd MS Inf.	1827-1912 Monr	Monr
RIGGAN, Joe	2nd MS Cav.	1843-1903 Monr	Monr
RIGGON, Thomas Benton	Harveys Scouts	1845-1913	Hind
RIGSBY, J. A. Sr.	20th MS Inf.	1848-1920 Scot	Scot
RIGSBY, William H.	Funsdons AL	1846-1915 AL	Tate
RILEY, E. M.	39th MS Inf.	1837-1917 Simp	Lawr
RILEY, Harrison	6th MS Inf.	1831-1903 Leak	Atta
RILEY, J. _.	56th AL Rangers	1833-___ AL	Laud
RILEY, James G.	1st MS Cav.	1818-1883 Atta	Atta
RILEY, James H.	28th MS Cav.	1843-1923 Warr	Forr
RILEY, James S.	43rd MS Inf.		Monr
RILEY, Jessie	2nd MS Inf.	___-1867	Lee
RILEY, John T.	4th MS Cav.	1845-1921 Copi	Atta
RILEY, Nathan	5th SC Inf.	1820-1863 SC	Itaw
RILEY, Patrick	18th MS Inf.	1837-1906 Yazo	Yazo
RILEY, R. T.	2nd MS Inf.	1837-1917 Tipp	Unio
RILEY, Walter	3rd MS Inf.	1824-1888 Tipp	Chic
RIMES, E. F.	6th & 15th MS Inf.	1834-1895	Copi
RIMES, J. F.	12th MS Inf.	1820-1885	Hind
RIMMER, C. H.	Poagues MS Art.	1831-1907 Madi	Madi
RIMMER, _. W.	Commissary	1827-1913	Madi
RIMMER, Hosea T.	Adams MS Cav.	1824-1908	Madi
RIMMER, J. A.	Poagues MS Art.	1829-1898 NC	Madi
RINE, J. D.	61st MS Lt. Art.	1833-1870 Warr	Warr
RINEHART, D. A.	12th MS Cav.	1820-1914 Noxu	Noxu
RINEHART, George M.	32nd MS Inf.	Tish	Alco
RINEWALT, Henderson H.	40th MS Inf.	1842-1928 Nesh	Scot
RING, Jerry	21st MS Inf.	1834-1912 IR	Warr
RIPLEY, Andy Wilson	22nd TN Inf.	1837-1878 TN	Bent
RISER, George	1st MS Inf.	1816-1897 Lawr	Hind
RISHER, C. C.	27th MS Inf.	1846-1917 Jasp	Jasp
RISHER, G. E.	40th MS Inf.	1831-1903 Jasp	Jone
RISHER, James W.	27th MS Inf.	1838-1924 Jasp	Jasp
RITCH, James	8th MS Cav.	1827-1912 AL	Calh
RITCHEY, David	2nd MS Inf.	1843-1923 Tipp	Newt
RITCHEY, John M.	14th MS Cav.	1836-1905 Lawr	Lawr
RITCHIE, Emanuel G.	7th MS Cav.	1836-1923 MS	Linc
RITCHIE, George W.	7th MS Inf.	1848-1916 Laud	Jasp
RITCHIE, Jacob	14th Cav.	1838-1932 Linc	Linc
RITTER, Anderson D.	1st MS Inf.	1836-1920 Monr	Monr
RITTER, John N.	16th AL Inf.		Monr
RITTER, T. L.	2nd MS Cav.	1826-1904 Laud	Monr
RITTER, William Y.	43rd MS Inf.	1833-1918 Itaw	Lee

Name	Unit	Dates	Col1	Col2
RIVERS, Douglas L.	LA			
	Prov. Marshall	1817-1862 VA	Adam	
RIVERS, G. W.	5th MS Inf.	1847-1904 Holm	Holm	
RIVERS, J. T.	10th GA Inf.	1845-1911 GA	Harr	
RIVERS, W. A. J.	41st MS Inf.	1836-1889 Itaw	Laud	
RIVES, John E.	12th MS Inf.	1839-1862 Linc	Clai	
RIVES, W. T.	14th MS Inf.	1836-1905 NC	Wins	
ROACH, J. A.	17th MS Ca.	1847-1924	Pear	
ROACH, J. M.	24th MS Cav.	1847-1924 MS	Harr	
ROACH, James A.	9th MS Cav.	1847-1924 MS	Harr	
ROACH, John	18th MS Inf.	1844-1920	Pike	
ROACH, John H.	26th MS Inf.	1840-1922 MS	Pren	
ROACH, Newton W.	23rd MS Inf.	1839-1916 Unio	Tipp	
ROACH, T. J.	7th MS Cav.	1846-1915 Unio	Tipp	
ROACH, Thomas J.	1st MS			
	Sharpshooters	1836-1863 MS	Copi	
ROAK, Thomas J.	4th MS Cav.	1829-1905 Amit	AmiT	
ROBB, Eugene A.	28th MS CaV.	1837-1910 Wash	Wash	
ROBB, Joseph Hamilton	2nd KY Cav.	1842-1919 KY	Wash	
ROBBINS, Alexander	2nd MS Inf.	1844-1929 MS	Mari	
ROBBINS, Almon	MS Lt. Art.	1843-1915	Hind	
ROBBINS, D. M.	6th MS Inf.	1844-1924	Rank	
ROBBINS, E. B.	31st MS Inf.	1833-1911 NC	Jone	
ROBBINS, Jefferson	19th AR Inf.	1842-1862 AR	Lafa	
ROBBINS, John C.	23rd MS Regt.	1844-1920 Pont	Unio	
ROBBINS, S. R.	14th Cav.	____-1907	Simp	
ROBBINS, Simon R.	3rd MS Inf.	1846-1917 Harr	Linc	
ROBBINS, Wiley D.	6th MS Inf.	1840-1907 AL	Rank	
ROBBINS, William J.	23rd MS Inf.	1842-1927 Pont	Unio	
ROBERSON, David C.	31st AL Inf.	1835-1914 AL	Unio	
ROBERSON, Frank	34th MS Inf.	1826-1918 GA	Tipp	
ROBERSON, George	17th MS Inf.		Hind	
ROBERSON, George B/H.	29th MS Inf.	1818-1886 MS	Tall	
ROBERSON, Peter	5th MS Inf.	1816-1901 Wayn	Wayn	
ROBERSON, Rich S.	34th MS Inf.	1833-1901 Tipp	Bent	
ROBERSON, W. E.	21st MS Inf.	1845-1912 Tall	Tall	
ROBERSON,				
Wm. Thomas Sr	23rd MS Inf.	1836-1914	Scot	
ROBERTS, A.	11th MS Cav.	1843-1924 MS	Kemp	
ROBERTS, A. A	18th MS Inf.	1843-1916	Hind	
ROBERTS, A. B/E.	4th MS Cav.	1846-1927 Pike	Pike	
ROBERTS, A. J.	46th MS Inf.	1845-1937 Scot	Rank	
ROBERTS, A. J.	44th MS Inf.	1830-1898 Amit	Amit	
ROBERTS, Aaron	4th AL Inf.	1832-1872 AL	Laud	
ROBERTS, Agrippa	4th MS Inf.	1842-1902 Holm	Holm	
ROBERTS, Alvin (AL)	State Troops	1825-1908 Gree	Gree	
ROBERTS, B. F.	15th MS Cav.	1843-1925 Gree	Wayn	
ROBERTS, B. M.	11th MS Cav.	1820-1886 Wins	Wins	
ROBERTS, Cal	Seven Star Art.		Hind	
ROBERTS, D. E.	7th TN Cav.	1836-1909 TN	Holm	
ROBERTS, Dennis	7th MS Inf.	1829-1881 Covi	JEFA	
ROBERTS, Duncan	27th MS Inf.	1841-1916 Newt	Jasp	

85

ROBERTS, Elisha	13th MS Inf.	Hind	Copi
ROBERTS, Ervin	3rd MS Inf.	1838-1915 MS	Jack
ROBERTS, Everett	2nd MS Cav.	1814-1888	Kemp
ROBERTS, F. F.	23rd MS Inf.	1847-1912	Hind
ROBERTS, Franklin Alex	4th AL Inf.	1836-1912 AL	Laud
ROBERTS, Frank P.	Saddle Making	1828-1925 Simp	Simp
ROBERTS, G. H.	5th MS Inf.	1841-1876 Monr	Monr
ROBERTS, G. T.	3th MS Inf.	1822-1890 TN	Monr
ROBERTS, George	39th MS Inf.	1837-1870 Holm	Holm
ROBERTS, George	4th MS Inf.	1828-1917 Holm	Holm
ROBERTS, George W.	33rd MS Inf.	1842-1910 Amit	Amit
ROBERTS, H. _.	14th MS Cav.	1825-1899 Pike	Pike
ROBERTS, H. C.	12th MS Cav.	1849-1920 Unio	Unio
ROBERTS, H. H.	2nd & 3rd		
	MS Inf.	1824-1908 Itaw	Monr
ROBERTS, Henry	24th MS Inf.	1822-1880 MS	Gree
ROBERTS, Houston	39th MS Inf.	1831-1891 Hind	Holm
ROBERTS, Isiah	13th MS Inf.	1833-1905 Scot	Jone
ROBERTS, J. C.	11th MS Cav.	1838-1869 MS	Kemp
ROBERTS, J. G.	20th MS Inf.	1845-1924 Leak	Leak
ROBERTS, James (Jim)	9th MS Inf.	1822-1901 MS	Gree
ROBERTS, James A.	15th MS Inf.	1837-1911 SC	Holm
ROBERTS, James S.	1st MS Lt. Art.	1829-1901 Yazo	Yazo
ROBERTS, John	45th MS Inf.	1836-1918 Pont	Unio
ROBERTS, John B.	1st MS Cav.	1809-1893 NC	Newt
ROBERTS, John C.	5th MS Inf.	1838-1919 Monr	Monr
ROBERTS, John G.	20th MS Inf.	1845-1924 Atta	Atta
ROBERTS, John I.	30th MS Inf.	1817-1879 MS	Leak
ROBERTS, John J.	24th MS Inf.	____-1900	Kemp
ROBERTS, John L.	8th MS Cav.	1840-1940 Lown	Pont
ROBERTS, John M.	3rd LA Cav.	1845-1925 Walt	Walt
ROBERTS, John M.	LA Cav.	1845-1925	Mari
ROBERTS, John R.	18th MS Cav.	1827-1915 Bent	Bent
ROBERTS, Levi	9th MS Inf.	1831-1895 Mars	Mars
ROBERTS, M. F.	20th MS Inf.	1844-1919	Newt
ROBERTS, M. L.	11st MS Cav.	1841-1897 MS	Kemp
ROBERTS, M. Y.	12th MS Cav.	1845-1930 Pont	Unio
ROBERTS, Moses	12th MS Cav.	1845-1930 Unio	Unio
ROBERTS, Perry	21st MS Inf.	1842-1904 Linc	Linc
ROBERTS, Robert M.	2nd MS Inf.	1837-1919	Lee
ROBERTS, Uriah S.	13th MS Inf.	1842-1926 AL	Leak
ROBERTS, W. F.	48th MS Inf.	1832-1914 AL	Unio
ROBERTS, W. M.	2nd MS Cav.	1842-1926	Choc
ROBERTS, W. V	154th TN Cav.	1840-1928 TN	Chic
ROBERTS, William B.	20th AR Inf.	1843-1913 AR	Tate
ROBERTS, William T.	2nd MS Cav.	1838-1925 Monr	Monr
ROBERTSON, A. J.	4th MS Cav.	1844-1876 Covi	Covi
ROBERTSON, _. H.	15th MS Inf.	1834-1898	Sunf
ROBERTSON, C. A.	35th MS Inf.	1848-1939 MS	Jone
ROBERTSON, Charles S.	1st TN Regt.	1830-1916 TN	Unio
ROBERTSON, D. A.	15th MS Inf.	1832-1921 TN	Harr
ROBERTSON, E. G.	Wheelers AL Cav.	1834-1905 AL	Alco

Name	Unit	Dates	State	County
ROBERTSON, F. O.	8th LA Inf.	1839-1862 LA		Warr
ROBERTSON. G. R. (Dr.)	Brookhaven Lt. Art.	1844-1938 Copi		Linc
ROBERTSON, Gaston	19th MS Inf.	1847-1929 Lafa		Lafa
ROBERTSON, George	17th MS Inf.	1821-1880 TN		DeSo
ROBERTSON, George Frank	4th MS Cav.	1812-1886 GA		Covi
ROBERTSON, George H.	1st MS Inf.	1832-1879 SC		Hind
ROBERTSON, Geo. Hanson	Baltimore Lt.Art.	1844-1899 MD		Lama
ROBERTSON, George J.	17th MS Inf.	1812-1871 Mars		Yalo
ROBERTSON, George J.	17th MS Inf.	1842-1910 Mars		Yalo
ROBERTSON, George W.	18th MS Cav.	1822-1892 Yalo		Yalo
ROBERTSON, Henry	4th MS Inf.	1847-1900 Choc		Choc
ROBERTSON, J. D.	7th MS Inf.	1816-1871 JeDa		JeDa
ROBERTSON, J. W.	2nd AL Inf.	18_-1910 AL		Nesh
ROBERTSON, James K. P.	23rd MS Inf.	1845-1887 Tipp		Tipp
ROBERTSON, James M. (Dr)	8th TN Cav.	1839-1898		DeSo
ROBERTSON, James S.	30th MS Inf.	1836-1908 Carr		Carr
ROBERTSON, Joe R.	35th MS Inf.	1837-1875 Atta		Holm
ROBERTSON, John	3rd SC Inf.	1845-1933 SC		Carr
ROBERTSON, John R.	36th MS Inf.	1829-1897		Copi
ROBERTSON, John Stewart	8th AL Inf.	1846-1921 AL		Lown
ROBERTSON, John T.	15th MS Inf.	1832-1877 Okti		Wins
ROBERTSON, John W. Sr.	1st MS Cav.	1844-1908 Pont		Pont
ROBERTON, Newton B.	7th MS Inf.	1837-1918 Fran		Amit
ROBERTSON, Norvel L.	4th MS Cav.	1831-1922 Copi		Covi
ROBERTSON, Ransom	24th MS Inf.	1833-1865 Gree		Gree
ROBERTSON, S. M.	4th MS Cav.	1848-1875 Copi		Covi
ROBERTSON, S. P.	6th SC Cav.	1845-1927 SC		Carr
ROBERTSON, Samuel Dixon	Medical Corps	1837-1910 SC		Yazo
ROBERTSON, Samuel P.	6th Cav.	1845-1927 SC		Carr
ROBERTSON, W. H.	30th MS Inf.	1842-1907 Clay		Clay
ROBERTSON, W. P.	5th MS Inf.	1842-1918 Nesh		Amit
ROBERTSON, William	24th MS Inf.	1828-1865 Gree		Gree
ROBERTSON, William Cary	7th MS Inf.	1839-1886		Covi
ROBERTSON, William D.	13th VA Cav.	1839-1863 VA		Holm
ROBERTSON, William F.	7th TN Inf.	1838-1894 TN		Tall
ROBERTSON, William H.	31st AL Inf.	1844-1862 AL		Lown
ROBERTSON, William M.	31st AL Inf.	18_5-1901 AL		Copi
ROBERTSON, William M.	7th MS Inf.	1823-1887 SC		JeDa
ROBERTSON, William N.	7th MS Inf.	1831-1918 Lawr		Lawr
ROBERTSON, William N.	1st MS Cav.	1847-1862		Copi
ROBERTSON, William T.	11th MS Inf.	1839-1918 Nesh		Kemp
ROBERTSON, William T.	4th MS Cav.	1832-1891 Jeff		Jeff
ROBERTSON, William W.	MS Cav.	1835-1918 Copi		Jone
ROBINETT, John R.	MS Lt. Art.			
ROBINSON, A. M.	2nd MS Inf.	1842-1872 Tish		Tish
ROBINSON, Berry	13th MS Inf.	1843-1929 Laud		Laud
ROBINSON, Charles F.	32nd MS Inf.	1841-1914 Alco		Alco
ROBINSON, E. A.	16th MS Inf.	1839-1897 NY		Wilk
ROBINSON, E. C.	48th MS Inf.	1845-1923 Atta		Harr
ROBINSON, G. H.	11th MS Inf.	1846-1885 Nesh		Kemp
ROBINSON, George	8th MS Inf.	1844-1923		Rank

ROBINSON, George E.	42nd AL Inf.	1844-1907 Itaw	Itaw
ROBINSON, George Murry	4th AL Cav.	1842-1923 AL	Noxu
ROBINSON, George Wash.	33rd MS Inf.	1829-1918 MS	Amit
ROBINSON, H. C.	8th MS Cav.	1848-___ AL	Clay
ROBINSON, H. H.	32nd MS Inf.	1824-1891 NC	Tipp
ROBINSON, Henry	3rd MS Inf.	1828-1897 GA	Newt
ROBINSON, I. A.	33rd MS Inf.	1825-1917 Amit	Amit
ROBINSON, J. F.	13th MS Inf.	1839-1901	Rank
ROBINSON, J. H.	8th MS Inf.	1840-1908 MS	Smit
ROBINSON, J. H. C.	48th MS Inf.	1844-1915 MS	Tish
ROBINSON, J. M.	35th MS Inf.	1838-1867 Clay	Clay
ROBINSON, J. O.	1st MS Inf.	1839-1924	Itaw
ROBINSON, J. P.	31st MS Inf.	1829-1896 Unio	Unio
ROBINSON, J. S.	15th MS Inf.	1844-1902 Choc	Atta
ROBINSON, J. T.	5th AL Cav.	1848-1935 AL	Gree
ROBINSON, J. W.	5th MS Inf.	1838-1922 SC	Chow
ROBINSON, James A.	14th MS Inf.	1844-1934 Wins	Harr
ROBINSON, James H.	26th MS Inf.	Tish	Alco
ROBINSON, Jim	15th MS Inf.	1849-1935 MS	Harr
ROBINSON, Joe (Dr.)	5th MS Inf.	Choc	Choc
ROBINSON, John	9th AL Cav.	1825-1899 AL	Tish
ROBINSON, John C.	11th MS Inf.	1837-1875 Lafa	Lafa
ROBINSON, John D.	7th MS Cav.	1839-1882 AL	Tipp
ROBINSON, John Fuzua	10th VA Inf.	1845-1912 VA	Lown
ROBINSON, John T.	5th AL Cav.	1848-___ AL	Monr
ROBINSON, John V.		1832-1862	Chic
ROBINSON, John W.	7th MS Inf.	1823-1881 NC	Hind
ROBINSON, L.	15th MS Inf.	1846-1930 SC	Choc
ROBINSON, L. R.	7th AL Cav.	1837-1919 MS	Tish
ROBINSON, L. S. P.	53rd NC Inf.	1838-1914 NC	Yalo
ROBINSON, Moses B.	33rd MS Inf.	1829-1919 Amit	Amit
ROBINSON, R.	11th AL Cav.	1835-1917 AL	Tish
ROBINSON, R. B.	18th MS Cav.	1844-1930	Pano
ROBINSON, R. B/H.	11th MS Inf.	1845-1930 Nesh	Lafa
ROBINSON, R. N.	41st MS Inf.	1843-1913 AL	Harr
ROBINSON, R. W.	5th MS Inf.	1827-1906 Laud	Laud
ROBINSON, Richmond Love	11th MS Inf.	1843-1889 Nesh	Kemp
ROBINSON, S. N.	26th MS Inf.	1845-1880 Tish	Alco
ROBINSON, S. T.	16th MS Cav.	1844-1911 Tish	Alco
ROBINSON, S. W.		1837-1908	Rank
ROBINSON, Shelby Dye	16th MS Inf.	1837-1902 Simp	Copi
ROBINSON, Sherwood S.	18th Cav.	1833-1925 AL	DeSo
ROBINSON, Simeon	21st MS Inf.		Rank
ROBINSON, Thomas	39th MS Inf.	1836-___	Newt
ROBINSON, Thomas	32nd MS Inf.	1841-1935 Tish	Alco
ROBINSON, Thomas A.	33rd MS Inf.	1846-1921 Amit	Amit
ROBINSON, Thomas E. H.	8th MS Inf.	1837-1910 NY	Perr
ROBINSON, Van W.	Powers MS Cav.	1839-1918 Amit	Amit
ROBINSON, Van W.	10th MS Cav.	1848-1934 Amit	Wilk
ROBINSON, W. C/G.	27th MS Inf.	1836-1862 Okti	Okti
ROBINSON, W. W.	4th MS Cav.	1834-1928 NC	Jone
ROBINSON, William	2nd MS Inf.	1833-1914	Tate

ROBINSON, William J.	9th MS Inf.	1829-1895	DeSo
ROBINSON, William M.	33rd MS Inf.	1839-1916 Pike	Copi
ROBINSON, William W.	6th MS Inf.	1842-1925 Rank	Forr
(ROBUCK, F. M. located after ROE)			
ROBUCK, William	29th MS Inf.	Lafa	Calh
ROBY, Harry	15th MS Inf.	1830-1925 Jack	Jack
ROBY, Timothy Kennedy	9th LA Inf.	1840-1913 LA	Pano
ROBY, W. A.	11th MS Cav.		Lown
ROCCA, F.	12th MS Inf.	1827-1900 Italy	Adam
ROCHELL, Henry G.	14th MS Inf.	1837-1906 Leflo	Lefl
ROCHESTER, William F.	7th MS Inf.	1826-1899 Unio	Unio
ROCKCO, John W.	24th MS Cav.	1837-1895 MS	Pike
ROCKWOOD, William M.	28th MS Cav.	1838-1878 Warr	Warr
RODGERS, D. W.	32nd MS Inf.	1836-1899 NC	Pren
RODGERS, J. H.	Chalmers Brig.	1848-1919 Carr	Mont
RODGERS, J. L.	9th LA Inf.	1844-1911 LA	Walt
RODGERS, J. W.	Woods Cav.	1842-1918 Yazo	Yazo
RODGERS, Jack	38th MS Cav.	1836-1914	JeDa
RODGERS, James Whitfield	34th MS Inf.	1834-1904	DeSo
RODGERS, John	1st MS Cav.	1841-1937 Lafa	Lafa
RODGERS, John W.	16th MS Inf.	1825-1879 MS	Smit
RODGERS, Joseph W.	MS Lt. Art.	183_-1896 Clar	Jack
RODGERS, T. P.	26th MS Inf.	1838-1909 Tish	Tish
RODGERS, Thomas	4th MS Inf.	1829-1863 AL	Holm
RODGERS, W. D.	Gen. Forrest	1848-1928 AL	Unio
RODRIQUEZ, Jose (Dr.)	10th MS Inf.	1817-1889 Adam	Fran
ROE, M. C/G.	35th MS Inf.	1827-1869 Wins	Laud
ROBUCK, F. M.	2nd AL Cav.	1834-1877 AL	Chic
ROEBUCK, George Nile	20th AL Inf.	1839-1862 AL	Chic
ROEBUCK, J. H.	2nd AL Cav.	1836-1862 AL	Chic
ROGAN, Charles B.	Herberts Batt.	1840-1863 Warr	Warr
ROGAN, Lloyd W.	18th MS Inf.	1846-1907 Hind	Warr
ROGERS, A. A.	1st MS Cav.	1847-1932 Calh	Calh
ROGERS, Alfred E.	6th MS Inf.	1838-1911 Smit	Smit
ROGERS, A. J.	46th MS Inf.	1838-1910	Rank
ROGERS, A. W.	43rd MS Inf.	1842-1863 MS	Monr
ROGERS, B. H.	7th MS Cav.	____-1893 Tish	Alco
ROGERS, B. L.	1st MS Cav.	1835-1911 Jone	Jone
ROGERS, D. C.	27th MS Inf.	1840-1908	Covi
ROGERS, D. W.	32nd MS Inf.		Alco
ROGERS, F. M.	14th MS Inf.	1816-1862 MS	Monr
ROGERS, George W.	1st MS Lt. Art.	1840-1903 Choc	Atta
ROGERS, George W.	1st MS Lt. Art.	1844-1888 LA	Copi
ROGERS, H. J.	38th MS Cav.	1832-1910 MS	Lawr
ROGERS, Henry C.	15th MS Inf.	1839-1922 Holm	Holm
ROGERS, Henry Clay	23rd MS Batt.	1846-1928 Amit	Wilk
ROGERS, Henry Clay	7th MS Inf.	1846-1920 Amit	Amit
ROGERS, J. G.	1st MS Cav.	1841-1927 SC	Smit
ROGERS, J. J.	41st MS Inf.	1846-1936 GA	Lee
ROGERS, James	38th MS Cav.	1835-1906 MS	Lawr
ROGERS, James	9th MS Inf.	1847-1927 Lafa	Lafa
ROGERS, James P.	1st MS Cav.	1819-1897 KY	Holm

ROGERS, J. Henry	9th MS Inf.	1847-1926 Mars	Rank
ROGERS, John C.	8th MS Inf.	1844-1924 Clar	Jasp
ROGERS, John J.	22nd MS Inf.		Carr
ROGERS, John T.	9th MS Cav.	1847-1922 Jack	Geor
ROGERS, Joseph	41st MS Inf.	1817-1912 MS	Lee
ROGERS, Joseph E.	7th MS Cav.	1819-1891 TN	Tipp
ROGERS, Joseph G.	3rd MS Inf.	1842-1925 Jack	Geor
ROGERS, Joseph T.	5th MS Inf.	1836-1921 Kemp	Laud
ROGERS, Josiah	46th MS Inf.	1827-1864 Covi	Covi
ROGERS, L. B.	9th MS Inf.	DeSo	Alco
ROGERS, L. W.	37th MS Inf.	Clar	Copi
ROGERS, Meshack	Stubbs MS Cav.	1847-1927 Covi	Covi
ROGERS, N. C.	1st SC Cav.	1838-1935	Lee
ROGERS, N. E.	1st MS Inf.	1847-1926 SC	Jone
ROGERS, Nick N.	1st MS Cav.	1844-1919 Noxu	Noxu
ROGERS, Norvell	27th MS Inf.	1830-1907 MS	Covi
ROGERS, P. A.	2nd MS Cav.	1842-1913 Laud	Laud
ROGERS, R. H.	1st MS Inf.	1839-1922 AL	Lee
ROGERS, Richard T.	43rd MS Inf.	1836-1879 Monr	Monr
ROGERS, Robert H.	1st MS Inf.	1839-1922	Lee
ROGERS, Robert F/P.	46th MS Inf.	1844-___ Smit	Simp
ROGERS, Samuel J.	2nd MS Inf.	1821-1899 MS	Copi
ROGERS, Seth	1st MS Lt. Art.	___-1891	Mont
ROGERS, T. L.	28th AL Inf.	1841-1862 AL	Chic
ROGERS, T. M.	6th MS Inf.	1833-1913	Scot
ROGERS, Thomas J.	5th MS Inf.	1845-1878 IR	Laud
ROGERS, Timothy	6th MS Inf.	1828-1902 MS	Covi
ROGERS, Timothy Lott	16th MS Inf.	1841-1891 MS	Forr
ROGERS, W. B.	18th MS Cav.	1834-1901 Smit	Bent
ROGERS, W. F.	Ashcrafts MS Cav.	1826-1892 MS	Rank
ROGERS, W. H.	11th AL Inf.	1842-1895 AL	Carr
ROGERS, W. J. T.	46th MS Inf.	1838-1902 Laud	Laud
ROGERS, W. V. S.	7th MS Cav.	1836-1922 Fran	Alco
ROGERS, W. W.	39th MS Inf.	1829-1893 GA	Newt
ROGERS, William Jr.	41st MS Inf.	1839-1911 Pont	Pont
ROGERS, William J. (Dr.)	26th MS Inf.	1829-1889 TN	Pren
ROGERS, William W.	7th MS Inf.	1839-1864 Lawr	Lawr
ROGILLIO, William F.	48th MS Inf.	1832-1912	Clai
ROCHELIO, W. T.	20th MS Inf.	1839-191_ Scot	Scot
ROLLER, George M.	42nd AL Inf.	1836-1911 AL	Tish
ROLLINS, J. G.	12th MS Inf.	___-1904	Clai
ROLLINS, Samuel Davis	28th MS Cav.	1846-1909 MS	Warr
ROLLINS, W. H.	7th TN Cav.	1836-1904	DeSo
ROLLINSON, S. _.	7th MS Inf.	1831-1897 Fran	Amit
ROMAN, R. A.	2nd MO Inf.	1849-1916 Lafa	Pont
ROMEDY, J. H.	Q. M. Corps	1829-1911 SC	Wins
ROMINE, Eli F.	6th MS Cav.	1830-1912 Lown	Alco
ROMINE, William S.	6th MS Cav.	1836-1899 Lown	Alco
RONE, Archibald Thomas	Stanfords Lt. Art.	1841-1922 MS	Gren
RONEY, Alfred M.	15th AL Inf.	1843-1914 AL	Jone

Name	Unit	Dates		
ROOK, B. F.	2nd MS Inf.	1839-1896		Lefl
ROOK, Ben. Franklin	2nd MS Inf.	1833-1918	Lee	Gren
ROOK, W. F.	20th MS Inf.	1848-1912	Atta	Atta
ROOKS, John	12th MS Cav.	1839-1905	Monr	Monr
ROPER, E. E.	1st MS Partisans	1838-1864	Tipp	Chic
ROPER, F. M.	42nd MS Inf.	1832-1907	Gren	Unio
ROPER, W. H.	10th MS Cav.	1843-1930	MS	Itaw
ROPER, W. Z.	5th MS Inf.	1840-1928	NC	Perr
ROSAMOND, J. S.	15th MS Inf.	1841-1914	SC	Choc
ROSAMOND, John R. W.	18th MS Cav.	1821-1912	SC	Gren
ROSAMOND, John S.	4th MS Inf.	1843-1911	Holm	Holm
ROSAMOND, Thomas S.	1st MS Cav.	1823-1908	Atta	Atta
ROSAMOND, V. B.	15th MS Inf .		Choc	Atta
ROSS, A. G.	15th MS Inf.	1844-1924	Atta	Harr
ROSE, M. F.	15th MS	1842-1909	Choc	Mont
ROSE, Miles W.	15th MS Inf.	1838-1908	Choc	Gren
ROSE, Robert T.	1st MS Inf.		Adam	Adam
ROSE, W. _.	Stanfords			
	Lt. Art.	1836-1908	Gren	Gren
ROSE, W. H.	7th MS Cav.	1824-1864		Hind
ROSE, W. H.	7th MS Cav.	1835-1876		Lefl
ROSE, William H.	7th MS Cav.	1838-1916	AL	Gree
ROSEBERRY, Charles R.	1st MS Inf.	1848-1913	Clar	Forr
ROSENBAUM, David	1st MS Cav.	1820-1892	GE	Laud
ROSENBAUM, Marx	1st MS Cav.	1819-1883	GE	Laud
ROSENBURG, Louis Sr.	12th MS Inf.	1819-1882	PO	Yazo
ROSENTHAL, Benjamin L.	2nd MS Cav.	1827-1889	Choc	Carr
ROSETTE, James B.	44th MS Inf.	____-18_3	Adam	Adam
(ROSS, A. G. located after ROSAMOND)				
ROSS, C. L.	3rd MS Inf.			Monr
ROSS, Calvin T.	15th AL Inf.	1845-19_2		Gren
ROSS, D. _.	1st MS Cav.	1826-1911	Pont	Tall
ROSS, David	29th MS Inf.	1813-1874	Yalo	Tall
ROSS, Edward J.	3rd MS Inf.	1845-1929	Copi	Clai
ROSS, Emmett L.	18th LA Inf.	1843-1891	LA	Madi
ROSS, F. C.	27th TN Inf.	1840-1924	NC	Monr
ROSS, F. Bolivar	11th MS Inf.	1828-1875	Nesh	Nesh
ROSS, Frank W.	15th MS Inf.	1846-1939		Jeff
ROSS, G. W.	11th AR Inf.	1847-1922	JeDa	JeDa
ROSS, George	1st AL Art.	1843-1932	GE	Harr
ROSS, George W.	17th MS Inf.	1839-1873	MS	Monr
ROSS, Grandville H.	23rd MS Inf.	1841-1909	Alco	Alco
ROSS, Hugh Thomas	3rd Inf.	1849-1925		Rank
ROSS, J. C.	Adam MS Cav.	1839-1918		Madi
ROSS, J. F.	31st MS Inf.	1843-1900	Calh	Calh
ROSS, J. M.	41st MS Inf.	1835-1916	MS	Laud
ROSS, James C.	Adams MS Cav.			Hind
ROSS, James E.	Adams MS Cav.	1844-1929		Hind
ROSS, J. S.	35th MS Inf.	1832-1918	Wins	Kemp
ROSS, John F.	Rivers NC Inf.	1847-1920	NC	Alco
ROSS, Thos. G.	1st MS Cav.	1848-1921		Rank
ROSS, W. C.	18th MS Inf.	1841-1881	MS	Yazo

ROSS, W. G.	1st AL Lt. Art.	1840-1920 AL	Harr
ROSS, William	18th MS Inf.	1808-1885 TN	Yazo
ROSS, William C.	39th MS Inf.	____-1863	Hind
ROSS, William Newton	23rd MS Inf.	1841-1911 Tish	Alco
ROTCH, G. W.	Richards Lt. Art.	1830-1904	Copi
ROTEN, Franklin	27th MS Inf.	1830-1885 Leak	Leak
ROTH, Morris	9th GA Inf.	1830-1914 GA	Monr
ROTHENBERGER, Frederick	38th MS Cav.	1830-1862 GE	Alco
ROUGH, Walter Albert	8th MS Inf.	1843-1864 SC	Scot
ROUNDSVILLE, William	48th MS Inf.	1840-1925 AL	Gren
ROUNDTREE, E. L.	40th MS Inf.	1840-1911 Kemp	Kemp
ROUNSAVILLE, Elias	24th MS Inf.	1845-1902 Gree	Gree
ROUSE, Burl	38th MS Cav.	1845-1901 Lama	Lama
ROUSE, B. Snow	9th MS Cav.	1839-1925 Jack	Geor
ROUSE, J. W.	9th MS Cav.	1820-1906 Jack	Jack
ROUSSEAU, William James	48th MS Inf.	1829-1908 TN	Okti
ROW, Vincent	4th MS Cav.	1826-1886 Wilk	Wilk
ROWAN, John	32nd MS Inf.	1832-1921	Lee
ROWAN, Josiah Kennedy	62nd TN Inf.	1838-1913 TN	Jone
ROWAN, Montgomery M.	24th MS Inf.	MS	Lown
ROWE, Ab__ Vernon	28th MS Cav.	1848-1926 Holm	Mont
ROWE, W. D.	Fowlers AL Batt.	1838-1915 Tall	
ROWELL, George W.	9th LA Inf.	1832-1909 LA	Walt
ROWELL, H. H.	8th MS Inf.	1841-1921 Jone	Jone
ROWELL, J. D.	8th MS Inf.	1845-1928 Jone	Jone
ROWELL, J. W.	8th MS Inf.	1845-1893 Clar	Clar
ROWELL, Samuel B.	42nd MS Inf.	1844-1924 Tate	Tate
ROWELL, W. B.	27th MS Inf.	1842-1909 Jasp	Jasp
ROWELL, William	46th MS Inf.	1831-1891	Covi
ROWELL, William F.	1st MS Cav.	1847-1893 Choc	Webs
ROWELL, William J.	2nd MS Cav.	1844-1907 SC	Tate
ROWLAND, H. Young	13th MS Inf.	1843-1915 SC	Hind
ROWLAND, I. M.	34th MS Inf.	1826-1907 Tipp	Tipp
ROWLAND, J. A.	34th MS Inf.	1836-1894 TN	Tipp
ROWLAND, James Henry	3rd MS Cav.	18_6-1891 TN	Mars
ROWLAND, Jim E.	20th MS Inf.	1844-1937 Wins	Warr
ROWLAND, Peter	43rd MS Inf.	1841-1894 Itaw	Pont
ROWLAND, Peter	2nd MS Inf.	1834-1918 Itaw	Pont
ROWLAND, Robert H.	29th MS Inf.	1841-1910 MS	Tall
ROWLAND, W. T.	13th TN Inf.	1837-1911 TN	Bent
ROWLEY, Hance	7th MS Inf.	1833-1905 Walt	Walt
ROWSE, J. _.	1st MS Inf.	1836-1914 Pont	Lafa
ROWSEY, W. H.	11th & 12th MS Cav.	1839-1911 Chic	Alco
ROWZEE, J. E.	41st MS Inf.	1836-1922 Pont	Pont
ROWZEE, John E.	41st MS Inf.	1837-1912 Pont	Pont
ROWZEE, Weston W.	2nd MS Cav.	1846-1927 GA	Newt
ROWZEE, William C.	2nd MS Cav.	1843-1923 GA	Newt
ROY, A.	3rd MS Inf.	1812-1890 ST	Jack
ROY, George Washington	3rd SC Cav.	1840-1923 MO	Hind
ROYAL, D.	28th MS Cav.	1836-1912 Gren	Yalo
ROYAL, William H. H.	1st MS Cav.	1840-1915	Lafa

ROYE, Henry C.	26th MS Inf.	1846-1899 Pont	Pont
ROYE, Joseph G. (Rev.)	1st MS Inf.	1839-1911 Pont	Pont
ROYE, Lemuel H.	41st MS Inf.	1823-1882 Pont	Pont
ROYSTER, Jay	Woods MS Cav.	1847-1922 Yazo	Yazo
ROZIER, William	5th MS Cav.	1832-1896 Carr	Lefl
RUBE, John A.	13th MS Inf.	1845-1902 MS	Newt
RUDY, Charles W.	42nd MS Inf.	1839-1915 AL	Tate
RUCKER, Abbott C.	34th MS Inf.	1827-1917 MO	Tipp
RUCKER, Charlie C.	7th MS Cav.	1848-1901 MS	Tipp
RUCKER, James T.	37th GA Inf.	1823-___ GA	Newt
RUCKER, Robert T.	62nd AL Inf.	1844-1912 AL	Pont
RUCKER, W. A.	2nd MS Cav.	1823-1908 Monr	Tipp
RUCKER, Wm. W.	18th MS Inf.	1841-1918 Madi	Madi
RUCKS, Lewis Taylor	18th MS Inf.	1841-1884 TN	Wash
RUDISILL, A. W.	4th TN Inf.	1830-1910 TN	Pano
RUFF, John J.	24th MS Inf.	1838-1912 Chic	Chic
RUFF, T. L.	41st MS Inf.	1839-1915 Tipp	Unio
RUFFIN, James	4th MS Cav.	1837-1919 Pano	Pano
RUFFIN, F. L.	14th MS Inf.	1838-1882 Okti	Okti
RUFFIN, Samuel W.	12th MS Cav.	1843-1890 Jasp	Jasp
RUMBLE, Stephen Edgar	7th MS Inf.	1837-1913 Amit	Adam
RUMPH, William P.	1st MS Inf.	1834-1862	Hind
RUNDBERG, John I.	16th MS Inf.	1811-1906 RI	Warr
RUNDLE, David Brainard	Fenners Batt.	1833-1900 NY	Warr
RUNGE, Louis A.	6th MS Regt.	1835-1877	Rank
RUNNELLS, C. _.	McLaurins Co.	1830-1881	Rank
RUNNELLS, Elias	6th MS Cav.	1815-19_	Simp
RUNNELLS, Ellis Joseph	6th MS Cav.	1827-1893	Rank
RUNNELLS, James F.	39th MS Inf.	1844-1924 Simp	Simp
RUNNELLS, Joseph	7th MS Inf.	1836-1918 MS	Perr
RUNNELLS, Samuel	37th MS Inf.	1825-1904 Clar	Simp
RUNNELLS, Samuel	39th MS Inf.	____-1906 Simp	Simp
RUSHING, Felix P.	14th MS Inf.	1832-1899 Okti	Okti
RUSHING, H.	1st MS Lt. Art.	18_1-1863	Lafa
RUSHING, Jack	2nd MS Inf.	____-1912	Amit
RUSHING, William N.	26th Ns. Inf.	1844-1924 MS	Pren
RUSHING, Nevell E.	33rd MS Inf.	1835-1909 Walt	Walt
RUSCOE, Alexander B.	43rd NC Inf.	1846-1925 NC	Carr
RUSH, Daniel	5th MS Inf.	1820-1881 Wins	Nesh
RUSH, G. T.	35th MS Inf.	1822-1901 Wins	Kemp
RUSH, James Calvin	35th MS Inf.	1845-1862 Wins	Kemp
RUSH, John W.	7th MS Inf.	1844-1909 Jone	Jone
RUSH, T. L.	38th MS Cav.	1841-1862 Clai	Clai
RUSH, W. M.	35th MS Inf.	1828-1874 Wins	Kemp
RUSH, W. V.	1st MS Cav.	1846-1916 Laud	Laud
RUSH, William G.	35th MS Inf.	1803-1876 NC	Kemp
RUSHIN, William	46th AL Inf.	1845-1937 AL	Okti
RUSHING, Andrew Jackson	34th MS Inf.	1839-1895	Lafa
RUSHING, Charles E.	5th MS Inf.	1819-1881	Laud
RUSHING, John C.	33rd MS Inf.	1820-1901 MS	Walt
RUSHING, John C.	38th MS Cav.	1840-1905 Rank	Scot
RUSHING, John J.	14th Conf. Cav.	1844-191_ Fran	Fran

RUSHING, Josephis O.	31st LA Inf.	1834-1909 LA	Linc
RUSHING, W. A.	33rd MS Inf.	1848-1916 MS	Walt
RUSHING, Wiley	33rd MS Inf.	1825-1905 Pike	Walt
RUSHING, William M.	46th AL Inf.	1841-1937 AL	Okti
RUSHTON, Obie E.	37th MS Inf.	1835-1891 MS	Jone
RUSKIN, W. N.	26th MS Inf.	1844-1924 Tish	Tish
RUSSEL, John A.	Bradfords Art.	1827-1901	Chic
RUSSELL, A. E.	33rd MS Inf.	1825-1911 Nesh	Nesh
RUSSELL, A. G.	37th MS Inf.	1834-1906 Wayn	Wayn
RUSSELL, A. H.	1st AL Inf.	1841-1862 AL	Lafa
RUSSELL, Christopher C.	16th Cav.	1846-1916	Rank
RUSSELL, D. W.	33rd MS Inf.	1839-1924	Leak
RUSSELL, Daniel R.	20th MS Inf.	1821-1870 Carr	Carr
RUSSELL, Daniel W.	33rd MS Inf.	1839-1924 Nesh	Nesh
RUSSELL, Ely Wells	48th MS Inf.	1848-1921	Hind
RUSSELL, F. B.	15th MS Inf.	1833-1889 Atta	Atta
RUSSELL, F. W.	14th MS Inf.	1843-1923 Okti	Okti
RUSSELL, Frank	39th MS Inf.	1842-1920	Newt
RUSSELL, Franklin	39th MS Inf.	1835-1881 MS	Newt
RUSSELL, George W.	8th & 13th MS Inf.	1829-1891 Newt	Newt
RUSSSLL, H. J.	15th MS Inf.	1844-1929	Mont
RUSSELL, Howell J.	4th MS Inf.		Carr
RUSSELL, Isaac Preston	6th MS Inf.	1848-1919	Rank
RUSSELL, J. A.	1st MS Inf.	1814-1878	Hind
RUSSELL, J. L.	6th & 15th MS Inf.	1836-1889 Rank	Laud
RUSSELL, J. M.	11th MS Cav.	1830-1906	Lown
RUSSELL, J. P. Sr.	6th MS Inf.	1839-1913 Rank	Rank
RUSSELL, James A.	43rd MS Inf.	1836-1904 Lafa	Lafa
RUSSELL, James R.	8th AL Inf.	1831-1906 AL	Kemp
RUSSELL, James W.	4th MS Inf.	1839-1878 Carr	Carr
RUSSELS, Jamess Wash.	4th MS Inf.	1842-1924 Choc	Copi
RUSSELL, J___	14th LA Inf.	1841-1918 LA	Lawr
RUSSELL, John	3rd MS Inf.	1815-1890 Rank	Rank
RUSSELL, John	16th MS Inf.	1835-___ ST	Adam
RUSSELL, John A.	41st MS Inf.	1839-1862	Pont
RUSSELL, John A.	Bradfords Art.	1843-1922 Pont	Pont
RUSSELL, John H.	26th MS Inf.	1840-1926 Tish	Tish
RUSSELL, John H.	5th MS Inf.	1820-1884 GA	Jasp
RUSSELL, John T.	27th LA Inf.	1837-1911 LA	Pont
RUSSELL, John L.	6th MS Inf.	1843-1862	Rank
RUSSELL, L. N.	13th MS Inf.	1838-1906 Linc	Linc
RUSSELL, Murdock	39th MS Inf.	1846-1923 GA	Newt
RUSSELL, Perry	41st MS Inf.	1826-1898 Noxu	Noxu
RUSSELL, T. L.	Bradfords Art.	1842-1924	Pont
RUSSELL, Truflay C.	61st MA Inf.	1845-1915 CN	Forr
RUSSELL, W. J.	33rd MS Inf.	1847-1921 Pike	Leak
RUSSELL, W. P.	7th AL Cav.	1837-1931 AL	Tish
RUSSELL, W. S.	31st MS Inf.	1849-1871	Rank
RUSSELL, William	23rd MS Inf.	1840-1917 Tish	Scot
RUSSELL, S. M.	7th AL Cav.	1842-1927 AL	Tish

94

RUSSUM, Benjamin Frank.	6th MS Inf.	1832-1893 Smit	Smit
RUSSUM, Henry Bascomb	19th MS Inf.	1844-1920 Noxu	Bent
RUTH, Starling D.	42nd MS Inf.	1829-1899 MS	Calh
RUTHERFORD, F. W.	15th MS Inf.	1837-1915 Atta	Atta
RUTHERFORD, J. H.	7th MS Cav.		Alco
RUTHERFORD, J. M.	34th MS Inf.	1834-1909 GA	Tipp
RUTHERFORD, Lindsey J.	1st MS Inf.	1843-190_ MS	Pren
RUTHERFORD, Thomas	34th MS Inf.	1837-1896	Sunf
RUTHERFORD, W. Barton	6th AL Inf.	1840-1914 Hanc	Hanc
RUTHERFORD, William F.	1st FL Inf.	1840-1935 FL	Ston
RUTHVEN, A. G.	Gamblins		
	MS Cav.	1818-1890 Kenp	Kemp
RUTLAND, Allen	46th MS Inf.	1813-1869	DeSo
RUTLEDGE, A. J.	34th MS Inf.	1836-1890 Lafa	Unio
RUTLEDGE, J.	16th MS Inf.	1835-1916 Tish	Tish
RUTLEDGE, J. J.	20th MS Inf.	1833-1915 Tish	Tish
RUTLEDGE, J. P.	36th MS Inf.	1843-1913 Copi	Linc
RUTLEDGE, Joseph	4th MS Cav.	1822-1912	Copi
RUTLEDGE, W. A.	11th MS Cav.	1846-1922 Pont	Chic
RUTLEDGE, W. C/G.	2nd MS Inf.	1841-1911 Tipp	Unio
RUTLEDGE, William	7th MS Inf.	1831-1916 Covi	Pike
RYAKS, Felix G.	7th MS Inf.	1845-19_ MS	Walt
RYAN, George W. (Rev.)	8th MS Inf.	1811-1898 Jasp	Jasp
RYALS, Hardy	2nd MS		
	Minute Men	1828-1906 Walt	Walt
RYALS, Jesse C.	7th MS Inf.	1840-1905 Mari	Mari
RYALS, John	7th MS Inf.	1834-1876 Mari	Walt
RYAN, Anthony	3rd MS Inf.	1842-1908 Jack	Jack
RYAN, Jacob	24th MS Inf.	1840-1933	Forr
RYAN, James	35th MS Inf.	1832-1901 Wins	Atta
RYAN, Jerry	Seven Star Art.	1843-1911 IR	Simp
RYAN, John	Vicksburg Lt.Art.	1828-1863 Warr	Warr
RYAN, John	LA Art.	1838-1883 LA	Warr
RYAN, John	3rd MS Inf.	1837-1907 Jack	Jack
RYAN, Louis	3rd MS Inf.	1837-1909 Jack	Jack
RYAN, Martin	3rd MS Inf.	1842-1913 Jack	Jack
RYAN, Milton	8th MS Inf.	1842-1916 Jasp	Jasp
RYAN, Thomas	2nd MS Inf.	1831-1891	Hind
RYAN, Z. J.	4th MS Inf.	1838-1893 Calh	Calh
RYE, A. H.	2nd MS Cav.	1840-1927 Monr	Monr
RYE, D. W.	2nd MS Cav.	1819-1863	Monr
RYE, John M.	43rd MS	1831-1910 Monr	Monr
RYE, S. Wesley	2nd MS Cav.	1828-1872 Clar	Monr
RYE, T. J.	2nd MS Inf.	1841-1880 MS	Pont
RYLE, J. J.	13th MS Inf.	1833-1897 GA	Newt
RYLES, Thomas	24th GA Inf.	1845-1926 GA	Mars
RYLE, William N.	14th GA Inf.	1837-1903 GA	Wayn
SADLER, A	1st MS Inf.	1839-1862 Monr	Monr
SADLER, Anderson D.	23rd MS Inf.	1836-1902 Tish	Lee
SADLER, B. F.	9th LA Inf.	1834-1919 LA	Harr
SADLER, Drury	17th MS Inf.	1830-1894 Mars	Mars

SADLER, John H.	35th MS Inf.	1849-1935 Nesh	Nesh
SADLER, L. A.	7th TN Inf.	1839-1919 Mars	Yazo
SADLER, Samuel O.	2nd MS Cav.	1832-1875 Tate	Tate
SADLER, Thomas	9th MS Cav.	1833-1881 Chic	Chic
SAGE, William Wallace	9th MS Inf.	1838-1907	DeSo
SALE, Eugene P.	43rd MS Inf.	1846-1901 Monr	Monr
SALE, John.B.	27th MS Inf.	1839-1876 Monr	Monr
SALLEY, D. J.	15th MS Inf.	1832-1918	Webs
SALLEY, James W.	15th & 45th MS Inf.	1843-1927 Carr	Webs
SALLIS, Joseph Melton	11th MS Cav.	1820-18_7	Atta
SALLIS, R. J.	15th MS Inf.	1830-1908 Atta	Atta
SALLIS, T. D.	15th MS Inf.	1828-1893 Atta	Atta
SALMON, David Daniel	40th SC Inf.	1843-1934 SC	Tate
SALMON, Joe M.	31st MS Inf.	1840-1910 Smit	Tate
SALMON, John A.	2nd MS Inf.	1822-1864 Pont	Pont
SALMON, T. A.	34th MS Inf.	1842-1909 Mars	Mars
SALMON, W. H.	7th MS Cav.	1845-1914 Madi	Unio
SALTER, D. S.	40th MS Inf.	1838-1910 Nesh	Nesh
SALTER, K.	42nd AL Inf.	1842-1863 AL	Lafa
SAMPLE, Calvin	2nd MS Inf.	1840-1928	Lee
SAMPLE, J. A.	Holmes Co. Ind.	1823-1908 SC	Holm
SAMPLE, J. R.	7th MS Inf.	1840-1915 MS	Pike
SAMPLE, W. B.	7th AL Cav.	1846-1920 AL	Tish
SAMUELS, R. H.	3rd MS Inf.	1836-1893	Hind
SANDEFER, A. B.	21st MS Inf.	1831-1925 Simp	Simp
SANDELL, John Wesley	39th MS Inf.	1829-1913 Pike	Pike
SANDERFORD, John H.	46/48th MS Inf.	1828-1882 Laud	Laud
SANDERS, A. B.	38th MS Cav.	1847-1910 MS	JEDAs
SANDERS, A. R.	3rd MS Cav.	1821-1893 Yalo	Yalo
SANDERS, Ammons	27th MS Inf.	Leak	Atta
SANDERS, Aron P.	3rd MS Cav.	1848-1921	Lafa
SANDERS, B. W.	40th MS Inf.	1832-1904 Leak	Leak
SANDERS, Benjamin F.	18th MS Cav.	1846-1915 MS	Mars
SANDERS, C. L.	38th MS Cav.	1846-1926 Lawr	Lawr
SANDERS, D. W. T.	20th MS Inf.	1833-190_ Atta	Atta
SANDERS, David	KY Rifles	KY	Atta
SANDERS, E. I.	1st AL Rifles	1844-1924 AR	Gree
SANDERS, Elkanah	18th MS Inf.		Atta
SANDERS, Ewel P.	12th MS Inf.	1837-1871	Copi
SANDERS, F. M.	33rd MS Inf.	1839-1921 Leak	Leak
SANDEER, Francis	11th MS Inf.	1847-1936 Okti	Okti
SANDERS, G. G.	31st MS Inf.	1839-1918	Okti
SANDERS, George W.	26th MS Inf.	1838-1928 AL	Pren
SANDERS, Harris	7th MS Cav.	1824-1917 NC	Tipp
SANDERS, Henry	26th MS Inf.	1840-1881 Pont	Pont
SAANDERS, Hiram	4th MS Inf.	1823-1908 Itaw	Itaw
SANDERS, I. H.	26th AL Inf.	1823-1908 AL	Lown
SANDERS, Ira A.	38th MS Cav.	1841-1911 Wilk	Wilk
SANDERS, J. P.	13th MS Inf.	1831-1927 Wayn	Harr
SANDERS, J. W.	35th MS Inf.	1839-1915 Okti	Lafa
SANDERS, James J.	15th MS Inf.	1832-1884 Wins	Wins

SANDERS, James N.	9th MS Inf.	1842-1877 Lafa	Lafa
SANDERS, Jasp	4th MO Cav.	1842-1906 MO	Lawr
SANDERS, Jeff W.	6th & 15th		
	MS Inf.	1840-1911 Leak	Atta
SANDERS, John	1st MS Inf.		Hind
SANDERS, John	17th MS Inf.	1828-1899 Chic	Chic
SANDERS, John	37th MS Inf.	1840-1911 Atta	Atta
SANDERS, John A.	38th MS Cav.	1827-1911 EN	Wilk
SANDERS, John R.	28th MS Cav.		Lown
SANDERS, John W.	10th MS Cav.	1832-1876	Pren
SANDERS, Lafayette	38th MS Cav.	1847-1913 MS	Lawr
SANDERS, M. P.	33rd MS Inf.	1844-1922 Leak	Leak
SANDERS, Mark A.	4th MS Cav.	Wilk	Wilk
SANDERS, Micajah	40th MS Inf.	1830-___ Leak	Leak
SANDERS, Nathan J.	38th MS Cav.	1842-1909 MS	Lawr
SANDERS, Owen	3rd MS Cav.	1805-2899 Atta	Atta
SANDERS, Peter	1st MS Cav.	1847-1911 Carr	Leak
SANDERS, Reuben	3rd MS Inf.	1821-1901	Monr
SANDERS, Robert M.	40th MS Inf.	1840-1921 GA	Jone
SANDERS, S. F.	22nd MS Inf.	1846-1926 Lawr	Harr
SANDERS, S. F.	22nd MS Inf.	1839-1914 Lawr	JEDA
SANDERS, Simeon L.	1st AR Inf.	1839-1908 AR	Alco
SANDERS, Sol	39th MS Inf.	1842-1902 Scot	Scot
SANDERS, T. J.	41st MS Inf.	1834-1920 Pont	Unio
SANDERS, T. J.	27th MS Inf.	1821-1903 SC	Atta
SANDERS, Thomas H.	Powers Cav.	1847-1910 Copi	Copi
SANDERS, Thomas J.	27th MS Inf.	1846-1921 Leak	Leak
SANDERS, W. B.	15th MS Inf.	1835-1886	Atta
SANDERS, W. C.	18th MS Inf.	1834-1906	Hind
SANDERS, W. G.	Powers MS Cav.	1841-1911	Kemp
SANDERS, W. H.	15th MS Inf.	1842-1865 Yalo	Chic
SANDERS, W. P.	12th MS Cav.	1845-1933 Wins	Atta
SANDERS, W. R.	7th AL Cav.	1833-1916 AL	Tish
SANDERS, W. S.	16th MS Inf.	1847-1924	Harr
SANDERS, William	15th MS Inf.	1843-1933 Atta	Atta
SANDERS, William	28th MS Cav.	1831-1874 Warr	Warr
SANDER, William Allen	5th MS Inf.	MS	Atta
SANDERS, William G.	Powers MS Cav.	1846-1921 Copi	
SANDERS, William J.	15th MS Inf.	1839-1870 Atta	Atta
SANDERS, William M.	15th MS Inf.	1846-1911 Atta	Holm
SANDERS, William M.	15th MS Inf.	1821-1893	Copi
SANDERS, Wm. A.	6th MS Inf.	1838-1911 MS	Leak
SANDERSON, A. J. (Dr.)	1st MS Lt. Art.	1825-1902 Clai	Carr
SANDERSON, A. W. B.	7th MS Inf.	1846-1908 Pike	Jone
SANDERSON, E. L.	Army CSA	1846-1936 Gren	Gren
SANDERSON, J. W.	7th MS Inf.	1832-1905 Jone	Jone
SANDERSON, Joseph W.	5th MS Inf.	1821-1874 MS	Rank
SANDERSON, William R.	46th MS Inf.	1836-1893 Wayn	Wayn
SANDIDGE, James M.	1st MS Cav.	1848-1907	Hind
SANDIDGE, P. F.	Coopers MS Inf.	1820-1892 TN	Rank
SANDIDGE, Robert	15th MS Inf.	1838-1911 Hind	Yazo
SANDIDGE, Thomas H.	1st MS Lt. Art.	1819-1881	Hind

SANDIFER, Absalom	36th MS Inf.	1839-1862 Copi	Holm
SANDIFER, J. D.	5th MS Inf.	1839-1921 Monr	Monr
SANDIFER, J. T.	Graves MS		
	Lt. Art.	1848-1903	Rank
SANDIFER, James M.	1st MS		
	Home Guards	1849-1883 MS	Walt
SANDIFER, Jim	1st MS Lt. Art.	1842-1871 Holm	Holm
SANDIFER, John	38th MS Cav.	1822-1892 Pike	Lawr
SANDIFER, John P.	36th MS Inf.	1849-1924	Copi
SANDIGE, Benj. L.	1st MS Art.	1830-1905 Yazo	Yazo
SANDIGE, William S.	Harveys Scotts	1848-1936 MS	Linc
SANDS, Nathaniel	35th MS Inf.	1838-1864 Okti	Chic
SANFORD, George Presley	59th VA.	1838-1921 TN	Kemp
SANFORD, George W.	7th MS Inf.	1845-1915 Pont	Unio
SANFORD, Hiram M.	8th AL Inf.	1839-1903 AL	Tish
SANFORD, J. B.	Gurleys AL Cav.	1845-190_ AL	Coah
SANFORD, J. D.	9th MS Cav.	1846-1923 Jone	Covi
SANFORD, J. T.	9th MS Cav.	1846-1923 Jone	Covi
SANFORD, James Allen	46th MS Inf.	1836-1923 Kemp	Kemp
SANFORD, Jesse H.	46th MS Inf.	1845-1928 Laud	Laud
SANFORDS, W.	1st MS		
	Sharpshooters	1821-1903 GA	Holm
SANSING, G. P. C.	2nd MS Cav.	1847-1918 Newt	Newt
SANSING, J. E/H.	8th MS Inf.	1843-1910 Laud	Newt
SANSING, P. W.	8th MS Inf.	1841-1919 Newt	Nesh
SANSING, William A.	8th MS Inf.	1839-1864	Nesh
SANSOM, William C.	1st MS Inf.		Monr
SAPPINGTON, R. A.	1st MS Cav.	1818-1897 Noxu	Pont
SARGENT, George	3rd LA Cav.	1832-1893	Nesh
SARRETT, H. J.	1st MS Cav.	____-1903	Hind
SARTAIR, W. A.	7th AL Cav.	1847-1910 Tish	Tish
SARTIN, Alfred	2nd MS Inf.	1819-1893	Copi
SARTIN, Crawford F.	8th MS Cav.	Yalo	Calh
SARTIN, J. G.	38th MS Cav.	1843-1868 Pike	Lawr
SARTIN, J. Obed	38th MS Cav.	1845-1931 Pike	Walt
SARTIN, James B.	38th MS Cav.	1832-1862 Pike	Walt
SARTIN, Leander	38th MS Cav.	1824-1902 Pike	Walt
SARTIN, Linus W.	17th LA Inf.	1847-1928 Pike	Walt
SARTIN, A. C.	11th MS Inf.	1838-____	Monr
SARTOR, G. W.	2nd MS Cav.	1817-1885 SC	Monr
SARTOR, J. C.	3rd MS Inf.		Monr
SARTOR, John	41st MS Inf.	____-1915	Monr
SARTOR, R. C.	11th MS Inf.	1838-1923 Monr	Harr
SARTOR, W. W.	12th MS Cav.	1845-1913 AL	Monr
SARTORIUS, Phillip	14th LA Inf.	1831-1913 LA	Warr
SARVER, J. W.	2nd TN Inf.	____-1862 TN	Lown
SASSER, Daniel V.	7th MS Inf.	1837-1906 MS	Linc
SASSER, Joseph	7th MS Inf.	1834-1902 Pike	Linc
SASSER, Stephen	7th MS Inf.	1824-1891	Copi
SASSER, William P.	7th MS Inf.	1846-1911 Fran	Linc
SATTERFIELD, Robt. F. L.	23rd MS Inf	1844-1927 Bent	Pren
SAUCIER, David	3rd MS Inf.	1840-1910 Jack	Jack

SAUCIER, Harry J.	Williams AL Inf.	1846-1929 AL	Hanc
SAUCIER, Henry	9th LA Inf.	1826-1884 MS	Harr
SAUIER, Henry E.	9th LA Inf.	1848-1926 MS	Harr
SAUCIER, J. Abner	20th MS Inf.	1845-1931 Harr	Harr
SAUCIER, John B.	3rd MS Inf.	1824-1900 Harr	Lama
SAUCIER, John Henry	1st AL Inf.	1847-1929	Hanc
SAUCER, Philip N.	3rd MS Inf.	1829-1886 Harr	Harr
SAUCIER, Pierre	3rd MS Inf.	1819-1895 Harr	Harr
SAUCIER, R.	20th MS Inf.	1844-1906 Harr	Harr
SAUL, Richard M.	37th MS Inf.	1843-1909 Laud	Jone
SAULS, Isaac Lane	22nd MS Inf.	1842-1931 MS	Lawr
SAILS, William Jasper	24th MS Cav.	1846-1918 Walt	Lawr
SAULS, J. Parham	24th MS Cav.	1846-1918 Lawr	Walt
SAULS, William Jasper	7th MS Inf.	1838-1881 Lawr	Lawr
SAUNDERS, Benjamin F.	2nd MO Inf.	1841-1900 MO	Tall
SAUNDERS, Hubbard Turner	6th MS Inf.	1846-1920 Holm	Okti
SAUNDERS, Lawrence W.	Warren Lt. Art.	1840-1895 Hind	Hind
SAUNDERS, Robert Leroy	3rd MS Inf.	1848-1920	Hind
SAUNDERS, William H.	27th MS Inf.	1819-1895 SC	Monr
SAUNDERS, Wm. Ragsdale	Foundry	1816-1904 Clay	Chic
SAVAGE, Alex T. M.	11th MS Cav.	1845-1896 Alco	Alco
SAVAGE, Giles	11th MS Cav.	1821-1907 Kemp	Alco
SAVAGE, Granvil	11th MS Cav.	1826-1895 Kemp	Alco
SAVAGE, J. _.	44th MS Inf.	1848-1916	Okti
SAVAGE, James Anderson	2nd MS Regt.	1825-1884 NC	Wins
SAVAGE, John W.	23rd MS Cav.	1838-1900 MS	Alco
SAVAGE, Josiah	31st MS Inf.	NC	Calh
SAVAGE, Z. F.	27th MS Inf.	1837-1882 Monr	Monr
SAVELL, Jasper	33rd MS Inf.	1837-1910	Nesh
SAWYER, Charles M.	1st MS Inf.	1838-1905 Adam	Adam
SAWYER, H. A.	2nd NC Inf.	1839-1921 NC	Atta
SAXON, John H.	14th MS Inf.	1832-1901 Clar	Scot
SAXON, Pressly H.	36th AL Inf.	1841-1907 AL	Wayn
SAXON, William	40th MS Inf.	1841-1920 Scot	Scot
SAXTON, I. G. (Dr.)	Hospital	1836-1929 Okti	Harr
SCALES, T. O.	8th AL Cav.	1846-1917 AL	Scot
SCALES, W. W.	11th MS Inf.	1846-1925 MS	Okti
SCALLY, H. P.	32nd MS Inf.	1846-1920 TN	Alco
SCALLY, W. H.	32nd MS Inf.	1828-1917 Alco	Tipp
SCANLAN, T. M.	8th MS Inf.	1846-1927 Newt	Forr
SCARBERRY, Joe	26th MS Inf.	1846-1912 Tish	Alco
SCARBOROUGH, A. J.	14th MS Inf.	1834-1883 Laud	Laud
SCARBOROUGH, A. L.	Brookhaven Art.	1817-1895 Lawr	Linc
SCARBOROUGH, Abner W.	15th MS Inf.	1841-1871 Atta	Atta
SCARBOROUGH, David	3rd MS Inf.	1841-1919 MS	Harr
SCARBOROUGH, Henry	7th MS Inf.	1841-1913 Mari	Mari
SCARBOROUGH, James	3rd MS Inf.	1822-1905 Wins	Wins
SCARBOROUGH, James Allen	22nd MS Inf.	1846-1907 Lawr	Lawr
SCARBOROUGH, John	3rd MS Inf.	1836-1913 Mari	Harr
SCARBOROUGH, P. L.	Wauls TX Inf.	1841-1862 TX	Lafa

SCARBOROUGH, W.	28th MS Cav.	1837-1910	Yalo	Atta
SCARBROUGH, David G.	14th MS Inf.	1837-1911		Newt
SCARBROUGH, Harmon	Lays MS Cav.	1846-1884		Rank
SCARBROUGH, T. P.	24th MS Inf.	1840-1929	MS	Webs
SCARBROUGH, M. M.	39th MS Inf.	1841-1872	Rank	Rank
SCARBROUGH, Richard	8th MS Inf.	1839-1903	Laud	Laud
SCARBROUGH, Richard J.	8th MS Inf.	1840-1928	Clar	Laud
SCARBROUGH, William	6th MS Cav.	1836-1864	Holm	Chic
SCARBUR, Wiley S.	15th MS Inf.	1836-1906	MS	Atta
SCHAEFER, Emile	3rd MS Inf.	1839-191_	MS	Yazo
SCHALLER, J. F.		___-1862		Lown
SCHENOWITZ, Wm. Fred	7th AL Inf.	1847-1929	AL	Harr
SCHENOWITZ, Wm. Fred.	7th AL Inf.	1844-1910	AL	Harr
SCHLENOIGT, Louis	Q. M. & Hosp	1829-1881	Laud	Laud
SCHMITT, Frederic	40th MS Inf.	1842-1901	Yazo	Yazo
SCHNOWENBERG, H. N.	12th MS Inf.	1822-1884	Jeff	Linc
SCHOOLER, H. H.	14th MS Inf.	1835-1909	Clar	Harr
SCHOOLER, John K.	35th MS Inf.	1828-1882	SC	Wins
SCHROCK, Abraham	7th MS Inf.	1838-1898	GE	Linc
SCHROCK, Jonas	15th MS Inf.	1833-1902	Holm	Lefl
SCHUMAN, H.	2nd TX Inf.	1842-1862	TX	Lafa
SOITZS, C. Hilliard	33rd MS Inf.	1824-1899	Nesh	Nesh
SCOGGIN, J. M.		1846-1932	AL	Jone
SCOOT, William	1st MS Lt. Art.	1821-1875		Laud
SCOTHORNE, William B.	Conners Lt. Art.	1835-1863	Adam	Adam
SCOTT, A. J.	Adams MS Cav.	1847-1886		Tate
SCOTT, C. C.	9th MS Inf.	1846-1926		DeSo
SCOTT, Charles	28th MS Cav.	1847-1916	Hind	Boli
SCOTT, Charles	2nd MS Inf.	1811-1864	TN	Hind
SCOTT, Edward M.	18th MS Inf.	1844-1909	MS	Hind
SCOTT, Emmit R.	40th MS Inf.	1845-1930	Leak	Leak
SCOTT, Francis	1st LA Heavy Art.	1833-1863	IR	Warr
SCOTT, George	Poagues MS Art.	1838-1903	NC	Madi
SCOTT, Israel S.	10th MS Inf.	1833-1901	Adam	Adam
SCOTT, J. H. Sr.	Quitman Lt. Art.	1841-1900	Adam	Adam
SCOTT, J. R.	8th MS Inf.	1835-1891	Leak	Leak
SCOTT, J. W.	42nd MS Inf.	1829-1884	MS	Pano
SCOTT, James A.	1st MS Inf.	1841-1907	DeSo	Tate
SCOTT, Jarret	11th TX Inf.	1839-1913	TX	Alco
SCOTT, Joe B.	6th MS Inf.	1836-1903	MS	Copi
SCOTT, John	33rd MS Inf.	1827-1880	Leak	Pont
SCOTT, John A.	42nd MS Inf.	1821-1885	Tate	Tate
SCOTT, John F.	Adams MS Cav.	1832-1869	Tate	Tate
SCOTT, John M.	9th MS Inf.	1840-1916		Tate
SCOTT, John R.	3rd MS Inf.	1811-1895	Lawr	Pont
SCOTT, John W.	1st MS Lt. Art.	1836-1897	MS	Jeff
SCOTT, Milas	41st AL Inf.	1842-1911		Okti
SCOTT, R. A.	10th AL Inf.	1842-1926	AL	Tish
SCOTT, R. K.	7th MS Inf.	1842-1905	Fran	Fran
SCOTT, R. K.	7th MS Inf.	1840-1905	Copi	Copi
SCOTT, Richard Watson	1st MS Lt. Art.	1846-1901	MS	Jeff
SCOTT, Robert M.	12th MS Inf.	1841-19_		Clai

SCOTT, Robert S.	10th TX Inf.	1832-___ TX	Monr
SCOTT, Samuel L.	7th MS Inf.	1846-1902 Fran	Fran
SCOTT, T. F.	16th MS Inf.	1842-18_6	Copi
SCOTT, W. S.	1st MS Cav.	1849-1914 Wins	Wins
SCOTT, W. W. (Dr.)	18th MS Inf.	1838-1897 AL	Copi
SCOTT, William Jasper	33rd MS Inf.	1846-1918 Fran	Pike
SCOTT, William T.	1st MS Cav.	1843-1935 Kemp	Pear
SCOTT, Z. J.	36th MS Inf.	1829-1903	Copi
SCOTTHORN, Henry O.	4th LA Inf.	1841-1908 Adam	Fran
SCOVEL, Benjanin F.	27th MS Inf.	1842-1931 LA	Jack
SCREWS, Archibald	46th MS Inf.	1846-1930 Yazo	Yazo
SCRIVINER, James E.	AL Lt. Art.	1846-1935 AL	Yalo
SCRIVNER, James J.	30th MS Inf.	1845-1925 Carr	Carr
SCROGGINS, C. M.	16th GA Inf.	1836-1919	Okti
SCROGGINS, J. M.	1st MS Lt. Art.	1840-1922 Carr	Carrl
SCROGGINS, Levi W.	1st MS Lt. Art.	1844-1910 Carr	Carr
SCRUGGS, A. T.	17th MS Inf.	1845-1933 Tish	Tish
SCRUGGS, E. F.	17th AL Inf.	1824-1907 AL	Laud
SCRUGGS, _. S.	17th MS Inf.	1834-1913 AL	Harr
SCRUGGS, Isham P.	28th MS Cav.	1828-1885 Carr	Carr
SCRUGGS, J. J.	28th MS Cav.	1848-19_0	Lefl
SCRUGGS, James M.	9th MS Inf.	1835-1876 Mars	Mars
SCRUGGS, John T.	28th MS Cav.	1846-1912 Carr	Mont
SCRUGGS, Julius T.	70th NC Inf.	1845-192_ NC	Pano
SCRUGGS, W. M.	28th MS Cav.	1845-1926 Carr	Carr
SCRUGGS, William	13th MS Cav.	1837-1912	DeSo
SCRUGGS, William M.	28th MS Cav.	1846-1926	Mont
SCUDAMORE, Robert	12th MS Inf.	1842-1931 EN	Adam
SCURR, W. B.	15th MS Inf.	1837-1909 Gren	Gren
SEAB, Augustus	14th MS Inf.	1846-1933 Fran	Adam
SEABROOK, D. O.	21st AL Inf.	1837-1907 AL	Gree
SEABROOK, John Pugh	38th AL Inf.	1846-1928 AL	Wayn
SEABROOK, John P.	38th AL Inf.	1842-1927 AL	Gree
SEAL, Anthony	38th MS Cav.	1829-1903 Pear	Pear
SEAL, August	3rd MS Cav.	1845-1933 Fran	Fran
SEAL, D.	38th MS Cav.	1835-1916 Hanc	Hanc
SEAL, D. B.	38th MS Cav.	1837-1911	Hanc
SEAL, James S.	3rd MS Inf.	1836-1906 MS	Pear
SEALE, Eli	11th MS Inf.	1831-1898 Nesh	Nesh
SEALE, J. E.	40th MS Inf.	1827-1897 Nesh	Nesh
SEALE, J. M.	14th MS Cav.	1845-1931 Fran	Fran
SEALE, James	14th MS Cav.	1845-1890 Fran	Fran
SEALE, Jerry	11th MS Inf.	1833-1918 Chic	Chic
SEALE, Paschal	14th MS Cav.	1829-1913 Fran	Fran
SEALE, Robert Ewing	22nd MS	1841-1925	Pike
SEALE, T. G.	7th MS Inf.	1846-1898 Fran	Fran
SEALE, Thomas	40th MS Inf.	1827-1891 Leak	Nesh
SEALE, William B.	1st MS Lt. Art.	1840-1920 Pont	Pont
SEALS, George G.	11th MS Inf.	1837-1903 Nesh	Nesh
SEALY, B. M.	43rd MS Inf.	1837-1906	Okti
SEARCY, Irwin	26th MS Inf.	1839-1880 MS	Pren
SEARCY, William Newton	42nd MS Inf.	1843-1921 MS	Pren

SEARLES, James M.	Miles TX Inf.	1835-1916 TX	Warr
SEARS, A. H.	6th MS Cav.	1846-1909 AL	Covi
SEATON, William	1st MS Inf.		Adam
SEAVEY, Eben Edwin	Brookhaven		
	Lt. Art.	1835-1894 GA	Linc
SEDBERRY, Shadrack	20th MS Inf.	1835-191_ Scot	Scot
SEELY, A. J.	2nd MS Inf.		Monr
SEEN, F. R.	25th LA Inf.	1840-1862 LA	Chic
SEGERS, Sherman P.	39th AL Inf.	1836-1909 AL	Linc
SEITZ, W. J.	Williams AL Inf.	1846-1909 AL	Okti
SEITZLER, Joseph	1st Lt. Art.	1841-1898 Holm	Holm
SELBY, Philip	37th MS Inf.	1836-1926 MS	Pano
SELBY, T. H.	2nd MS Cav.	1841-1913 Newt	Newt
SELBY, Thomas J.	4th AL Cav.	1833-1914 AL	Tish
SELBY, William C.	35th MS Inf.	1832-1898 Kemp	Yazo
SELF, H. G.	5th Inf.	1838-1862 Chic	Chic
SELF, Reuben	58th AL Inf.	1844-1927 AL	Pont
SELLERS, Benjamin G.	6th & 37th		
	MS. Inf.	1833 1923	Copi
SELLERS, Calvin	8th MS Inf.	1828-1898 Wayn	Wayn
SELLERS, Irvine	7th MS Inf.	1827-1899 Covi	Covi
SELLERS, John A.	27th MS Inf.	1833-1922 MS	Jone
SELLERS, T. G.	48th MS Inf.	1831-1892	Okti
SELLERS, William A.	8th MS Inf.	1843-1862 MS	Smit
SELPH, Montgomery	2nd MS Inf.	1837-1917	Bent
SELSER, James E.	MontgonerysCav.	1835-1889	Hind
SEMMES, J. L.	36th Inf.	1827-1917 Laud	Laud
SEMMES, James Minor	28th MS Cav.	1837-1899 Gren	Pano
SENTER, John A.	24th MS Inf.	1831-1870 Itaw	Itaw
SERVICE, Thomas	49th CarolinaInf.	1815-1876 NC	Leak
SESSIONS, C. Columbus	21st AL Inf.	1842-1909 AL	Noxu
SESSIONS, J. F.	36th MS Inf.	1838-1896 Copi	Linc
SESSIONS, J. W.	Perrys State		
	Troops	1846-1918 Bent	Scot
SESSIONS, Joseph	18th MS Inf.	1837-1870 Adam	Holm
SESSIONS, Joseph Godfrey	36th MS Inf.	1847-1927 Linc	Linc
SESSUMS, Jacob	46th MS Inf.	1833-1909 Newt	Scot
SETTLE, J. R.	11th MS Cav.	1844-1934 Alco	Alco
SETTLE, John T.	9th MS Inf.	1827-1870 DeSo	Alco
SETTLE, T. F.	23rd MS Inf.	1834-1911 TN	Harr
SEUTER, Robert T.	24th MS Inf.	1842-1931 Itaw	Itaw
SEVIER, Henry Clay	1st MS Lt. Art.	1830-1892 Clai	Atta
SEWELL, John	41st MS Inf.	1844-1928 Pont	Pont
SAXTON, Elijah	2nd MS Cav.	1818-1905 Clar	Clar
SEXTON, John F.	1st MS Inf.	1844-1921	Copi
SEYMOUR, Henry	3rd MS Inf.	1845-1924 Jack	Jack
SEYMOUR, John	3rd MD Cav.		Jack
SEYMOUR, Moses	3rd MS Inf.	1838-1893 Jack	Jack
SEYMOUR, Samour	9th MS Cav.	1829-1911 Jack	Jack
SHACKELFORD, Dan G.	26th MS Inf.	1831-____ MS	Hind
SHACKELFORD, David H.	5th MS Inf.	1830-1865 Nesh	Nesh

Name	Unit	Dates		
SHACKELFORD, J. F.	Berrys MS Cav.	1846-1919	Laud	Laud
SHACKELFORD, James A.	5th MS Inf.	1844-1909	Carr	Carr
SHACKELFORD, W. A. H.	26th MS Inf.	181_-1902	Tish	Tish
SHACKELFORD, William M.	26th MS Inf.	1829-1914	MS	Pren
SHACKLEFORD, James M.	48th MS Inf.	1837-1912	Itaw	Lown
SHACKLEFORD, John W.	11th MS Inf.	1841-1871	Carr	Carr
SHACKLEFORD, Lee (Dr.)	Surgeon	1833-1878	Laud	Laud
SHAFFER, A. J.	35th MS Inf.	1839-1926	Clay	Clay
SHAIFER, A. K.	1st MS Lt. Art.	1833-1921	Clai	Clai
SHAMBERGER, Riley	37th MS Inf.	1821-1889		Laud
SHAMBLIN, B. _.	26th MS Inf.	1826-1906	Tish	Pren
SHAMBLIN, Lark S.	26th MS Inf.	1837-1880	MS	Pren
SHANANHAN, M. W.	9th MS Inf.	1342-1887	Mars	Tate
SHANDS, Edwin	24th MS Inf.	1833-1917	MS	Pont
SHANDS, Garvin Dugan	6th SC Cav.	1844-1917		Tate
SHANKLE, T. B.	2nd MO Cav.	1847-1911		Pano
SHANNON, Columbus F.	6th MS Inf.	1845-1911	Laud	Laud
SHANNON, George Wash.	19th MS Cav.	1845-1923	Yalo	Yalo
SHANNON, Henry J.	38th MS Cav.	1843-1910	Clai	Linc
SHANNON, John	MS Cav.	1836-1901	Laud	Laud
SHANNON, Moses M.	34th AL Inf.	1820-1910	AL	Scot
SHANNON, William H.	Q. M. Corps	1840-1923	Laud	Laud
SHARKEY, Greenwood	5th & 28th MS Cav.	1829-1873	Yalo	Tall
SHARKEY, H. Clay	3rd & 18th MS Inf.	1844-1934		Hind
SHARP, Allen	22nd MS Inf.	1836-1882	Lawr	Lawr
SHARP, D. H.	23rd MS Cav.	1849-1936	Amit	Amit
SHARP, Eli	7th MS Inf.	1844-1925	Scot	Leak
SHARP, F. M.	5th MS Inf.	1831-1894	AL	Wins
SHARO, H. E.	1st MO Inf.	1828-1862	MO	Chic
SHARP, Henry C.	5th MS Cav.	1842-1917	Laud	Laud
SHARP, Hines	10th MS Cav.	1836-1880		Amit
SHARP, Hugh	5th MS Inf.	1844-190	Laud	Laud
SHARP, John F.	5th MS Inf.	1826-1906	AL	Wins
SHARP, J. W.	43rd MS Inf.	1844-1921		Okti
SHARP, J. W.	16th MS Cav.	1845-1916	Chic	Lown
SHARP, Jacob H.	43rd MS Inf.	1833-1907	Lown	Lown
SHARP John F.	28th MS Cav.	____-1920		Scot
SHARP, Joseph H.	4th AL Cav.	1844-1927	AL	Tate
SHARP, Martin Demore	26th MS Inf.	1841-1906	Tish	Tish
SHARP, Sam	31st TN Inf.	1838-1906	TN	Alco
SHARP, Thomas I.	10th MS Inf.	1847-1911	Lown	Lown
SHARP, Tom Jeff ▪	31st TN Inf.	1845-1923	TN	Alco
SHARP, W. L.	35th MS Inf.	1823-1906	Nesh	
SHARP, W. M.	28th MS Cav.	1835-1908		Scot
SHARPE, F. M.	MS Inf.	1847-19__		Harr
SHARPE, George Hind	Powers MS Cav.	1837-1929	MS	Jack
SHAW, B. B.	9th TN Inf.	1845-1930	TN	Alco
SHAW, Daniel A.	3rd MS Regt.	1829-1909		Rank
SHAW, F. M.	19th MS Inf.	1837-1913	Mars	Mars
SHAW, George Patrick	56th AL Cav.	1839-1915	AL	Wayn

Name	Unit	Dates		
SHAW, H. W.	29th MS Inf.	1835-1909 DeSo	Tate
SHAW, J. D. (Rev.)	2nd MS Cav.	1833-1866	Boli
SHAW, J. D.	5th MS Cav.	1846-1910 Carr	Carr
SHAW, John M.	29th MS Inf.	1823-1905 Yalo	Yalo
SHAW, John Morgan	29th MS Inf.	1819-1908 MS	Yalo
SHAW, John R.	33rd MS Inf.	1835-1929	Webs
SHAW, Robert N.	11th MS Inf.	1839-1878 Noxu	Noxu
SHAW, W. L.	10th MS Inf.	1843-1915 Lee	Adam
SHAW, W. M.	8th MS Inf.	1835-1906 Newt	Nesh
SHAW, William	30th MS Inf.	1833-1918 Carr	Mont
SHAW, Willis Jesse	2nd MS Inf.	1834-1905 MS	Pont
SHAWKS, J. J. (Rev.)	4th MS Inf.	1842-1916 Holm	Harr
SHEYS, D. H.	23rd MS Cav.	1849-1936 Amit	Amit
SHEALY, John	48th MS Inf.	1843-1915 Warr	Copi
SHEARER, P. W.	3rd & 45th MS Inf.	1837-1926 AL	Lefl
SHEARER, Phares Waldo	45th MS Inf.	1837-1926 MS	Warr
SHEARER, Thomas N.	1st AL Inf.	1844-1924 AL	Okti
SHEARMAN, N. _.	2nd MS Cav.	1830-1904 Jasp	Jone
SHEDD, C/G. W.	13th MS Inf.	1843-1909 AL	Harr
SHEDD, George	13th MS Inf.	1836-1898 MS	Laud
SHEDD, T. A.	20th AL Inf.	1841-1918	Rank
SHEDD, W. H.	41st MS Inf.	1845-1900 Laud	Nesh
SHEEGOG, James Gowen	11th MS Inf.	1836-18_9 TN	Lafa
SHEEL, James D.	11th MS Inf.	1839-1912 SC	Monr
SHEELEY, Thomas C.	8th MS Inf.	1832-1916 Jasp	Newt
SHEELY, J. C.	4th MS Cav.	18_5-1920	Rank
SHEELY, William H. M.	8th MS Inf.	1841-192_ Jasp	Newt
SHEELY, William W.	27th MS Inf.	1843-1907 Linc	Tall
SHEFFIELD, F.	2nd MS Cav.	1845-1940 Calh	Calh
SHEFFIELD, G. F.	3rd LA Inf.	1841-1862 LA	Lafa
SHEFFIELD, W. M.	28th AL	1819-1902 AL	Itaw
SHEFFIELD, William M.	30th AL Inf.	1841-1916 AL	Itaw
SHEFFIELD, William S.	11th MS Cav.	1847-1926	Itaw
SHELBURN, James P.	37th MS Inf.	1832-1905 EN	Laud
SHELBY, B. M.	16th MS Cav.	1821-1903 FL	Holm
SHELBY, William L.	3rd MS Inf.	1848-1923	Laud
SHELBY, Winchester	39th Inf.	1827-1873 TN	Rank
SHELEY, A. C. N.	21st MS Inf.	1834-1882 Tall	Tall
SHELL, John J.	12th MS Cav.	1823-1887 SC	Monr
SHELL, Morgan	31st MS Inf.	183_-18_9 Chic	Chic
SHELL, P. W.	MS Inf.	1841-1924 MS	Chic
SHELLEY, Anderson	24th MS Cav.	1845-1913 Atta	Atta
SHELLEY, Thomas W.		1819-1864 KY	Adam
SHELTON, D. T.	31st MS Inf.	1828-1903 MS	Pont
SHELTON, David J.	21st MS Inf.	1842-1924 Wilk	Adam
SHELTON, Elijah A.	17th MS Inf.	1833-1893	DeSo
SHELTON, George D.	37th MS Inf.	1842-1899 AL	Warr
SHELTON, George William	1st MS Cav.	1821-1867	Rank
SHELTON, Jacob L.	11th MS Inf.	1827-1891 Pont	Unio
SHELTON, James	1st & 3rd MS Cav.	____-1884	Hind

104

Name	Unit	Dates/Place	County
SHELTON, John L.	33rd MS Inf.	1835-1891 Pont	Unio
SHELTON, Samuel Mosby	12th MS Inf.	1837-1908 VA	Warr
SHELTON, Thomas P.	31st MS Inf.	1834-1882 MS	Pont
SHELTON, Whitten	2nd MS Cav.	1826-1907 Laud	Lee
SHELTON, Willis	23rd MS Inf.	1843-1907 Tipp	Tipp
SHEPARD, Joseph H.	5th MS Inf.	1845-1932 MS	Kemp
SHEPHARD, Benj. Frank.	32nd MS Inf.	1843-1923 Pren	Pren
SHEPHEARD, Littlen J.	36th AL Inf.	1832-1906 Gree	Geor
SHEPHERD, Anderson	11th MS Cav.	1845-1878 MS	Kemp
SHEPHERD, D. W.	11th MS Cav.	1847-1904 MS	Kemp
SHEPHERD, Isaac	15th MS Inf.	Calh	Calh
SHEPHERD, James M.	4th MS Cav.	1848-1933	Yalo
SHEPHERD, Jerry D.	4th MS Inf.	1837-1926 Calh	Calh
SHEPHERD, _. _.	28th MS Cav.	1837-1889	Leak
SHEPHERD, Richard B.	Drews LA Cav.	1839-1878 Wilk	Wilk
SHEPHERD, Thomas	37th MS Inf.	1833-1903 Clar	Clar
SHEPHERD, Thomas Henry		1850-1934 Kemp	Holm
SHEPPARD, A. D.	Jeff Davis Cav.	1834-1907 MS	Harr
SHEPPARD, F. M.	3rd MO Inf.	1844-1923 MO	Webs
SHEPPARD, Robert Clayton	1st MS Lt. Art.	1835-1892 Yazo	Yazo
SHEPPARD, W. A.	6th MS Inf.	1840-190_	Rank
SHEPPERD, John	36th MS Inf.	1820-___ Gree	Geor
SHERBET, S. D.	1st AL Res.	1846-1921 AL	Monr
SHERMAN, Elijah	11th MS Cav.	1826-1892 Okti	Okti
SHERMAN, John Lewis	11th MS Inf.	1839-1894 Okti	Okti
SHERMAN, John W.	Woods Cav.	1846-1925 MS	Simp
SHERMAN, William	42nd MS Inf.	1836-1914 AL	Calh
SHERROD, George	1st MS Cav.	1832-1887 Noxu	Noxu
SHERROUSE, C. M.	AL Inf.	1845-1935 LA	Harr
SHETTLES, D. P.	2nd MS Inf.	1841-1923 Pont	Pont
SHETTLES, _. W.	5th MS Regt.	1844-1863 Wins	Pont
SHEWMAKE, Carroll	33rd MS Inf.	1837-1914 Choc	Webs
(SHEYS located after SHAWKS)			
SHIELD, J. S.	40th MS Inf.	1833-1906	Laud
SHIELD, James Surget	Forrests Cav.	1847-1909 Adam	Adam
SHIELDS, Bisland	Jeff Davis Cav.	1838-1911	Jeff
SHIELDS, Charles Lee		1846-1872 LA	Adam
SHIELDS, F. H.	5th MS Inf.	1846-1912 MS	Atta
SHIELDS, James H.	6th MS Inf.	1831-1909	Rank
SHIELDS, John R.	43rd MS Inf.	1847-1895	Hind
SHIELDS, Richard	6th MS Inf.	1829-1889	Rank
SHIELDS, Robert Andrew	33rd MS Inf.	1828-1905 Pano	Pano
SHIELDS, Samuel J.	11th MS Inf.	1838-1921 MS	Lown
SHIELDS, Thomas R. Jr.	28th MS Cav.	1833-1873	Jeff
SHIELDS, William	11th MS Inf.	1835-1912 Lown	Lown
SHIELDS, Wilmer	Navy	1817-1879 LA	Adam
SHILLING, I. N.	16th Cav.	1837-1925 Pren	Unio
SHINAULT, J. L.	Adams MS Cav.	18_3-1929 Mars	Mars
SHINAULT, J. L.	1st MS Cav.	1832-191_ Lafa	Lafa
SHINE, E. C.	4th Inf.	1843-1917 Holm	Holm
SHINE, John T.	29th MS Inf.	1811-1873 Holm	Holm

SHINGLEUR, James A.	Gen. Frenchs Aide	1839-1895	SC	Hind
SHINN, C. M.	1st MS Cav.	1846-1927	MS	Pano
SHINNALL, S. B.	23rd MS Inf.	1844-1921	GA	Tipp
SHINPACK, William H.	Blythes MS Cav.	1826-1890	DeSoto	
SHIPP, C. W.	1st MS Inf.	1842-1903	Lafa	Lafa
SHIPP, D.	Houghs MS Cav.			Copi
SHIPP, Joe		1842-1917	Holm	
SHIPP, Samuel S.	9th MS Inf.	1843-1906	Lafa	Yazo
SHIRLEY, W. W.	37th MS Inf.	1830-1907	Clar	Clar
SHIVER, Oliver W.	4th MS Cav.	1824-1885	Carr	Lefl
SHIVERS, James E.	18th MS Inf.	1844-1927	MS	Madi
SHIVERS, James McLaurin	4th AL Inf.	1843-1922	Perr	Pear
SHOCKLEY, Thonas H.	13th MS Inf.	1843-1924	Nesh	Newt
SHOEMAKE, _.	46th MS Inf.	____-1915	Covi	Covi
SHOEMAKER, Derias	16th MS Inf.	1844-1862	Jasp	Jasp
SHOEMAKER, Henry Clay	4th MS Inf.	1847-19_9	Leak	Holm
SHOEMAKER, J. A. J.	37th AR Inf.			Leak
SHOEMAKER, Farmer	16th MS Inf.	1840-1862	Jasp	
SHOEMAKER, P.	23rd AL Art.	1839-1904	AL	Wayn
SHOFFNER, Jacob	18th MS Inf.	1837-1880	MS	Bent
SHONE, Joseph A.	2nd MS Inf.	1828-1897	Tipp	Bent
SHOOK, C. C.	26th MS Inf.	1846-1913	Tish	Tish
SHOOK, Michael	1st AL Cav.	1834-1904	Tish	Tish
SHOOK, Noah	42nd MS Inf.	1840-1932	Yalo	Tall
SHORES, C. C.	21st MS Inf.	1839-1911	MS	Harr
SHORES, Joseph D.	6th FL Inf.	1843-1915	FL	Covi
SHORES, Moses Bonner	8th TN Inf.	1838-1878	TN	Tall
SHORT, Albert L.	17th MS Inf.	1839-1915	MS	Pren
SHORT, E. T.	42nd MS Inf.	1836-1912	MS	Noxu
SHORT, Edward F.	38th MS Cav.	1846-1888	Clai	Jeff
SHORT, Hezekiah	38th MS Cav.	1820-1900	Clai	Jeff
SHORT, John T.	34th MS Inf.	1842-1918	Lafa	Pont
SHORT, Thomas	7th MS Inf.	1830-1912	Covi	Covi
SHORT, William H.	12th MS Inf.	1840-1910	Holm	Pano
SHOTTS, David H.	5th MS Inf.	1842-1921	Kemp	Kemp
SHOTTS, H. I.	20th MS Inf.	1845-1914	Newt	Newt
SHOTWELL, Bour_on Sr.	1st MS Lt. Art.	1829-1883		Hind
SHOTWELL, Ruben	21st MS Inf.	1842-1911	MS	Quit
SHOWS, J. H.	7th MS Inf.	1825-1892	Jone	Jone
SHOWS, J. J.	7th MS Inf.	1830-1882	Jone	Jone
SHOWS, John P.	24th Cav.	1824-1899	Wayn	Wayn
SHOWS, Norwell R.	39th MS Inf.	1839-1862	Simp	Lawr
SHOWS, William Irvine	8th MS Inf.	1836-1899	Simp	Simp
SHRADER, A. J.	1st KY Cav.	1838-1927	KY	Linc
SHRADER, James A. C.	24th AL Inf.	1833-1909	AL	Shar
SHROCK, J. C.				Lown
SHROSHIRE, Jack	38th MS Cav.	1835-1928	Wilk	Wilk
SHROPSHIRE, Robert A.	62nd AL Inf.	1846-1885		Okti
SHROPSHIRE, Robert D.	14th MS Inf.			Lown
SHUFORD, Franklin B.	VA Hospital	1820-1891	Mars	Mars
SHUFORD, Thomas Selwyn	33rd MS Inf.	1845-1919	MS	Coah

106

SHUMAKER, Henry C.	35th MS Inf.	1833-1917 Atta	Wins
SHUMAKER, J. M.	40th MS Inf.	1847-1934 Nesh	Nesh
SHUMAKER, P. B.	4th MS Inf.	1838-1922 Atta	Wins
SHUMATE, _. M.	11th MS Cav.	1846-1893 Tall	Kemp
SHUMATE, James Taylor	35th MS Inf.	1843-1880 Kemp	Kemp
SHUMATE, John E.	5th MS Cav.	1844-1928 Carr	Carr
SHUMATE, John Edward	5th MS Cav.	1844-1928 Carr	Lefl
SHUMATE, P. L.	Stanfords Lt. Art.	1838-1885 Yalo	Gren
SHUMBERT, W. I.	43rd MS Inf.	1838-1926 Lee	Lee
SHURDEN, John E.	35th MS Inf.	1845-1900 Okti	Okti
SHURLDS, Henry	1st MS Inf.	1827-1887	Hind
SHURLDS, Robert	Smyths Cav.	1834-1892	Hind
SHURLEY, J. R.	3rd MS Inf.	1842-1925 Yazo	Yazo
SHUTE, Elihu	1st SC Inf.	1836-1878 SC	Carr
SHUTE, Sylvester	30th MS Inf.	1829-1914 Carr	Carr
SHUTTLESWORTH, R. F.	10th AL Art.	1837-1898 AL	Atta
SIBLEY, G. W.	6th GA Inf.	1843-1921 GA	Pont
SIBLEY, Horace	46th MS Inf.	1840-1910 Warr	Warr
SIBLEY, J. _.	28th MS Cav.	1825-1891 VA	Mont
SIDDON, J. D.	1st MS Lt. Art.	1826-1881 SC	Holm
SIDDON, S. J.	Lomax Lt. Art.	1847-1911 Holm	Holm
SIDE, Mose	18th AR Inf.	1834-1908 AR	Holm
SIDES, Tobias	Blacksmith	1824-195 NC	Mars
SIEBE, Henry T.	36th MS Inf.	1841-1862	Copi
SIEBE, James G.	6th MS Inf.	1836-1914	Copi
SIGMAN, John Bernard	7th TN Cav.	1830-1896 TN	Mars
SIGREST, Charles	Brookhaven Lt. Art.	1846-1917 Scot	Scot
SIGREST, M. V.	Brookhaven Lt. Art.	1842-1905 Scot	Scot
SIGREST, Meloy Ganes	20th MS Inf.	1841-1910	Rank
SIKES, A. J.	48th MS Inf.	1839-1917 Okti	Okti
SIKES, C. S.	48th MS Inf.	1837-1890 Okti	Okti
SIKES, James	16th MS Inf.	1833-1893 Simp	Simp
SIKES, Jason	33rd MS Inf.	1825-1906 Nesh	Nesh
SIKES, Richard W.	48th MS Inf.	1833-1896 MS	Okti
SILLERS, Joseph	Montgomerys State Troops	1824-1865 Boli	Boli
SIMMONS, B.	39th MS Inf.	1844-1920	Copi
SIMMONS, B. F.	27th MS Inf.	1835-1908 Perr	Forr
SIMMONS, Caswell	17th MS Inf.	1827-1892 Unio	Unio
SIMMONS, Cyrus S.	7th MS Inf.	1841-1920 MS	Walt
SIMMONS, D. W.	6th MS Inf.	1838-1904	Copi
SIMMONS, David	6th MS Inf.	1824-1880	Hind
SIMMONS, David W.	6th & 15th MS Inf.		Hind
SIMMONS, _. _.	33rd MS Inf.	1821-1871 Nesh	Laud
SIMMONS, G. B/H.	13th MS Inf.	1830-1909 Laud	Laud
SIMMONS, G. B/H.	23rd MS Inf.	1843-1924 Laud	Laud
SIMMONS, G. W.	14th & 48th MS Inf.	1841-____ AL	Clay
SIMMONS, George W.	2nd MS Inf.	1831-1898	Copi

SIMMONS, Henry G.	7th MS Inf.	1827-1915	Pren
SIMMONS, Henry L.	29th MS Inf.	1823-1894 MS	
SIMMONS, J. E/H.	33rd MS Inf.	1835-1905 Nesh	Laud
SIMMONS, J. J.	39th MS Inf.	1836-1922 MS	Pike
SIMMONS, J. J.	2nd MS Inf.	1838-1906	Pont
SIMMONS, J. M.	4th MS Cav.	1824-1905 Copi	Pike
SIMMONS, James M.	4th MS Cav.	____-1913 MS	Pike
SIMMONS, J. W.	17th MS Inf.	1840-1920 GA	Lama
SIMMONS, James	5th MS Inf.	1828-1892	Pren
SIMMONS, James	38th MS Cav.	1832-1930 Pike	Walt
SIMMONS, James	6th MS Cav.	1845-1900 MS	Alco
SIMMONS, James E.	18th LA Inf.	1842-1916 LA	Walt
SIMMONS, James L.	21st MS Inf.	1822-1904 Tall	Laud
SIMMONS, James L.	21st MS Inf.	1840-1925 Yalo	Coah
SIMMONS, James W.	6th MS Inf.	1831-1865	Jasp
SIMMONS, John D.	38th MS Cav.	1840-1903 MS	Walt
SIMMONS, Sam A.	24th MS Cav.	1845-1915	Jeff
SIMMONS, Thomas	40th AL Inf.	1816-____ AL	Laud
SIMMONS, W. A.	26th MS Inf.	1836-1914 SC	Monr
SIMMONS, W. H.	40th AL Inf.	1841-1935 AL	Scot
SIMMONS, Wm. C.	13th MS Reg.	1842-1920 Laud	Laud
SIMMONS, W. R.	38th MS Cav.	1821-1904 Pike	Pike
SIMMONS, William	11th NC Inf.	1835-1905 VA	Harr
SIMMONS, William	13th MS Inf.		Hind
SIMMONS, William W.	6th MS Inf.	1843-1924 Copi	Amit
SIMPSON, Allen J.	40th MS Inf.	1844-1909 Leak	Leak
SIMPSON, Arrington W.	AL Cav.	1834-1904 AL	Laud
SIMPSON, Charles N.	3rd MS Inf.		Monr
SIMPSON, Charles Thomas	31st MS Inf.	Choc	Choc
SIMPSON, George A.	2nd MS Inf.	1829-1905 Pont	Pont
SIMPSON, George _.	15th MS Inf.	1839-1862 SC	Mont
SIMPSON, John _.	1st MS Lt. Art.	1836-1912 SC	Mont
SIMPSON, John Calhoun	41st MS Inf.	1843-1938 Pont	Bent
SIMPSON, James	Adams MS Cav.	1842-1916 Madi	Madi
SIMPSON, Malakiah	1st MS Inf.	1818-1893	Leak
SIMPSON, Robt. W.	18th MS Inf.	1834-1876 Madi	
SIMPSON, Sidney Smith	18th MS Inf.	1846-1928 MS	Madi
SIMPSON, T. B.	21st MS Inf.	1839-1924 Unio	Unio
SIMRALL, G. H.	16th MS Inf.	1845-1911 Wilk	Warr
SIMRALL, G. M.	1st MS Cav.	1844-1919 Warr	Warr
SIMS, Augustus (Dr.)	20th MS Inf.	1832-1892 Scot	Scot
(SIMS, B. C. located after SISSON)			
SIMS, B. D.	27th MS Inf.	1830-1911	Okti
SIMS, Benjanin Calhoun	9th & 12th MS Cav.	1845-1910 Monr	Monr
SIMS, Drew	46th MS Inf.	1844-1923	Scot
SIMS, G. R.	5th AL Inf.	1842-1932 AL	Itaw
SIMS, G. R.	39th MS Inf.	1843-1916 Newt	Newt
SIMS, J. C.	43rd MS Inf.	1839-1912 Monr	Lee
SIMS, J. H.	46th MS Inf.	____-1938	Scot
SIMS, J. J.	1st MS Lt. Art.	1835-1884 Yazo	Yazo
SIMS, James	17th MS Inf.	1816-1903 Mars	Mars

SIMS, John D.	39th MS Inf.	1832-1904 Newt	Newt
SIMS, John M.	12th MS Inf.	1835-1886 Linc	Lawr
SIMS, Lyergus	31st MS Inf.	1831-1865 Chic	Chic
SIMS, Miles	7th MS Inf.	1838-1916 Jone	Jone
SIMS, P. H/H.	11th MS Inf.	1836-1862 Chic	Chic
SIMS, S. W.	26th MS Inf.	1834-1911 AL	Lafa
SIMS, Stanton	38th MS Cav.	1834-1881 Wilk	Wilk
SIMS, W. A.	2nd MS Cav.	1846-1917 MS	Laud
SIMS, W. J.	1st MS Inf.	1838-1908 Itaw	Itaw
SIMS, W. J.	13th MS Inf.	1839-1910 Laud	Laud
SIMS, W. T.	Scotts LA Cav.	1847-1928 LA	Wilk
SIMS, William W.	6th MS Inf.	1833-1899	
SINCLAIR, Alexander H.	18th MS Inf.	1838-1881 SC	Rank
SINCLAIR, Charles L.	24th MS Inf.	1831-18_1 Kemp	Kemp
SING, W. J.	22nd MS Inf.	1832-1915 DeSo	Harr
SING, Will J.	22nd MS Inf.	____-1934	DeSo
SINGLAR, Thomas J.	4th AL Inf.	183_-1917 AL	Laud
SINGLETARY, Daniel	3rd MS Inf.	1818-1897	Rank
SINGLETARY, Francis	39th MS Inf.	1828-1889	Rank
SINGLETON, O. R.	18th MS Inf.	1814-1889 Madi	Madi
SINGLETARY, Thomas	6th MS Inf.	1836-1909	Rank
SINGLETARY, Thomas M.	Lays MS Cav.	1848-1934 MS	Jeff
SISK, A. T.	3rd MS Inf.	1817-1879 Nesh	Monr
SISK, William A.	22nd MS Inf.	1844-1911 Monr	Chic
SISLOFF, Henry	3rd MS Inf.	1818-1893 Lefl	Leflo
SISSON, C. A.	2nd MS Cav.	1845-1904 Pont	Atta
SISSON, J.(Dr.)	14th MS Inf.	1836-1918 Wins	Nesh
SISSON, William E.	2nd MS Cav.	1840-1878 MS	Newt
SIMS, B. C.	11th MS Inf.	1839-1862 Chic	Chic
SISTRUNK, D. W.	4th MS Cav.	1843-1922 Lawr	Lawr
SISTRUNK, George W.	36th MS Inf.	1827-1889	Copi
SISTRUNK, Nicholas	38th MS Cav.	1847-1905 Lawr	Lawr
SISTRUNK, W. M.	40th MS Inf.	1844-1907 Leak	Leak
SISTRUNK, William W.	1st MS Inf.	1822-1890 MS	Lama
SITTON, W. M.	4th AL Inf.	1844-1896 AL	Alco
SIVILS, Balus Darls	6th MS Inf.	1824-1884 Leak	Leak
SIVLEY, William Rufus	3rd MS Inf.	1843-1895	Hind
SKEAHAN, Thomas H.	5th MO Inf.	1840-1875 Linc	Linc
SKELTON, William B.	31st MS Inf.	1815-1894 Choc	Webs
SKELTON, William	37th MS Inf.	1837-1911 MS	Laud
SKIFFINGTON, M. L.	22nd MS Inf.	1828-1868 IR	Warr
SKINNER, E. L.	13th MS Inf.	1838-1883 Kemp	Kemp
SKINNER, Emanuel G.	36th MS Inf.	____-1903	Newt
SKINNER, Enoch	26th MS Inf.	1843-1926 Pont	Unio
SKINNER, Frederick	22nd MS Inf.	1833-1884 EN	Jeff
SKINNER, Joshua	28th MS Cav.	1847-1915 NC	Wash
SKINNER, Richard L.	31st MS Inf.	1838-1910 Pont	Pont
SKINNER, W. F.	4th MS Inf.	1833-1923 Carr	Mont
SKINNER, W. H.	7th AL Cav.	1846-1917 AL	Tish
SKINNER, W. M.	7th AL Cav.	1840-1914 AL	Tish
SKINNER, William D.	37th MS Inf.	1839-1884 Clar	Laud
SKINNER, Young	24th MS Inf.	1818-18_9 Chic	Chic

SKIPPER, J. W.	1st MS Cav.	1838-1890 Kemp	Kemp
SKIPPER, Z. L.	23rd AL Inf.	1843-1935 AL	Forr
SKIPWOHTH, Nathaniel G.	1st MS Lt. Art.	1848-1913 Issa	Hind
SLADE, Charles	7th MS Inf.	1832-1905 MS	Lama
SLADE, Daniel	7th MS Inf.	1830-1899 Mari	Lama
SLADE, John J.	1st MS Inf.	1832-1910 GA	Pike
SLADE, S. _.	7th MS Inf.	1843-1916 Mari	Lama
SLADE, William	21st MS Inf.	1845-1930 Mari	Lama
SLATON, U. W.	7th MS Inf.	1827-1891	Wayn
SLATER, George W.	8th MS Inf.	1848-1910 Warr	Warr
SLATON, Augustus M.	35th MS Inf.	1830-1865 Kemp	Kemp
SLATON, James R. (Dr.)	32nd GA Inf.	1835-1889 GA	Tate
SLAUGHTER, Thomas Jack.	2nd MS Cav.	1841-1916 MS	Wayn
SLAUGHTER, William A.	30th MS Inf.	1826-1885	Laud
SLAVEN, Charles	28th MS Cav.	1831-1885 Carr	Carr
SLAWSON, William	2nd MS Cav.	1824-1888 Wins	Wins
SLAY, A. D.	16th or 18th MS Inf.	1848-1921	Copi
SLAY, Alex Jr.	40th MS Inf.	1831-1866	Copi
SLAY, Erasmus	1st MS Cav.	1826-1884	Copi
SLAY, James	36th AL Inf.	1848-1925 AL	Gree
SLAY, James K.	Powells State Troops	1847-1927 Lama	Lama
SLAY, Leonidas	Powers MS Cav.	1846-1868	Copi
SLAY, N.	16th MS Inf.	1836-1907	Copi
SLAY, N. W.	6th MS Inf.	1830-1889	Copi
SLAY, T. J. Sr.	Powers MS Cav.	1847-1885	Copi
SLAYTON, Oliver H. P.	32nd GA Inf.	1832-1917 GA	Tate
SLEDGE, George William	Stanfords Lt.Art.	1841-1919 Carr	Mont
SLEDGE, Norfleet Ruffin	28th MS Cav.	1839-1910 Yalo	Pano
SLEDGE, Oliver D.	1st MS Cav.	1840-1909 Carr	Pano
SLIGH, H. T.	30th AL Inf.	1843-1932 AL	Chic
SLOAN, John N.	45th MS Inf.	1829-1897 Pont	Pont
SLOAN, Theodore Bolivar	21st MS Inf.	1830-1917 SC	Unio
SLOAN, W. R.	18th MS Cav.	1845-1923	Lafa
SLOUGH, John Nelson	3rd MS Inf.	1847-1915 Yazo	Lafa
SMALL, George W.	6th MS Cav.	1841-1883 MS	Alco
SMALL, H. J. (Dr.)	1st MS Cav.	1836-1916 Carr	Mont
SMALL, James F.	6th MS Cav.	1838-1894 MS	Alco
SMALLWOOD, A. A.	Woods MS Cav.	1847-1918	Rank
SMALLWOOD, W. T.	1st Cav.	1846-1897 Unio	Unio
SMART, A.	1st MS Inf.	1836-190_ Adam	Adam
SMEDES, Thonas Marshall	21st MS Inf.	1843-1908 Warr	Warr
SMILEY, John M.	24th MS Cav.	1828-1922	Wayn
SMILEY, Jim	33rd MS Inf.	1845-1909 Amit	Amit
SMILEY, Nathaniel F.	33rd MS Inf.	1842-1922 Amit	Amit
SMITH, A. C.	15th MS Inf.	1830-1912	Webs
SMITH, A. J.	42nd AL Inf.	1833-1904 AL	Jone
SMITH, A. J.	13th TN Inf.	1830-1901 TN	Bent
SMITH, A. J.	3rd MS Inf.	1833-1903	Warr
SMITH, A. M.	35th MS Inf.	1831-1897 MS	Newt
SMITH, A. R.	2nd MO Inf.	1838-1921 MO	Yalo

SMITH, A. S. (Dr.)	4th MS Cav.	1848-1921	Pike	Pike
SMITH, A. U. (Dr.)	46th GA Cav.	1815-1895	GA	Laud
SMITH, A. W.	33rd MS Inf.	1844-1929	Linc	Linc
SMITH, A. W.	4th LA Inf.	1844-1908	MS	Adam
SMITH, Abner	17th MS Inf.	1804-1879	Chic	Chic
SMITH, Albert S.	16th VA Inf.	1842-1919		Lafa
SMITH, Alexander	1st MS Lt. Art.	1812-1883	Yazo	Yazo
SMITH, Alford	4th AL Art.	1823-1889	FL	Geor
SMITH, Allen H.	33rd MS Inf.	1841-1923	Linc	Linc
SMITH, Allen W.	33rd MS Inf.	1831-1905	Linc	Linc
SMITH, Alvin W.	39th MS Inf.		Simp	Simp
SMITH, Andrew J.	3rd MS Inf.	1842-1911		Pear
SMITH, Andrew J.	29th MS Inf.	1815-1886		DeSo
SMITH, Andrew J.	13th MS Inf.	1828-1913	AL	Newt
SMITH, Andrew Jackson	3rd MS Inf.	183_-1900	Jasp	Jasp
SMITH, Angus W.	1st MS Lt. Art.	1843-1928	Jeff	Jeff
SMITH, Archie	39th MS			Rank
SMITH, Archie E.	39th MS Inf.			Simp
SMITH, Archibald	1st MS Lt. Art.	1843-1913	Jone	Jone
SMITH, Augustus M.	4th MS Cav.	1838-1915	MS	Copi
SMITH, Austin W.	4th LA Inf.		Adam	Adam
SMITH, B. A.	6th MS Inf.	1834-1910		Copi
SMITH, B. B.	5th MS Inf.	1818-1882	Laud	Laud
SMITH, B. F.	40th MS Inf.	1845-1932	Jone	Jone
SMITH, Barney	11th & 36th MS Inf.	____-1896		Simp
SMITH, Ben	40th MS Inf.			Leak
SMITH, Benjamin Frank.	5th MS Cav.	1846-1910	NC	Mont
SMITH, Henj. Lafayette	14th & 43rd MS Inf.	1842-1933	Lown	Clay
SMITH, Benj. Lankford	5th MS Inf.	1833-1912	Laud	Lama
SMITH, Benjamin M.	40th MS Inf.	1830-1905	Laud	Nesh
SMITH, Berry	32nd MS Inf.	1834-1909	Tipp	Tipp
SMITH, Brantley H.	33rd MS Inf.	1835-1919	Linc	Linc
SMITH, Britton	2nd FL Reg.	1800-1866	FL	Holm
SMITH, Byron	1st GA Cav.	1843-19_6	GA	Amit
SMITH, C. C.	7th MS Inf.	1842-1922	Amit	Amit
SMITH, C. C.	12th MS Inf.	1842-1917	Laud	Laud
SMITH, C. P.	33rd MS Inf.	1835-1909	Linc	Linc
SMITH, C. S.	18th MS Cav.	1846-1930		Pear
SMITH, Calvin	26th MS Inf.	1834-1920	Tish	Alco
SMITH, Calvin J.	9th MS Inf.	1840-1894		Mars
SMITH, Canvas	7th MS Inf.	1837-1914	Clar	Clar
SMITH, Carroll S.	Poagues MS Art.	1842-1903		Madi
SMITH, Charles M.	Woods MS Cav.	1838-1910	Covi	JEDA
SMITH, Christopher R.	Adams Cav.	1832-1903		Copi
SMITH, D. B.	4th MS Cav.		Tish	Alco
SMITH, D. H.	2nd MS Cav.	1847-1925	SC	Monr
SMITH, D. O.	Inf.	1849-1905	MS	Rank
SMITH, D. P.	27th MS Inf.	1839-1927	MS	Jone
SMITH, D. W.	28th MS Cav.	1830-1894	MS	Walt
SMITH, Daniel	39th MS Inf.		Simp	Simp

111

SMITH, Daniel	9th MS Inf.	1828-1900	Lafa	Lafa
SMITH, Daniel F.	37th MS Inf.	1840-1898	Jone	Jone
SMITH, Dave	15th MS Inf.	1836-1910	Atta	Atta
SMITH, David	7th MS Inf.	1837-1909	Clar	Laud
SMITH, E. C.	41st MS Inf.	1828-1907	AL	Monr
SMITH, E. J.	24th MS Cav.	____-1911		Clai
SMITH, E. T.	33rd MS Inf.	1833-1918	Amit	Amit
SMITH, Edward	1st MS Inf.	1817-1887		Hind
SMITH, Edward	3rd MS Inf.	1834-1912	!Hanc	Pear
SMITH, Edward Earl	31st MS Inf.	1818-1897	Chic	Chic
SMITH, Edward W. (Dr.)	15th MS Inf.	1829-1880	Choc	Yalo
SMITH, Elder R. A.	6th & 36th MS Inf.	1835-1937		Newt
SMITH, Elihah	12th MS Cav.	1842-1902	NC	Pren
SMITH, Elijah G.	37th MS Inf.	____-1888		Coah
SMITH, Enoch Harry	6th MS Cav.	1836-1907	MS	Alco
SMITH, Enoch Hunt	29th MS Inf.	1823-1896	VA	Gree
SMITH, Ephram H.	23rd MS Inf.	1827-1864	SC	Tipp
SMITH, F. M.	2nd MS Inf.	1840-1919		Unio
SMITH, F. S.	43rd MS Inf.	1838-1902	MS	Kemp
SMITH, F. Q.	16th & 35th MS Inf.	1835-1919		Sunf
SMITH, Fred P.	4th & 41st MS Inf.	1844-1920	GA	Pren
SMITH, G. B.	40th MS Inf.	1822-1894	Laud	Nesh
SMITH, G. N.	19th MS Inf.	1840-1913	MS	Lown
SMITH, G. W.	15th MS Inf.	1840-1904	Choc	Choc
SMITH, G. Albert	14th MS Lt. Art.	1846-1935		Copi
SMITH, George	16th MS Inf.	1840-1921	MS	Walt
SMITH, George R.	36th AL Inf.	1840-1894	AL	Wayn
SMITH, George T.	35th MS Inf.	1843-1914	Wins	Wins
SMITH, George W.	9th MS Cav.	1847-1916	Gree	Gree
SMITH, George W.	1st MS Cav.	1844-1926	Covi	Simp
SMITH, George W.	43rd AL Inf.	1839-1903	AL	Pont
SMITH, George W.	1st MS Cav.	1848-1932		Pear
SMITH, George W.	3rd MS Cav.	____-1899		Yazo
SMITH, George W.	36th or 38th MS Cav.	1848-1919	Pike	Lawr
SMITH, George W.	4th MS Inf.	1842-1923	Atta	Atta
SMITH, George Washington	9th Inf.	18_2-1923		Madi
SMITH, George Whitfield	1st MS Cav.	1840-1911	SC	Okti
SMITH, Geratius N.	1st MS Cav.	1839-1926	Carr	Carr
SMITH, Gilbert L.	22nd MS Inf.	1835-1895		Lefl
SMITH, Gregory T.	6th MS Cav.	1846-1907	Lown	Alco
SMITH, H. C.	28th MS Cav.	1812-1884		Mont
SMITH, H. J.	2nd MS Inf.	1833-1935	SC	Tipp
SMITH, H. P.	8th MS Inf.	1838-192_	MS	Simp
SMITH, H. R.	16th MS Inf.	1839-1912	Copi	Harr
SMITH, H. R.	20th MS Inf.	1827-1900	Wins	Wins
SMITH, Hamilton	11th MS Cav.		Tall	Alco
SMITH, Hardy (Rev.)	3rd MS Inf.	1838-1919	MS	Pear
SMITH, Harvey W.	2nd MS Inf.	1838-1917	GA	Tipp

Name	Unit	Dates		Location
SMITH, Hector	37th MS Inf.	1836-1932	MS	Jone
SMITH, Henry	39th MS Inf.		Simp	Hind
SMITH, Henry	9th LA Cav.	1847-1914	MS	Walt
SMITH, Henry	39th MS Inf.	1845-1875	Simp	Lawr
SMITH, Henry B.	1st MS Cav.	1809-1871		Kemp
SMITH, Henry C.	44th MS Inf.	1839-1912	JEDA	Tate
SMITH, Henry C.	34th MS Inf.	1844-1895	Tipp	Tipp
SMITH, Henry Clay	Commissary Dept.	18_2-1917	Laud	Laud
SMITH, Henry Clay	49th TN Inf.	1844-1912	TN	Alco
SMITH, Henry H.	37th MS Inf.	____-1916		Smit
SMITH, Henry L.	16th MS Inf.	1835-1908	MS	Lafa
SMITH, Henry Lewis	31st MS Inf.	1842-1918	Choc	Choc
SMITH, Henry Warren	37th MS Inf.	1827-189_		Wayn
SMITH, Hiram	38th MS Cav.	1825-1900		Pear
SMITH, Hiram	21st MS Inf.	1826-1904	Wilk	Wilk
SMITH, H. Simeon	8th & 27th MS Inf.	1832-1906	Jone	Jone
SMITH, I. A.	10th MS Inf.	____-1916		Copi
SMITH, Ike	2nd Partisan Rangers			Kemp
SMITH, Ira	3rd MS Cav.	1843-1922		Hind
SMITH, Ira	18th MS			Rank
SMITH, Ira Foster	6th MS Inf.	1834-1912	MS	Smit
SMITH, Irvin	6th MS Inf.	1847-1923	Pike	Linc
SMITH, Isaac	2nd MS Inf.	1841-1918	Gree	Gree
SMITH, Isaac A.	14th MS Cav.	1843-1911	Fran	Fran
SMITH, Isaac _.	7th MS Cav.	1844-1912	AL	Tipp
SMITH, Isham A. J.	1st MS Inf.	1835-1876	Mars	Linc
SMITH, Isiah W.	5th MS Cav.	1831-1871	Holm	Holm
SMITH, J. A.	3rd MS Inf.	1825-1888		Rank
SMITH, J. C.	46th MS Inf.	1834-1910	MS	Laud
SMITH, J. C.	13th MS Inf.	1843-1892	Laud	Laud
SMITH, J. D.	8th MS Cav.	1834-1905	Chic	Chic
SMITH, J. Davidson (Dr.)	4th LA Inf.	1841-1883	Adam	Adam
SMITH, J. E.	3rd MS Cav.	1844-1915	Copi	Linc
SMITH, J. F.	41st MS Inf.	1837-1916	Pont	Unio
SMITH, J. F.	6th MS Inf.	1840-1886	Copi	Linc
SMITH, J. H.	14th MS Inf.	1841-1900	Okti	Noxu
SMITH, J. H.	11th MS Cav.	184_-1924		Noxu
SMITH, J. H.	15th MS Inf.	1842-1908	Atta	Atta
SMITH, J. J.	13th MS Inf.	1821-1877	MS	Laud
SMITH, J. J.	18th MS Inf.	1837-1903		Rank
SMITH, J. J. W.	3rd MS Inf.	1845-1917	MS	Mars
SMITH, J. L.	2nd MS Cav.	1835-1905	GA	Newt
SMITH, J. L.	2nd MS Inf.	1841-1891	Pont	Pont
SMITH, J. L.	2nd MS Inf.	1841-1912	Tish	Alco
SMITH, J. L.	18th MS Inf.	1827-1898	Yazo	Yazo
SMITH, J. L.	35th MS Inf.	1839-1897		Okti
SMITH, J. P.	MS Inf.	1837-1918	Laud	Laud
SMITH, J. Tipton	29th MS Inf.	1834-1866	Tall	Tall
SMITH, J. V.	33rd MS Inf.	1840-1916		Mont
SMITH, James	38th MS Inf.	1845-1921	Clai	Mari

113

Name	Unit	Years		
SMITH, James M.	8th MS Inf.	1842-1923	Unio	Nesh
SMITH, Janes O.	17th MS Inf.	1840-19_	Chic	Chic
SMITH, James W.	41st MS Inf.	1847-1863	MS	Monr
SMITH, J. Andrew	9th MS Inf.	1847-1910	Gree	Gree
SMITH, J. Mell (Dr.)	29th MS Inf.	1831-1927	Yalo	Yalo
SMITH, J. Monroe	15th MS Inf.	1842-1901	Choc	Yalo
SMITH, John	Lamsdens Art.	1839-1862	Monr	Monr
SMITH, John F.	8th MS Inf.	1835-1910	Jone	Jone
SMITH, John H.	2nd MS Inf.	1829-1861	Tipp	Unio
SMITH, Joseph	22nd SC Inf.	1845-1903	SC	Unio
SMITH, Perry C.	7th MS Inf.	1836-1915	Fran	Fran
SMITH, Peter B/H.	8th MS Inf.	1807-1884	Smit	Smit
SMITH, Robert R.	2nd MS Inf.	1846-1888	GA/TN	Tipp
SMITH, Thomas W.	38th MS Cav.	1846-1919	Holm	Holm
SMITH, Jack K.	1st MS Inf.	1847-1937		Nesh
SMITH, Jacob O.	42nd MS Inf.	1822-1900	Gren	Gren
SMITH, James	8th MS Inf.	1829-1891		Newt
SMITH, James	41st MS Inf.	1836-1904	Pont	Pont
SMITH, James A.	13th MS Inf.	1838-1863	MS	Wayn
SMITH, James A.	7th MS Inf.	1831-1876	Perr	Linc
SMITH, James Argyle	32nd MS Regt.	1832-1901		Hind
SMITH, James C.	1st MS Inf.	1831-1905		Copi
SMITH, James F.	5th MS Inf.	1830-1916	Monr	Alco
SMITH, James K.	33rd MS Inf.	1845-1925	Lawr	Linc
SMITH, J. H.	33rd MS Inf.	1842-1863	Fran	Lafa
SMITH, James H.	11th MS Inf.	1844-1904	Lafa	Lafa
SMITH, James H.	6th MS Inf.	1828-1862	Yazo	Yazo
SMITH, James K.	5th MS Inf.	1847-1928	Wins	Alco
SMITH, James M.	7th MS Inf.	1836-1916	Clar	Laud
SMITH, James M.	41st MS Inf.	1845-1923	Itaw	Monr
SMITH, James M.	9th LA Inf.	1840-___		Jeff
SMITH, James M.	13th MS Inf.	1845-192_	Pont	Pont
SMITH, James _.	39th MS Inf.	1842-1920	Pren	JEDA
SMITH, James P.	20th MS Inf.		Atta	Atta
SMITH, James P.	20th MS Inf.	1840-1911	MS	Leak
SMITH, James W.	3rd MS Inf.	1844-1894	MS	Hanc
SMITH, James W.	1st MS Res.	1845-1925	Pear	Pear
SMITH, Jeff	Baxters MS Cav.	1839-1921	Tish	Alco
SMITH, Jeremiah	36th MS Inf.	1831-1906		Copi
SMITH, Jesse M.	3rd MS Inf.	1849-1935	Simp	Pear
SMITH, Jessie Martin	2nd MS Inf.	1813-1904	AL	Monr
SMITH, Jim	24th MS Inf.		Kemp	Kemp
SMITH, Jobe R.	9th AL Cav.	1847-1928	AL	Choc
SMITH, Joe H.	2nd MS Cav.	1848-1927	Tipp	Tipp
SMITH, Joe	6th TN Inf.	1842-1936		Lee
SMITH, Joe H.	6th TN Inf.	1842-1936	TN	Lee
SMITH, John	10th MS Inf.	1832-1904	Clai	Clai
SMITH, John	39th MS Inf.	1843-1902	Rank	
SMITH, John	39th MS Inf.			Simp
SMITH, John	2nd MS Inf.	1843-1921	Tipp	Unio
SMITH, John A.	10th MS Inf.	1843-1869	Clai	Linc
SMITH, John A.	11th MS Cav.	1837-1902	Chic	Alco

114

Name	Unit	Dates	
SMITH, John C.	4th MS Inf.	1840-1894 Covi	Covi
SMITH, John D.	8th MS Inf.	1828-1900 Clar	Clar
SMITH, John Dunn	39th MS Inf.	1846-1900	Copi
SMITH, John E.	20th MS Inf.	1837-1916 Atta	Atta
SMITH, John F.	39th MS Inf.	1833-1895	Rank
SMITH, John F.	8th & 45th MS Inf.	____-1864	Hind
SMITH, John H.	21st MS Inf.	1840-1910 TN	Alco
SMITH, John H.	26th MS Inf.	1845-1913 MS	Alco
SMITH, John J.	42nd MS Inf.	1840-18_4 Pren	Pren
SMITH, John K.	12th MS Cav.	1837-1878 Tall	Tall
SMITH, John L.	5th MS Cav.	1824-1870 TN	Mont
SMITH, John L.	24th MS Inf.	1839-1911 MS	Lown
SMITH, John P.	63rd GA Inf.	1849-1926 GA	Nesh
SMITH, John P.	9th MS Inf.	1842-1910 MS	Wayn
SMITH, John T.	16th MS Inf.	1821-1885	Copi
SMITH, John S.	24th MS Inf.	1822-1865 Gree	Gree
SMITH, John T.	34th MS Inf.	1846-1902 MS	Hind
SMITH, John W.	24th MS Inf.	1839-1928 Kemp	Kemp
SMITH, John W.	26th MS Inf.	1834-1899	Pren
SMITH, John W.	39th MS Inf.		Rank
SMITH, Jones	24th AL Inf.	1844-1918 AL	Shar
SMITH, Joseph	2nd MS Inf.	1841-1912 Monr	Alco
SMITH, Joseph Sr.	12th MS Inf.	1842-1894 Lawr	Lawr
SMITH, Joseph A.	38th MS Cav.	1836-1903 Hanc	Pear
SMITH, Joseph B.	32nd MS Inf.	____-1899 Tish	Alco
SMITH, Joshua Jackson	42nd MS Inf.	1832-1911 Gren	Yalo
SMITH, Joshua R.	8th MS Inf.	1836-1904 Laud	Laud
SMITH, Josiah A.	18th MS Inf.	1840-1869 MS	Madi
SMITH, L. M.	1st MS Inf.	1848-1930 Pont	Unio
SMITH, Lang Q.	1st GA Cav.	1846-1902 GA	Amit
SMITH, Lazros	14th MS Inf.	1831-1892 Laud	Laud
SMITH, Leroy A.	3rd MS Cav.	1846-1871 Yalo	Lafa
SMITH, Levi	4th MS Cav.	1840-1905 Lown	Alco
SMITH, Louis P.	8th MS Cav.	1848-1925 NC	Madi
SMITH, Madison	14th Heavy Art.	1848-1923 Linc	Linc
SMITH, Malcom C.	37th MS Inf.	1845-1894 Jasp	Jone
SMITH, Marshall H.	3rd SC Art.	____-1915 SC	Wash
SMITH, Martin	Pettus Art.	1827-1912	Linc
SMITH, Martin	Woods MS Cav.	1832-1913 Covi	JEDA
SMITH, Martin N.	35th MS Inf.	1842-1862	Kemp
SMITH, Martin Thomas	1st MS Lt. Art.	1833-1914 Yazo	Yazo
SMITH, Martin VanBuren	Smiths MS Lt. Art.	1841-1890 Laud	Laud
SMITH, Melton West	18th MS Inf.	____-1900	Yazo
SMITH, N. B.	1st MS Inf.	1846-1887	Hind
SMITH, N. J.	1st State Troops	1841-1921	Hind
SMITH, N. J.	26th AL Inf.	1842-1933 SC	Wins
SMITH, N. N.	2nd MS Regt.	1822-1899 Fran	Fran
SMITH, Nathan	39th MS Inf.	____-1863 Simp	Simp
SMITH, Nathan Alexander	2nd TX Rifles	1842-1920 TX	Quit
SMITH, Nathaniel H.	18th MS Inf.	1838-1926	Rank

SMITH, Nimrod	3rd MS Inf.	184_-1935 MS	Pear
SMITH, Noah E.	30th MS Inf.	____-1880 Gren	Carr
SMITH, Norris	36th MS Inf.	1842-___ MS	Newt
SMITH, Obdiah	4th & 11th MS Inf.	1829-1919 Monr	Okti
SMITH, Oliver	14th MS Inf.	1835-1923 Laud	Scot
SMITH, Oliver M.	36th MS Inf.	1838-1912 Scot	Adam
SMITH, P. B.	2nd MS Inf.	1845-1925 Monr	Lee
SMITH, P. M.	33rd MS Inf.	1834-1892 Fran	Linc
SMITH, P. S.	3rd Cav.	1822-1901 Yalo	Yalo
SMITH, Pete	4th MS Cav.	1847-1936	Pear
SMITH, Peter	4th MS Cav.	1837-1908 Simp	Simp
SMITH, Pleasant M.	18th MS Inf.	1843-1902 NC	Madi
SMITH, R. A.	26th MS Inf.	1832-1914 GA	Unio
SMITH, R. A.	36th MS Inf.	1835-1920 MS	Newt
SMITH, R. E.	33rd MS Inf.	1840-1919 Fran	Linc
SMITH, R. H.	17th MS Inf.	1833-1900 MS	Alco
SMITH, R. H.	39th MS Inf.		Rank
SMITH, R. H.	17th MS Inf.	1826-1904	Hind
SMITH, Ransom D.	9th MS Inf.	1845-1929 Gree	Gree
SMITH, Reddick	7th MS Inf.	1836-1906 Jasp	Jasp
SMITH, Richard H.	22nd MS Inf.	1837-1862 Amit	Amit
SMITH, Robert A.	10th MS Inf.	1837-1862 ST	Hind
SMITH, Robert B.	9th MS Inf.	Tish	Alco
SMITH, Robert C.	19th MS Inf.	1833-1882 Lafa	Lafa
SMITH, Robert M. (Dr.)	7th MS Inf.	1826-1877 Fran	Fran
SMITH, Rolly	29th MS Inf.	1822-1873 Monr	Tall
SMITH, Ruben	5th MS Inf.	1829-1898 MS	Laud
SMITH, S.	2nd MS Cav.	1842-1908	Newt
SMITH, S. V.	17th MS Cav.	1843-1872 Gree	Gree
SMITH, Sam H.	5th MS Inf.	____-1907 AL	Madi
SMITH, Samuel J.	24th MS Inf.	1817-1900 Gree	Gree
SMITH, Samuel J.	7th MS Cav.	1845-1911 Tipp	Bent
SMITH, Sanuel _.	17th MS Inf.	1825-1900 Lafa	Lafa
SMITH, Seborn	40th MS Inf.	1830-1885 Laud	Nesh
SMITH, Stanford S.	27th MS Inf.	1844-1909 Linc	Tall
SMITH, Stephen S.	33rd MS Inf.	1843-1905 MS	Fran
SMITH, Stephen Taylor	4th GA Inf.	1848-1927 GA	Pren
SMITH, T. A.	41st MS Inf.	1842-1862 Pont	Pont
SMITH, T. A.	41st MS Inf.	1842-1916 Pont	Pont
SMITH, Therreo P.	13th MS Inf.	1841-1893 MS	Madi
SMITH, Tilnan	8th MS Inf.	1837-1911 Laud	Nesh
SMITH, Thomas	18th MS Inf.	1836-1918 Madi	Madi
SMITH, Thomas D.	42nd MS Inf.	1836-1903 Carr	Carr
SMITH, Thomas Hunter	2nd MS Inf.	1833-1901 Lawr	Lawr
SMITH, Thomas Marion	15th Conf. Cav.	1845-1864 MS	Wayn
SMITH, Thomas R.	10th AL Cav.	1832-1914 AL	Tish
SMITH, Thomas Robertson	42nd MS Inf.	MS	Calh
SMITH, Tillman	37th MS Inf.	____-1912	Newt
SMITH, V. B.	50th TN Inf.	1835-1914 TN	Lafa
SMITH, Vance	11th MS Inf.	1845-1924	Lee
SMITH, W. A.	21st MS Inf.	1841-1932 Copi	Linc

116

SMITH, W. A.	1st MS Cav.	1814-1890 Carr	Carr
SMITH, W. A. L.	57th MS/AL Inf.	1839-1927 MS	Simp
SMITH, W. B.	13th MS Inf.	1840-1882	Laud
SMITH, W. A.	37th MS Inf.	1842-1921 Smit	Harr
SMITH, W. B.	1st MS Inf.	1814-1904	Rank
SMITH, W. D.	8th MS Inf.	1841-1904	Smit
SMITH, W. D.	3rd MS Cav.	1820-1889	Hind
SMITH, W. D.	41st MS Inf.	1838-1923 Monr	Monr
SMITH, W. G.	41st MS Inf.	1822-1897 AL	Monr
SMITH, W. H.	6th MS Inf.	1822-1912 Scot	Monr
SMITH, W. J.	9th MS Cav.	1845-1927 MS	Harr
SMITH, W. J.	37th MS Inf.	1846-1910 Perr	Jone
SMITH, W. J.	9th MS Inf.	1844-1907 DeSo	Gree
SMITH, W. L.	8th MS Inf.	1821-1901	Smit
SMITH, W. L.	33rd MS Inf.	1840-1909 MS	Fran
SMITH, W. M.	10th MS Inf.	1828-1903	Copi
SMITH, W. O.	41st MS Inf.	1845-1917 AL	Monr
SMITH, W. P.	23rd MS Cav.	1846-1920 Linc	Linc
SMITH, W. R.	1st MS Lt. Art.	1840-1886 Kemp	Linc
SMITH, W. R.	7th AL Cav.	1827-1901 Tish	Tish
SMITH, W. R.	8th MS Inf.	1826-1904	Newt
SMITH, W. R.	1st Lt. Art.	1808-1889 Choc	Choc
SMITH, W. T.	4th MS Inf.	1837-1877 Calh	Calh
SMITH, W. T.	15th MS Inf.	1848-1923 Atta	Linc
SMITH, W. Z.	18th MS Inf.	1841-1910 Yazo	Hump
SMITH, Wade	Brookhaven Lt. Art.	1820-1895 Lawr	Linc
SMITH, Watson C.	24th MS Cav.	1845-1915	Copi
SMITH, Wellington	1st MS Lt. Art.	____-1890 MS	Yazo
SMITH, Wesley Marion	6th MS Inf.	1830-1919 NC	Rank
SMITH, Whiting W.	4th MS Inf.	1813-1888 VA	Holm
SMITH, Wiley	Brookhaven Lt. Art.	1806-1882 GA	Amit
SMITH, Wiley M.	2nd MS Cav.	1848-1916 Monr	Monr
SMITH, Wiley P.	42nd MS Inf.	1835-1892 Yalo	DeSo
SMITH, Wilford Carroll	29th MS Inf.	1834-1876 MS	Tall
SMITH, William	5th MS Inf.	1835-1889 Wayn	Wayn
SMITH, William	8th MS Inf.	1802-1889 Smit	Simp
SMITH, William	39th MS Inf.		Rank
SMITH, William	4th MS Inf.	1829-1913 Atta	Yazo
SMITH, William	12th MS Inf.	1846-1916 Lawr	Linc
SMITH, William	Gun Boat McRae	1836-1911 Harr	Harr
SMITH, William Sr.	33rd MS Inf.	1805-1882 MS	Amit
SMITH, William	2nd TN Cav.	1829-1924 EN	Harr
SMITH, William	4th MS Inf.	1825-1888 Holm	Holm
SMITH, William	30th LA Inf.	1835-1911 LA	Atta
SMITH, William _.	28th MS Cav.	1833-187_ Yalo	Sunf
SMITH, William Cephas	Adams MS Cav.	1843-1934 TN	Tate
SMITH, William F.	2nd MS Inf.	1833-1898 Pont	Pont
SMITH, William Hardy	3rd AL Res.	1837-1911 AL	Tish
SMITH, William Harvey	11th MS Regt.	1835-1904	Hind

SMITH, William Henderson	Brookhaven Lt. Art.	1842-1865 Lawr	Linc
SMITH, William J.	11th MS Inf.	1843-1911 MS	Lown
SMITH, William J.	10th MS Inf.	1845-1930	Copi
SMITH, William J.	Adams MS Cav.	1846-1918 Madi	Madi
SMITH, William J.	38th MS Cav.	1843-1910 Pike	Pike
SMITH, William J.	16th MS Inf.	1844-1919 Atta	Atta
SMITH, William L.	15th MS Inf.	1835-1911 LA	Atta
SMITH, William L.	9th LA Cav.	1845-1929 MS	Walt
SMITH, William M.	1st MS Inf.	1843-1907	Hind
SMITH, William M.	38th MS Cav.	1839-1917 Hanc	Pear
SMITH, William Milton	1st MS Lt. Art.	1834-1885 Linc	Linc
SMITH, William Mondson	3rd MS Cav.	1837-1922 Gren	Gren
SMITH, William P.	33rd MS Inf.	1833-1902 Amit	Amit
SMITH, William Pinky	Gillis MS Cav.	1843-1934 MS	Lama
SMITH, Willis	5th MS Inf.	1838-1915 Linc	Linc
SMITH, Wm.	8th MS Regt.	1840-1919	Hind
SMITH, Wm. T.	4th MS Inf.	1837-1877 Calh	Calh
SMITH, Wyley	33rd MS Inf.	1844-1921 Linc	Linc
SMITH, Z. (Buck)	7th MS Cav.	1845-1924 MS	Tipp
SMITH, Z. F.	7th VA Inf.	1840-1934 VA	Clar
SMITH, Zachariah	7th MS Cav.	1825-1908 MS	Tipp
SMITHERMAN, John	29th AL Inf.	1841-1921 AL	Pont
SMITHHART, W. O.	1st MS Lt. Art.	1844-1897 Warr	Yazo
SMYLIE, B. S.	LA Cav.	1838-___ LA	Amit
SMYTH, Ed.	28th MS Cav.	1847-1917 Wins	Noxu
SMITHHART, Abner	40th MS Inf.	1840-1909 Kemp	Scot
SMITHART, Thomas Jeff.	46th MS Inf.	1837-1911 Warr	Warr
SMYLIE, John	2nd MS Cav.	1830-1910 Choc	Choc
SMYTH, Edwin H.	28th MS Cav.	1845-191_ MS	Noxu
SMYLIE, John M.	3rd MS Inf.	1841-1912 MS	Hind
SMYLIE, Joseph Calhoun	Powers Regt.	1847-1926 Copi	Forr
SMYLIE, R. W.	2nd MS Regt.	1817-1905 MS	Fran
SMYLY, Charles F.	2nd MS Cav.	1843-1924 Newt	Newt
SMYTHE, George A.	14th MS Lt. Art.	1826-1880 EN	Hind
SMYTHE, George J.	16th MS Inf.	1849-1893 EN	Hind
SMYTH, J. S. (Dr.)	6th MS Inf.	1819-1886 Leak	Leak
SMYTH, Julian Marshall	Adams MS Cav.	Leak	Atta
SMYTHE, Zachary F.	15th VA Cav.	1840-1934 GE	Clar
SMYTHE, Zachary Fernando	56th AL Cav.	1840-1934 GE	Laud
SNEED, Archibald J.	Smythes MS Cav.	1847-1919 Yazo	Madi
SNELL, John A.	8th MS Cav.	1847-1915 Lown	Lown
SNIDER, A. B.	33rd MS Inf.	1843-1917 Unio	Unio
SNIDER, Andrew J.	33rd MS Inf.	1837-1914 MS	Unio
SNIPES, Sion	19th MS Inf.	1833-1909 Pont	Unio
SNIPES, W. A.	4th MS Inf.	1834-1911	Webs
SNOW, Eli	20th AL Inf.	1841-1912 AL	Alco
SNOWDEN, C/G.	37th MS Inf.	1846-1915 Clar	Wayn
SNOWDEN, Holder B.	16th Conf. Cav.	1846-1880 VA	Monr
SNOWDEN, James A.	11th MS Inf.	1806-1895 VA	Monr
SNOWDEN, W. P.	11th MS Inf.	1837-1910 Noxu	Noxu

SNYDER, I/J. A.	Powers Cav.	1848-1909	Hind
SOCKWELL, W. M.	42nd GA Inf.	1840-1928 GA	Jone
SOJOURNER, A. H.	Jeff Davis Legion	1833-1922 MS	Adam
SOJOURNER, B. H.	4th MS Cav.	1829-1900	Copi
SOJOURNER, M. U.	36th MS Inf.	1833-1913	Copi
SOJOURER, S. D.	36th MS Inf.	1820-1899	Copi
SOJOURNER, William	Jeff Davis Legion		Adam
SOJOURNER, William W.	25th LA Inf.	1841-1862 LA	Lafa
SOLIS, Felix	3rd LA Inf.	1834-1863 LA	Warr
SOLOMON, J. H.	29th MS Inf.	1832-1902	DeSo
SOLOMON, J. H.	37th AL Inf.	1841-1921 AL	Smit
SOLOMON, Jacob	1st MS Cav.	1845-1898 Rank	Laud
SOLOMON, James M.	23rd MS Inf.	Tish	Alco
SOMERFORD, Loaminx	3rd MS Cav.	1828-1918 Chic	Monr
SONES, B/D. J.	9th MS Cav.	1841-1915 MS	Pear
SONES, F.	17th MS Cav.	1814-1875 MS	Pear
SONES, W. H.	40th MS Inf.	1824-1902 TN	Leak
SONTHEIMER, Jacob	5th MS Cav.	1819-1886 Holm	Holm
SONTHEIMER, Solomon	5th MS Cav.	1825-1890 GE	Holm
SORRELS, Robert Brown	18th MS Cav.	1843-1922 Tate	Pano
SORTER, William D.	37th MS Inf.	1840-1863 Jasp	Jasp
SOUTER, Franklin	1st MS Cav.	1829-1902 Pont	Pont
SOUTER, William L.	1st MS Cav.	1831-1915 Pont	Pont
SOUTH, Ira	7th MS Inf.	1845-1938 SC	Tipp
SOUTH, J. H.	17th MS Inf.	1846-1937 AL	Tipp
SOUTH, John	17th MS Inf.	1841-1906	Tish
SOUTHERLAND, W. A.	Provost Guards	1846-1885 Unio	Unio
SOUTHWARD, W. A.	7th AL Cav.	1840-1911 AL	Tish
SOUTHWICK, W. C.	21st MS Inf.	1837-1911 Yalo	Yalo
SOWEL, John W.	19th TN Inf.	1839-1909 TN	Pano
SOWELL, James Monroe	24th MS Inf.	1829-1911 SC	Gree
SPAIN, Aaron	32nd MS Inf.	1837-1922 TN	Pren
SPAIN, Alec	32nd MS Inf.	1838-1921 TN	Pren
SPAIN, Henry W.	32nd MS Inf.	1841-1919 MS	Pren
SPAIN, James W.	32nd MS Inf.	1847-1907 Pren	Pren
SPAIN, John W.	11th MS Cav.	1846-1924 NC	Pren
SPANN, Augustus	6th & 15th MS Inf.	1820-1864 GA	Rank
SPANN, Robert W.	41st MS Inf.	1829-1899 Noxu	Jack
(SPARKMAN, A. P. & Levi located after SPARKS)			
SPARKMAN, W. A.	40th MS Inf.	1838-1881 Leak	Leak
SPARKS, A. _.	14th MS Art.	1836-1916	Harr
SPARKS, Alex B.	Powers Art.	1841-1863 LA	Hind
(SPARKS, C. through James located after SPECKS)			
SPARKS, Marion	43rd MS Inf.	1836-1913 Lafa	Lafa
SPARKS, William P.	41st MS Inf.	1843-1912 Itaw	Monr
SPARKS, William T.	40th AL Inf.	1830-1898	Scot
SPARROW, J. G.	Warren Lt. Art.	1831-1898 Warr	Warr
SPEAKE, Ben	41st MS Inf.	1839-1900 AL	Madi
SPEAKS, _	39th MS Inf.	1836-___ Hind	Madi
SPEARS, David F.	33rd MS Inf.	1812-1908 MS	Nesh
SPEARS, Eli G.	42nd MS Inf.	1838-1878 Gren	Gren

Name	Unit	Dates	State	Place
SPEARS, Frank M.	1st MS Inf.	1840-1900 MS	Gren
SPEARS, J. W.	4th MS Cav.	1837-1915 Yalo	Yalo
SPEARS, James G.	1st NC Inf.	1840-1931 NC	Lafa
SPEARS, James Madson	1st MS Inf.	1841-1906 MS	Gren
SPEARS, P. W.	30th MS Inf.	1837-1912 Yazo	Lafa
SPEARS, Richard	11th MS Cav.	1846-1929 MS	Nesh
SPEARS, Samuel K.	19th TN Inf.	1835-1905 TN	Harr
SPEARS, Thomas E.	12th MS Cav.	1845-___ Monr	Monr
SPEARS, Wesly W.	27th LA Inf.	1845-1933 LA	Kemp
SPEARSE, G. W.	40th MS Inf.	1840-1914 MS	Harr
SPECK, J. E.	17th MS Inf.	1845-1915 MS	Unio
SPECK, W. P.	2nd MS Cav.	1847-1923 Pont	Unio
SPECKS, C.	7th MS Cav.	1838-1908 TN	Tipp
SPARKS, David S.	2nd MS Inf.	1816-1905 AL	Monr
SPARKS, Elijah	1st MS Inf.	1837-1917 Pont	Lafa
SPARKS, I. E.	12th MS Cav.	1820-1892 MS	Lee
SPARKS, James W.	14th SC Inf.	1839-1911 SC	Pano
SPARKMAN, A. P.	16th MS Inf.	1841-1913 Pike	Pike
SPARKMAN, Levi Beeman	28th MS Cav.	1846-1940 NC	Boli
SPEED, B. T.	Stubbs MS Cav.	1834-1910 MS	Covi
SPEED, J. W.	Stubbs MS Cav.	1843-1913 Covi	Covi
SPEED, James M. Sr.	6th MS Inf.	1818-1896 Covi	Covi
SPEED, James Monroe Jr.	6th MS Inf.	1842-1932 Covi	Covi
SPEED, W. E.	Stubbs MS Cav.	1815-1879 MS	Covi
SPEEDE, Andrew	19th AL Inf.	1847-1928 AL	Chic
SPEER, Alexander	3rd MS Cav.	1821-1870	Rank
SPEIGHTS, Archie S.	7th MS Inf.	1848-1925 MS	JEDA
SPEIGHTS, Franklin	38th MS Cav.	1836-1866 Lawr	Lawr
SPEIGHTS, Levi	38th MS Cav.	182_-1935 Clai	Lawr
SPEIGHTS, A. Wilken	7th MS Inf.	1828-1885 Lawr	Lawr
SPELL, J. V.	1st MS Lt. Art.	1829-1906 Holm	Holm
SPELL, W. F.	8th MS Inf.	1838-1905 Covi	Covi
SPENCE, F.	4th MS Inf.	1824-1906 Yalo	Lafa
SPENCE, J. F.	1st MS Cav.	1838-1916 Itaw	Itaw
SPENCE, John F.	1st MS Cav.	1838-1916 MS	Itaw
SPENCE, O. H.	12th MS Inf.	1838-1897 AL	Copi
SPENCER, A. H.	1st MS Cav.	1840-1913 Pont	Pont
SPENCER, Albert A.	43rd MS Inf.	1840-1910	Webs
SPENCER, Chas. W.	35th MS Inf.	1823-1899 AL	Kemp
SPENCER, Elijah Harrison	11th MS Inf.	1841-1892 Carr	Carr
SPENCER, Frank S.	30th MS Inf.	1844-1914 Holm	Holm
SPENCER, Giles	26th MS Inf.	1840-1926 MS	Tipp
SPENCER, James G.	Cowans MS	1844-1926 Clai	Clai
SPENCER, James M.	11th MS Inf.	1846-1892 Carr	Carr
SPENCER, John W.	24th MS Inf.	1840-1923 Itaw	Itaw
SPENCER, N. E.	12th MS Inf.	1847-1924 Lawr	Linc
SPENCER, O. S.	41st & 43rd AL Inf.	1832-1905 AL	Pont
SPENCER, Tobe	12th MS Inf.	1826-1908 MS	Pren
SPENCER, W. R.	7th MS Inf.	1837-1909 Pike	Pont
SPENCER, William	32nd MS Inf.	Tish	Alco

Name	Unit	Dates / Place	Co.
SPENCER, William H.	Jeff Davis MS Cav.	1843-1923 VA	Jeff
SPENGLER, Antone H.	Lays MS Cav.	1846-1904	Hind
SPENGLER, Frank	48th MS Inf.	1848-1919 MS	Hind
SPENGLER, Hubert	1st MS Inf.	1820-1900 FR	Hind
SPERIER, Alcide	3rd MS Inf.	1838-1885 LA	Harr
SPERIER, Paul Adolph	3rd MS Inf.	1839-1908 LA	Harr
SPIARS, James Sr.	1st MS Cav.	1818-1895 Yazo	Isaq
SPICKARD, J. H.	2nd MS Cav.	1846-1935 Webs	Clar
SPIERS, Alex	38th MS Cav.	1829-1907 Hanc	Pear
SPIERS, I. M.	3rd MS Inf.	1820-1892 MS	Newt
SPIERS, J. W.	1st MS Inf.	1836-1903 MS	Leak
SPIERS, Robert R.	43rd MS Inf.	1838-1916 Lown	Lown
SPIERS, Samuel S.	38th MS Cav.	1837-1911 Hanc	Pear
SPIGHT, Thomas	38th MS Cav.	1839-1906	Pear
SPIGHT, Thomas	23rd MS Inf.	1841-1924 Tipp	Tipp
SPILLAN, John	33rd MS Inf.	1838-1864 Amit	Amit
SPILLMAN, Robert	12th KY Cav.	1839-1864 KY	Lee
SPINKS, Charles S.	36th MS Inf.	1845-1912 Newt	Newt
SPINKS, Enoch Ephrian	35th MS Inf.	1835-1911 Laud	Laud
SPINKS, J. N.	39th MS Inf.	1829-1910 Pike	Pike
SPINKS, John Clarke	13th MS Inf.	1826-1903 Laud	Clar
SPINKS, John Lyod.	24th MS Inf.	1847-1903 Monr	Laud
SPINKS, Raleigh W.	35th MS Inf.	1833-1875 Wins	Kemp
SPINKS, William G.	39th MS Inf.	1832-1924 Pike	Pike
SPINKS, Windsor J.	35th MS Inf.	1832-1868 Wins	Kemp
SPIVEY, J. M.	33rd MS Inf.	1833-1907 Nesh	Nesh
SPIVEY, W. G/O.	33rd MS Inf.	1838-1916 Leak	Newt
SPIVY, Moses R.	15th MS Inf.	1841-1898 Carr	Madi
SPRADLEY, William W.	6th MS Inf.	1843-1913 Simp	Jasp
SPRADLING, William J.	31st MS Inf.	1832-1900 MS	Calh
SPRAGGINS, H. C.	24th AL Regt.	___-1920	Hind
SPRAGGINS, M. E.	2nd MS Cav.	1823-1900 Chic	
SPRATT, N. B. (Dr.)	14th MS Inf.	1843-1920 Monr	Monr
SPRAYBERRY, George W.	3rd TN Cav.	1846-1935 TN	Calh
SPHICK, A. H.	4th MS Cav.	1840-1916 Copi	Pike
SPHINGE, George	7th MS Inf.	1833-1908 Fran	Fran
SPRINGER, Daniel	3rd MS Inf.	1840-1862 Hanc	Chic
SPRINGER, Ira	6th MS Cav.	1841-1915 Alco	Alco
SPRINGER, J. S.	2nd MS Inf.	1815-1888 Tipp	Bent
SPRINGER, Joel	24th MS Inf.	1848-___ Chic	Chic
SPRINGFIELD, A. T.	43rd MS Inf.		Monr
SPRINKLE, Henry	Army CSA		Adam
SPROLES, H. F.	1st MS Lt. Art.	1844-1912 Holm	Hind
SPROLES, John W.	29th MS Inf.	1825-1899 Holm	Holm
SPROULE, Johnston	35th MS Inf.	1831-1890 IR	Hind
SPROULE, Robert	1st MS Art.	IR	Hind
SPROUSE, Martin	Nitro Works	1826-1914 GA	Tish
SPRUILL, Benjamin L.	18th MS Inf.	1837-1916 NC	Madi
SPRUILL, James A.	41st AL Inf.	1843-1930 AL	Lown
SPURGEON, J. P.	28th MS Cav.	1846-1934 Adam	Yalo
SPURGEON, W. M.	8th MS Cav.	1846-1928 Yalo	Choc

Name	Unit	Dates	Col1	Col2
SPURLOCK, T. J.	33rd MS Inf.	1839-1920 Amit	Amit
SPURLOCK, Thomas Jeff.	1st LA Cav.	1830-1915 LA	Amit
STACK, W. T.	45th MS Inf.	1842-1921 Pont	Unio
STACK, W. T.	3rd MS Inf.	1842-1921	Tipp
STACKHOUSE, Ervin M.	36th MS Inf.	1846-1902	Copi
STACKHOUSE, Henry C.	16th MS Inf.		Copi
STACKHOUSE, Samuel H.	24th MS Cav.	1839-1882	Copi
STACY, I. D.	31st MS Inf.	Calh	Calh
STACY, John	26th MS Inf.	1837-1919 Tish	Tish
STACY, L. C.	15th MS Inf.	1842-1920 Choc	Choc
STAFFORD, Amzi	43rd MS Inf.		Monr
STAFFORD, Archie	15th MS Inf.	1827-1895 Carr	Mont
STAFFORD, Edward W.	27th MS Inf.	1834-1903 Jasp	Jasp
STAFFORD, Joseph Henry	1st MS Lt. Art.	1845-1922 Warr	Boli
STAFFORD, Neal (Dr.)	4th MS Inf.	1825-1898 Carr	Mont
STAGG, William E.	9th MS Cav.	1832-1892	Wayn
STAGGS, John	3rd AL Cav.	1843-1935 AL	Lown
STALLINGS, John Floyd	MS Art.	1838-1890 Clar	Clar
STALLINGS, John W.	14th MS Inf.	1842-1878	Okti
STAMPER, J. C.	39th MS Inf.	1823-1906 Newt	Newt
STAMPER, M. W.	8th MS Inf.	1838-1918 MS	Newt
STAMPER, T. H.	8th MS Inf.	1839-1899 MS	Newt
STAMPLLY, C. Q.	4th MS Cav.	1838-1906 Copi	Jeff
STAMPS, Isaac Davis	21st MS Inf.	1828-1863 Wilk	Wilk
STAMPS, J. J.	33rd MS Inf.	1832-1910 Pike	Linc
STANALAND, B. F.	57th GA Inf.	1830-1863 GA	Warr
STANDARD, J. F.	1st MS Lt. Art.	1839-1920 Warr	Warr
STANDFORD, John M.	19th MS Inf.	1843-1862 Warr	Tish
STANDFORD, Stephen	19th MS Inf.	1835-___ Warr	Wash
STANDARD, Wesley	Adams MS Cav.	1837-1877 Warr	Warr
STANDIFER, F. L. (Dr.)	3rd MS Inf.	1842-1924 Simp	Simp
STANDLEY, B. F.	22nd MS Inf.		Carr
STANDROD, William S.	20th MS Inf.		Carr
STANFORD, Auren W.	Adams MS Cav.	1832-1894 Madi	Madi
STANFORD, Frank	Jeff Davis Cav.	1842-1899 Chic	Chic
STANFORD, Henry G.	16th AL Inf.	1842-1921 AL	Monr
STANFORD, J. F.	41st MS Inf.	1837-1894 Lee	Lee
STANFORD, J. W.	1st MS Lt. Art.	1846-1924 Pont	Pont
STANFORD, James W.	11th MS Inf.	1845-1924	Lee
STANFORD, John T.	11th MS Inf.	1834-1909 Carr	Carr
STANFORD, Samuel	11th MS Inf.	1803-1883 Carr	Carr
STANFORD, Thomas P.	41st MS Inf.	Pont	Calh
STANFORD, W. _.	31st MS Inf.	1820-1900 Pont	Pont
STANFORD, Willian M.	10th MS Inf.	1840-1929 Tipp	Tipp
STANGLEY, John B.	15th MS Inf.	1837-1925 Atta	Atta
STANLEY, E. P.	13th MS Inf.	1837-1900 VA	Holm
STANSBURY, David M.	4th KY Cav.	1841-1924 KY	Jeff
STANSEL, W. R.	10th GA Inf.	1844-1912 GA	Tipp
STANTON, Aaron	1st MS Inf.	1840-1918 Mars	Adam
STANTON, James S.	4th MS Cav.	1847-1921 Unio	Unio
STANTON, John	10th & 31st MS Inf.	1841-1923 Tish	Unio

122

STANTON, Thomas S.	1st MS Cav.	1843-1864 Noxu	Noxu
STANTON, Thomas W.	36th MS Inf.	1826-1904 Laud	Laud
STANTON, William	10th MS Inf.	1840-1908 Adam	Hind
STAPLES, R. J.	24th MS Cav.	1847-1921 Clay	Clay
STAPLES, Willian G.	24th MS Inf.	1822-1881 NC	Mont
STAPP, A. M.	4th MS Inf.	1843-1911 Atta	Linc
STAPP, C. C.	4th MS Cav.	1844-1925	Copi
STARK, Thomas T.	2nd MS Inf.	1821-1906 Pont	Pont
STARKER, John H.	15th MS Inf.	1828-1887	Holm
STARKES, John H.	20th MS Inf.	1837-1920 SC	Wins
STARKS, John F.	33rd MS Inf.	1829-1908 SC	Tipp
STARLING, Francis M.	16th MS Inf.	1843-1921 MS	Wayn
STARLING, James M.	14th MS Inf.	1827-1898 Wayn	Wayn
STARNES, C. W.	19th MS Inf.	1834-1912 MS	Lafa
STARNES, D. M.	26th MS Inf.	1830-1899 AL	Lafa
STARNES, Samuel S.	3rd MS Inf.	1848-1905	Copi
STARNER, Seth H.	17th MS Inf.	1842-1902	DeSo
STARY, Willie Harvey	46th MS Inf.	1831-1915	Rank
STATHAM, M. C. H/H.	4th MS Cav.	1838-1876 Pike	Walt
STATHAM, Walter Scott	15th MS Inf.	1832-1862 Gren	Gren
STATON, Norfleete	36th MS Inf.	1831-1876 GA	Newt
STAUB, Henry	10th MS Inf.	1833-1904 Warr	Clai
STEADMAN, Edwin B.	2nd MS Cav.	1842-1862 Choc	Choc
STEADMAN, George	2nd MS Cav.	1840-1878 Choc	Choc
STEAN, W.	2nd MS Inf.	1841-1910 Itaw	Atta
STEARNES, Emory C.	14th MS Inf.	1836-1914 Wayn	Wayn
STEDMAN, Edwin R.	2nd MS Cav.	1834-1883	Hind
STEDMAN, R.	2nd MS Cav.	1830-1885 Choc	Choc
STEEDE, Abner C.	9th MS Cav.	1828-1901 Jack	Jack
STEEL, Thomas	NC Inf.	NC	Carr
STEELE, Andrew	39th MS Inf.	1831-1905 Pike	Fran
STEELE, Archie	6th MS Inf.	1818-1879	Copi
STEELE, Benton	7th MS Inf.	1835-1909 Fran	Amit
STEELE, Isaac C.	2nd MS Inf.	1827-1916 Calh	Calh
STEELE, J. D.	11th AL Cav.	1835-1896 AL	Tall
STEELE, Jos. C.	10th MS Inf.	1839-1902 Clai	Adam
STEELE, J. R.	11th MS Inf.	1841-1900 Alco	Alco
STEELE, S. E.	5th MS Inf.	1818-1899 MS	Nesh
STEELE, W. M.	21st MS Inf.	1833-1904 Tall	Tall
STEEN, Elias E.	3rd MS Inf.	1827-1863	Rank
STEEN, James	10th MS Inf.	1843-1901	Copi
STEEN, W. R.	1st MS Lt. Art.	1840-1924 Choc	Atta
STEEN, W. T.	26th SC Inf.	1845-1926 SC	Alco
STEEN, W. W.	6th MS Inf.	1844-1925	Rank
STEEN, William G.	6th MS Inf.	1839-1909	Rank
STEEN, William Thomas	26th SC Inf.	1838-1900 SC	Alco
STEGALL, Columbus	41st MS Inf.	1841-1922 Pont	Pont
STEGALL, James M.	41st MS Inf.	1830-1924 Pont	Pont
STEGALL, Jerry G.	41st MS Inf.	1838-1896 Pont	Pont
STEGALL, Thomas M.	41st MS Inf.	1830-1908 Pont	Pont
STEGALL, W. M.	3rd MS Inf.	1819-1898 Itaw	Monr
STEGALL, Willian T.	2nd MS Cav.	1834-1915 Pont	Pont

Name	Unit	Dates		
STEGER, J. P.	12th MS Cav.	1837-1886	Tish	Alco
STEINWEINDER, B. B.	MS Lt. Art.	1842-1911	MS	Laud
STEINWEINDER, J. R.	21st AL Inf.	1829-1908	Clar	Laud
STEINWINDER, J. F.	22nd AL Inf.	1844-1924	AL	Forr
STEINWINDER, James E.	22nd Inf.	1827-1907	AL	Jone
STENNETT, George L.	10th MS Cav.	1824-189_	MS	Pren
STENNETT, Thomas A.	10th MS Cav.	1835-1902	MS	Pren
STENNETT, William W.	32nd MS Inf.	1833-1915	MS	Pren
STENNIS, Adam T.	32nd AL Inf.	1819-1878	AL	Laud
STEPHEN, William Lewis	19th MS Inf.	1836-1897		Jeff
STEPHENS, C. W.	35th MS Inf.	1843-1928	Clay	Clay
STEPHENS, Dauz W.	8th MS Inf.	1838-1863	KY	Smit
STEPHENS, E. S.	35th MS Inf.	1840-1906		Nesh
STEPHENS, E. S. (Rev.)	4th MS Inf.	1838-1907	Nesh	Laud
STEPHENS, Elijah	MS Lt. Art.	1846-1917		Tate
STEPHENS, Francis M.	30th MS Inf.	1842-___	Atta	Noxu
STEPHENS, Harrison A.	2nd MS Inf.	1822-1862	Tipp	Tipp
STEPHENS, J. L.	41st MS Inf.	1844-1898		Rank
STEPHENS, J. P.	13th MS Inf.	1849-1929	Atta	Atta
STEPHENS, John	2nd MS Cav.	1840-1913	Newt	Newt
STEPHENS, John M.	35th MS Inf.	1826-1904	Nesh	Kemp
STEPHENS, John Riley	12th MS Cav.	1824-1906	Itaw	Itaw
STEPHENS, Joseph Marion	32nd MS Reg.	1842-1923	MS	Pren
STEPHENS, Joseph S.	1st MS Lt. Art.	1840-1909		Jeff
STEPHENS, M. H.	28th MS Cav.	1838-1913	Monr	Monr
STEPHENS, Marcus D.	17th MS Inf.	1829-1911	Yalo	Yalo
STEPHENS, P. T.	20th MS Inf.	1841-1919	Atta	Atta
STEHENS, R. B.	12th MS Cav.	1826-1891	Pont	Unio
STEPHENS, R. M.	2nd & 13th MS Inf.	1834-1888	Pont	Pont
STEPHENS, Richard	3rd MS Inf.	1823-1873	KY	Yazo
STEPHENS, S. S.	15th TN Cav.	1845-1931	TN	Monr
STEPHENS, T. S.	35th MS Inf.	1831-1897	Nesh	Kemp
STEPHENS, Thomas	2nd MS Cav.	1841-1924	MS	Newt
STEPHENS, Thomas M.	7th MS Inf.	1820-1900	Mari	Webs
STEPHENSON, James W.	26th MS Inf.	____-1904	Tish	Alco
STEPHENSON, John W.	Adams MS Cav.	1839-1886	Tate	Tate
STEPHENSON, Marcus L.	48th MS Inf.	1846-1864	NC	Warr
STEPHENSON, Thomas J.	48th MS Inf.	1844-1912	NC	Warr
STEPHISON, S. T.	17th LA Inf.	1842-1862	LA	Lafa
STERLING, John A.	38th MS Cav.	1846-1900	MS	Simp
STERLING, John A.	38th MS Cav.	1843-1901	Lawr	Covi
STERLING, Vinson P.	7th MS Inf.	1836-1904	Amit	Amit
STEVENS, A. H.	3rd & 22nd MS Inf.	1848-1933		Copi
STEVENS, Alexander L.	14th MS Inf.	1843-1904	MS	Wins
STEVENS, B. L.	7th FL Inf.	1849-1928	FL	Mont
STEVENS, Clark	11th MS Cav.	1829-1894	SC	Wins
STEVENS, Edward B.	1st MS Cav.	1844-1901	Pano	Pano
STEVENS, F. Marion	15th MS Inf.	1840-1889	Shar	Shar
STEVENS, General P.	14th MS Inf.	1836-1862	SC	Wins
STEVENS, George W.	14th MS Inf.	1844-1900	Wins	Wins

STEVENS, Henry G.	15th MS Inf.	1819-1888 Warr	Shar
STEVENS, J. A.	14th MS Inf.	1843-1910 Lown	Clay
STEVENS, J. A. C.	9th MS Inf.	1825-1898 DeSo	Tate
STEVENS, J. W.	1st MS Lt. Art.	18_-1882 Holm	Holm
STEVENS, James H.	12th LA Inf.	1835-1902 TN	Pike
STEVENS, Joel	48th MS Inf.	1834-1891 Warr	Warr
STEVENS, John	2nd MS Inf.	1836-1915 AL	Lee
STEVENS, John A.	14th MS Inf.	1843-___ Lown	Clay
STEVENS, Johnathan	5th AL Cav.	1825-1924 AL	Itaw
STEVENS, John Oscar	15th MS Inf.	1829-1891	Shar
STEVENS, John P.	6th MS Inf.	1835-1908 NC	Hind
STEVENS, Joseph H/R	14th MS Inf.	1838-1914 Lown	Lown
STEVENS, Leroy	39th MS Inf.	1845-1915 Pike	Lefl
STEVENS, Lycurgus A.	22nd MS Inf.	1839-1918	Copi
STEVENS, P. J.	32nd AL Inf.	1844-1908 AL	Laud
STEVENS, R. M.	8th MS Inf.	1845-1923 MS	Harr
STEVENS, Robert H.	3rd MS Inf.	1840-1924 Yazo	Yazo
STEVENS, S. E.	18th MS Inf.	1837-1876	Rank
STEVENS, Thomas	14th MS Inf.	1832-1912 SC	Wins
STEVENS, Thomas L.	14th MS Inf.	1825-1917 SC	Holm
STEVENS, W. H.	9th MS Inf.	1843-1930 DeSo	Harr
STEVENS, William	1st MS Inf.	1841-1900 Tish	Itaw
STEVENS, William D.	2nd MS Cav.	1838-1903 SC	Wins
STEVENS, Willian R.	Walters MS Lt. Art.	1820-1900 Wayn	Wayn
STEVENS, Wylie H.	8th MS Cav.	1811-1872 Tall	Tall
(STEVENSON, Alex located after STEWART, A. J.)			
STEVENSON, David	2nd MS Cav.	1838-1908 IR	Choc
STEVENSON, J. A.	2nd Partisans	1847-1913 Calh	Chic
STEVENSON, J. L.	23rd MS Inf.	Tish	Alco
STEWARD, J. W.	27th AL Inf.	1828-1898 AL	Tish
STEWART, A.	11th MS Inf.	1835-1904 Nesh	Nesh
STEWART, A. C.	34th MS Inf.	1822-1874	DeSo
STEWART, A. J.	3rd TX Cav.	1841-1862 TX	Lafa
STEVENSON, Alex	32nd MS Inf.		Hind
STEWART, Alexander P.	TN Army	1821-1908 TN	Harr
STEWART, Anderson A.	31st MS Inf.	1845-1921 Calh	Calh
STEWART, Arden	5th MS Inf.	1829-1916	Nesh
STEWART, B. F.	40th MS Inf.	1827-1915 Nesh	Nesh
STEWART, Benj. F.	41st MS Inf.	1836-1920 Noxu	Noxu
STEWART, Benson	2nd MS Inf.	1833-190_ Pont	Pont
STEWART, D. H.	43rd MS Inf.	1840-1909 SC	Lown
STEWART, D. W.	35th MS Inf.	1841-1893 Wins	Kemp
STEWART, Duncan	MS Cav.	1836-1905 Wilk	Wilk
STEWART, E.	9th AL Inf.	1843-1919 AL	Itaw
STEWART, E. T.	1st MS Lt. Art.	1841-1863 Adam	Adam
STEWART, F. M.	10th AL Cav.	1848-1919 AL	Yalo
STEWART, G. F.	1st MS Lt.Art.	Adam	Adam
STEWART, George	7th MS Inf.	1835-1925 ST	Pike
STEWART, H.	3rd MS Cav.		Hind
STEWART, H. C.	5th MS Inf.	1844-1919 Nesh	Nesh

STEWART, Hiram G.	Mitchells MS Cav.	1847-191_	Pear	Pear
STEWART, J. A.	35th MS Inf.	1839-1915	Wins	Wins
STEWART, J. B.	3rd MS Inf.	1838-1921	Harr	Newt
STEWART, J. C.	21st MS Inf.	1837-1898	Wilk	Wilk
STEWART, J. H.	4th MS Inf.	1842-1876	Calh	Calh
STEWART, J. M.	33rd MS Inf.	1842-1909	Amit	Amit
STEWART, J. M.	35th MS Inf.	1818-1906	AL	Madi
STEWART, J. M.	41st MS Inf.	1839-1908		Harr
STWART, J. M.	24th MS Inf.	1846-1906	Lown	Tall
STEWART, J. N.	42nd MS Inf.	1828-1903	Yalo	Webs
STEWART, J. T.	8th MS Cav.	1845-1933	GA	Newt
STEWART, J. W.	3rd TN Inf.	1838-1872	TN	Alco
STEWART, Jacob Cooper	44th GA Inf.	1845-1906	Clar	Laud
STEWART, James	Made Uniforms	1811-1895	IR	Choc
STEWART, James A.	34th MS Inf.	1844-1921	Mars	Tate
STEWART, James D.	Militia	____-1905		Hind
STEWART, James _.	34th MS Inf.	1827-1869	Mars	Bent
STEWART, John	33rd MS Inf.	1841-1921	Amit	Amit
STEWART, John	38th MS Cav.	1849-1933	MS	Hanc
STEWART, John A.	35th MS Inf.	1825-1895	Nesh	Leak
STEWART, John J.	2nd LA Inf.	1840-188	LA	Warr
STEWART, John M.	38th MS Cav.	1844-1916	Pear	Pear
STEWART, Leonard C.	20th MS Inf.	1840-1899	MS	Monr
STEWART, Marion	36th MS Inf.	1842-1899	MS	Scot
STEWART, Martin	7th MS Inf.	1825-1905	MS	Mari
STEWART, Moody B.	2nd MS Inf.	1813-1885	Monr	Monr
STEWART, N. S.	6th AL Inf.	1837-1915	AL	Harr
STEWART, R. J. (Rev.)	22nd MS Inf.	1847-1919	Amit	Amit
STEWART, Rea	36th MS Inf.	1837-1896		Copi
STEWART, Robert A.	23rd MS Inf.	1840-1919	AL	Tipp
STEWART, Samuel	Madison Lt. Art.	1833-1921	IR	Rank
STEWART, Samuel W.	19th MS Inf.	1840-1926	MS	Pano
STEWART, Sebron	33rd MS Inf.	1833-1915	Linc	Linc
STEWART, T. P.	12th MS Inf.	1840-1923	Clai	Harr
STEWART, W. C.	19th MS Inf.	1842-1917	Noxu	Kemp
STEWART, W. E.	10th MS Inf.	1841-1895		DeSo
STEWART, W. _.	27th MS Inf.	1845-1932	MS	Jone
STEWART, W. M.	2nd MS Inf.	1845-1918	Tish	Alco
STEWART, W. Calvin	7th MS Inf.	1845-1923		Pear
STEWART, Weekly	19th MS Inf.	1821-1898		DeSo
STEWART, Wm. H.	Jeff Davis Cav.	1839-1889	Adam	Adam
STEWART, William	33rd MS Inf.			Hind
STEWART, William C.	44th AL Inf.	1845-1913	AL	Wins
STEWART, William G.	35th MS Inf.	1846-1886	Wins	Kemp
STEWART, William Henry	1st MS Lt. Art.	1828-1891	Adam	Adam
STEWART, William J.	33rd MS Inf.	1834-1880	Amit	Amit
STEWART, William J.	33rd MS Inf.	1843-1918	Linc	Linc
STEWART, William Wallace	34th MS Inf.	1846-1927	MS	Lafa
STIGLER, Ben	1st Bat. S. S.	1830-1910	AL	Holm
STIGLER, Edward B.	29th MS Inf.	1830-1903	Holm	Holm
STIGLER, Isaac R.	5th MS Cav.	1834-1881	Holm	Holm

Name	Unit	Dates		
STIGLER, James M.	25th MS Inf.	1830-1919		Sunf
STIGLER, James Monroe	29th MS Inf.	1835-1900	Holm	Holm
STIGLER, John Hamilton	_8th MS Cav.	1843-1909	Holm	Holm
STIGLER, Simon	1st MS Bat. S. S.	1838-1863	Holm	Holm
STIGLER, William George	12th MS Inf.	1844-1919	Holm	Sunfr
STILES, Edward Howard	12th MS Inf.	1843-1892		Jack
STILL, Charles	Martins AL Inf.	1827-1908		Clar
STILL, Daniel	42nd MS Inf.	1827-1901	Pano	Pano
STILL, James H.	18th MS Cav.	1832-1897	MS	Tate
STILL, John W.	9th MS Inf.	1845-1923	DeSo	Pano
STILLMAN, George T.	41st AL Inf.	1841-1901	AL	Chic
STILLMAN, John H.	35th MS Inf.	1837-1899		Okti
STILLMAN, William	50th TN Inf.	1841-1863	TN	Lafa
STINGLE, Harry	15th MS Inf.	1841-186_		Lafa
STINGLEY, D. W.	40th MS Inf.			Atta
STINGLEY, George P.	30th MS Inf.	1843-1910	Atta	Atta
STINGLEY, Joseph W.	30th MS Inf.	1834-1905	Holm	Atta
STINSON, Anderson	34th MS Inf.	1845-1909	TN	Mars
STINSON, John	5th MS Inf.	1825-1910	Laud	Laud
STINSON, Joseph	1st MS Lt. Art.	1834-1900	TN	Mont
STINSON, Thomas A.	41st AL Inf.	1845-1910	AL	Lown
STINSON, William B.	18th MS Inf.	1839-1906	Madi	Madi
ST. JOHN, Charles	Gen. Johnsons Staff	1832-1917	Madi	Madi
STOATE, Joseph	23rd MS Inf.	1831-1903		Lafa
STOATES, Joseph	23rd MS Inf.	1833-186_	Pont	Lafa
STOCKDALE, Thomas R.	16th MS Inf.	1828-1899	Pike	Pike
STOCKETT, Peter M.	16th MS Inf.	1842-1901	Wilk	Wilk
STOCKMAN, J. R.	4th LA Inf.			Adam
STOCKMAN, S. D.	10th MS Inf.		Adam	Adam
STOCKSTILL, David W.	3rd MS Inf.	1818-1887	Jack	Pear
STOCKSTILL, George W.	3rd MS Inf.	1842-1927	Jack	Pear
STOCKSTILL, T. J.	38th MS Cav.	1844-1921	Pear	Pear
STOCKSTILL, T. J. T.	9th MS Cav.	1846-1912	Pear	Pear
STOCKSTILL, Thomas J.	9th MS Cav.	1840-1872	Pear	Pear
STOCKSTILL, W. Alonzo	3rd MS Inf.	1842-1930	MS	Pear
STOCKTON, J. S.	2nd MS Inf.	1845-1910	Tish	Tish
STOCKTON, R. N.	3rd MS Inf.	1814-1896	TN	Monr
STOCKTON, W. E.	1st MS Lt. Art.		Adam	Adam
STODDARD, A. A.	20th MS Inf.	1824-1898	OH	Lefl
STOGNER, Joseph M.	19th MS Inf.	____-1884		Tall
STOGNER, William	2nd MS Inf.	1823-1901	MS	Walt
STOKES, Daniel T.	63rd GA. Inf.	1844-191_	GA	Newt
STOKES, David J.	24th AL Inf.	1845-____	AL	Jack
STOKES, E. A.	Adams MS Cav.	1823-1906	Madi	Madi
STOKES, H. C.	5th MS Inf.	1826-1901	Holm	Holm
STOKES, James R.	6th AL Inf.	1841-1914	AL	Scot
STOKES, Joseph D.	20th AL Inf.	1841-1925	AL	Kemp
STOKES, L.	2nd MS Inf.	1814-1889	Noxu	Yazo
STOKES, P. R.	5th MS Inf.	1821-1893	Wins	Wins
STOKES, Richard J.	30th MS Inf.	1839-1920		Mont
STOKES, Sanders W.	2nd MS Inf.	1846-1927	MS	Lee

Name	Unit	Dates		
STOKES, Thomas Jeff.	11th MS Inf.	1839-1932	MS	Lown
STOKES, Thomas S.	20th AL Inf.	1846-1827	AL	Kemp
STOKES, W. F.	3rd AL Inf.	1845-1926	AL	Harr
STOKES, Wiley Allen	23rd MS Inf.	1846-1924	GA	Tipp
STOKES, William F.	20th AL Inf.	1845-1925	AL	Scot
STOKES, William L.	46th MS Inf.	1843-1918	VA	Kemp
STOMPLEY, T. S.	23rd Cav.	1848-1902	Fran	Fran
STONE, A. J.	40th MS Inf.	1841-1888	Leak	Leak
STONE, A. P.	2nd MS Cav.	1845-1914	Laud	Lee
STONE, C. H. (Dr.)	Jeff Davis Legion	1806-1864	Adam	Adam
STONE, Caleb W.	2nd MS Cav.	1840-1894	Itaw	Monr
STONE, Carroll	9th MS Inf.	1846-1876	Madi	Madi
STONE, D. A.(Dr.)	2nd MS Inf.	1846-1925		Lee
STONE, H. D.	5th MS Cav.	1821-1875	SC	Mont
STONE, Henry	MS Cav.	1837-1887	Wilk	Adam
STONE, Henry Clay	22nd MS Inf.	1843-1893		DeSo
STONE, I. B.	Fords MS Cav.	1801-1862	Carr	Carr
STONE, J. D.	1st AL Art.	1846-1901	AL	Laud
STONE, J. L.	18th MS Cav.	1836-1895	MS	Lee
STONE, J. T.	3rd MS Inf.	1850-1913		Harr
STONE, James	9th MO Inf.	1837-1906	KY	Wash
STONE, James Boyd	43rd MS Inf.	1831-1913		Mont
STONE, John H.	16th MS Inf.	1846-1921	Chic	Chic
STONE, John H.	2nd MS Cav.	1845-1921	Monr	Chic
STONE, John M.	1st AL Inf.	1835-1905	AL	Laud
STONE, John Marshall	2nd MS Inf.	1830-1900	Tish	Tish
STONE, N. Y.	37th MS Inf.	1844-1911	Laud	Laud
STONE, Perry S.	Poagues Art.	1844-1878	Madi	Madi
STONE, R. S.	28th MS Cav.	1844-1925		DeSo
STONE, R. W.	2nd MS Inf.	1848-1932	MS	Lee
STONE, Robert Reuben	45th MS Inf.	1843-1905	Mars	Mars
STONE, T. S.	3rd TN Inf.	1842-1863	TN	Lafa
STONE, Thomas M.	Morgans KY Cav.	1839-1879	KY	Wash
STONE, W. T.	Ballentines MS Cav.	1831-1900	Carr	Carr
STONE, Walter Wilson	8th MS Inf.	1840-1930		Hind
STONE, William	Jeff Davis Legion	1846-1901	AL	Laud
STORM, Edward	28th MS Cav.	1843-1904	GE	Wash
STORM, John	Brookhaven Lt. Art.	1812-1882	FR	Linc
STOREY, A. F.	26th AL Inf.	1833-1904		Nesh
STORMANT, W. D.	32nd MS Inf.	1840-1916	Tish	Tish
STORY, A. J.	11th AL Inf.	1840-1903	AL	Lown
STORY, Samuel	14th TX Inf.	1843-1862	TX	Lown
STORY, Thomas	23rd MO Inf.	1837-1917	SC	Tipp
STORY, Thomas H.	10th AL Inf.	1842-1934	AL	Harr
STOUT, C. W.	5th MS Cav.	1843-1939	Carr	Carr
STOUT, John S.	2nd KY Inf.	1831-1892	Harr	Harr
STOVALL, C. S.	26th MS Inf.	1826-1909	GA	Harr
STOVALL, Charles A.	13th MS Inf.	1837-1916	Clar	Clar
STOVALL, Columbus C.	24th MS Inf.	1838-1923	Chic	Chic
STOVALL, G. J.	4th MS Inf.	1832-____	Mont	Mont

128

STOVALL, H. T.	4th MS Regt.	1841-1917 Carr	Hind
STOVALL, Harrison P.	24th MS Inf.	1846-1926 Chic	Chic
STOVALL, John A.	11th MS Inf.		Kemp
STOVALL, W. G.	Jeff Davis		
	MS Cav.	1843-19 Lawr	Chic
STOVALL, Warren	15th MS Inf.	1823-1902	Mont
STOWERS, James Campbell	4th MS Cav.	1846-1914	Jeffn
STOWERS, John C.	Jeff Davis Legion	1832-1902 MS	Adam
STOWERS, Let E.	4th LA Inf.	1832-1863 LA	Clai
STOWERS, Lewis Edward	LA Inf.	1840-1863 LA	Clai
STOWERS, William J.	11th MS Inf.	1841-190_ Lafa	Lafa
STRAHAM, William L.	1st MS Cav.	1830-1908	Covi
STRAIN, Brice Blackburn	2nd MS Inf.	1840-1897 AL	Unio
STRAIN, Cyrus	4th AL Inf.	1847-1921	Pont
STRAIN, Cyrus F.	4th AL Cav.	1846-1886 AL	Pont
STRAIN, Cyrus Franklin	4th AL Cav.	1846-1922 AL	Pont
STRAIN, James H.	2nd MS Inf.	1813-1894 Pont	Unio
STRAIN, James Henderson	2nd MS Inf.	1842-1926 AL	Lee
STRAIT, James L. H.	1st MS Cav.	1850-___ MS	Wins
STRAIT, Leonard S.	7th MS Inf.	1845-1936 Fran	Linc
STRATTON, Floyd W.	7th MS Inf.	1839-1904 VA	Amit
STRATTON, Sidney V.	1st MS Lt. Art.	1845-1921 Adam	Adam
STRATTON, W. J.	26th AL Inf.	1846-___ AL	Clay
STRATTON, William Jeff.	26th AL Inf.	1847-1912 AL	Lefl
STRAUS, Benjamin	27th MS Inf.	1830-1908 Perr	Perr
STRAUSS, Henry	10th MS Inf.	1830-1904 FR	Hind
STRAVAPORDA, Dennis	3rd MS Inf.	1839-1934 MS	Harr
STREALE_, L. A.	10th KY Inf.	1844-1912 KY	Warr
STREATER, J. B.	30th MS Inf.	1845-1940 Carr	Carr
STREET, Archibald McB.	26th MS Inf.	1840-1926 NC	Pren
STREATER, J. T.	30th MS Inf.	1821-1890 Carr	Carr
STREET, Benjamin C.	2nd & 5th		
	MS Inf.	1820-1901 MS	Wayn
STREET, Donald Jr.	26th MS Inf.	1844-1929 NC	Warr
STREET, Hugh McQueen	28th MS Inf.	1833-1920 NC	Pren
STREET, J. J.	22nd MS Inf.	1824-1916 Tipp	Tipp
STREET, Joseph M.	14th MS Inf.	1840-1924 Lown	Lown
STREET, N. B.	10th MS Inf.	1828-1882 Yazo	Yazo
STREET, S. A.	2nd MS Cav.	1848-1906 Tipp	Sunf
STREET, Sidney Bryan	8th MS Cav.	1843-1929 AL	Lown
STREET, Thomas Parke	33rd MS Inf.	1839-1917 Clai	Amit
STREETER, Edmond C.	42nd MS Inf.	MS	Calh
STRIBBLING, M. F.	17th MS Inf.	1834-1926	Harr
STRIBBLING, Mathew C.	31st MS Inf.	1832-1913 Calh	Calh
STRILING, J. M.	5th MS Inf.	1812-1885 Nesh	Nesh
STRIBLING, James Harris	36th MS Inf.	1822-1880 Scot	Nesh
STRIBLING, O. P.	31st MS Inf.	1814-1897 AL	Chic
STRIBLING, Shelton R.	14th TN Cav.	1835-1914 TN	Lown
STRIBLING, W. J.	5th MS Inf.	1843-1911 MS	Nesh
STRIBLING, William B.	40th MS Inf.	1816-1863 Nesh	Nesh
STRICKER, Brotherton	Warren Lt. Art.	1844-1905 KY	Warr
STRICKLAND, A. J.	26th MS Inf.	1843-1913 MS	Tish

STRICKLAND, Albert G.	26th MS Inf.	1833-1902 GA	Pren
STRICKLAND, B. P.	26th MS Inf.	1826-1901 Alco	Alco
STRICKLAND, E.	31st MS Inf.	1841-1925 Choc	Harr
STRICKLAND, E.	31st MS Inf.	1846-1929 Choc	Webs
STRICKLAND, Ed	6th MS Cav.		Alco
STRICKLAND, Frank S.	14th MS Cav.	1838-1917 Pike	Pike
STRICKLAND, G. W.	26th MS Inf.	1845-1921 Alco	Alco
STRICKLAND, H. L.	1st MS Cav.	1848-1926	Jone
STRICKLAND, J. E.	31st MS Inf.	1843-1903 Choc	Webs
STRICKLAND, J. W.	1st MS Lt. Art.	Adam	Adam
STRICKLAND, Josephus C.	9th LA Inf.	1835-1917 Pike	Pike
STRICKLAND, R. P.	26th MS Inf.	1843-1902 Tish	Alco
STRICKLAND, S. S.	46th MS Inf.	1822-1895 Wayn	Wayn
STRICKLAND, T. N.	1st MS Inf.	1816-1878 Adam	Adam
STRICKLANND, W. G. N.	1st MS Art.	1822-1868 MS	Yazo
STRICKLAND, William M.	9th MS Inf.	1823-1908 Mars	Mars
STRICKLEN, A. J.	7th AL Cav.	1843-1913 AL	Tish
STRICKLIN, Edmond W.	2nd MS Inf.	1834-1892 NC	Tipp
STRICKLIN, J. T.	2nd MS Inf.	1838-1880 Pont	Bent
STRINGER, B. W.	8th MS Inf.	1844-1905 Smit	Covi
STRINGER, J. D.	37th MS Inf.	1843-1898 Jasp	Jasp
STRINGER, J. S.	7th MS Inf.		Copi
STRINGER, Jackson W.	7th MS Inf.	____-1863 Mari	Mari
STRINGER, James M.	38th MS Regt.	1834-1915	Hind
STRINGER, John S.	37th MS Inf.	1841-	Newt
STRINGER, Mose	7th MS Inf.	1843-1936 Lawr	Harr
STRINGER, Moses	Withers Art.	1846-1936	Harr
STRINGER, S. D.	12th MS Cav.	____-1908 Smit	Smit
STRINGER, W. M.	7th MS Inf.	184_-1910 Smit	Jasp
STRINGER, Wade A.	37th MS Inf.	1843-1924 MS	Jasp
STHINGER, Wiley W.	1st MS Cav.	1845-1927 Smit	Smit
STRINGER, William B.	8th MS Inf.	1839-1926 Smit	Smit
STRINGFELLOW, John R.	5th MS Inf.	1828-1910 Chic	Chic
STRONG, Henry	6th MS Inf.	1827-1906 Copi	Copi
STRONG, Hugh Anderson	1st MS Cav.	1847-1916 Copi	Copi
STRONG, J. R.	1st MS Lt. Art.	1831-1903	Hind
STRONG, John	6th MS Inf.	1829-1897	Copi
STRONG, Thomas	36th MS Inf.	182_-1904 Copi	Copi
(13 cards were blurred and unreadable)			
STRUM, Benjamin	35th MS Inf.	18__-190 Nesh	Nesh
STUARD, J. A.	23rd GA Inf.	1834-1922 GA	Harr
STUART, Joseph B.	MS Minute Man	1828-1889 Copi	Lama
STUART, S. M.	21st AL Inf.	1840-1924 AL	Harr
STUART, S. M.	14th TX Inf.	1843-1862 TX	Lown
STUART, Vardy L.	16th MS Inf.	1832-1908 Smit	Smit
STUART, William	3rd MS Inf.	____-1876	Hind
STUART, William Clark	Bradfords Scouts	1846-1940 Wilk	Wilk
STUBLEFIELD, A. B.	12th KY Cav.	GA	Rank
STUBBLEFIELD, A. M.	18th MS Inf.	1840-1880 MS	Yazo
STUBBLEFIELD, Calvin B.	1st MS Lt. Art.	1833-1862 Yazo	Yazo
STUBBLEFIELD, David	1st MS Lt. Art.	1826-1909 Yazo	Yazo
STUBBLEFIELD, Marlin	1st MS Lt. Art.	1818-1893 Yazo	Yazo

STUBBLEFIELD, Robert	2nd MS Cav.	1843-1890 MS	Calh
STUBBLEFIELD, William H.	1st MS Lt. Art.	1820-1907 Yazo	
STUBBS, Henry A.	1st TN Inf.	1830-1907 GA	Tipp
STUBBS, T. H.	16th Conf. Cav.	1819-1902 Simp	Covi
STUBBS, T. _.	7th MS Cav.	1848-1917 Scot	Scot
STUBBS, W. W.	16th MS Cav.	1845-1931 Smit	Smit
STUCKEY, Daniel	1st MS Inf.	1817-1890	Smit
STUCKEY, Enoch	38th MS Cav.	1843-1922 MS	JEDA
STUCKEY, R. B.	7th MS Inf.	1837-1917	Rank
STUCKEY, S. W.	3rd LA Inf.	1839-1911 LA	Laud
STUCKY, E. D.	4th MS Cav.	1844-___ Simp	Simp
STUDDARD, A. J.	2nd MS Cav.	1847-1915 Laud	Monr
STUDDARD, Samuel S.	3rd MS Inf.	1814-1881 Itaw	Monr
STURDIVANT, A. B.	5th MS Inf.	1841-1862 Monr	Lown
STURDIVANT, Ransom	12th MS Inf.	1830-1886 MS	Yazo
STURDIVANT, William C.	2nd TN Inf.	1846-1931 Tate	Tate
STURGIS, A. J.	16th MS Inf.	1820-1906 SC	Copi
STURGIS, William A.	36th MS Inf.	1847-1866	Copi
STYLES, W. _.	16th MS Inf.	Adam	Adam
SUBER, J. _.	23rd MS Inf.	1839-1924 MS	Pont
SUDDETH, Alexander D.	23rd MS Inf.	1821-1905	Coah
SUDDUTH, H. P.	1st MS Cav.	1846-1889 Pont	Pont
SUDDUTH, Jefferson D.	30th MS Inf.	1833-1900 Carr	Carr
SUGG, Lemuel	14th MS Inf.	1846-1906 Chic	Chic
SUGG, Lucius D.	LA Cav.	1845-1924 MS	Coah
SUGG, Wiley C. Sr.	19th MS Cav.	1805-1863	Webs
SUGG, Wiley Calhoun Jr.	19th MS Cav.	1843-1920	Webs
SUGG, William G.	8th MS Cav.	1845-1870 Choc	Webs
SUGG, William G.	8th MS Cav.	1846-1929 Lown	Webs
SUGGS, H. T.	3rd MS Inf.	1818-1911 Calh	Calh
SUGGS, John D.	2nd MS Cav.	1822-1863 AL	Monr
SUITER, Morman	32nd MS Inf.	1830-1913 Alco	Alco
SULLIVAN, A. J.	23rd MS Cav.	1833-1914 Copi	Fran
SULLIVAN, Alexander	Stubbs MS Cav.	1847-1937 Smit	Smit
SULLIVAN, Algernon L.	19th MS Inf.	1840-18__ Pano	Pano
SULLIVAN, Charles A.	48th MS Inf.	1835-1882	Okti
SULLIVAN, Daniel D.	8th MS Inf.	1839-1916 Smit	Smit
SULLIVAN, George W.	6th MS Cav.	1822-1885	Hind
SULLIVAN, J. S.	35th MS Inf.	1840-1926 Wins	Wins
SULLIVAN, Jack J.	39th MS Inf.	1834-1913 AL	Copi
SULLIVAN, James A.	3rd MS Inf.	1825-1895 Monr	Monr
SULLIVAN, Jessie	35th MS Inf.	1834-1876 NC	Wins
SULLIVAN, Jim R.	9th MS Inf.	1843-1924 Mars	Mars
SULLIVAN, John E.	4th MS Inf.	1839-1922 Yalo	Tate
SULLIVAN, Joseph	39th MS Inf.	1841-1934 Smit	Smit
SULLIVAN, Joseph	39th MS Inf.	1818-1895 Simp	Smit
SULLIVAN, Joseph E.	43rd MS Inf.	1845-1919 Pont	Pont
SULLIVAN, Lewis S.	39th MS Inf.	Simp	Simp
SULLIVAN, Loden	46th MS Inf.	1844-1898 Covi	JEDA
SULLIVAN, Mark	8th MS Regt.	1830-1913 MS	Smit
SULLIVAN, Monroe	40th AL Inf.	1836-1909 AL	Scot
SULLIVAN, R. L.	20th MS Inf.	1841-1892	Laud

Name	Unit	Dates	State	County
SULLIVAN, Samuel R.	8th MS Inf.	1838-1917 MS	Smit
SULLIVAN, W. G.	24th MS Inf.	1824-1908 Itaw	Itaw
SULLIVAN, W. J.	Breckenridge MS Cav.		Adam
SULLIVAN, W. T. J.	Army	1829-1911	Hind
SULLIVAN, William H.	1st MS Inf.	1840-1915 MS	Monr
SULLIVAN, William J.	1st MS Inf.	1839-1870 Adam	Adam
SULLIVANT, Jesse	27th MS Inf.	1835-1910 Linc	Tall
SULLIVANT, Wiley	3rd MS Inf.	1838-1878	Okti
SUMERALL, Archie	Turners Art.	____-1894 Clar	Clar
SUMERALL, Joseph H.	3rd MS Inf.	1843-1908	Copi
SUMERFORD, W. D.	1st MS Inf.	1836-1903 Tish	Itaw
SUMMERFORD, L.	3rd Ashcrafts Regt.	1828-1918 Monr	Monr
SUMMERFORD, William C.	1st MS Inf.	1813-1891 MS	Itaw
SUMMERS, Archellis	33rd MS Inf.	1845-1931 Linc	Linc
SUMNER, John	16th MS Inf.	____-1862 SC	Smit
SUMMERS, G. B.	20th MS Inf.	1829-1905 Leak	Leak
SUMMERS, George W.	17th MS Inf.	1846-1863	Copi
SUMMERS, Gwin D.	33rd MS Inf.	1839-1871 Lawr	Lawr
SUMMERS, H. A.	27th MS Inf.	1841-1910 Linc	Tall
SUMMERS, J. C/G.	17th MS Inf.	18_3-1926	Harr
SUMMERS, Jesse	33rd MS Inf.	1837-1923 Holm	Lee
SUMMERS, Joshua	33rd MS Inf.	184_-1918 Lawr	Lawr
SUMMERS, Robert	36th MS Inf.	1846-1930 Scot	Scot
SUMMERS, Smith Jr.	27th MS Inf.	1843-1912 Linc	Scot
SUMMERS, T. A.	14th TN Inf.	1845-1915 TN	Harr
SUMMERS, W. C.	1st MS Inf.	1848-1927	Harr
SUMMERS, Zepaneah	33rd MS Inf.	1810-1877 Lawr	Linc
(SUMNER, John located after SUMMERS, Archellis)			
SUMNER, W. H.	18th TN Inf.	1840-1901 TN	Warr
SUMRALL, Allen	3rd MS Inf.	1841-1879	Copi
SUMRALL, D.	Turners MS Art.	1847-1913 Clar	Harri
SUMRALL, Dan	1st LA Inf.	1845-1923 MS	Lama
SUMRALL, E. F. (Dr.)	Jeff Davis Cav.	1837-1885 Wayn	Covi
SUMRALL, Elisha	36th MS Inf.	1828-1875	Copi
SUMRALL, Elisha Woods	2nd MS Inf.	1848-1932 MS	Jasp
SUMRALL, Henry	7th MS Inf.	1827-1906 Jone	Jone
SUMRALL, J. J.	MS Lt. Art.	1842-1910 Clar	Laud
SUMRALL, John	38th MS Cav.	1842-1894 Clai	Mari
SUMRALL, John	MS Lt. Art.	1842-1917 Clar	Lama
SUMRALL, W. W.	7th MS Inf.	1839-1911 Jone	Jone
SUMRALL, William	Seven Star Art.	1835-1884	Copi
SURATT, John L.	16th TN Inf.	1848-1923	Lee
SURATT, John M.	2nd MS Inf.	1828-1875 Alco	Alco
SURRATT, J. L.	4th MS Inf.	1844-1923 MS	Pren
SURRATT, William H.	12th MS Cav.	1843-1925 TN	Pren
SUTHERLAND, Daniel	Adams MS Cav.	1843-1877 Madi	Madi
SUTHERLAND, P. R.	4th MS Cav.	1843-1930 Madi	Harr
SUTHERLAND, William W.	2nd TN Inf.	1844-1909 MO	Pren
SUTTLE, John	3rd MS Inf.	1822-1885 Wins	Wins
SUTTLE, Samuel S.	3_ MS Inf.	1834-____ Smit	Wins
SUTTLES, M.	8th AL Inf.	1838-1907 AL	Kemp

SUTTON, David S.	33rd MS Inf.	18__-1927	Lawr	Lawr
SUTTON, J. M.	20th MS Inf.	1827-1894	Linc	Linc
SUTTON, James H.	2nd MS Inf.	1826-1900	Linc	Linc
SUTTON, James M.	2_ MS Inf.	1846-1864	Wins	JEDA
SUTTON, James M.	28th MS Cav.	1806-1883	PA	Wash
SUTTON, John Carr	41st AL Inf.	1848-1912	AL	Webs
SUTTON, M. L.	39th MS Inf.	1842-193_	Hanc	Lawr
SUTTON, Marquis L.	39th MS Inf.	1842-1932	Sims	Lawr
SUTTON, Shelby	3rd MS Inf.	1826-1880		Chic
SUTTON, Thomas Jeff	28th MS Cav.	____-1906	Wash	Boli
SUTTON, Wayne	6th & 15th MS Inf.	1842-1917		Rank
SWAFFER, Sanders	4th MS Inf.	1819-1886	Calh	Calh
SWAFFORD, J. P.	8th & 19th MS Cav.	____-1913		Hind
SWAFFORD, T. A.	8th TN Inf.	1832-1911	TN	Lee
SWAIN, J. C.	7th MS Inf.	1840-1919	Tipp	Unio
SWAIN, Joseph D.	5th MS Cav.	1823-1875	Carr	Mont
SWAIN, Richard A.	7th MS Cav.	1842-1890	Pont	Unio
SWAIN, W. H.	12th MS Inf.	1832-1909	MD	Adam
SWALES, H. G.	Hardages Battery	1847-1934	MS	Leak
SWAN, Henry	1st LA Art.	1837-1883	Pike	Pike
SWAN, Janes	1st MS Cav.	____-1921		Hind
SWAN, W. G.	Simpins AL Inf.	1836-1905	AL	Chic
SWANN, D. F.	31st TN Inf.	1837-1863	TN	Warr
SWANN, Henry Macon	3rd Vol. Cav.	18_2-1907	MS	Hind
SWANN, Thomas T.	13th MS Inf.	1825-1870		Hind
SWANZY, G. W.	24th MS Inf.	1845-1920	Lown	Lown
SWANZY, _. A.	24th & 43rd MS Inf.	1832-1917	Lown	Lown
SWAYZE, Henry	10th MS Inf.	1841-1862	Adam	Adam
SWAYZE, Hardy S.	1st MS Lt. Art.	1842-1921	Yazo	Yazo
SWAYZE, Prentiss	18th MS Inf.	1840-1892	Yazo	Yazo
SWAYZE, O. H.	1st MS Lt. Art.	1844-1917	MS	Yazo
SWEARINGEN, _. L.	7th MS Inf.	1834-1914	Amit	Amit
SWEARINGEN, Thomas	7th MS Inf.	1841-1937	Amit	Amit
SWEARINGON, James M.	35th MS Inf.	1842-___	Wins	Kemp
SWEARINGON, Morgan M.	24th MS Inf.	1838-1892	Kemp	Kemp
SWEARINGON, W. _.	13th MS Inf.		Kemp	Kemp
SWEAT, Noah	38th MS Cav.	1822-1885	Hanc	Alco
SWEATMAN, David Luke	15th MS Inf.	183_-1920	MS	Mont
SWEATT, T. P.	4th MS Inf.	1850-1934	Atta	Atta
SWETT, Charles	1st MS Lt. Art.	1828-1910	Warr	Warr
SWETT, Daniel Jr.	Warren Lt. Art.	1804-1878	MA	
SWIFT, Thomas	41st MS Inf.	1836-1901	Noxu	Noxu
SWIGERT, J. M.	8th MS Inf.	1831-1877	Smit	Smit
SWILLEY, B. F.	39th MS Inf.	1837-1912		Copi
SWILLEY, Samuel	1st LA Inf.	1828-1903	GA	Ston
SWINDLE, Wid.	43rd AL Inf.	1840-1898	AL	Itaw
SWINDOLL, T. J.	24th MS Inf.	1841-1920	Choc	Webs
SWINNEY, E. M.	29th MS Inf.	1842-1930	Atta	Atta
SWINNEY, John	38th MS Cav.	1839-1921	MS	

SWINNEY, S. M.	Armstrongs Cav.	1844-1930 SC	Pren
SWITZER, William M.	14th MS Inf.	1847-1868 Monr	Laud
SYKES, Columbus	43rd MS Inf.	1832-1865 Monr	Monr
SYKES, Edward	10th MS Inf.	1838-1922 AL	Lown
SYKES, Ethelred Lundy	5th MS Inf.	1846-1915 Monr	Monr
SYKES, Eugene Octavius	14th MS Inf.	1843-1911 MS	Monr
SYKES, Joseph Augustus	17th MS Inf.	1834-1863 Monr	Monr
SYKES, Lawson W.	Gen. Graggs Aide	1841-1864 AL	Monr
SYKES, Lucian Melvill	5th MS Inf.	1838-1879 AL	Monr
SYKES, Richard L. (Dr.)	44th MS Inf.	1840-1912 Lown	Lown
SYKES, Solon M.	15th MS Inf.	1832-1899	Mont
SYKES, S. Turner	11th MS Cav.	1838-1916 Monr	Monr
SYKES, Thomas Barrett	20th MS Inf.	1824-1894 AL	Monr
SYKES, W.	3rd MS Inf.	1844-1918 Copi	Copi
SYKES, Walter L.	5th MS Cav.	1837-1863 AL	Monr
SYKES, W. Granville	43rd MS Inf.	____-1931 AL	Monr
SYKES, William E.	43rd MS Inf.	1835-1864 Lown	Lown
SYLVESTER, Albert G.	15th MS Inf.	1850-1931 MS	Perr
SYLVESTER, James H. A.	23rd AL Inf.	1828-1901	Hanc
SYLVESTER, John Quinn	Steeds MS Cav.	1849-1933 MS	Gree
SYNDER, Caleb Hurst	3rd LA Cav.	1840-1911 LA	Adam
TABB, Daniel D.	8th MS Cav.	1846-1914 MS	Chic
TABB, John W.	18th MS Inf.	1846-1935 Hind	Harr
TABOR, A. J.	24th AL Inf.	1842-1938 AL	Lafa
TABOR, Edwin M.	9th LA Cav.	1828-1900 LA	Wilk
TABOR, William Henry	6th MS Inf.	Wins	Choc
TACKETT, J. P.	16th MS Inf.	1822-1891 AL	Holm
TACKETT, John	Holmes Co. Ind.	1815-1891 AL	Holm
TACKETT, Thomas L.	11th AL Cav.	1844-1900 Alco	Alco
TADLOCK, M. D. C.	11th AL Inf.	1843-1908 AL	Scot
TADLOCK, John W. (Rev.)	11th AL Inf.	1844-____ AL	Scot
TAFT, William M.	8th MS Cav.	184_-1929 Laud	Laud
TAGGART, George W.	3rd AL Regt.	1842-1927 AL	Jack
TAGGART, _. L.	Jeff Davis Inf.	1836-1879 Noxu	Wins
TALBERT, I. S.	1st MS Inf.	1848-192_ Laud	Laud
TALBERT, J. A.	4th MS Inf.	1831-1918 Amit	Amit
TALBERT, J. W.	41st MS Inf.	1847-1929 MS	Laud
TALBERT, Polk	4th MS Cav.	1845-1928	Amit
TALBERT, Thomas W.	27th LA Inf.	1834-1924 LA	Amit
TALBOT, Jerry	11th MS Inf.	1844-1929	Carr
TALBURT, T. A.	1st AR Inf.	1838-1862 AR	Chic
TALIFERRO, Charles	1st TN Cav.	1840-1924 MS	Harr
TALLAFERRO, John D.	6th MS Cav.	____-1862	Lown
TALLEFERRO, Charles	1st TN Cav.	1841-1913	Nesh
TALLEY, C. S.	10th GA Cav.	1846-1927 Madi	Harr
TALLEY, John	35th MS Inf.	1842-1913	Webs
TALLEY, Tom	14th MS Inf.	184_-1923 Nesh	Wins
TALLIAFERRO, Richard T.	42nd MS Inf.	1831-1901 Carr	Carr
TALLISON, Leslie Lee	AL Cadets	1847-1927 AL	Tish
TANKERSLEY, David S.	30th MS Inf.	1829-1913 Lafa	Lafa
TANKERSLEY, C/G. P.	17th MS Inf.	1830-1873 MS	Lafa

Name	Unit	Dates	Location
TANKERSLEY, George Perry	1st MS Cav.	1832-1907 SC	Tish
TAPP, E.	23rd MS Inf.	1824-1909 AL	Tipp
TANNEHILL, J. T.	2nd MS Inf.	___-1874	Mari
TANNEHILL, John T.	6th AL Inf.	1845-1906 AL	Covi
TANNEHILL, N. W.	6th AL Inf.	1843-1909 AL	Covi
TANNER, Charles W.	15th MS Inf.	___-1903	Mont
TANNER, G. W.	Powers Cav.	1847-1923 MS	Copi
TANNER, J. A.	1st MS Inf.	1845-1926 Monr	Monr
TANNER, John M.	9th MS Cav.	1820-1878 MS	Jack
TANNER, L.	15th MS Inf.	1830-1888	Rank
TANNER, Thomas	17th MS Cav.	1829-1899 MS	Jack
TANNER, W.	Powers Cav.	1847-___ Copi	Copi
TAPLEY, Charles Price	39th MS Inf.	1842-1914	Hind
TAPLEY, John	Adams Cav.	1830-1900	Hind
TAPP, Levi	32nd MS Inf.	1833-1925	Lee
TAPP, V. J.	4th AL Inf.	1832-1916 AL	Tipp
TAPPER, Joseph	33rd MS Inf.	1828-1903 Pano	Pano
TAPSCOTT, Lucas L.	2nd MS Inf.		Monr
TARBUTTON, A. J.	16th MS Inf.	1834-1903	Copi
TARDY, George H.	33rd LA Art.	1839-1902 GA	Jack
TARDY, T. H.	27th MS Inf.	1843-1927 MS	Harr
TARLTON, Frank A.	35th MS Inf.	1837-1923 Lown	Lown
TARPLEY, John Estelle	18th MS Inf.		Hind
TARTT, John C.	3rd MS Inf.		Monr
TARVER, B. _.	6th MS Inf.	1827-1868 Leak	Leak
TARVER, J. _.		___-1906	Adam
TARVER, Lott	3rd MS Inf.	1830-1931 MS	Amit
TARVER, Thomas B.	3rd MS Inf.	1847-1926	Atta
TARZETTI, Angelo	S. S. Ozark	1834-1902 Italy	Harr
TASSELL, J. B.	31st TN Inf.	1827-1910 TN	Alco
TATE, Enoch	38th MS Cav.	1827-1889 Holm	Holm
TATE, E. R.	38th MS Cav.	183_-18_7	Pear
TATE, H. M.	23rd MS Inf.	1833-1906 Tipp	Unio
TATE, Harry B.	2nd MS Cav.	1840-1926 Pont	Pont
TATE, Henry Nathaniel	23rd MS Inf.	1843-1911 Tipp	Unio
TATE, J. K. P.	14th LA Inf.	1846-1912 LA	Amit
TATE, Jessie	5th AL Inf.	1833-1923 AL	Monr
TATE, Josiah	4th MS Inf.	1834-1902 Leak	Leak
TATE, Mitchell	3rd MS Cav.	1811-1878	DeSo
TATE, Robert	1st MS Lt. Art.	1833-1904 Yazo	Yazo
TATE, Robert	1st MS Lt. Art.	1843-1905 Yazo	Yazo
TATE, T. A. J.	38th MS Cav.	1828-1904	Pear
TATE, T. J.	3rd MS Cav.	1824-1902 Holm	Holm
TATE, Uriah	18th MS Inf.	1832-1892 Holm	Holm
TATE, W. F.	35th MS Inf.	1845-1911 SC	Wins
TATE, Z. H.	2nd MS Inf.	1834-1914 Calh	Unio
TATOM, A. L.	37th AL Inf.	1841-1862 AL	Lown
TATOM, Joseph Warren	3rd MS Inf.	1844-1903	Hind
TATUM, Daniel	2nd MS Cav.	1823-1892 AL	Monr
TATUM, E. W.	2nd MS Cav.	1828-1879 AL	Monr
TATUM, George W.	3rd AL Cav.	1844-1936 AL	Alco
TATUM, James Marion	38th MS Cav.	1847-1933 Wilk	Amit

TATUM, John	23rd MS Inf.	1833-1909 SC	Tipp
TATUM, John Q.	18th MS Cav.	1849-1932 Yalo	Yalo
TATUM, Joshua	3rd MS Cav.	1829-1884 Lafa	Newt
TATUM, R. T.	7th MS Cav.	1837-1909 GA	Tipp
TAYLOR, A.	35th MS Inf.	1833-190_ Wins	Wins
TAYLOR, A. A.	35th MS Inf.	1831-1909 Wins	Wins
TAYLOR, Alonzo H.	26th MS Inf.	1820-1889 Tish	Alco
TAYLOR, Andrew J.	5th MS Inf.	1840-1894 Choc	Choc
TAYLOR, Andrew Jackson	11th TN Inf.	1834-1906 TN	Tish
TAYLOR, B. F.	45th AL Inf.	1840-1928 AL	Forr
TAYLOR, Calvin	32nd MS Inf.	1843-1889 Tish	Alco
TAYLOR, Calvin A.	32nd MS Inf.	1813-1891 Tall	Alco
TAYLOR, Daniel	15th Conf. Cav.	1831-1914 AL	Wayn
TAYLOR, David Madison	9th MS Inf.	1844-1928 DeSo	Tate
TAYLOR, Ed	8th MS Inf.	1836-1908	Covi
TAYLOR, Edward M.	3rd AL Cav.	1837-1914	Jack
TAYLOR, F. _.	8th MS Cav.	1840-1902 Yalo	Yalo
TAYLOR, G. B.	2nd MS Cav.	1823-1880 Monr	Monr
TAYLOR, G. R.	4th MS Inf.	1842-1930	Mont
TAYLOR, G. T.	35th MS Inf.	1832-1918 Wins	Wins
TAYLOR, G. W.	4th MS Cav.	1847-1931 Calh	Calh
TAYLOR, George W.	Griffins SC Inf.	1845-1931 SC	Carr
TAYLOR, Greenwood W.	Ballentines MS Cav.	1847-1931 Gren	Gren
TAYLOR, H. B.	Armstrongs Home Guards	1847-1926 MS	Calh
TAYLOR, Harlan Mercer	18th MS Cav.	1828-1902	Hind
TAYLOR, Hilary Lafayette	3rd TX Inf.	1843-1915 TX	Yazo
TAYLOR, J. G.	1st MS Cav.	1844-1909 Alco	Alco
TAYLOR, John C.	22nd MS Inf.	1839-1913 Lafa	Unio
TAYLOR, John J.	11th TN Inf.	1835-1909 TN	Tish
TAYLOR, J. K.	4th MS Inf.	1842-1922 Calh	Harr
TAYLOR, J. M.	26th MS Inf.	1842-1919 Pren	Pren
TAYLOR, J. M.	46th MS Inf.	1841-1907	Rank
TAYLOR, J. M. (Dr.)	26th MS Inf.	1827-1895 Alco	Alco
TAYLOR, J. M. G.	41st MS Inf.	1838-1905 MS	Pont
TAYLOR, J. N.	31st MS Inf.	1844-1911 Choc	Atta
TAYLOR, J. P.	3rd AL Inf.	1835-1905	Nesh
TAYLOR, J. R.	7th AL Inf.	1830-1926 AL	Jack
TAYLOR, J. S.	19th MS Inf.	1838-1893	Mars
TAYLOR, J. W.	19th MS Cav.	1841-1909 Calh	Pano
TAYLOR, Jacob C.	11th MS Inf.	1827-1903 Lafa	Lafa
TAYLOR, James	5th MS Inf.	1827-1890	Hind
TAYLOR, James Albert	37th MS Inf.	1844-1909 Monr	Scot
TAYLOR, James C.	39th MS Inf.	1846-19_ Simp	Simp
TAYLOR, James H.	15th MS Sharpshooters	1847-1897 Carr	Carr
TAYLOR, James _.	4th MS Inf.	1831-1922 Carr	Carr
TAYLOR, James W.	15th MS Inf.	1831-1918 MS	Mont
TAYLOR, Jefferson	14th MS Inf.	1825-1877 Monr	Monr
TAYLOR, Joe P.	3rd MS Cav.	1846-1923	DeSo
TAYLOR, John	13th MS Inf.	1830-1864 Wayn	Wayn

Name	Unit	Dates	County
TAYLOR, John	10th MS Inf.	____-1878	Itaw
TAYLOR, John Allen	1st MS Cav.	1845-1920 Madi	Madi
TAYLOR, John L.	41st MS Inf.	1831-1892 Pont	Pont
TAYLOR, John P.	23rd MS Inf.	1840-1916 Tipp	Unio
TAYLOR, John Speed	Pettus Flying Art.	1848-1862 Pano	
TAYLOR, John T.	3rd AL Inf.	1845-1882 AL	Laud
TAYLOR, J. W.	26th MS Inf.	MS	Alco
TAYLOR, John W.	29th MS Inf.	Yalo	Calh
TAYLOR, Joseph Lane	11th MS Inf.	1838-1877 Noxu	Lafa
TAYLOR, Leroy F.	11th MS Cav.	1844-1917 Itaw	Lee
TAYLOR, P. W.	48th MS Inf.	1840-1883	Hind
TAYLOR, Peter	46th MS Inf.	1835-1888 Wayn	Wayn
TAYLOR, Priestley	46th MS Inf.	1843-1898 AL	Laud
TAYLOR, R. A.	8th & 19th MS. Cav.	1845-1887 Calh	Calh
TAYLOR, R. F.	Powers Cav.	1848-1900	Copi
TAYLOR, Reuben E.	2nd MS Cav.	1822-____	Monr
TAYLOR, Robert	3rd TN Inf.	1847-1909 Laud	Laud
TAYLOR, Samuel	3rd MS Inf.	1847-1937 MS	Harr
TAYLOR, T. J.	6th MS Inf.	1841-1909	Rank
TAYLOR, T. J. Sr.	44th MS Inf.	1833-1910 Lown	Pano
TAYLOR, Thomas T.	2nd MS Inf.	1833-1917 Monr	Monr
TAYLOR, T. Turner	18th MS Inf.	1839-1921 MS	Madi
TAYLOR, W. E.	Ballentines MS Inf.	1847-1930 VA	Pano
TAYLOR, W. H.	12th MS Inf.		Hind
TAYLOR, Wallace	38th MS Cav.	1845-1918 Holm	Holm
TAYLOR, William A.	5th MS Inf.	____-1916	Newt
TAYLOR, William _.	11th AL Cav.	1844-1914 DeSo	Monr
TAYLOR, William E.	6th MS Inf.		Hind
TAYLOR, William E.	12th SC Inf.	1844-1936 SC	Hind
TAYLOR, William L.	8th MS Inf.	1821-1898 Newt	Jone
TAYLOR, William M.	1st MS Inf.	1841-1913 Mars	Tate
TAYLOR, Wm.	3rd MS Inf.	1812-1898 AL	Alco
TAYLOR, W. O.	1st LA Inf.	1845-1926 LA	Atta
TAYLOR, W. W.	42nd MS Inf.	1844-1917 MS	Calh
TAYLOR, W. W.	37th VA Inf.	1847-1922 VA	Lama
TAYLOR, William	2nd MS Cav.	1815-1876 Clar	Gren
TAYLOR, Zack	21st MS Inf.	1848-1922 Tall	Alco
TAYLOR, Zack	1st SC Legion	1849-____ SC	Carr
TEAGUE, Barney	Adams MS Cav.	1835-1903 IR	Warr
TEAGUE, Sallis	12th MS Cav.	1839-1895 Holm	Atta
TEASDALE, C. H. (Dr.)	1st TX Cav.	1845-1935	Copi
TEASDALE, Howard M.	43rd MS Inf.	1843-1924 Lown	Lown
TEASLEY, John	3rd MS Inf.	1829-1869	Rank
TEAT, James Henry	40th MS Inf.	1842-1905 Atta	Atta
TEBOW, John	22nd MS Inf.	1794-1873 MS	Amit
TEDFORD, James M.	5th MO Inf.	1835-1914 MO	Linco
TEER, Eli	MS Cav.	1844-1931 Kemp	Kemp
TELLER, Emanuel	18th NC Inf.	1835-1911 NC	Warr
TELLER, William T.	1st MS Inf.	1844-1888 Laud	Laud

Name	Unit	Dates	County
TEMPLE, Calvin Mont.	2nd MS Inf.	1846-1882 Noxu	Kemp
TEMPLE, J. A.	37th MS Inf.	1843-1925 MS	Harr
TEMPLE, James M.	7th MS Inf.	1832-1891 Fran	Fran
TEMPLES, L. J.	37th MS Inf.	1842-1917 Jone	Jone
TEMPLES, Rowan	7th MS Inf.	1832-1904 Fran	Fran
TEMPLES, A. F.	20th MS Inf.	1841-1929 Atta	Atta
TEMPLES, Calvin L.	14th Conf. Cav.	1831-1898 MS	Fran
TEMPLETON, F. N.	39th MS Inf.	1843-1912 Amit	Amit
TEMPLETON, J. F.	21st MS Inf.	1835-1871 Warr	Warr
TEMPLETON, J. Matt.	39th MS Inf.	1835-1900	Clai
TEMPLETON, S. A.	35th MS Inf.	1839-1876	Okti
TEMPLETON, Thomas A.	44th MS Inf.	1820-1896 Copi	Copi
TEMPLETON, William J.	20th MS Inf.	1841-1910 AL	Monr
TEMPLETON, W. Scott	39th MS Inf.	1847-1929 Copi	Copi
TENHET, C. L.	43rd MS Inf.	1833-1881 Lown	Choc
TENHET, William L.	3rd MS Inf.	1839-1920 Harr	Choc
TENNISON, Hiram A.	26th MS Inf.	1839-1923 SC	Pren
TENNISON, J. A.	3rd MS Cav.	1835-1906 Tall	Tall
TEPI, F. A.	9th MS Inf.	1832-1874 Mars	Mars
TERRAL, James Edward	7th MS Inf.	1846-1897 Covi	Covi
TERRALL, A. J.	14th & 29th MS Inf.	1837-1870	Hind
TERRALL, Samuel	37th MS Inf.	1835-1903 Clar	Clar
TERREL, W. C.	28th MS Cav.	1832-19_	Hind
TERRELL, D. _.	16th MS Cav.	1846-1870 Monr	Monr
TERRELL, G. L.	2nd MS Cav.	1832-1921 Choc	Choc
TERRELL, Griffin F.	4th MS Cav.	1830-1890 Amit	Amit
TERRELL, Harvey	Garlands MS Cav.	1822-1900	Copi
TERRELL, Henry Clay	12th MS Cav.	1847-1935 MS	Sunf
TERRELL, J. A.	4th MS Cav.	1832-1890 Amit	Amit
TERRELL, J. D.	7th Inf.	1841-1905 MS	JEDA
TERRELL, Jasper D.	7th MS Inf.	1841-1905 Covi	JEDA
TERRELL, John J.	19th MS Inf.	1836-1931 Lafa	Pano
TERRELL, Louis _.	18th MS Inf.	182_-1907	Hind
TERRELL, Vernon L.	4th MS Cav.	1832-1894	Copi
TERRELL, William Henry	41st MS Inf.	1838-1932 Calh	Lafa
TERRELL, William A.	45th MS Inf.	1836-1863 Amit	Amit
TERRELL, William H.	Capt. Rucks Co.	1814-1887	Hind
TERRY, A. J.	36th MS Inf.	1839-1906	Copi
TERRY, B. T. (Dr.)	28th MS Cav.	1825-1863 AL	Carr
TERRY, C. M.	4th & 29th MS Inf.	1836-1924 MS	Calh
TERRY, George W.	5th MS Inf.		Monr
TERRY, Hampton H.	29th MS Inf.	1833-1909 Calh	Calh
TERRY, J. A.	18th MS Inf.	1843-1924 Hind	Copi
TERRY, J. J.	16th AL Inf.	1819-1926 AL	Unio
TERRY, J. W.	3rd MS Inf.	____-1866 Kemp	
TERRY, John	41st MS Inf.	1825-1895 Lafa	Kemp
TERRY, L. S.	15th MS Inf.	1828-1893 Atta	Atta
TERRY, Newton	Adams MS Cav.	1848-1913	Jeff
TERRY, Roland G.	36th MS Inf.	1843-1918 Copi	Pike

Name	Unit	Dates/Place	Place
TERRY, S. D.	1st MS Inf.	1820-1899 MS	Leak
TERRY, Thomas J.	36th MS Inf.	1833-1876 Copi	Laud
TERRY, W. M.	Powers MS Cav.	1828-1897	Kemp
TERRY, William H.	4th MS Inf.	1844-1911 Calh	Chic
TERRY, William H.	19th MS Inf.	1841-1912 Jeff	Jeff
TERRY, William M.	3rd MS Cav.	1825-1912 Yalo	Yalo
TEUNNISON, George	22nd MS Inf.	1841-1925 Lawr	Lawr
TEW, D. B.	10th MS Inf.	1844-1916 Clai	Fran
TEW, Jonathan	3rd MS Cav.	1843-1931 Smit	Clar
TEW, Osburn	37th MS Inf.	1842-1935 Clar	Clar
TEW, Samuel	7th MS Inf.	1837-1912 Clar	Clar
TEW, William Washington	Hodges MS Cav.	1831-1878 Nesh	Wins
THACKERSON, Robert J.	31st MS Inf.	1829-1902	Choc
THAMES, C. P.	1st MS Inf.	1826-1875	Rank
THAMES, John	15th Conf. Inf.	1844-1901 Simp	Simp
THAMES, Samuel Monroe	30th AL Inf.	1835-1918 AL	Warr
THAMES, Shadric A.	39th MS Inf.	1835-1873 Simp	Simp
THAMES, W. G.	28th MS Cav.	1847-1925	Rank
THARP, Daniel B.	33rd MS Inf.	1842-1892	Webs
THARP, John H.	33rd MS Inf.	1812-1886 Choc	Webs
THARPE, James S.	42nd MS Inf.	1834-1923 Yalo	Gren
THATCH, David	9th MS Inf.	1837-1911 Jasp	Jasp
THAXON. A. M.	Arsenal in AL	1846-1925 AL	Scot
THAXTON, _. D.	10th MS Inf.	184_-1926 Covi	Covi
THEDFORD, George W.	14th MS Lt. Art.	1833-1904 Pano	Pano
THERRELL, E.	8th & 9th MS Cav.	1819-1906 Calh	Calh
THERRELL, James W.	44th MS Inf.	1843-1905	Webs
THERRELL, James Wm.	44th MS Inf.	1844-1928	Webs
THERRELL, John F. (Dr.)	16th MS Inf.	1840-1904 Wilk	Wilk
THERRELL, William M.	8th MS Inf.	1842-1929 Clar	Clar
THIBODAUX, Francois	26th LA Inf.	18__-1862 LA	Warr
THIGPEN, J. C.	18th MS Inf.	1840-1916	Hind
THIGPEN, James	37th MS Inf.	1847-193_ Jasp	Jasp
THIGPEN, J. S.	6th MS Inf.	1831-1922 Jone	Jone
THIGPEN, Joel J.		1837-1875	Hind
THIGPEN, Louis	3rd MS Inf.	1844-1916	Hanc
THIGPEN, Nathan	33rd MS Inf.	1844-1923	Hanc
THIGPEN, Nathan	3rd MS Inf.	1841-1912 Hanc	Pear
THOMAS, A. C.	34th MS Inf.	1839-1900	Laud
THOMAS, A. M.	33rd MS Inf.	1846-1905 MS	Leak
THOMAS, A. W.	39th MS Inf.	1848-1915 Rank	Harr
THOMAS, Andrew Jackson	27th MS Inf.	1836-1917 Perr	Perr
THOMAS, Ansela J.	4th MS Cav.	1832-1904	Rank
THOMAS, Bucker W.	4th TN Inf.	1842-1923 TN	Tish
THOMAS, C. C.	12th MS Inf.	Adam	Adam
THOMAS, C. Fred	28th MS Cav.	Adam	Adam
THOMAS, Charles M.	19th MS Inf.	1828-1905 NC	Noxu
THOMAS, D. H.	1st MS Cav.	1833-1910 NC	Noxu
THOMAS, D. R.	2nd MS Cav.	1831-1862 Monr	Monr
THOMAS, Daniel A.	14th MS Inf.	1823-____ MS	Choc
THOMAS, Dye Wesley	7th TN Cav.	1843-1928 TN	Coah

139

THOMAS, Eligah	8th MS Inf.	1834-1927 MS	Wayn
THOMAS, F. M.	39th MS Inf.	1821-1888	Copi
THOMAS, G. W.	38th MS Regt.	1842-1902 Madi	Madi
THOMAS, Green	20th MS Inf.	1842-1902 Mont	Mont
THOMAS, Isham Irving	46th MS Inf.	1844-1911 Rank	Rank
THOMAS, J. M.	40th GA Inf.	1830-1906 SC	Harr
THOMAS, J. M.	1st MS Inf.	1847-1916 Leak	Leak
THOMAS, J. M.	37th AL Inf.	1837-1917 AL	Laud
THOMAS, J. O.	Adams MS Cav.	1842-1921 Okti	Okti
THOMAS, J. P.	15th MS Inf.	1843-1920 Gren	Carr
THOMAS, James A.	5th MS Inf.	1843-1929 MS	Nesh
THOMAS, James M.	20th MS Inf.	1847-1913 MS	Scot
THOMAS, James R.	30th GA Inf.	1833-1913 GA	Newt
THOMAS, James W.	3rd MS Inf.	1837-___ Harri	Jack
THOMAS, John	44th MS Inf.	1833-1894	DeSo
THOMAS, John L.	7th MS Cav.	1835-1908 MS	Linc
(THOMAS, John located after THOMAS, William E.)			
THOMAS, Johnson	31st MS Inf.	Choc	Carr
THOMAS, Joseph	39th MS Inf.	1840-1926 IR	Harr
THOMAS, Joseph W.	16th Inf.	1816-1891 NC	Smit
THOMAS, Julius Havis	7th MS Inf.	1843-1922 Fran	Harr
THOMAS, M. J.	32nd MS Inf.	1841-1926 GA	Tipp
THOMAS, Micajah	18th MS Cav.	1845-1920 Tipp	Bent
THOMAS, P. B.	1st MS Lt. Art.	1824-1892 TN	
THOMAS, R. B.	6th MS Cav.	1846-1928 Clay	Clay
THOMAS, R. F.	10th MS Inf.	1832-1911 Itaw	Itaw
THOMAS, Richard	31st MS Inf.	1828-1903 Chic	Chic
THOMAS, Richard	3rd AR Inf.	1842-186_ AR	Lafa
THOMAS, Samuel B.	36th MS Inf.	1825-1907 Copi	Hind
THOMAS, Stanley O.	1st MS Lt. Art.	Adam	Adam
THOMAS, W. A.	29th AL Inf.	1844-1915 AL	Chic
THOMAS, W. C.	3rd MS Inf.	1821-1873 Itaw	Monr
THOMAS, W. T.	17th AL Inf.	1844-1930 AL	Harr
THOMAS, W. W.	23rd MS Inf.	1838-1926 CARO	Pren
THOMAS, William A.	35th MS Inf.	1839-1918 Kemp	Kemp
THOMAS, William F.	60th GA Inf.	1846-1916 GA	Holm
THOMAS, W. _.	MS Inf.	1831-1906 Choc	Atta
THOMAS, William	Powers MS Cav.	1839-1925	Fran
THOMAS, William	4th MS Inf.	1806-1868 SC	Holm
THOMAS, William	3rd MS Inf.	1822-1873	Rank
THOMAS, William	36th or 38th MS Inf.	1832-1871	Copi
THOMAS, William E.	3rd MS Inf.	1841-1883 MS	Gree
THOMAS, John	5th MS Inf.	1822-1908 AL	Jasp
THOMAS, John A.	2nd MS Cav.	1830-1909	Webs
THOMAS, John A. (Dr.)	30th MS Cav.	1818-1891	Webs
THOMAS, John Frederick	5th MS Inf.	1824-1903 VA	Wins
THOMAS, William H.	5th MS Inf.	1831-1906 VA	Wins
THOMAS, William N.	14th & 48th MS Inf.	1845-1906	Okti
THOMAS, Wyche	3rd GA Cav.	1827-1923 GA	Pano
THOMASON, Sam H.	26th MS Inf.	1814-1892	Lee

Name	Unit	Dates		Place
THOMASON, Sam H.	26th MS Inf.	1848-1925	Itaw	Lee
THOMASSON, J. C.	1st AL Inf.	1832-1917	AL	Unio
THOMASSON, J. J.	35th MS Inf.	1830-1872	AL	Wins
THOMPKINS, Stephen	1st MS Cav.	1839-1879	Noxu	Noxu
THOMPKINS, Willie	30th VA Inf.	1832-1895	VA	Laud
THOMPSON, A. E.(Dr.)	4th LA Inf.	1834-1897	LA	Linc
THOMPSON, A. H. S.	7th MS Inf.	1845-1930	Perr	Perr
THOMPSON, Abraham A.	37th MS Inf.	1827-1870	Laud	Laud
THOMPSON, Abram B.	5th MS Inf.	1823-1886	Calh	Unio
THOMPSON, Alexander	33rd MS Inf.	1824-1878	MS	Amit
THOMPSON, Benzamin F.	8th MS Inf.	1846-1927	Laud	Laud
THOMPSON, Charlie	44th MS Inf.	____-1908	Amit	Amit
THOMPSON, Charles T.	22nd MS Inf.	1831-1906	Amit	Wilk
THOMPSON, Cicero	11th MS Inf.	1837-1902	Carr	Carr
THOMPSON, D. A.	3rd Minute Men	1828-1872		Monr
THOMPSON, D. S.	4th MS Inf.	1820-1861	Atta	Atta
THOMPSON, David B.	37th MS Inf.	1842-1899	Jasp	Jasp
THOMPSON, E. M.	27th LA Inf.	1843-1928	MS	Mont
THOMPSON, Edward	4th MS Inf.	1841-1924	Choc	Choc
THOMPSON, Elijah J.	44th MS Inf.	1842-1862	MS	Lafa
THOMPSON, F. M.	35th MS Inf.	1835-1900		Okti
THOMPSON, Ford W.	15th MS Inf.	18_3-1862	Carr	Mont
THOMPSON, G. L.	37th MS Inf.	1838-1873	Laud	Laud
THOMPSON, George	6th MS Inf.	1843-1932	Okti	Okti
THOMPSON, H. B.	32nd GA Inf.	1835-1911	GA	Atta
THOMPSON, Henry H.	Withers Art.	____-1863		Jack
THOMPSON, Henry T.	35th MS Inf.	1825-1898	Lown	Lown
THOMPSON, I. J.	26th AL Inf.	1846-1928	AL	Monr
THOMPSON, J. A.	2nd MS Cav.	1847-1913	Monr	Monr
THOMPSON, J. A.	22nd MS Inf.	1819-1904	MS	Lafa
THOMPSON, J. H.	Hams MS Cav.	1821-1905		Rank
THOMPSON, J. J.	27th TN Inf.	1839-1862	TN	Chic
THOMPSON, J. L.	15th MS Inf.	1843-____	Choc	Clay
THOMPSON, J. L.	3rd MS Inf.	1842-1925		Harr
THOMPSON, J. N.	40th MS Inf.	1818-1892	Atta	Atta
THOMPSON, J. R.	14th MS Inf.	1841-1908	MS	Monr
THOMPSON, J. S.	7th MS Inf.	1846-1923	Jasp	Covi
THOMPSON, J. T.	41st MS Inf.	1837-1893	Chic	Chic
THOMPSON, J. W.	37th AL Inf.	1835-1913	AL	Pren
THOMPSON, J. W.	26th MS Inf.	1836-1893	Tish	Tish
THOMPSON, J. W.	44th MS Inf.	1838-1869	Chic	Chic
THOMPSON, J. W.	Govt. Shop	1842-1930	Simp	Simp
THOMPSON, Jack F.	31st MS Inf.	1841-1917	Chic	Chic
THOMPSON, James Henry	6th MS Inf.	1838-____		Simp
THOMPSON, James S.	12th MS Cav.	1833-1886	Monr	Monr
THOMPSON, James Shockley	40th MS Inf.	1847-1923	Jasp	Jone
THOMPSON, James Thomas	11th MS Inf.	1837-1893	Chic	Chic
THOMPSON, James W.	1st MS Cav.	1842-1923	Okti	Okti
THOMPSON, Jesse Jr.	19th MS Inf.	1841-1906		Copi
THOMPSON, Jessie F.	Woods Regt.	1848-1915	MS	JEDA
THOMPSON, J. Lee	3rd MS Cav.	1837-1917	Holm	Holm

THOMPSON, John	3rd MS Inf.	1840-1933 Harr	Harr
THOMPSON, John Astor	Jeff Davis Cav.	1838-1910 GA	Laud
THOMPSON, John B.	37th MS Inf.	1832-1915	Clar
THOMPSON, John Floyd	Seven Star Art.	1848-1919	Copi
THOMPSON, John H.	10th MS Inf.	1850-1927	Hind
THOMPSON, John H.	1st MS Cav.	1846-1921	Forr
THOMPSON, John Henry	AL Lt. Art.	1846-1925 AL	Laud
THOMPSON, John I.	8th MS Cav.	1809-1876 Lown	Chic
THOMPSON, John J.	6th MS Cav.	1839-___ Covi	Simp
THOMPSON, John M.	7th MS Inf.	1822-1902 Amit	Amit
THOMPSON, John Mitchell	21st MS Inf.	1836-1878 Tall	Tall
THOMPSON, John Newton	8th MS Inf.	1848-1935 GA	Smit
THOMPSON, John P.	15th MS Inf.	1839-1925 Carr	
THOMPSON, John T.	14th MS Inf.	1839-1918 Okti	Okti
THOMPSON, Joseph G.	11th MS Cav.	1827-1898 Wins	Lown
THOMPSON, Joseph	1st MS Cav.	1839-1919 Pont	Tall
THOMPSON, Joseph White	10th MS Inf.	1827-1890 Hind	Copi
THOMPSON, Julian	3rd MS Cav.	1845-1913 NC	Madi
THOMPSON, L. _.	26th MS Inf.	1839-1914 Alco	Alco
THOMPSON, L.	3rd MS Inf.	1837-1919 AL	Gree
THOMPSON, L. R.	35th MS Inf.	1837-1875 Okti	Okti
THOMPSON, L. T.	2nd MS Cav.	1818-1899	Chic
THOMPSON, M. _.	40th AL Inf.	1840-1911 Itaw	Laud
THOMPSON, M. J.	14th MS Inf.	1845-1910 Monr	Laud
THOMPSON, M. _.	1st AL Art.	1829-1901 AL	Laud
THOMPSON, Marvel	15th MS Inf.	1843-1862 Carr	Mont
THOMPSON, N. H.	18th MS Inf.	1836-1886	Madi
THOMPSON, O. F.	Comforts MS Inf.	1836-1923	Okti
THOMPSON, O. W.	43rd MS Inf.	1830-1890 Itaw	Unio
THOMPSON, R.	43rd MS Inf.	1841-1905 MS	Monr
THOMPSON, R. _.	24th MS Cav.	1847-1935 Copi	Hind
THOMPSON, R. J.	12th MS Cav.	1835-1910 MS	Tall
THOMPSON, R. P.	37th MS Inf.	1836-1905 Laud	Laud
THOMPSON, Reddick	44th MS Inf.	1844-1914 Amit	Amit
THOMPSON, Robert	Moores AL Inf.		Monr
THOMPSON, Roland B.	44th MS Inf.	1846-1909 Amit	Amit
THOMPSON, Silas H.	33rd MS Reg.	1824-1912 Amit	Amit
THOMPSON, T. J.	41st MS Inf.	1839-1916	Hind
THOMPSON, Thomas	37th MS Inf.	1832-1890 Laud	Laud
THOMPSON, Thomas J.	Adams MS Cav.	1848-1937 MS	Warr
THOMPSON, Thomas N.	6th MS Inf.	1840-1913 Simp	Simp
THOMPSON, W. B.	5th Regt. State Mil.	1820-1884 Pont	Unio
THOMPSON, W. B.	20th MS Regt.	1838-1926	Newt
THOMPSON, W. D.	22nd MS Inf.	1839-1911 Linc	Fran
THOMPSON, W. E.	1st AL Cav.	1838-1918 AL	Scot
THOMPSON, W. _.	Powers Cav.	1848-1903 LA	Mont
THOMPSON, W. P.	38th MS Cav.	1841-1906 Newt	Copi
THOMPSON, William	1st MS Lt. Art.	1830-1883	Jeff
THOMPSON, William	15th MS Inf.	Carr	Carr
THOMPSON, William	22nd MS Inf.	1839-1916 MS	Lawr
THOMPSON, William Garrett	9th MS Inf.	1842-1927 DeSo	Alco

142

THOMPSON, William G.	9th MS Inf.	1842-1927 MS	Tipp
THOMPSON, William H.	39th MS Inf.	1836-1899	Rank
THOMPSON, William _.	7th MS Inf.	1830-1898 Mari	Mari
THOMPSON, William J.	4th MS Cav.	1838-1898 Covi	JEDA
THOMPSON, William L.	7th MS Cav.	1848-1929 Tipp	Tipp
THOMPSON, William Lewis	34th MS Inf.	1846-1929 Tipp	Bent
THOMPSON, William S.	2nd Inf.	1818-___	Simp
THOMPSON, William W.	24th MS Inf.	1833-1900 Gree	Gree
THOMPSON, William White	1st AL Art.	1828-1914 AL	Laud
THORN, James E.	6th MS Inf.	1841-1916 Smit	Smit
THORNBERRY, John W.	31st MS Inf.	1843-1930 MS	Itaw
THORNBURG, James	MS Cav.	1836-1875 Adam	Adam
THORNE, Michazy Benkin	Capt. Newmans AL	1848-1934 AL	Tish
THORNE, W. H.	8th AL Cav.	1845-1917 AL	Pano
THORNELL, A. H.	44th MS Inf.	1840-1918 Leak	Leak
THORNHILL, Asa D.	3rd MS Cav.	1832-1905 MS	Walt
THORNHILL, J. M. (Dr.)	7th MS Vol.	183_-1906 Pear	Pear
THORNHILL, John C.	4th MS Cav.	1828-1899 Lawr	Linc
THORNHILL, John J.	33rd MS Inf.	1838-1916 Lawr	Pear
THORNHILL, John S.	14th MS Inf.	1844-1904 Simp	Walt
THORNHILL, Jonathan L.	4th MS Cav.	1832-1906 SC	Walt
THORNLEY, Joseph T.	12th MS Cav.	1843-1905 Monr	Monr
THORNTON, Benjamin F.	Blythes MS Inf.	1830-1919 Clay	Clay
THORNTON, Benjamin F.	15th Conf. Regt.	1831-1895 Smit	Smit
THORNTON, Charles C.	Myricks Art.	1837-1917 Holm	Holm
THORNTON, Daniel	46th Inf.	1844-1924 MS	Smit
THORNTON, E. J.	33rd MS Inf.	1839-1916 Leak	Leak
THORNTON, G. _.	45th MS Inf.	1822-1891	Pren
THORNTON, Henry J.	38th MS Cav.	183_-1897 Scot	Scot
THORNTON, J. J.	8th MS Inf.	1833-1904 Newt	Newt
THORNTON, J. M.	15th MS Inf.	1835-1930 Yalo	Pont
THORNTON, J. Z.	33rd AL Inf.	1846-1909 MS	Calh
THORNTON, James E.	8th MS Inf.	1838-1863 Newt	Newt
THORNTON, Jeff L.	2nd MS Cav.	1836-1907 Tate	Tate
THORNTON, John	40th MS Inf.	1831-1916 Atta	Atta
THORNTON, John Jones	6th MS Inf.	1826-1886 VA	Harr
THORNTON, Pickens S.	37th MS Regt.	1840-1909 SC	Jasp
THORNTON, R. C.	2nd MS Cav.	1819-1882	Newt
THORNTON, W. C.	2nd MS Inf.	1846-1919 MS	Newt
THORNTON, William M.	6th MS Cav.	1819-1889	Smit
THRAILKILL, Morgan	14th & 43rd MS Inf.	1834-1907 Monr	Monr
THRASH, D. L.	15th MS Inf.	1842-1901	Leak
THRASH, Eli	4_ AL Inf.	1821-1910 AL	Laud
THRASH, W. E.	4th LA Inf.	1840-1924 LA	Harr
THRASHER, C. C.	22nd AL Inf.	1844-1916 AL	Leak
(THRASHER, J. W. located after TRAPP)			
THREADGILL, James P.	31st MS Inf.	1846-1915 Atta	Atta
THREADGILL, Sam George	1st MS Cav.	1840-1936	Mont
THREATT, Elijah H.	35th MS Inf.	____-1909	Newt
THREATT, Nathaniel	26th AL Inf.	1842-1914 MS	Monr

Name	Unit	Dates		
THROWER, John Edward	6th MS Cav.	1846-1911	Lown	Lown
THURMAN, Abel	39th MS Inf.	1837-1911	Lawr	Lawr
THURMAN, Daniel	8th MS Inf.	1847-1929	MS	Harr
THURMAN, Elijah	36th MS Inf.	1842-1897	Laud	Simp
THURMAN, F. M.	39th MS Inf.	1837-1918	Simp	Simp
THURMAN, George W.	39th MS Inf.	1844-1910	Simp	JEDA
THURMAN, W. W.	2nd TN Cav.	1843-1914	TN	Lee
THWEATT, William J.	9th AR Inf.	1842-1911	AR	Atta
TIBBS, James A.	6th MS Inf.	1836-1880	Scot	Scot
TIBLIER, Emile	3rd MS Inf.	1838-1923		Jack
TIBLIER, Eugene	3rd MS Inf.	1843-1930	Harr	Harr
TICER, J. P.	2nd MS Inf.	1836-1927	Tipp	Unio
TIDWELL, A. J.	28th MS Cav.	1830-1879	Carr	Carr
TIDWELL, James F.	1st MS Lt. Art.	1837-1901	SC	Mont
TIDWELL, Levi	35th MS Inf.	1828-1905	Nesh	Nesh
TIDWELL, Samuel	15th TN Cav.	1848-1930	TN	Bent
TIERCE, James	17th MS Inf.	1840-1926	Yalo	Yalo
TIERNEY, J. P.	Englishs Batt.	1832-1904	IR	Adam
TIERNON, Thomas J.	10th MS Inf.	1831-186_	Clai	Clai
TIGERT, _._.	2nd MS Inf.	1847-1920	Tipp	Tipp
TIGRETT, D. P.	2nd MS Inf.	1827-1896	GA	Tipp
TILGHMAN, Lloyd	26th MS Inf.	____-1863		Hind
TILL, T. M.	6th & 15th MS Inf.	1848-1924		Rank
TILLERY, Daniel W.	4th MS Cav.	1839-1923	Amit	Amit
TILLERY, John L.	5th MS Inf.	1843-1871	Amit	Amit
TILLERY, Thomas Richard	4th MS Cav.	1842-1914	Wilk	Wilk
TILLMAN, Hayden Dallas	6th & 15th MS Inf.	1846-1920		Copi
TILLMAN, J. R.	6th MS Inf.	1837-1907		Copi
TILLMAN, James A.	Powers MS Cav.	1830-1901	MS	Copi
TILLMAN, James D.	37th MS Inf.	1842-1932	MS	Laud
TILLMAN, John	1st MS Inf.	1842-1884	Tish	Yalo
TILLMAN, John E/F.	6th MS Inf.	1843-1911	Copi	Copi
TILLMAN, N. P.	24th MS Inf.	1847-1931	Copi	Copi
TILLMAN, Rufus	37th MS Inf.	1833-1895	Laud	Laud
TILLMAN, Thomas	8th MS Inf.	1845-1923		Newt
TILLSON, J. W.	6th MS Inf.	1844-1924	Smit	Smit
TILTON, Joshua Atwood	8th AL Inf.	1835-1911	MS	Wilk
TIMBERLAKE, H. C.	53rd VA Inf.	1835-1888		Hind
TIMBES, James L.	12th MS Cav.	1840-1899	GA	Pren
TIMMS, John	37th MS Inf.	1847-1906	Clar	Clar
TIMS, O. H.	7th MS Inf.	1835-1917	Clar	Clar
TIMS, Timothy	8th MS Inf.	1827-1900	MS	Smit
TINDALL, George	20th MS Inf.	1844-____	Monr	Monr
TINDALL, W. M.	15th MS Inf.	1835-1916	Carr	Carr
TINDELL, J. H.	15th Conf. Cav.	1848-1929	Harr	Harr
TINDEL, W. R.	40th MS Inf.	1830-1899	Atta	Nesh
TINER, J. P.	33rd MS Inf.	1830-1925	Nesh	Nesh
TINGLE, B. F.	13th MS Inf.	1835-1910	Perr	Perr
TINGLE, T. W.	3rd MS Inf.	1827-1903	GA	Newt
TINGLE, W. P.	36th MS Inf.	1833-1917	Carr	Carr

144

TINNIN, David G.	MS Inf.	1838-1914	Hind
TINNIN, H. P.	Maxeys MS. Cav.	1827-1893	Rank
TINNIN, James	2nd MS Cav.	184_-1926 MS	Laud
TINNONE, James M.	33rd MS Inf.	1830-1931 MS	Harr
TINSLEY, A. G.	5th MS Inf.	1847-1936 Kemp	Nesh
TINSLEY, Charles B.	35th MS Inf.		Kemp
TINSLEY, Fred J.	5th MS Inf.	1825-1906	Kemp
TINSLEY, Henry G.	35th MS Inf.	1836-1909 AL	Laud
TIPPETT, J. L.	27th MS Inf.	1840-1900 Jone	Pano
TIPTON, J. H.	26th MS Inf.	1833-1899 MS	Tish
TISDALE, E. W.	8th MS Inf.	1839-1920 Jone	Jone
TISDALE, W. H.	8th MS Inf.	1847-1916 Jasp	Harr
TISDALE, Zachary Taylor	3rd MS Inf.	1847-1923 Jone	Jone
TODD, Aaren	8th MS Inf.	1836-1921 Jone	Jone
TODD, George W.	8th MS Inf.	1825-1911 MS	Newt
TODD, James	41st MS Inf.	1814-1888 Pont	Pont
TODD, James K. Polk	8th MS Cav.	1842-1909 Bent	Bent
TODD, James T.	41st MS Inf.	1841-1895 Pont	Pont
TODD, James William	Bledsoes AL Art.	1839-1890 AL	Laud
TODD, V.	46th MS Inf.	1833-1924 Newt	Wins
TODD, W. B.	Bealls GA Inf.	1847-1906 GA	Monr
TODD, Washington	14th TN Cav.	1825-1884 TN	Bent
TOLBERT, H. R.	41st MS Inf.	1843-1924 Laud	Leak
TOLBERT, Thomas R.	35th MS Inf.	1838-1922 Kemp	Kemp
TOLER, H. H.	16th MS Inf.	1842-1916 Lawr	Lawr
TOLER, J. H.	33rd MS Inf.	184_-1907 Amit	Amit
TOLER, Theodore Eugene	11th AR Inf.	1848-1936 Amit	Amit
TOLER, W. A.	1st MS Cav.	1846-1928	Copi
TOLER, W. Franklin	7th MS Inf.	1843-1912 Amit	Amit
TOLES, John W.	GA Inf.	1847-1928 GA	Kemp
TOMERNICK, James A.	5th TN Cav.	1846-1930 TN	Tish
TOMLIN, A.	2nd MS Cav.	1823-1907 Pont	Itaw
TOMLIN, I. P.	40th MS Inf.	1832-1915 Atta	Atta
TOMLINSON, W. C.	8th AL Cav.	1832-1906 AL	Webs
TOMLINSON, W. S.	Stanfords Lt. Art.	1837-1910 Yalo	Gren
TOMPKINS, George H.	1st MS Art.	1833-1905 KY	Warr
TONEY, William D.	33rd MS Inf.	1823-1890 Pano	Lafa
TOOMBS, Allen H.	1st AR Inf.	1830-1897 TN	Tate
TOOMBS, G. M.	Montgomerys Scouts	1847-1912 Copi	Holm
TOOMEY, John	24th MS Cav.	1836-1915 MS	Wayn
TOOTLE, George W.	9th MS Cav.	1844-1914 Jack	Jack
TORREY, James A.	1st MS Lt. Art.	1827-1899 Jeff	Fran
TORREY, James Harding	4th MS Cav.	1846-1881	Hind
TORREY, R. D.	2nd MS Cav.	1822-1887	Jeff
TOUCHSTONE, J. L.	32nd AL Inf.	1839-1906 AL	Jone
TOUCHSTONE, T. N.	4th MS Cav.	1846-1915 Simp	Simp
TOUPS, Felicien	26th LA Inf.	1843-1862 LA	Warr
TOWERY, Wade H.	5th MS Inf.		Monr
TOWNES, James A.	27th MS Inf.	1844-1914 MS	Tall
TOWNES, John Charles	22nd MS Inf.	1836-1907	Lefl

TOWNES, John Leigh	29th MS Inf.	1841-1930 Yalo	Gren	
TOWNS, Wm. A.	Adams Cav.	1835-1908 GA	Linc	
TOWNSEND, A. C.	2nd MS Cav.	1848-1938 Scot	Scot	
TOWNSEND, A. F.	28th MS Cav.	1843-1892 Mont	Mont	
TOWNSEND, A. J.	1st MS Inf.	1827-1905	Rank	
TOWNSEND, A. T.	3rd MS Cav.	1846-1891 Choc	Choc	
TOWNSEND, Allen	4th MS Inf.	1819-1891	Mont	
TOWNSEND, Andrew J.	15th MS Inf.	1834-___ MS	Mont	
TOWNSEND, E. C.	2nd MS Cav.	1831-1902 Tate	Tate	
TOWNSEND, _. D.	40th MS Inf.	1842-1914 Atta	Atta	
TOWNSEND, J. _.	4th MS Inf.	1829-1886 Carr	Gren	
TOWNSEND, J. W.	28th MS Cav.	1843-1900		
TOWNSEND, James David	4th MS Inf.	1850-1932 Carr	Gren	
TOWNSEND, James J.	48th MS Inf.	1837-1911	Nesh	
TOWNSEND, James W.	2nd MS Cav.	1844-1865 Scot		
TOWNSEND, L. M.	1st MS Inf.	1825-1884	Copi	
TOWNSEND, W. S.	40th MS Inf.	1835-1916 Nesh	Nesh	
TOWRY, E. W.	2nd MS Cav.	1843-1891 Monr	Monr	
TRAHAN, Eugene	1st LA Hvy. Art.	1837-1863 LA	Warr	
TRAMELL, S. C.	11th AL Vol.	1843-1928 AL	Kemp	
TRAMMELL, John	7th AL Cav.	1829-1908 AL	Tish	
TRANTHAM, D. G.	1 MS Lt. Art.	1835-1892 Choc	Alco	
TRAPP, Benjamin F.	Perrins Cav.	1845-1896 Nesh	Nesh	
TRA_ H, W. E/F.	4th LA Inf.	1848-1924 Amit	Harr	
THRASHER, J. W.	10th AL Inf.	1847-1897 AL	Chic	
TRAVIS, J. A.	27th MS Inf.	1844-1930 Jasp	Forr	
TRAVIS, E. S.	27th MS Inf.	1836-1937 Forr	Forr	
TRAVIS, J. Q.	16th MS Inf.	1832-1907 Pike	Pike	
TRAVIS, N. A.	7th MS Inf.	1841-1936 Amit	Amit	
TRAVIS, Seth	5th MS Inf.	1822-1893 Jasp	Jasp	
TRAVIS, W. W.	33rd MS Inf.	1840-1914	Hind	
TRAWICK, C. C.	6th MS Inf.	1823-1907 AL	Laud	
TRAWICK, O. L.	3rd MS Inf.	1826-1890	Rank	
TRAWEEK, W. B.	Jeff Davis Art.	1845-1934 Adam	Harr	
TRAYLOR, David	39th MS Inf.	1840-1881	Rank	
TRAYLOR, William H.	28th AL Inf.		Monr	
TRAYLOR, Willis R.	39th MS Inf.	1828-1872	Rank	
TRAYNHAM, Felix G.	1st MS Inf.	1834-1886 Itaw	Monr	
TREADWAY, William	1st MS Cav.	1829-1917	DeSo	
TREADWELL, B. _. (Dr.)	5th MS Cav.	1814-1891 Holm	Holm	
TREADWELL, David	33rd MS Inf.	1835-1905 Leak	Leak	
TREADWELL, Isaac	27th MS Inf.	1828-1894 Leak	Leak	
TREANOR, Thos.	1st MS Lt. Art.	1833-1878 IR	Warr	
TRAHERN, Richard	7th AL Inf.	1848-1939 AL	Harr	
TRESCOTT, Austin A.	21st MS Reg.	1837-1929 OH	Warr	
TREST, Samuel C.	7th MS Inf.	1832-1923 Jone	Jone	
TREVILION, Absalom L.	2nd MS Cav.	1825-1910 Wilk	Wilk	
TREVILION, S. M.	2nd MS Cav.	1846-1913 Jeff	Wilk	
TRE_MLIN, H. L.	29th MS Inf.	1828-1896 Tall	Tall	
TRIBBLE, Dick	16th MS Inf.	1843-1912 SC	Gren	
TRIBBLE, G. W.	3rd MS Cav.	1821-1901 Gren	Gren	
TRIBBLE, James M.	21st MS Inf.	1842-1925 Tall	Tall	

Name	Unit	Dates		
TRICE, John M.	35th MS Inf.	1838-1891	Wins	Wins
TRICE, Robert Lindsay	42nd MS Inf.	1821-1894	Monr	Lee
TRICE, Stephen J.	Whites AL Cav.	1839-1909	AL	Clar
TRIGG, John I.	13th MS Inf.	1839-1909	Wayn	Wayn
TRIGG, William F.	36th MS Inf.	1829-1895	Wayn	Wayn
TRIGG, Wm. Sylvester	38th AL Vol.	1843-1927	AL	Madi
TRIGG, Wyndham R.	28th MS Cav.	1834-1904	VA	Wash
TRIM, James L.	41st AL Inf.	1833-1911	AL	Tish
TRIMAR, G. T.	9th AL Inf.	1838-1909	AL	Alco
TRIMBLE, Harlan A.	129th VA Inf.	1839-1923	IN	Coah
TRIMBLE, Lee	19th MS Inf.	1831-1910	Jeff	Fran
TRIMBLE, W. A.	Adams MS Cav.	1838-1862	LA	Jeff
TRIPLETT, Francis M.	Breastwork Crew	1830-1863	SC	Wins
TRIPLETT, G. W.	13th MS Inf.	1823-1898	Leak	Leak
TRIPLETT, Glover B.	11th MS Inf.	1826-1911	SC	Noxu
TRIPLETT, J. M.	35th MS Inf.	1830-1914	Nesh	Leak
TRILPETT, N. D.	14th MS Inf.	1839-1926	SC	Wins
TRIPLETT, Nimrod D.	Breastwork Crew	1838-1926	SC	Wins
TRIPLETT, S. R.	46th MS Inf.	1827-1902	MS	Kemp
TRIPP, J. W.	40th MS Inf.	1836-1890		Leak
TRIPP, James	18th MS Inf.	____-1920		Hind
TROTTER, Alex	37th MS Inf.	1840-1928	Clar	Clar
TROTTER, Alpha Peebles	5th MS Cav.	1846-1909	Choc	Mont
TROTTER, T. R. (Dr.)	Stanfords Lt. Art.	1837-1914	Carr	Mont
TROTTER, W. H.	2nd MS Cav.	1816-1874		Hind
TROUP, Walter W.	2nd MS Regt.	1830-1890	Monr	Monr
TROWBRIDGE, Albert	1st MS Lt. Art.	1812-1863	Warr	Warr
TRULY, Richard H.	4th LA Batt.	1833-1904	Jeff	Jeff
TRUSSELL, Benjamin F.	40th MS Inf.	1844-1939	MS	Nesh
TRUSSELL, J. R.	31st MS Inf.	1834-1893	Choc	Choc
TRUSSELL, James	4th MS Inf.	1830-1874	MS	Choc
TRUSSELL, T. N.	4th MS Inf.	1840-1932	MS	Choc
TRUSTY, J. F.	15th MS Inf .	1840-1903	Yalo	Yalo
TSCHUDI, Milchior	15th TN Inf.	1842-1905	TN	Monr
TUBB, Alfred W.	43rd MS Inf.	1844-1929	Monr	Monr
TUBB, Benson Jr.	43rd MS Inf.	1833-1902	Monr	Monr
TUBB, Benson Sr.	14th MS Inf.	1814-1898	AL	Monr
TUBB, C. M.	43rd MS Inf.	____-1889		Monr
TUBB, J. P.	2nd MS Cav.	1828-1870	Kemp	Monr
TUBB, James N.	43rd MS Inf.	____-1892		Monr
TUBB, Jeptha	3rd & 43rd MS Inf.	1835-1893		Monr
TUBB, John S.	14th MS Inf.	1837-1901	Monr	Monr
TUBB, W. L. Sr.	14th MS Inf.	1843-1921	Monr	Monr
TUBB, W. W.	43rd MS Inf.	1839-1897	Monr	Monr
TUBBS, David D.	19th MS Inf.	1839-1908	Lafa	Lafa
TUBBS, George W.	14th MS Inf.	1842-1921	Monr	Monr
TUBBS, M. W.	Davis 28th AL	____-1917		Rank
TUCKER, A. Lunsford	40th MS Inf.	1826-1896	MS	Leak
TUCKER, Ben C.	19th MS Inf.	1846-1924	MS	Tate
TUCKER, C. R.	31st MS Inf.	1828-1911	Calh	Calh

Name	Unit	Dates		
TUCKER, Caleb E.	Forests MS Cav.	1846-1916	Mars	Mars
TUCKER, E. J.	40th MS Inf.	1840-1888	Madi	Madi
TUCKER, E. W.	1st MS Cav.	___-1928		Hind
TUCKER, Ellis	33rd MS Inf.	1836-1914	Leak	Leak
TUCKER, G. R.	2nd AL Cav.	1837-1892	AL	Laud
TUCKER, Hardin E.	38th NC Inf.	1844-1900	NC	Pren
TUCKER, Henry Thomas	10th MS Inf.	1843-1923	TN	Tuni
TUCKER, I. R.	15th MS Inf.	1833-1908		Atta
TUCKER, J. _.	Adams MS Cav.	1823-1880	Madi	Madi
TUCKER, J. D.	24th TN Inf.	1841-1862	TN	Lown
TUCKER, J. S.	2nd AL Cav.	1839-1909	AL	Laud
TUCKER, James A.	11th AL Cav.	1831-1901	AL	Tish
TUCKER, John _.	28th MS Cav.			Monr
TUCKER, M. M.	7th MS Inf.	1838-1913	Jone	Jone
TUCKER, Marcus L.	2nd MS Cav.	1827-1909		Pren
TUCKER, R. D.	32nd MS Inf.	1848-___	Pont	Scot
TUCKER, Robert Levi	1st MS Cav.	1846-1917	Warr	Warr
TUCKER, Robert William	10th MS Inf.	1841-1914	TN	Tuni
TUCKER, S. J.	41st MS Inf.	1833-1904	Pont	Pont
TUCKER, Theophelus I.	18th VA Inf.	1841-1917	VA	Yalo
TUCKER, Thomas Emmett	11th MS Inf.	1843-1861		Mars
TUCKER, W. M.	2nd & 20th MS Cav.	1845-1929	Laud	Harr
TUCKER, William	33rd MS Inf.	1837-1906	Leak	Leak
TUCKER, William H. (Rev)	22nd MS Inf.	1840-1889	Amit	Amit
TUCKER, Wm. Forester	11th MS Inf.	___-1881	NC	Chic
TUCKER, Wm. J.	9th TX Cav.	1846-1929	TX	Harr
TUFF, M.	14th MS Inf.	1841-1918	MS	Monr
TULL, William Baylus	9th LA Inf.	1838-1919	LA	Pike
TULLOS, C. J.	6th MS Inf.	1845-1924	Smit	Smit
TULLOS, Cisiar W.	8th MS Inf.	1845-1930	Smit	Smit
TULLOS, J. N.	1st MS Lt. Art.	1836-1912	Choc	Choc
TULLOS, Jackson W.	8th MS Inf.	1839-1927	Smit	Smit
TULLOS, Richard	4th MS Cav.	1826-___		Simp
TULLOS, Steven	33rd MS Inf.	1832-1906		Nesh
TULLOS, Temple R.	41st MS Inf.	1847-1925	Nesh	Nesh
TULLOS, William A.	33rd MS Inf.	1834-1910		Nesh
TUMLINSON, W. C.	8th AL Inf.	1847-1924	AL	Okti
TUNNELL, John	12th MS Cav.	1813-1865	Monr	Monr
TUNNELL, S. C.	43rd MS Inf.	1844-1904	Monr	Monr
TUNNELL, Thomas Loyd	43rd MS Inf.	1837-1911	Lown	Lown
TURBEVILLE, E. _.	11th MS Inf.	1841-1891	Monr	Monr
TURBEVILLE, J. W.	15th Conf. Cav.	1810-1879	Monr	Monr
TURBEVILLE, Jesse	1st & 6th MS Inf.		Rank	Rank
TURMAN, J. M.	43rd MS Inf.	1842-1921	AL	Monr
TURNAGE, Albert J.	7th MS Inf.	1843-1913	MS	JEDA
TURNAGE, Asbury	40th MS Inf.	1843-1926	MS	Leak
TURNAGE, Mills Preston	7th MS Inf.	1843-1929		JEDA
TURNER, Abner _.	Woods MS Cav.	1846-1898	Simp	Simp
TURNER, Beauford A.	19th MS Inf.	1838-1862	Lafa	Lafa
TURNER, Ben Franklin	Woods MS Cav.	1846-1929	Yazo	Lawr
TURNER, D. W.	Breckenridges MS Cav.			Adam

148

TURNER, J. H.	41st GA Inf.	1831-1906 GA	Gren
TURNER, J. H.	41st GA Art.	1832-1934 GA	Harr
TURNER, J. L.	8th MS Inf.	1847-1923	Scot
TURNER, James A.	35th MS Inf.	1845-1925 MS	Nesh
TURNER, James C.	7th AL Cav.	1840-1901 AL	Tish
TURNER, James David	32nd MS Inf.	1848-1937 Tish	Alco
TURNER, James _.	4th MS Inf.	1835-1886 Carr	Carr
TURNER, Jessie H.	12th MS Cav.	1837-1907 Monr	Monr
TURNER, John	11th MS Cav.	1823-1908 AL	Shar
TURNER, John C.	40th MS Inf.	1833-1909 Atta	Atta
TURNER, John H.	11th MS Cav.	1836-1863 Kemp	Alco
TURNER, John H.	4th & 41st GA Inf.	1843-1925 GA	Harr
TURNER, John Robert	34th MS Inf.	1827-1863 Lafa	Lafa
TURNER, John _.	4th MS Inf.	1833-1913 Carr	Carr
TURNER, John T.	4th MS Inf.	1840-1888 Carr	Carr
TURNER, Joseph J.	15th MS Inf.	1833-1910 Atta	Atta
TURNER, L. J.	5th MS Inf.	1805-1884 MS	Choc
TURNER, Lewis	41st MS Inf.	1832-1910 MS	Okti
TURNER, Robert Hood	3rd MS Cav.	1825-1922 Gren	Gren
TURNER, Roe	7th AL Cav.	1847-1911 AL	Tish
TURNER, Simon W.	4th MS Inf.	1837-1900 Carr	Carr
TURNER, T. A.	1st MS Cav.	1847-1909 Leak	Leak
TURNER, Thomas T.	Prison Guard	1822-1904 SC	Holm
TURNER, W. A.	6th MS Inf.	1836-1892 Leak	Leak
TURNER, W. C.	5th MS Inf.	1842-1913 Wins	Carr
TURNER, W. H.	12th MS Inf.	1843-1926 Clai	Warr
TURNER, W. I.	22nd AL Inf.	1837-1929 AL	Pont
TURNER, W. J.	18th MS Cav.	1848-1896 AL	Leak
TURNER, W. W.	13th TN Inf.	1838-1862 TN	Lown
TURNER, Walter S.	4th MS Inf.	1843-1920 Carr	Mont
TURNER, Wiley T.	37th MS Inf.	1837-1893 Clar	Newt
TURNER, William	32nd MS Inf.	1820-1877 Tish	Alco
TURNER, William C.	1st MS Inf.	Adam	Adam
TURNER, William Emerson	2nd MS Inf.	1837-1896 TN	Lee
TURNER, William H.	40th MS Inf.	1829-1916 Atta	Atta
TURNER, Wm. James Frank	14th MS Art.	1836-1907 Pano	Tall
TURNER, William K.	30th MS Inf.	1832-1903 Carr	Carr
TURNER, William Sanders	4th MS Inf.	1844-1927 Carr	Carr
TURNER, W. Tom	34th MS Inf.	1847-1929 Lafa	Chic
TURNIPSEED, D. B.	38th MS Cav.	1826-1910 AL	Harr
TURNIPSEED, George _.	33rd MS Inf.	1831-1911 Amit	Amit
TURNIPSEED, J.	3rd MS Regt.	1825-1904 SC	Wins
TURNIPSEED, J. M.	5th MS Inf.	1838-1908 MS	Choc
TURNIPSEED, O. F.	24th MS Cav.	1839-1925 Clai	Clai
TURNNER, George W.	24th Inf.	1830-1902 Gree	Gree
TURNNER, James S.	Steeds MS Cav .	1827-1906 Gree	Gree
TURNNER, L. P.	24th MS Inf.	1833-1907 MS	Gree
TURNNER, Louis	9th MS Inf.	1820-1904 MS	Gree
TURNNER, William	9th MS Inf.	1822-1912 MS	Gree
TURPIN, James Archer	Dardens Army of TN	1845-1918 Jeff	Adam

TURPIN, T. W.	33rd MS Inf.	1839-1921	Pano	Lafa
TUTOR, Jeff D.	17th MS Cav.	1845-1916	Pont	Pont
TUTTON, Joseph Benj.	21st AR Inf.	1838-1881	AR	Lawr
TWINER, J. M.	18th MS Inf.	1836-1912	MS	Harr
TWINER, Joseph	12th LA Inf.	1847-1926		Copi
TWINER, Joseph A.	Woods MS Cav.	1841-1922	Yazo	Yazo
TWITCHELL, Jeduthan L.	10th MO Inf.	1842-1930	MO	Sunf
TYE, John Fletcher	1st MS Lt. Art.	1832-1907	NC	Holm
TYLER, Henry Clay	18th MS Inf.	1829-1887	Yazo	Yazo
TYLER, J. M. Sr.	1st MS Cav.	1822-1898		Linc
TYLER, James _. P.	1st MS Lt. Art.	1846-1905	Atta	Atta
TYLER, James M.	15th MS Inf.	1847-1928	Carr	Linc
TYLER, Julius M.	1st MS Cav.	1848-1915	Linc	Linc
TYLER, John P.	15th MS Inf.	1843-1890	Carr	Mont
TYLER, M.	42nd MS Inf.	1831-1909	Lawr	Mont
TYLER, Redwin _.	14th MS Inf.	1832-18_		Clar
TYLER, W. H.	1st MS Lt. Art.	1847-1916	Carr	Mont
TYLER, William Ira	1st MS Lt. Art.	1838-1906	Atta	Atta
TYLER, William M.	42nd MS Inf.	1828-1863	Lawr	Mont
TYNER, James Polk	33rd MS Inf.	184_-1923	Nesh	Nesh
TYNER, James W.	59th AL Inf.	1843-1920	AL	Jone
TYNER, John D.	40th MS Inf.	1832-1889	FL	Jasp
TYNES, John W.	38th MS Cav.	1827-1904		Walt
TYRE, Elijah E.	12th MS Inf.	1832-1879	MS	Pren
TYREE, James	4th LA Inf.	1844-1889	LA	Adam
TYRONE, H. _.	22nd MS Inf.	1824-1898	Lawr	JEDA
TYRONE, Parkman	7th MS Inf.	1843-1924	Pike	Lawr
TYSON, A. L.	36th MS Inf.	1837-1909		Copi
TYSON, James O.	12th MS Inf.	1839-1906	Mars	Mars
TYSON, L. V.	36th MS Inf.	1835-1920		Copi
TYSON, W. F.	4th NC Cav.	1846-1923	NC	Alco
ULMER, James Madison	40th MS Inf.	1836-1873	Jasp	Clar
ULMER, William Adam	13th MS Regt.	1838-1895	Laud	Simp
UNDERWOOD, George Wash.	26th MS Inf.	1837-1904	MS	Pren
UNDERWOOD, James M.	22nd MS Inf.	1832-1906	Amit	Amit
UNDERWOOD, M. V.	43rd TN Inf.	1837-1927		Tish
UNDERWOOD, R. C.	36th MS Inf.	1843-18_5	Unio	Scot
UNDERWOOD, Richard P.	3rd MS Inf.	1825-1909		Hind
UNDERWOOD, W. C.	1st MS Inf.	1845-1916	MS	Smit
UNDERWOOD, William L.	16th Conf. Cav.	1826-1891	Itaw	Itaw
UNGER, James D.	15th MS Inf.	1823-189_	Holm	Holm
UPSHAW, Drew	46th MS Inf.	1829-1907	Wayn	Wayn
USRY, Stevens C.	Kellys State Troops	1845-1930		Yalo
USSERY, John M.	24th MS Inf.	1840-1917	Lown	Lown
UTLEY, James Robert	7th AL Cav.	1845-1921	AL	Tish
UTLEY, John N.	9th MS Inf.	1841-1918		Lafa
VALENTINE, David	14th MS Inf.	1840-1863	Okti	Okti
VALENTINE, J. I.	7th MS Inf.	1838-1916	Jone	Jone

VALENTINE, James Alex.	3rd MS Inf.	1815-1877		Oktl
VALENTINE, M. B.	7th MS Inf.	1838-1917	Jone	Jone
VALENTINE, R. H.	27th MS Inf.	1843-1924	Jone	Jone
VALLIANT, Franklin	28th MS Cav.	1831-1886	AL	Wash
VALLIANT, John _.	17th MS Inf.	1837-1904	Chic	Chic
VANCE, Calvin Brooks	14th MS Art.	1842-1926	Pano	Pano
VANCE, David	8th MS Inf.	18_5-1911	IR	Newt
VANCE, George W.	15th & 30th MS Inf.	1847-___	Carr	Carr
VANCE, Hutson	Thames Cav.	1847-1933	Newt	Newt
VANCE, J. H.	29th MS Inf.	1840-1915	Calh	Calh
VANCE, J. J.	2nd MS Cav.	1809-1879	GA	Newt
VANCE, J. N.	4th MS Inf.	1847-1933	Calh	Calh
VANCE, James	2nd MS Cav.	1836-1927	Newt	Newt
VANCE, John	MS Inf.	1845-1926	Newt	Laud
VANCE, John D.	3rd MS Cav.	1829-1897	Gren	Gren
VANCE, John W.	29th MS Inf.	1845-1870		DeSo
VANCE, John W.	Stanfords Lt. Art.	1848-___	Gren	Gren
VANCE, Joseph William	2nd MS Inf.	1848-1933	ME	Ston
VANCE, K. E.	3rd MS Inf.	1848-1933	Calh	Calh
VANCE, Robert T.	9th LA Inf.	1843-1925	LA	Wilk
VANCE, Thomas Jeff.	4th MS Inf.	1846-___		Mont
VANCLEAVE, R. _.	1st MS Lt. Art.	1840-___	Yazo	Jack
VANCLEVE, Madison R.	1st MS Lt. Art.	1839-1919	Hind	Yazo
VANDEFORD, John B.	6th MS Cav.	1832-1893	Lown	Alco
VANDENVENDER, W. W.	Jeff Davis Legion	1847-1926	MS	Kemp
VANDERBERG, D. C/G.	Hospital Corps	1825-1906	PA	Warr
VANDERBURG, J. C.	Adams Cav.	1846-1927	Yazo	Harr
VANDERFORD, A. T.	2nd MS Cav.	1844-1920	Alco	Alco
VANDERFORD, J. J.	12th MS Inf.	1830-1911	Holm	Alco
VANDERFORD, John	6th MS Cav.	1843-1905	Lown	Alco
VANDERFORD, N.	2nd MS Cav.	1843-1905	Kemp	Alcor
VANDERVENDER, J. S.	Jeff Davis Legion	1841-1907	Kemp	Kemp
VANDEVANDER, James K.	32nd MS Inf.	1843-1923	AL	Pren
VANDEVANDER, William L.	12th MS Cav.	1847-1912	MS	Pren
VANDEVENDER, J.	Jeff Davis Legion	1830-1912	Kemp	Kemp
VANDIKE, James	12th MS Inf.	184_-1920	Warr	Harr
VANDIVER, _. M.	26th AL Inf.	1832-1922	AL	Lown
VANDIVER, William S.	SC Rifles	1840-1862	SC	Chic
VAN DORN, Earl	Army	1824-1863	Clai	Clai
VANDYKE, Joseph A.	12th MS Inf.	1846-___	Adam	Adam
VAN EATON, H. S.	16th MS Inf.	1826-1898	Wilk	Wilk
VANHORN, George D.	7th AR Inf.	1840-1913	AR	Chic
VANLANDINGHAM, George	19th MS Cav.	1824-1907	Calh	Calh
VANLANDINGHAM, H. J.	35th MS Inf.	1838-1907	Clay	Clay
VANLANDINGHAM, James D.	42nd MS Inf.	1797-1861	Calh	Calh
VANLANDINGHAM, Moses E.	42nd MS Inf.		Calh	Calh
VANLANDINHAM, J. W.	2nd MS Cav.		Tate	Choc
VANN, William Woosley	42nd MS Inf.	1839-1920	Oktl	Oktl

Name	Unit	Dates		
VAN NORMAN, A. L.	22nd MS Inf.	1838-1917	Amit	Laud
VAN NORMAN, Garnet	7th MS Inf.	1839-1894	Amit	Amit
VAN NORMAN, S. T.	7th MS Inf.	1837-1905	Amit	Amit
VANNOROEN, John W.	33rd MS Inf.	1842-1918	Pike	Walt
VANVALKENBURG, T. D.	5th AR Inf.	1841-1921	NY	Harr
VANZANT, James L.	4th MS Cav.	1841-1916		Simp
VARDAMAN, James A.	Seven Star Art.	1828-1895	Copi	Copi
VARNADO, E. M.	33rd MS Inf.	1843-1917	Amit	Pike
VARNADO, ___	17th MS Cav.	1832-1875	Hanc	Pear
VARNADO, P. H.	3rd LA. Inf.	1846-1927	LA	Pike
VARNADO, William Leander	22nd MS Inf.	1835-1917	Warr	Pike
VARNELL, E.	6th MS Inf.	1843-1914	Jasp	Jasp
VANNER, Capel Perry	3rd SC Inf.	1841-1923	SC	Tate
VARNER, F. W.	56th AL Rangers	1835-1916	AL	Wayn
VARNER, L. C.	1st MS Inf.	1840-1910	MS	Wins
VARNER, William M.	20th MS Inf.	1837-1922	Scot	Scot
VASSER, Elijah J.	14th & 43rd MS Inf.	1838-1871	Monr	Monr
VAUGHAN, Edward Rallons	1st MS Lt. Art.	1842-1925	Yazo	Holm
VAUGHN, A. J.	45th MS Inf.	1835-1928	Copi	Hind
VAUGHN, Andrew A.	27th MS Inf.	1833-1912	MS	Jack
VAUGHN, Calep P.	1st MS Cav.		Madi	Hind
VAUGHN, D.C.	36th MS Inf.	1832-1872		Copi
VAUGHN, George M.	31st MS Inf.	1844-___	Choc	Choc
VAUGHN, George W.	43rd MS Inf.		Monr	Monr
VAUGHN, J. A.	26th MS Inf.	1845-1932		Noxu
VAUGHN, Henry Briggs	4th MS Cav.	1849-1930	Adam	Adam
VAUGHN, J. H.	Powers Cav.	1834-1884	Clai	Clai
VAUGHN, J. I.	11th AL Inf.	1842-1927	AL	Yalo
VAUGHN, J. L.	4th AL Inf.	1841-1892	AL	Lee
VAUGHAN, J. N.	2nd MS Inf.	1842-1862	Warr	Lafa
VAUGHAN, James M.	26th MS Inf.	1828-1886	AL/MS	Pren
VAUGHAN, L. H.	20th TX Inf.	1842-1929	TX	Smit
VAUGHAN, W. S.	15th MS Inf.	1831-1920	Holm	Linc
VAUGHN, James	18th MS Inf.	1842-1908	Yazo	Yazo
VAUGHN, James C.	1st MS Inf.	1840-1911	Pont	Pont
VAUGHN, Jerome B.	2nd MS Cav.	1833-1889	MS	Calh
VAUGHN, Joel E.	43rd MS Inf.	1830-1909		Okti
VAUGHN, John	26th MS Inf.	1840-1933	Kemp	Noxu
VAUGHN, John Smith	Jeff Art.	1826-1906	TN	Wash
VAUGHN, Joseph W.	16th MS Inf.	1846-1925	Clai	Lown
VAUGHN, Samuel Cicero	1st & 43rd MS Inf.	1827-1906		Okti
VAUGHN, Thomas A. W.	38th MS Cav.	1838-1866	Wilk	Adam
VAUGHN, Willis	6th MS Inf.	1841-1924	MS	Scot
VAUGHT, W. C.	39th MS Inf.	1841-1913	Pike	Pike
VAUGHT, W. W.	4th MS Cav.	1815-1895	Pike	Pike
VEAL, Columbus C.	2nd GA Cav.	1846-1929	GA	Atta
VEASEY, J. B.	Vaiden Lt. Art.	1844-1928	Carr	Atta
VEASEY, William J. Sr.	9th MS Inf.	1820-1899	MS	Tate
VEAZEY, Benjamin F.	5th MS Inf.	1845-1929	AL	Tate
VEAZEY, William J. Jr.	42nd MS Inf.	1844-1885	MS	Tate

VEITCH, W. T.	Nelsons AL Art.	184_-1901 AL	Holm
VEST, John A.	16th MS Inf.	1845-1901	Copi
VEST, W. B.	3rd VA Cav.	1847-1928	DeSo
VICK, Allen F.	34th MS Inf.	1836-1920 Mars	Mars
VICKORY, Alford J.	15th MS Inf.	1837-1896 Yalo	Yalo
VIGE, Edmond	28th LA Inf.	1840-1862 LA	Warr
VINCE, J. R.	7th MS Inf.	1832-1920 MS	Walt
VINCENT, Thomas	1st MS Inf.	Pont	Pont
VINE, Henry	7th MS Inf.	1846-1920 Amit	Amit
VINES, Thomas	29th MS Inf.	1834-1913 AL	Harr
VINES, William	31st AL Inf.	1832-___ AL	Lafa
VINING, T. G.	1st LA Inf.	1839-1916 LA	Copi
VINSON, A. G.	6th AL Inf.	AL	Kemp
VINSON, George W.	45th AL Inf.	1843-1913 AL	Scot
VINSON, J. L.	7th AL Inf.	1844-1912 AL	Tish
VINSON, John	10th MS Inf.	1829-1920	DeSo
VINSON, Luther S.	Hams MS Cav.	1848-1929	DeSo
VINSON, Nathan	37th MS Inf.	1828-1900	Clar
VINSON, R. B.	64th GA Inf.	1842-1922 GA	Lafa
VINSON, S. H.	28th MS Cav.	1833-1916	Rank
VINSON, William	1st MS Inf.	1827-1894 NC	Laud
VIRDEN, Alexander	1st MS Inf.	1814-1892	Hind
VIRDEN, Huron W.	S. D. Lees Escort	1846-1920 Madi	Madi
VIRDEN, Sam	1st MS Inf.	1829-1902	Hind
VIVERETT, James	6th MS Cav.	1847-1927 Nesh	Nesh
VOIGT, Ward	4th MS Cav.	1849-1936	Hind
VOSBURG, W. M.	21st MS Inf.	1835-1898 Warr	Warr
VOWELL, Valintine	14th MS Inf.	1836-18_ AL	Wins
VOWELL, Vineyard	14th MS Inf.	1837-1915 Wins	Wins
VOYLES, E. E.	14th AL Cav.	1837-1905 AL	Alco
VOYLES, Jasper W.	26th MS Inf.	1839-1923 Tish	Alco
VOYLES, Washington	26th MS Inf.	1824-1885 Tish	Alco
VURCANNON, F.	Gibbons Art.	1837-1923	Harr
WACKENHEIM, Simon	49th TN Inf.	1838-1911 GE	Warr
WACTOR, Johnny W.	14th MS Inf.	1820-1906 Clar	Fran
WADDELL, A. P.	24th MS Inf.	1844-1936	Clay
WADDELL, Alex	13th MS Inf.	1829-1910 Kemp	Kemp
WADDELL, Edmond Burke	Stockdales MS Cav.	1834-1886 CT	Rank
WADDELL, Wallington	Stockdales MS Cav.	1843-1920	Rank
WADDILL, V. J.	28th MS Cav.	1829-1895	Hind
WADDLE, Jessie	MS Inf.	1814-1892	Itaw
WADDLE, Jessie	24th MS Inf.	1814-1892 Chic	Itaw
WADDLE, W. O.	22nd MS Inf.	1846-1930	Itaw
WADDLINGTON, A. P.	30th MS Inf.	1840-1926 Carr	Mont
WADE, Alfred J.	45th MS Inf.		Copi
WADE, B. H.	31st MS Inf.	1843-1914 GA	Lee
WADE, Ben	1st MS Inf.	Adam	Adam
WADE, D. W.	7th MS Inf.	1830-1908 Jone	Jone
WADE, Dunbar Bisland	Jeff Art.	1843-1908 Jeff	Jeff

WADE, E. B.	7th MS Inf.	1838-1894 Jone	Jone
WADE, E. M.	36th MS Inf.	1844-1930	Copi
WADE, Hamp	37th MS Inf.	1825-1904	Forr
WADE, Henry	Walkers TN Inf.	1842-1863 TN	Lafa
WADE, J. T.	2nd MS Inf.	1826-1875 Pont	Pont
WADE, J. R.	43rd MS Inf.	1835-1921	Webs
WADE, James I.	7th MS Inf.	1842-1915 MS	Jasp
WADE, James W.	15th MS Inf.	1803-1869 Holm	Holm
WADE, John A.	Seven Star Art.	1836-1881	Copi
WADE, John M.	31st MS Inf.	1849-1897	Atta
WADE, John Rives	4th SC Inf.	1834-1905 SC	Jeff
WADE, Micajah	Seven Star Art.	1838-1862 Copi	Copi
WADE, S. J.	7th MS Inf.	1837-1888	Covi
WADE, Samuel T.	Steeds MS Cav.	1827-1890 MS	Gree
WADE, Seaborn L.	15th MS Inf.	1836-1899 Atta	Atta
WADE, Seaton	45th MS Inf.		Copi
WADE, Wm. D.	3rd MS Inf.	1837-1901	Hind
WADE, Watson R.	15th MS Inf.	1838-1904 Atta	Atta
WADE, William B.	4th MS Inf.		Lown
WADLINGTON, J. C.	11th MS Inf.	1840-1865 Carr	Lefl
WADLINGTON, T. R.	28th MS Cav.	1847-1872 Carr	Lefl
WADSWORTH, John C.	1st MS Cav.	1839-1925 Carr	Carr
WAFFORD, Alberry S.	8th & 19th MS Cav.	1846-1921	Okti
WAFFORD, Davis T.	31st MS Inf.	184_-1937	Webs
WAGATHA, Adam Martin	30th LA Inf.	1844-1924 LA	Harr
WAGES, J.	1st MS Inf.	1839-1906 Tipp	Unio
WAGES, P. G.	45th MS Inf.	1837-1914 Unio	Unio
WAGGONER, J. Merrel	18th MS Inf.	1835-1908 Leak	Leak
WAGGONER, S. G.	18th MS Inf.	1840-1899 Leak	Leak
WAGGONER, W. C.	1st Inf.	1848-1924 Leak	Leak
WAGNER, A. B.	13th MS Inf.	1833-1910 Laud	Laud
WAGNER, D. M.	15th MS Inf.	1840-1915 Yalo	Yalo
WAGNER, William B.	15th MS Inf.	1833-1869 Yalo	Yalo
WAHL, John M.	9th MS Inf.	1843-1898 Warr	Warr
WAILES, Levin	38th MS Cav.	1839-1889 Wilk	Adam
WAINWRIGHT, William	1st MS Inf.	1825-1884	Copi
WAIT, Pierce M. B.	1st MS Cav.	1847-1914 Pano	Tate
WAIT, Roehanbeom L.	Adams MS Cav.	1845-1878 Pano	Tate
WAITES, Gilbert M.	8th MS Inf.	1834-1918 AL	Jasp
WAITES, James	1st AL Inf.	1842-1870 AL	Alco
WALBERG, Louis	9th MS Batt'n.	1836-1907 GE	Lown
WALDEN, A. T.	43rd MS Inf.	1838-1887 Monr	Monr
WALDEN, James M.	41st AL Inf.	1826-1892 AL	Yalo
WALDEN, T. B.	36th MS Inf.	1821-1906	Copi
WALDON, A. B.	32nd MS Inf.	1828-1877 SC	Tipp
WALDON, Isaac	2nd MS Inf.	1835-1907 SC	Tipp
WALDRIP, J. M.	34th MS Inf.	1841-1921 Mars	Yalo
WALDROP, Archic	43rd MS Inf.	1822-1882 AL	Chic
WALDROP, Henry L.	2nd MS Cav.	1843-1927 MS	Pano
WALDROP, W. F.	22nd MS Inf.	1834-1917 Lafa	Pont

Name	Unit	Dates		Rank
WALDROP, William M.	6th MS Inf.			Rank
WALDRUP, George M.	8th MS Inf.	1835-1922 Jasp		Jasp
WALDRUP, J. F.	2nd MS Rangers	1842-1916 MS		Pano
WALDRUP, William Thomas	18th MS Cav.	1846-1927 Pano		Pano
WALES, John Ellis	Adams Cav.	1843-1917		Holm
WALKER, A. S.	38th MS Cav.	1831-1910 Pike		Pike
WALKER, Albert G.	Stubbs MS Cav.	1848-1937 MS		Simp
WALKER Alexander A.	2nd MS Cav.	1828-1895 Choc		Alco
WALKER, Alford Raymond	2nd MS Inf.	1840-1888 Lee		Lee
WALKER, Benjamin G.	37th MS Inf.	1839-1917 AL		Perr
WALKER, Benjamin _.	2nd MS Inf.	1842-1918 Tipp		Tipp
WALKER, Benjamin F.	Adams MS Cav.	1824-1876		Tate
WALKER, Benjamin L.	MS Art.	1838-18_ Laud		Laud
WALKER, Charles G.	5th LA Inf.	1834-1898 LA		Wash
WALKER, Christopher M.	14th Conf. Cav.	1848-1930 Pike		Pike
WALKER, Cicero	11th MS Inf.			Lown
WALKER, D. W.	7th MS Inf.	1845-___		JEDA
WALKER, David	Steeds MS Cav.	1833-1921 MS		Ston
WALKER, David M.	1st MS Lt. Art.	1845-1906 MS		Pike
WALKER, Elisah	2nd MS Cav.	1827-1886 Laud		Laud
WALKER, F. M.	6th MS Inf.	1836-1924		Rank
WALKER, Freeman	23rd MS Inf.	1843-1911 Tish		Bent
WALKER, George	3rd MS Inf.	1839-1915 AL		Holm
WALKER, George A.	16th MS Inf.	1836-1903 Wilk		Wilk
WALKER, George W.	39th Inf.	1834-1882 Copi		Simp
WALKER, George Wash.	44th MS Inf.	18_0-1900 MS		Harr
WALKER, H. W.	9th MS Inf.	1842-1907 DeSo		Tate
WALKER, Henry W.	3rd State Troops	1826-1893 Okti		Okti
WALKER, Horatio	14th MS Inf.	1848-1936 AL		Harr
WALKER, Isaac W.	2nd MS Cav.	1840-1928 GA		Newt
WALKER, Ivy	8th MS Inf.	1839-1896 Smit		Smit
WALKER, J. H.	1st MS Lt. Art.		LA	Adam
WALKER, J. M.	11th MS Cav.	1842-1906 Tall		Alco
WALKER, J. W.	Quitmans Lt. Art.			Adam
WALKER, J. Abner	20th MS Inf.	1836-1931 MS		Harr
WALKER, James	8th MS Inf.	1830-1899		Newt
WALKER, James E.	2nd MS Inf.	1837-1912 Bent		Bent
WALKER, James H.	16th MS Inf.	1837-1915 Wilk		Wilk
WALKER, James L.	19th MS Inf.	1844-1921 MS		Lafa
WALKER, James M.	9th MS Inf.	___-1865		DeSo
WALKER, James M.	2nd MS Cav.	1818-1897 MS		Okti
WALKER, James M.	3rd MS Inf.	1838-1920 Simp		Simpn
WALKER, James Motheral	10th MS Inf.	1834-1895 Tate		Tate
WALKER, James Oliver	14th MS Inf.	1842-1923 DeSo		Clar
WALKER, James R.	17th MS Inf.	1837-1909 Mars		Mars
WALKER, Jeremiah	1st MS Lt. Art.	1833-1878 Linc		Linc
WALKER, Joel P.	9th MS Inf.	1840-1915		DeSo
WALKER, Joel P.	13th MS Inf.	1840-1898 Laud		Laud
WALKER, John	32nd MS Inf.	1832-1871 Alco		Alco
WALKER, John	Navy	1834-1907 PA		Harr
WALKER, John B.	1st MS Lt. Art.	1820-___ Choc		Choc
WALKER, John D.	2nd MS Cav.	1843-1918 Laud		Laud

WALKER, John E.	22nd MS Inf.	1815-1897 Amit	Amit
WALKER, John H.	23rd MS Inf.	1843-1922 Tipp	Tipp
WALKER, John J.	23rd MS Inf.	1842-1916 Tipp	Unio
WALKER, John M.	4th MS Inf.	1834-1879	Pren
WALKER, John W.	31st TN Inf.	1835-1915 Tish	Tish
WALKER, Joseph B.	38th MS Cav.	1843-1883 Wilk	Wilk
WALKER, Josiah W.	MS Cav.	1819-1893 MS	Alco
WALKER, J. Reuben	17th MS Inf.	1838-1909	Mars
WALKER, M. C.	31st TN Inf.	1841-1893 TN	Alco
WALKER, M. T.	2nd MS Cav.	1840-1916 MS	Newt
WALKER, M. V.	11th MS Cav.	1835-1889 Kemp	Alco
WALKER, Madison	37th MS Cav.	1833-1923 AL	Jasp
WALKER, N. E.	Courier	1847-1928	Atta
WALKER, Nicholas L.	14th MS Inf.	1845-1935	Amit
WALKER, Pleasant A.	16th MS Inf.	1840-1893 Simp	Simp
WALKER, Phillip Marion	7th MS Cav.	1848-1904 MS	Pren
WALKER, Q. M.	20th AL Inf.	1830-1912 AL	Kemp
WALKER, R. B.	1st MS Lt. Art.	1838-1879 Adam	Adam
WALKER, Richard E.	9th & 34th MS Inf.	1837-1898 Mars	Mars
WALKER, Richard P.	2nd MS Cav.	1843-1918 Laud	Laud
WALKER, Robert	1st MS Lt. Art.	1838-1879 Adam	Adam
WALKER, S.	40th AL Cav.	1833-1883 AL	Wayn
WALKER, S.	6th MS Inf.	1834-190_ Simp	Simp
WALKER, S. J.	2nd MS Cav.	1828-1910 Laud	Laud
WALKER, Samuel B.	1st MS Inf.	1838-1878 Pont	Pont
WALKER, Silas Cicero	38th MS Cav.	1843-1915 Pike	Pike
WALKER, Stephen	42nd MS Inf.	____-1862	Mars
WALKER, T. H.	38th MS Regt.	1846-1920	JEDA
WALKER, Theodore	2nd TN Inf.	1838-1909	Pont
WALKER, Thomas H.	4th MS Inf.	1847-1934	Yalo
WALKER, Thomas M.	18th MS Inf.	1839-1864 Madi	Madi
WALKER, Thos.	26th MS Inf.		Alco
WALKER, W. D.	9th & 10th MS Inf.	1832-1906 Warr	Warr
WALKER, W. H.	3rd VA Cav.	1836-1915 Jasp	Jasp
WALKER, Wm. H.	2nd MS Cav.	1821-1896 Laud	Laud
WALKER, W. K.	Englishs MS Art.	Adam	Adam
WALKER, W. L.	24th MS Inf.	1834-1890 Chic	Chic
WALKER, W. L.	7th MS Inf.	1836-1913 Pike	Pike
WALKER, W. W.	8th MS Inf.	1841-192_ MS	Leak
WALKER, William	4th MS Inf.	1846-1908	Rank
WALKER, William H.	13th MS Inf.	1847-1923 Laud	Nesh
WALKER, William W.	18th MS Cav.	1847-1917	Tish
WALKER, William W.	19th MS Inf.	1836-1907 Lafa	Lafa
WALKER, Willis	8th MS Inf.	1835-1909 Wayn	Wayn
WALL, A. E. (Dr.)	16th MS Inf.	1838-1912 MS	Harr
WALL, D. G.	12th MS Inf.	1833-1882 MS	Amit
WALL, David Jerone	14th MS Cav.	1847-1916 MS	Amit
WALL, E. J.	8th MS Inf.	1839-1916 Laud	Forr
WALL, George W.	18th MS Cav.	1839-1905 Bent	Bent
WALL, J. A.	36th MS Inf.	1831-1910 Newt	Newt

156

Name	Unit	Dates	Birth	Death
WALL, James M.	42nd MS Inf.	1838-1898 Yalo	Warr	
WALL, John H.	33rd MS Inf.	1836-1889 Amit	Amit	
WALL, Mike	8th MS Inf.	1847-1940 Jasp	Lama	
WALL, T. J.	14th MS Inf	1839-1907 Jasp	Newt	
WALL, Thomas C. H.	34th MS Inf.	1820-1865 Bent	Bent	
WALL, W. C.(Dr.)	23rd NC Inf.	1837-1910	DeSo	
WALLS, W. W.	23rd MS Inf.	1834-1882 Pont	Unio	
WALL, William Henry	12th MS Inf.	1838-1910 Holm	Pano	
WALL, William J.	19th MS Inf.	1837-1880 Bent	Bent	
WALL, Young	8th & 10th MS Cav.	1842-1915 MS	Scot	
WALLACE, A. G.	18th MS Inf.	1837-1902	Copi	
WALLACE, A. J.	34th Inf.	1829-1900 Mars	DeSo	
WALLACE, A. M.	10th MS Inf.	1840-1875	Itaw	
WALLACE, Asa T.	28th MS Cav.	1840-____ Carr	Carr	
WALLACE, Charles R.	1st MS Inf.	1839-1913	Nesh	
WALLACE, D. C.	Davenports MS Cav.	181_-1899	Laud	
WALLACE, D. W. P.	10th MS Inf.	1841-1889 Itaw	Itaw	
WALLACE, F. J.	18th MS Inf.	1840-1897	Rank	
WALLACE, Hamilton	12th MS Cav.	1833-1901 SC	Pren	
WALLACE, J. A.	44th MS Inf.	1827-1899 MS	Yazo	
WALLACE, J. C.	20th MS Inf.	1847-1931 MS	Scot	
WALLACE, J. C.	6th MS Inf.	1835-1888 Carr	Carr	
WALLACE, J. D.	7th MS Inf.	1829-1925 Pike	Linc	
WALLACE, J. F.	29th MS Inf.	1843-1924 Atta	Holm	
WALLACE, James Henry	9th MS Inf.	1835-1915	Tate	
WALLACE, James _.	4th MS Cav.	1842-1925 Itaw	Itaw	
WALLACE, Joel R.	16th MS Inf.	1820-1896 Copi	Hind	
WALLACE, John H.	7th MS Cav.	1844-19__ Lawr	Lawr	
WALLACE, John M.	44th MS Inf.	1836-1909 Lown	Lown	
WALLACE, M. _.	39th MS Inf.	1841-1863 Pike	Lafa	
WALLACE, M. R.	MS Art.	1816-1877 Pont	Pont	
WALLACE, _. H.	23rd MS Inf.	1841-1885 Coah	Pano	
WALLACE, Stanford	Adams MS Cav.	1832-1887 Scot	Scot	
WALLACE, Stevens G.	40th MS Inf.	1845-____ Atta	Scot	
WALLACE, T. A.	Adams MS Cav.	1831-1896 Leak	Leak	
WALLACE, Thomas D. (Rev)	13th MS Inf.	1843-1909 AL	Wins	
WALLACE, V. H.	13th MS Cav.	1841-1908 Atta	Atta	
WALLACE, W. A.	39th MS Inf.	1840-1890	Rank	
WALLACE, W. P.	39th MS Inf.	1840-1927 MS	Fran	
WALLACE, Walter P.	9th MS Inf.	1839-1918 Madi	Madi	
WALLACE, Zack	7th MS Inf.	1838-1910 Pike	Linc	
WALLAGE, Thomas	Adams Cav.	1822-1868 Yazo	Yazo	
WALLDREP, Samuel	30th AL Inf.	1828-1909	Okti	
WALLER, Geo. Patterson	12th MS Inf.	1846-1929 Hind	Lown	
WALLER, H. A.	2nd GA Cav.	1832-____	Newt	
WALLER, Jasber	37th MS Inf.	1843-1924 Clar	Forr	
WALLER, John S.	40th AL Inf.	1841-1916 AL	Wayn	
WALLER, Robert	8th MS Inf.	1837-1909 Clar	Laud	
WALLER, William M.	40th MS Inf.	1846-1931 Lawr	Lawr	
WALLER, William W.	1st MS Lt. Art.	1845-1935 Yazo	Yazo	

WALLEY, A. Pink	27th MS Inf.	1832-1903 Perr	Perr
WALLEY, George W.	46th MS Inf.	1841-1905 Gree	Gree
WALLEY, J. M.	24th MS Inf.	1822-1908 MS	Gree
WALLEY, James S.	20th MS Inf.	1835-1924 Jasp	Jasp
WALLEY, Richard H.	3rd MS Inf.	1829-1910 Gree	Gree
WALLEY, William M.	Steeds Cav.	1826-1907 Gree	Gree
WALLIS, David	28th AL	1842-1918 MS	Itaw
WALLIS, Josiah	23rd MS Inf.	1821-1904 MS	Pren
WALLIS, W. A.	28th MS Cav.	1842-1904 LA	Harr
WALLS, A. J.	31st AL Inf.	1839-1914 AL	Pont
WALLS, J. F.	29th MS Inf.	1846-1929 Yazo	Yazo
WALLS, John	22nd AL Inf.	1829-1907 Pont	Pont
WALLS, Z.	8th MS Inf.	1832-1915	Scot
WALSH, Hiram	39th MS Inf.	1835-1912	Rank
WALSH, Peter	28th MS Cav.	1836-1886 IR	Adam
WALSTON, T. S.	20th MS Inf.	1844-1914 Harr	Harr
WALTERS, A.	3rd MS Inf.	1836-1912 Newt	Nesh
WALTERS, Albert	3rd MS Regt.	1825-1892	Rank
WALTERS, Charles J.	4th MS Cav.	183_-1925	Rank
WALTERS, David	4th AL Inf.	1821-1912 SC	Harr
WALTERS, Dawson	9th MS Inf.	1830-1914 Jack	Geor
WALTERS, E. H/N.	6th MS Inf.	1846-1923	Rank
WALTERS, J. W.	16th MS Inf.	1846-1929 MS	Harr
WALTERS, John	2nd MS Cav.	1827-1912 MS	Monr
WALTERS, John _. _.	6th & 15th MS Inf.	1836-1912	Rank
WALTERS, Lewis W.	16th MS Cav.	1844-1918	Smit
WALTERS, Luke	4th MS Inf.	1842-1931	Rank
WALTERS, Moses	8th MS Inf.	1829-1887 Rank	Jone
WALTERS, R. _.	8th MS Inf.	1841-1911 Jone	Jone
WALTERS, Sam W.	27th MS Inf.	1840-1915 MS	Jack
WALTERS, Theodore	9th LA Inf.	1844-1903 Hanc	Hanc
WALTERS, William	24th MS Inf.		Monr
WALTERS, William H.	40th MS Inf.	1842-1922 Nesh	Nesh
WALTHALL, Edward Carey	Army of TN	1831-1898 VA	Mars
WALTHALL, Rufus Peyton	26th MS Inf.	1842-1894 MS	Pren
WALTHALL, William Thomas	12th AL Inf.	1820-1899 VA	Warr
WALTMAN, John J.	14th MS Inf.	1834-1906 Clar	Scot
WALTON, Charles A.	18th MS Inf.	1817-1902	Hind
WALTON, Charlie	Warren Lt. Art.	1841-1891 Warr	Warr
WALTON, Edwin S.	Pettus MS Art.	1833-1909 Pano	Pano
WALTON, Green B.	36th MS Inf.	1821-1902 Newt	Nesh
WALTON, George	32nd MS Inf.	1840-1900 MS	Pren
WALTON, George Lee	25th LA Inf.	1830-1909 AL	Adam
WALTON, George W.	Mobile Dragoons	1837-1905 AL	Covi
WALTON, I. N.	33rd MS Inf.	1847-1916 MS	Leak
WALTON, J. S. J.	12th MS Inf.	1831-1910 Holm	Atta
WALTON, James	29th MS Regt.	1839-1862 Holm	Holm
WALTON, John C.	36th MS Inf.	1837-1908 Nesh	Nesh
WALTON, John J.(Dr.)	2nd MS Inf.	1834-1876 Clar	Jasp
WALTON, John T.	29th MS Inf.	1831-1899 Holm	Holm
WALTON, Joseph Plummer	28th MS Cav.	1841-1922 Holm	Holm

Name	Unit	Dates		
WALTON, Samuel L.	12th AR S. S.			Hind
WALTON, Simon A.	18th MS Inf.	1847-1924		DeSo
WALTON, Timothy	Stubbs Cav.	1847-1927		Hind
WALTON, William Dyke	43rd MS Inf.	1839-1907	MS	Monr
WALTON, William Henry	3rd MS Cav.	1848-1880	MS	Hind
WAMBLE, James	8th MS Cav.	1841-1866	Lown	Chic
WAMBLE, John T.	20th MS Inf.	1840-1920	TN	Monr
WAMBLE, Thomas J.	2nd MS Cav.			Monr
WANSLEY, Augustus	36th MS Inf.	1823-1898	Newt	Newt
WANSLEY, R. R.	2nd MS Cav.	1825-1908	Newt	Newt
WARD, Albert G.	5th MS Cav.	1821-1864	MS	Tate
WARD, Amos	10th MS Inf.	1838-1920	GA	Okti
WARD, Andrew M.	4th MS Cav.	1836-1862	MS	Pont
WARD, Benjamin Franklin	11th MS Inf.	1835-1920	NC	Mont
WARD, Charles	36th MS Inf.	1841-1916		Walt
WARD, Charles C.	14th MS Inf.	1844-1863	Lown	Lown
WARD, Charles H.	36th MS Inf.	1847-1929		Hind
WARD, Charles W.	4th LA Inf.	1841-1902	EN	Adam
WARD, D. J.	5th MS Inf.			Rank
WARD, E. A.	1st MS Inf.	1823-188_	Rank	Kemp
WARD, Frank	6th MS Cav.	1846-192_	Itaw	Sunf
WARD, G. W.	1st MS Lt. Art.	1833-1910	Yazo	Yazo
WARD, J. C.	5th MS Inf.	1841-1916	MS	JEDA
WARD, J. W.	20th MS Inf.	1836-1890	AL	Wins
WARD, Jackson	Streets MS Cav.	1835-1918	Lawr	Jack
WARD, James C. (Dr.)	7th TN Inf.	1834-1915	TN	Monr
WARD, Joe M.	3rd MS Cav.	___-1915		Smit
WARD, John	24th MS Inf.	1840-1894	GA	Warr
WARD, John F.	20th MS Inf.	1843-1898	MS	Shar
WARD, John M.	Lays MS Cav.	1848-1932	Atta	Atta
WARD, John M.	6th SC Cav.	1835-1888	SC	Copi
WARD, M. I.	40th AL Inf.	1846-1912	AL	Jone
WARD, Milton E.	8th AL Cav.	1846-1934	Clar	Jone
WARD, Needham W.	34th MS Inf.	1838-1908	Tate	Tate
WARD, R. E.	38th MS Cav.	1839-1917	Wilk	Wilk
WARD, R. P.	10th AL Inf.	1833-1880	AL	Chic
WARD, Richard	3rd NC Inf.	1841-1917	Gree	Geor
WARD, Robert A.	5th MS Cav.	1821-1885	VA	Mont
WARD, Robert F.	9th & 42nd MS Inf.	1841-___	Pano	Tate
WARD, Steve R.	8th & 19th MS Cav.	1840-1924		Okti
WARD, Thomas	Adams MS Cav.	1830-1893	Madi	Madi
WARD, Thomas J.	4th MS Cav.	1834-1916	MS	Pont
WARD, Thomas N.	1st MS Inf.		Pano	Calh
WARD, Thomas T.	42nd MS Inf.	1842-1873	MS	Calh
WARD, W. A.	4th MS Cav.	1831-1893	Leak	Leak
WARD, W. A.	14th MS Inf.	1843-1927	GA	Clay
WARD, W. B.	9th LA Inf.	1834-1920	LA	Mari
WARD, W. C.	4th MS Cav.	1827-1891	MS	Pont
WARD, W. J.	1st MS Cav.		MS	Calh
WARD, W. T. (Dr.)	28th MS Cav.	1829-1876	NC	Mont

WARD, William	40th MS Inf.	1832-1902 Nesh	Kemp
WARD, William Baker	11th MS Inf.	1835-1928 Monr	Monr
WARD, William Tolbert	8th MS Inf.	1812-1880 SC	Smit
WARDELL, W. B.	1st & 2nd MS Inf.	1848-1916 Pont	Tate
WARDEN, William	2nd MS Inf.	1838-1915 Pear	Pear
WARDLAW, Samuel Watt	7th SC Inf.	1836-1894 SC	Lafa
WARDLAW, W. A.	22nd MS Inf.	1843-1910 Warr	Pano
WARDLOW, J. W. Sr.	32nd MS Inf.	1840-1916 Tish	Alco
WARDLOW, Zack A.	22nd MS Inf.	1844-1928 Hind	Hind
WARDSWORTH, A. G.	GA Art.	1842-1920 GA	Leak
WARE, A. W.	39th MS Inf.	1832-1908 Simp	Simp
WARE, J. L.	18th MS Inf.	1847-1938 MS	Hind
WARE, Frank M.	8th MS Inf.	____-1893	Smit
WARE, J. H.	18th MS Inf.		Rank
WARE, J. M.	14th MS Inf.	1826-1895 Okti	Okti
WARE, J. W. (Dr.)	2nd MS Inf.	1839-1927 Pont	Harr
WARE, J. W. (Dr.)	2nd MS Inf.	1839-1928 Tish	Harr
WARE, James H.	20th MS Inf.	1842-1862 Monr	Monr
WARE, John R.	22nd MS Inf.	1819-1900 Carr	Carr
WARE, John T.	2nd MS Inf.	1847-1902 Monr	Monr
WARE, John S.	39th MS Inf.	1843-1920 Newt	Newt
WARE, Robert G.	36th MS Inf.	1821-1901 AL	Leak
WARE, S. W. (Dr.)	2nd MS Inf.	1838-1928 Tish	Harr
WARE, Sedley Lynch	6th MS Inf.	1848-1866	Hind
WARE, Thompson P.	46th MS Inf.	1811-1865 KY	Rank
WARE, Thomas N.	17th AL Inf.	1825-1904 AL	Leak
WARE, W. A.	Army	1840-1912 Hind	Hind
WARE, W. T.	31st AL Inf.	1839-1908 Pont	Pont
WARE, William H.	3rd MS Inf.	1820-1909 Monr	Monr
WARE, William Lynch	38th MS Cav.	1843-1878	Hind
WARE, William Z.	MS Art.	1830-1862 Pont	Pont
WARFIELD, Elisha	2nd AR Inf.	1838-1894 KY	Adam
WARFIELD, William P.	28th MS Cav.	1843-1886 MD	Tuni
WARING, Thomas G.	6th MD Cav.	1830-1909 MD	Walt
WARNER, Austin	Alcorn Inf.	1837-1910 Warr	Warr
WARNER, J. A.	28th NC Inf.	1838-1909 NC	Holm
WARNER, John D.	33rd MS Inf.	1838-1905 Pike	Pike
WARNER, Levi	1st Conf. Inf.	1838-1910 SC	Wins
WARREN, Abel Green	9th MS Cav.	1839-1881 MS	Laud
WARREN, Arthur	27th MS Inf.	1834-1909 MS	Pont
WARREN, Charley	2nd MS Cav.	AL	Kemp
WARREN, J.	17th AR Inf.	1843-1862 AR	Lafa
WARREN, J. H.	32nd MS Inf.	1838-1906 Tish	Alco
WARREN, James A.	35th MS Inf.	1837-1918 Nesh	Nesh
WARREN, James Calloway	36th MS Inf.	1831-1864 MS	Kemp
WARREN, Jim W.	6th MS Inf.	1830-1908 Scot	Linc
WARREN, John	39th MS Inf.	1830-1894	Rank
WARREN, Joseph	27th MS Inf.	1830-1911 MS	Hind
WARREN, Joseph J.	3rd MS Cav.	1815-1893	Jeff
WARREN, L. B.	1st MS Lt. Art.	1835-1903 Yazo	Yazo
WARREN, M. P.	36th MS Inf.	1842-1909 MS	Scot

160

Name	Unit		
WARREN, Mark M.	35th MS Inf.	1833-1880 Nesh	Nesh
WARREN, R. Key	26th MS Inf.	184_-1933 Kemp	Kemp
WARREN, Ruben	18th MS Inf.	1820-1889 Yazo	Yazo
WARREN, Silas	3_ MS Inf.	1838-1911 Scot	Scot
WARREN, William	7th MS Inf.	1835-1887 Mari	Mari
WARREN, William H.	35th MS Inf.	1828-1910 Nesh	Nesh
WARWICK, George W.	4th MS Cav.	1841-1929 Fran	Fran
WARWICK, R. W.	17th GA Inf.	1846-1929 GA	Leak
WARWICK, W. R.	17th GA Inf.	1845-1905 GA	Leak
WASH, A. P.	36th MS Inf.	1822-1909 MS	Newt
WASH, P. M.	8th MS Inf.		Newt
WASH, R. L.	36th MS Inf.	1825-1896	Newt
WASHBURN, L.	6th MS Inf.	1824-1906	Rank
WASHBURN, Thomas (Dr.)	22nd MS Inf.	1837-1901 IL	Mont
WASHINGTON, Warner R.	20th MS Inf.	1840-1924 MS	Harr
WASSER, Charles	1st MS Lt. Art.	1839-1910 Yazo	Yazo
WATERS, A. T.	3rd MS Inf.	1840-1907 Newt	Laud
WATERS, Edmund M.	6th MS Inf.	1845-1881 Smit	Smit
WATERS, Hamilton	Adams MS Cav.	1835-1907 Warr	
WATFORD, James A.	1st MS Troops		Rank
WATFORD, John A.	1st MS Inf.	1839-1865	Rank
WATKINS, A. W.	5th MS Inf.	1843-1913 Nesh	Nesh
WATKINS, A. James	26th AL Inf.	1816-1889 AL	Webs
WATKINS, Allen	11th MS Cav.	1847-1914 Kemp	Clay
WATKINS, Andrew Jackson	26th AL Inf.	1832-1898 AL	Webs
WATKINS, Benjamin	40th MS Inf.	1836-1917 Leak	Leak
WATKINS, Benjamin Frank	4th MS Cav.	1842-1906 Clai	Jeff
WATKINS, Charles H.	24th MS Inf.	1842-1917 Kemp	Kemp
WATKINS, Charles W.	27th MS Inf.	1843-1908 TN	Pano
WATKINS, Enoch M.	40th MS Inf.	Atta	Atta
WATKINS, Erskine	39th MS Inf.	1838-1910 AL	Hind
WATKINS, Fearn	40th MS Inf.		Leak
WATKINS, G. W.	5th MS Inf.	1846-1900 Nesh	Laud
WATKINS, H. C/G.	49th MS Inf.	1831-1894 AL	Leak
WATKINS, Henry	4th TN Inf.	1842-1917 TN	Tish
WATKINS, J. C.	10th Regt. Cav.	1847-19_	Clai
WATKINS, J. K.	5th MS Inf.	1840-1910 Laud	Laud
WATKINS, J. L.	Stanfords MS Art.	1842-1910 Yalo	Gren
WATKINS, J. T.	6th MS Inf.	1849-1930 AL	Smit
WATKINS, James W.	9th MS Cav.	1827-1914 Tish	Tish
WATKINS, James W.	9th MS Inf.	1842-1902 Mars	Mars
WATKINS, Jerry M.	43rd MS Inf.	1838-1918 Kemp	Kemp
WATKINS, Jessie	5th MS Inf.	1810-1884 Nesh	Nesh
WATKINS, John L.	4th AL Inf.	1841-1912 AL	Clay
WATKINS, John R.	2nd MS Cav.	1816-1892 Clay	Clay
WATKINS, John William	8th MS Inf.	1843-1862 Smit	Smit
WATKINS, Leigh A.	11th MS Cav.	1834-1898	Hind
WATKINS, Marshall	16th Inf.	1827-1864 Smit	Smit
WATKINS, Porter	6th MS Inf.	1845-1910 Leak	Leak
WATKINS, Richmond	40th MS Inf.	1836-1909 Leak	Leak
WATKINS, Thad	40th MS Inf.	1847-1928 MS	Nesh

WATKINS, Thad H.	44th MS Inf.	1832-1908 NC	Clay
WATKINS, Thomas Henry	4th MS Cav.	1848-1894 Clai	Jeff
WATKINS, Thornton T.	6th MS Inf.	1826-1920 AL	Harri
WATKINS, W. D. Sr.	59th VA Inf.	1818-1894 VA	Kemp
WATKINS, W. J.	7th MS Cav.	1847-1894 NC	Mars
WATKINS, Wiley D. Jr.	27th VA Inf.	1839-1900 VA	Kemp
WATKINS, Wm. Augustus	4th MS Cav.	1838-1915	Copi
WATKINS, Willis	5th MS Inf.	1844-1870	Nesh
WATLINGTON, Cornelius	Lees Army of VA	1842-1930 VA	Hind
WATLINGTON, Henry Clay	18th MS Cav.	1849-1935	Forr
WATLINGTON, W. F.	1st MS Lt. Art.	1813-1894 Yazo	Yazo
WATLINGTON, W. J.	1st MS Lt. Art.	1843-1905 Yazo	Yazo
WATSON, Albert	3rd AL Cav.	1832-1924	Pear
WATSON, Augustus C.	Watsons Lt. Art.	1824-1900 Jeff	Adam
WATSON, B. E.	31st MS Inf.	1841-1926 Choc	Choc
WATSON, Benjamin D.	14th MS	1844-1920 GA	Holm
WATSON, F. E.	Adams MS Cav.	1844-1917 Lown	Clay
WATSON, F. _.	17th AL Inf.	1843-1919 Laud	Laud
WATSON, George K.	14th MS Inf.	1847-1894 Clar	Jone
WATSON, H. R.	27th AL Inf.	1832-1894 AL	Tish
WATSON, J. M.	37th MS Inf.	1847-1901 Laud	Laud
WATSON, J. R. (Dr.)21st MS Inf.		1839-1922 Wilk	Holm
WATSON, J. R.	18th MS Cav.	1849-1915	Covi
WATSON, Jim	21st MS Inf.	1828-1897 NC	Holm
WATSON, John Archibald	36th AL Inf.	1831-1891 GA	Holm
WATSON, John C.	15th MS Inf.	1839-1881	Webs
WATSON, John F.	37th MS Inf.	1836-1905 Laud	Laud
WATSON, John J.	35th MS Inf.	1833-1904 Kemp	Kemp
WATSON, John M.	46th MS Inf.		Covi
WATSON, John T.	43rd MS Inf.		Monr
WATSON, Joseph H.	Holmes Co. Ind.	1818-18_ NC	Holm
WATSON, O. C.	35th MS Inf.	1840-1920 Wins	Wins
WATSON, O. T.	35th MS Inf.	1829-1897 AL	Wins
WATSON, R. I.	16th GA Inf.	1839-1931 SC	Lefl
WATSON, R. I.	36th MS Cav.	1840-1935 MS	Harr
WATSON, Samuel E.	3rd MS Cav.	1818-1876	Carr
WATSON, Samuel	22nd MS Inf.	1830-1902	Hind
WATSON, W. H.	4th MS. Inf.	1845-1930 Calh	Harr
WATSON, W. R. C.	1st MS Lt. Art.	1832-1906 Jeff	Jeff
WATSON, Wheeler	9th MS Cav.	1848-1911 MS	Monr
WATSON, William	20th Inf.	1813-1894 Harr	Harr
WATSON, William D.	32nd GA Inf.	1846-___ GA	Newt
WATT, C. B.	14th MS Inf.	1836-1907 Okti	Okti
WATT, Robert	Moodys LA Art.	1839-1911 LA	Clai
WATT, Thomas J.	2nd MS Inf.	1827-1907 Calh	Unio
WATT, Robert H.	48th MS Inf.	1839-1911 Warr	Warr
WATTS, A. B.	37th NC Inf.	1846-1928 NC	Alco
WATTS, A. J.	Bradfords Art.	1848-1940	Pont
WATTS, Bert S.	56th AL Inf.	1839-1914 AL	Covi
WATTS, Dallas	2nd MS Inf.	1847-1913	Rank
WATTS, Ephram	Brookhaven Lt. Art.	1840-1911 Lawr	Linc

WATTS, G. W.	28th MS Cav.	1841-1911 IL	Mont
WATTS, George	4th MS Cav.	1842-1893 Pear	Pear
WATTS, Francis Marion	7th MS Inf.	1833-1926 Covi	Covi
WATTS, G. W.	7th MS Inf.	1838-1900 Covi	Covi
WATTS, J. C.	14th MS Inf.	1834-1906	Clar
WATTS, J. J.	Stubbs Cav.	1845-1932 Copi	Copi
WATTS, J. R.	5th MS Inf.	1844-1929 Kemp	Wins
WATTS, J. T.	36th MS Inf.	1827-1901 Newt	Newt
WATTS, James	36th MS Inf.	1845-1920	Scot
WATTS, James	10th MS Inf.	1829-1902 Rank	Laud
WATTS, James	2nd MS Inf.	1826-1889 Tish	Alco
WATTS, James	48th MS Inf.	1843-1885 Covi	Mari
WATTS, John	3rd MS Inf.	1841-1884	Rank
WATTS, John Dickerson	21st MS Inf.	1845-1923 Warr	Sunf
WATTS, John L.	7th MS Inf.	1847-1922 Mari	Mari
WATTS, Joseph W.	1st La. Cav.	1834-1917 AL	Holm
WATTS, Jubal J. (Dr.)	46th MS Inf.	1831-1905 Newt	Scot
WATTS, Malachi	31st MS Inf.	1844-1916	Pont
WATTS, Nelson	37th MS Inf.	1840-1898 Newt	Jasp
WATTS, Olcott S.	13th MS Inf.	1844-1882 Kemp	Amit
WATTS, Richard L.	2_ MS Inf.	1844-1910 Holm	Hump
WATTS, Samuel B.	10th MS Inf.	1843-1931 Rank	Laud
WATTS, Thomas	24th MS Cav.	1823-1886 Pike	Linc
WATTS, Van B.	27th MS Inf.	1840-1916 Linc	Linc
WATTS, W. C.	4th MS Cav.	1845-1927	Pear
WATTS, Whi_	32nd MS Inf.	1846-1928 NC	Alco
WAUGH, R. W.	8th MS Cav.	1840-1900 Calh	Pont
WAULARD, Benjamin F.	38th AL Inf.	1841-1919 Gree	Gree
WAX, W. T.	12th MS Cav.	1842-1919 AL	Monr
WAYATT, Francis A.	28th MS Cav.	1841-1899 Yalo	Holm
WAYCASTER, Phillip A.	4th MS Cav.	1837-1909 Jeff	Monr
WEATHERALL, A. D.	18th MS Cav.	1827-1887	DeSo
WEATHERALL, George	2nd MS Cav.	1830-1896	Pont
WEATHERALL, John I.	2nd MS Cav.	1821-1865	Pont
WEATHERALL, _. W.	1st MS Cav.	1820-1896 Pont	Pont
WEATHERBEE, John _.	19th MS Cav.	1819-1901 MS	Calh
WEATHERBY, George M.	12th MS Cav.	1816-1900 Holm	Holm
WEATHERBY, Jesse T.	4th MS Inf.	1836-1914 NC	Tipp
WEATHERFORD, Henry P.	46th MS Inf.	1836-1909 Laud	Nesh
WEATHERFORD, W. G.	2nd MS Cav.	1846-1926 Laud	Forr
WEATHERLAND, William	15th MS Inf.	1845-1937 Holm	Holm
(WEATHERLY, Joseph M. located after WEATHERSBY)			
WEATHERSBY, George	4th MS Cav.	1843-1898 Copi	JeDa
WEATHERSBY, George _.	28th MS Cav.	1843-1891	Rank
WEATHERSBY, H. E.	33rd MS Inf.	1834-1864 Amit	Amit
WEATHERSBY, Hatten I.	33rd MS Inf.	1837-1896 Amit	Amit
WEATHERSBY, James T.	4th MS Cav.	1831-1893	Copi
WEATHERSBY, Joseph	7th MS Inf.	1839-1924 MS	Smit
WEATHERSBY, S. C.	7thMS Inf.	1842-1906 Fran	Amit
WEATHERSBY, Seaborn L.	33rd MS Inf.	1836-1883 Amit	Amit
WEATHERSBY, Warren W.	6th MS Inf.	1845-1908 Copi	Simp
WEATHERSBY, William	22nd MS Inf.	1847-1876	Hind

Name	Unit	Dates	Place
WEATHERSBY, William (Dr.)	22nd MS Inf.	1836-1883 Lawr	Lawr
WEATHERLY, Joseph M.	13th MS Inf.	1846-1892 Atta	Atta
WEAVER, A. C.	2nd MS Inf.	1847-189_ MS	Wayn
WEAVER, Daniel T.	2_ MS Inf.	1805-18_0 Yalo	Yalo
WEAVER, James H.	2nd MS Cav.	1812-1903 SC	Choc
WEAVER, James Henderson	2nd MS Cav.	1842-1900 Monr	Monr
WEAVER, Jess W.	5th MS Inf.	1841-1895 Monr	Chic
WEAVER, John R.	8th MS Inf.	1826-1894	Newt
WEAVER, R. L.	25th VA Inf.	1839-1913 AL	Harr
WEAVER, S. L.	2nd MS Cav.	1830-1907 Choc	Choc
WEBB, A. G.	7th MS Inf.	1843-1926 Marl	Marl
WEBB, Allen J.	40th MS Inf.	1831-1913 MS	Nesh
WEBB, G. D.	40th MS Inf.	1840-1912 AL	Jone
WEBB, George	20th MS Inf.	1848-1936	Clar
WEBB, George F.	33rd MS Inf.	1818-1902 MS	Amit
WEBB, Henry F.	36th AL Inf.	1838-1878 AL	Laud
WEBB, J. J.	20th MS Inf.	1830-1913 EN	Hind
WEBB, J. _. _.	33rd MS Inf.	1833-1890 Amit	Amit
WEBB, James R.	36th AL Inf.	1845-1881 AL	Laud
WEBB, John Addison	4th MS Inf.	1843-1924 VA	Hind
WEBB, John B.	4th MS Inf.	1824-1902 TN	Mont
WEBB, John Thomas	22nd MS Inf.	1851-1936 MS	Lafa
WEBB, John R.	24th MS Inf.	1822-1923 Itwa	Itaw
WEBB, John _.	24th MS Inf.	1841-1930 Itaw	Itaw
WEBB, Joshua Prewett	40th MS Inf.	1837-1925 Wins	Wins
WEBB, Lawrence	3rd MS Inf.	1827-1909 Tish	Alco
WEBB, Peyton S.	4th MS Inf.	1837-1934 TN	Mont
WEBB, R. A.	11th AL Inf.	1844-1927 AL	Lee
WEBB, R. L.	35th MS Inf.	1840-1921 MS	Choc
WEBB, Stephen M.	55th TN Inf.	1828-1862 NC	Pren
WEBB, Thompson B.	6th & 15th MS Inf.	1844-1890 MS	Rank
WEBB, W. H.	33rd MS Inf.	1843-1921 Amit	Amit
WEBB, W. H.	4th MS Inf.	1845-1919 TN	Lefl
WEBB, W. J. Sr.	2nd TN Cav.	1828-1907 TN	Monr
WEBB, William	3rd & 33rd MS Inf.		Hind
WEBB, William	3rd MS Inf.	1842-1929 Jack	Jack
WEBB, Willie F.	5th MS Cav .	1845-1862 TN	Mont
WEBB, William Harrell	22nd MS Inf.	1843-1915 Amit	Amit
WEBB, William R.	1st MS Inf.	1838-1923	Copi
WEBB, William T.	11th MS Inf.	183_-1919 AL	Lafa
WEBER, Charles S.	17th MS Inf.	1833-1901 Mars	Mars
WEBSTER, Alfred A.	2nd MS Cav.	1842-1912	Monr
WEBSTER, Daniel F.	4th MS Cav.	1844-1919 SC	Lafa
WEBSTER, Frank W.	41st MS Inf.	1839-1902 Pont	Pont
WEBSTER, Henry David	8th NC Inf.	1839-1905	Rank
WEBSTER, James W.	5th MS Inf.	1843-___	Monr
WEBSTER, Napoleon B.	1st MS Lt. Art.	1846-1915 Warr	Warr
WEBSTER, Peter R.	6th MS Inf.	1837-1925 Simp	Simp
WEBSTER, W. E.	5th AL Inf.	1836-1905 AL	Wins

164

Name	Unit	Dates	County
WEDGEWORTH, Christopher	37th MS Inf.	1838-1906 Jasp	Smit
WEDGEWORTH, H. J.	5th MS Inf.	1837-1907 Nesh	Nesh
WEDGEWORTH, J. W.	16th MS Inf.	1841-1935 Adam	Harr
WEDGEWORTH, Joel W.	35th MS Inf.	1817-1892	Laud
WEDGEWORTH, L.	35th MS Inf.	1821-___ Nesh	Laud
WEDGEWORTH, W. S.	37th MS Inf.	1843-1931 Jasp	Jasp
WEED, Allen W.	9th & 43rd MS Inf.	1829-1904	Pano
WEEKS, A. R.	40th MS Inf.	1835-1920 Atta	Atta
WEEKS, D. D.	1st MS Art.	1836-1916 Carr	Harr
WEEKS, James	27th AL Inf.	1829-1910 AL	Okti
WEEKS, James H/M.	36th MS Inf.	1843-1911	Copi
WEEKS, John	40th MS Inf.	1835-1920 Atta	Atta
WEEKS, John _.	42nd MS Inf.	1838-1918 Calh	Calh
WEEKS, Joseph P.	Seven Star Art.		Copi
WEEKS, Joseph P.	42nd MS Inf.	1845-1918 Calh	Calh
WEEKS, N. H.	21st AL Inf.	1832-1908 AL	Choc
WEEKS, W. T.	4th MS Cav.	1832-1919 Copi	Choc
WEEMS, Alexander	4th MS Inf.	1839-1889 GA	Leak
WEEMS, Alonzo James	7th MS Inf.	1846-1912 AL	Jone
WEEMS, Anderson	16th MS Inf.	1840-1865 Adam	Choc
WEEMS, B. S.	4th MS Inf.	1834-1912 Leak	Leak
WEEMS, Edward L.	5th GA Cav.	1839-1909 GA	Tate
WEEMS, Edward T.	4th MS Inf.	1835-1888 Holm	Holm
WEEMS, J. F.	2nd MS Inf.	1841-1927	Lee
WEEMS, James M.	4th MS Inf.	1809-1873 Holm	Holm
WEEMS, Robert L.	2nd MS Cav.	1828-1908 Clar	Clar
WEEMS, Sam Wesley	1st MS Lt. Art.	1822-1907 AL	Holm
WEEMS, W. J.	37th MS Inf.	1845-1930 Smit	Scot
WEIR, Cornelius G.	1st MS Cav.	1843-1869 Carr	Carr
WEIR, Joe T.	4th LA Inf.	1843-1914 Adam	Adam
WEIR, John	44th MS Inf.	1833-1900 Carr	Carr
WEIR, R. S.	1st MS Cav.	1835-1907 Carr	Carr
WEIR, Thomas H.	Stanfords Lt. Art.	1836-1902 Yalo	Gren
WEISSINGER, James M.	5th MS Cav.	1845-1931	DeSo
WEISSINGER, William S.	MS Art.	1847-1931	DeSo
WELBORN, F. G.	51st GA Inf.	1838-1928 AL	Leak
WELBORN, J. G.	7th MS Inf.	1829-1901 GA	Jone
WELBORN, P. C.	1st MS Cav.	1846-1914 Jone	Jasp
WELCH, A. M.	Pogues Art.	1837-1912 Madi	Madi
WELCH, Albert J.	24th MS Cav.	1842-1924	Copi
WELCH, B. H/R.	2nd KY Cav.	1833-1909 SC	Harr
WELCH, Caleb	7th MS Inf.	18_-1886 Covi	Covi
WELCH, Dennis	3rd MS Inf.	1827-1907 Newt	Newt
WELCH, H. A.	31st MS Inf.	1839-1903 AL	Yalo
WELCH, I. B.	Jeff Davis Cav.	1831-1903	Rank
WELCH, J. G.	17th MS Cav.	1824-1916 Clar	Clar
WELCH, James F.	4th LA Inf.	1842-1904 IR	Adam
WELCH, James _.	19th MS Inf.	1845-191_ Lafa	Lafa
WELCH, Joseph M.	7th MS Inf.	1846-1927 Covi	Covi

WELCH, Ransom J.	7th MS Inf.	1841-191_ Covi	Covi
WELCH, Richard	7th MS Inf.	1824-1902 Covi	Covi
WELCH, Thomas G.	4th MS Cav.	1831-1875	Copi
WELCH, W. H.	21st AL Inf.	1842-1905 AL	Laud
WELCH, W. M.	7th MS Inf.	1837-1908 Jone	Jone
WELDON, Thos.	16th MS Inf.	1816-1865 IR	Adam
WELFORD, Henry	36th AL Inf.	1841-1926 Gree	Geor
WELFORD, Joel	36th AL Inf.	1845-1938 MS	Geor
WELLBORN, Aaron	7th MS Inf.	1824-1924 Jone	Laud
WELLBORN, D. M. (Dr.)	7th MS Inf.	1824-1910 Jone	Laud
WELLBORN, E. J.	15th GA Inf.	1830-1911 GA	Laud
WELLBORN, Gideon	17th MS Inf.	1845-1913 Mars	Mars
WELLBORN, W. K.	Greens KY Art.	1844-1924 KY	Harr
WELLS, Anderson	15th MS Inf.	1838-1905 Okti	Wins
WELL, B. R.	18th MS Inf.	1838-1895 MS	Hind
WELLS, Benjamin	8th MS Inf.	1838-1906 Newt	Wins
WELLS, C. D.	19th MS Inf.	1843-1928 MS	Pano
WELLS, E. S.	13th TN Inf.	1837-1904 TN	Bent
WELLS, Eph	22nd MS Inf.	1831-1870	Hind
WELLS, Frank	17th MS Inf.	1835-1935 Lee	Mars
WELLS, G. H.	33rd MS Inf.	1843-1911 Leak	Leak
WELLS, James Alexander	13th AL Inf.	1845-1927 AL	Yalo
WELLS, John	10th MS Inf.	1837-1887 Adam	Adam
WELLS, John	8th MS Inf.	1835-1921 Jasp	Lown
WELLS, John W.	48th AL Inf.	1832-1911 AL	Yalo
WELLS, L. M.	18th MS Inf.	1835-1883	Hind
WELLS, Lucius	18th MS Inf.	1825-18_5	Copi
WELLS, Martin	23rd MS Inf.	1849-1934 Tipp	Harr
WELLS, Martin M.	2nd MS Inf.	1837-1903 Pont	Pont
WELLS, N. Alex	3rd MS Inf.	1830-1862	Hind
WELLS, Nathaniel	15th TN Cav.	____-1914	Pike
WELLS, Nathaniel Porter	3rd MS Inf.	1831-1907 Hind	
WELLS, Nim M.	6th MS Inf.	1845-1919 Rank	Lown
WELLS, Reuben Thomas	1st MS Cav.	1848-1926 Lown	
WELLS, Sam H/N.	31st MS Inf.	1844-1915	Webs
WELLS, Thos. B.	10th MS Inf.	1839-1904 Adam	Adam
WELLS, Thomas J.	3rd MS Cav.	1848-1922	Hind
WELLS, W. _.	1st AL Inf.	184_-1862 AL	Lafa
WELLS, W. Calvin	22nd MS Inf.	1844-1914 MS	Hind
WELLS, William G.	11th MS Inf.	1842-1912 Lown	Copi
WELLS, William H.	12th AL Cav.	1848-1925 AL	Monr
WELLS, William M.	1st MS Lt. Art.	1808-1871	Hind
WELLS, Wm. Lewis	10th & 12th MS Inf.	18_2-1919 Adam	Adam
WELLS, William W.	12th AL Cav.	1848-1923 AL	Monr
WELSH, Dempsey	8th MS Inf.	183_-1906	Nesh
WELSH, James W.	11th MS Inf.	1827-1898 Nesh	Nesh
WELSH, W. A.	20th MS Inf.	1831-1886 MS	Scot
WELSH, Wm. T.	1st MS Cav.	1847-1910 Pont	Laud
WELSH, William A.	26th MS Inf.	1840-1875 Tish	Tish
WENTWORTH, W. M.	7th MS Inf.	1816-1889 Fran	Fran
WESSON, James M.	Wessons Art.	1848-1925	Copi

Name	Unit	Dates		
WESSON, James Madison	Wessons Art.	1815-1899		Hind
WEST, A. B.	1st MS Cav.	1845-1919	Itaw	Itaw
WEST, A. M.	Q. M. C.	1813-1894	AL	Mars
WEST, Albert	36th MS Inf.	1843-1927		Copi
WEST, Anderson	12th MS Inf.	1842-1911	Holm	Holm
WEST, C. D.	3rd MS Inf.	1825-1875	Wins	Wins
WEST, D. F.	1st MS Cav.	1845-1923	Carr	Linc
WEST, Daniel	24th MS Inf.	1824-1910	Wayn	Wayn
WEST, David M.	2nd MS Cav.	1845-1921	Choc	Monr
WEST, F. H.	12th MS Inf.	1840-1893	WV	Adam
WEST, George W.	1st MS Inf.	1831-1907	Lafa	Lafa
WEST, H. J.	6th & 15th MS Inf.	1835-1862		Copi
WEST, J. A.	41st MS Inf.	1828-1909	Pont	Pont
WEST, J. T. Sr.	56th AL Cav.	1841-1903	AL	Wayn
WEST, J. W.	1st MS Inf.	1837-1897	MS	Lee
WEST, James A.	41st MS Inf.	1827-1909	Pont	Pont
WEST, John Sr.	56th AL Inf.	1822-1896	AL	Wayn
WEST, John Foster	18th MS Inf.	1839-1904	Jeff	Jeff
WEST, John M.	1st MS Lt. Art.	1847-1883	Holm	Holm
WEST, John M.	19th MS Inf.	1813-1892	Lafa	Lafa
WEST, John Sidney	4th MS Cav.	1822-1899	Tipp	Tish
WEST, John W.	24th MS Inf.	1843-1905	Gree	Gree
WEST, Lemuel Augustus	5th & 12th MS Inf.	1845-1911	Holm	Holm
WEST, Matthew M.	12th MS Inf.	1842-1932		Copi
WEST, N. C.	30th MS Inf.	1834-1895	Carr	Carr
WEST, Osborn F.	18th MS Inf.	1827-1879	SC	Tate
WEST, Phillip F.	12th MS Inf.	1840-1862		Copi
WEST, R. D.	5th MS Cav.	1837-1898	Holm	Holm
WEST, Rufus	35th MS Inf.	1842-1910	Okti	Wins
WEST, Stephen	56th AL Cav.	1826-1909	Wayn	Wayn
WEST, T. F/P.	4th MS Cav.	1848-1914		Lafa
WEST, T. S. (Rev.)	13th MS Inf.	1836-___		Hind
WEST, W.	14th & 46th MS Inf.	1838-1914	Laud	Lama
WEST, W. H.	14th MS Inf.	1842-1906	Laud	Laud
WEST, W. S.	18th MS Inf.	1829-1902		Hind
WEST, W. T.	1st & 43rd MS Inf.	1837-1909	Itaw	Monr
WEST, William	5th MS Inf.	1841-1901	MS	Kemp
WEST, William B.	43rd MS Inf.	1836-1920	Monr	Monr
WEST, William G.	19th MS Inf.	1840-1915	Tipp	Bent
WEST, Wilson	13th MS Inf.	1826-1900	Wayn	Wayn
WEST, Winston E.	9th MS Inf.	1845-1895		Wash
WEST, Zebulon	43rd MS Inf.	1828-1871	Monr	Monr
WESTBROOK, A. N.	33rd MS Inf.	1832-1893	Fran	Fran
WESTBROOK, Benjamin H.	45th MS Inf.	1846-1931	MS	Amit
WESTBBOOK, E. S. T.	45th MS Inf.	1848-1917	Pike	Amit
WESTBROOK, James	3rd MS Inf.	1829-1900		Chic
WESTBROOK, Joseph G.	TN Lt. Art.	1834-1921	TN	Clay

WESTBROOK, Seaborn Jones	3rd MS Inf.	1840-1916 Jack	Amit
WESTBROOK, Z. W.	6th MS Cav.	1847-1922 Lown	Lown
WESTBROOK, Zachariah T.	12th MS Cav.	1836-1910 Mars	Mars
WESTERFIELD, C.	5th MS Cav.	1819-1882 Wins	Scot
WESTMORELAND, F. W.	11th MS Cav.	1831-1888 Pont	Lee
WESTMORELAND, J. M.	34th MS Inf.	1838-1913 Pont	Pont
WESTMORELAND, James P.	10th MS Inf.	1842-1872 Pont	Lee
WESTMORELAND, Jerome	2nd MS Inf.	1838-1910 TN	Lee
WESTMORELAND, William M.	46th MS Inf.	1832-1917 Simp	Simp
WESTMORELAND, William W.	AL Cadets	1846-1922 AL	Lown
WESTON, Horatio _.	9th MS Cav.	1833-186 Hanc	Hanc
WESTON, Robert _.	42nd AL Inf.	1836-1869 AL	Wins
WESTON, W. _.	42nd AL Inf.	1842-1863 AL	Lafa
WESTROPE, D. _.	1st MS Lt. Art.	1829-19_ Clai	
WETHERSBEE, J. A.	11th MS Inf.	1823-1910 Wayn	Wayn
WHALEN, G.	16th MS Inf.	Adam	Adam
WHALAN, John	14th LA Inf.	1826-1906 IR	Adam
WHALEN, R.	16th MS Inf.		Adam
WHALEY, Truman	Capt. Berrys	1847-1927 GA	Mars
WHARTON, C/O. R.	154th TN Inf.	1834-1918 TN	Harr
WHARTON, Richard	154th TN Inf.	1843-1935	Lee
WHARTON, Thomas J.	33rd MS Inf.	1817-1900 TN	Hind
WHATLEY, D. P.	10th MS Inf.	1827-1913 Copi	Newt
WHATLEY, John	2nd MS Cav.	1844-1911 Clar	Geor
WHATLEY, Terrell	17th MS Cav.	1838-19_ AL	Gree
WHEAT, Alphes A. (Dr.)	12th KY Inf.	1834-1917 KY	Tall
WHEAT, James A.	9th MS Cav.	1830-1910 MS	Pear
WHEAT, William	9th MS Cav.	1831-1891 MS	Pear
WHEELER, Augustus S.	24th MS Cav.	1847-1917 Copi	Shar
WHEELER, Erastus (Dr.)	27th MS Inf.	1840-1900	Forr
WHEELER, James F.	1st & 2nd MS Inf.	1824-1906 Carr	Lefl
WHEELER, John	32nd MS Inf.	1841-1862 Alco	Alco
WHEELER, John W.	26th AL Inf.	1845-1914 AL	Tish
WHEELER, T. W.	10th & 29th MS Inf.	1831-1906	DeSo
WHEELER, W. H.	9th MS Inf.	1838-1921	DeSo
WHEELESS, George W.	24th MS Cav.	1839-1928 Clai	Clai
WHEELOCK, Alpheus	1st MS Vol.	1819-1863 Adam	Adam
WHEELOCK, Altheron	1st MS Inf.	1824-1881 VT	Adam
WHEELOCK, W. C.	10th MS Inf.		Adam
WHELAN, Peter	18th MS Inf.	1831-1900 Madi	Madi
WHERRY, Samuel	12th MS Inf.	1845-1908 Holm	Holm
WHETSTONE, Rollins C.	Powers Cav.	1845-1939 LA	Wilk
WHETSTONE, Telfair Mead	38th MS Cav.	1846-192 Wilk	Wilk
WHIDDON, Bentman	7th MS Inf.	1840-1896 Mari	Lama
WHIDDON, John	3rd MS Inf.	1847-1916 Lama	Lama
WHIP, Jacob	21st MS Inf.	1838-1880 Wilk	Wilk
WHISENANT, SC	2nd MS Cav.	1833-1865 MS	Choc

WHITAKER, Alexander	31st MS Inf.	1845-1910 Chic	Monr
WHITAKER, Claiborn G.	37th MS Inf.	1834-1886 MS	Wayn
WHITAKER, I. R.(Dr.)	Whitakers		
	Cav. Scouts	1834-1909 Hind	Hind
WHITAKER, James	Forrest Cav.	1847-1925 Wilk	Wilk
WHITAKER, L. P.	43rd MS Inf.	1831-1906 Monr	Monr
WHITAKER, Nolan S.	16th MS Inf.	1839-1893 MS	Wilk
WHITAKER, W. W.	19th TN Inf.	1849-1933 MS	Tish
WHITAKER, Warden G.	1st MS Lt. Art.	1832-1925 Warr	Warr
WHITAKER, William	44th MS Inf.	1839-1911 Amit	Amit
WHITAKER, William B.	18th TN Inf.	1838-1916 TN	Laud
WHITE, A. C.	17th MS Inf.	1804-1881	DeSo
WHITE, Andrew Jackson	1st AL Inf.	1843-1919 AL	Tish
WHITE, Archibald	Powers Cav.	18_2-1897 Wilk	Wilk
WHITE, Benjamin G.	21st MS Inf.	1838-1910 Wilk	Wilk
WHITE, Benjamin Stirling	6th TX Cav.	____-1892	Hind
WHITE, C. W.	41st MS Inf.	1847-1892 MS	Choc
WHITE, Ceder (Cato)	31st MS Inf.	1833-189_	Webs
WHITE, David L.	4th MS Cav.	1827-1910	Rank
WHITE, Edgar Allen	11th TN Cav.	1848-1938 TN	Jasp
WHITE, Edward Gaines	29th MS Inf.	1840-1862 Pano	Pano
WHITE, Eli Z.	11th MS Inf.	1839-1890 NY	Carr
WHITE, Elipha	Q. M. C.		
	Transport	1838-1902 Madi	Madi
WHITE, F. M.	4th MS Inf.	1839-1924 Holm	Holm
WHITE, Francis H.	21st MS Inf.	1836-1919 Wilk	Wilk
WHITE, G. B.	4th MS Inf.	1835-1909 Atta	Atta
WHITE, George W.	19th MS Inf.	1835-1903 Lafa	Lafa
WHITE, Green Berry	8th MS Inf.	1835-1894 Laud	Laud
WHITE, Harper J.	6th MS Inf.	1840-1908 MS	Copi
WHITE, J. B.	48th MS Inf.	1837-1921	Rank
WHITE, J. H.	2nd MS Cav.	1836-1929 MS	Pano
WHITE, J. H.	Warren Lt. Art.	1830-1911 MS	Warr
WHITE, J. J.	45th MS Inf.	1843-1925 MS	Laud
WHITE, J. J.	8th MS Inf.	1841-191_ Jasp	Chic
WHITE, J. J.	39th MS Inf.	1830-1912 Pike	Pike
WHITE, J. K. P.	41st MS Inf.	1843-1930 Laud	Laud
WHITE, J. M.	12th MS Inf.	1819-1903 Lawr	Linc
WHITE, J. S.	12th MS Inf.	1830-1910 Warr	Pont
WHITE, J. W.	37th MS Inf.	1836-1909 AL	Clar
WHITE, Jacob W.	38th MS Cav.	1830-1913 GA	Perry
WHITE, James	26th MS Inf.	1833-1911 Tish	Tish
WHITE, James W.	17th MS Inf.	1848-1926 Tish	Tish
WHITE, John A. Sr..	5th MS Inf.	1836-1910 MS	Amit
WHITE, James D.	42nd MS Inf.	1843-1926 MS	Calh
WHITE, James Daniel	30th MS Inf.	1832-1863 Atta	Atta
WHITE, James Daniel	1st MS Cav.	1841-1915 MS	Leak
WHITE, James F.	2nd MS Cav.	1830-1900 Lawr	JEDA
WHITE, John H.	11th MS Cav.	1842-1906 Kemp	Alco
WHITE, John _.	11th MS Inf.	1845-1922 Lown	Harr
WHITE, James L.	45th MS Inf.	1832-1888 Wins	Wins
WHITE, John Long	1st MS Lt. Art.	1835-1928 MS	Linc

Name	Unit	Dates	State	County
WHITE, John P.	20th MS Inf.	1826-1899 SC	Wins
WHITE, John T.	4th AL Inf.	1839-1918 AL	Pren
WHITE, John W.	8th MS Inf.	1824-1863 MS	Jasp
WHITE, John W.	6th MS Inf.	1836-1913 MS	Scot
WHITE, Joseph	36th MS Inf.	1827-1907 GA	Newt
WHITE, Joseph	13th & 21st MS Inf.	1842-1910 Tall	Atta
WHITE, Joseph	31st MS Inf.	1824-1891 Chic	Chic
WHITE, Joseph R.	2nd MS Inf.	1842-1917 MS	Lafa
WHITE, Joseph Warren	Powers MS Cav.	1840-1939 AL	Ston
WHITE, J. Thomas	14th Conf. Cav.	1835-1905 TN	Tipp
WHITE, Leonard J.	Peytons MS Cav.	1847-1911 MS	Linc
WHITE, Lorene (Dr.)	3rd MS Inf.	Hind	Hind
WHITE, Lorenza D.	38th MS Cav.	1830-1915 Wilk	Wilk
WHITE, M. P.	4th MS Inf.	1840-1910 Calh	Calh
WHITE, Mitchell	33rd MS Inf.	1840-1863 Lawr	Lawr
WHITE, Moses L.	8th MS Cav.	1836-1908 Pren	Pren
WHITE, N. E.	18th TN Inf.	1840-1862 TN	Lown
WHITE, Ollen	_1st MS Inf.	182_-188_ MS	Chic
WHITE, Owen F.	Hughes MS Cav.	1830-1916	Hind
WHITE, P. (Rev.)	32nd AL Inf.	1821-1880 AL	Laud
WHITE, P. S. (Dr.)	5th MS Inf.	1839-1898 Lown	Noxu
WHITE, R. B.	15th MS Cav.	1845-1911 Holm	Holm
WHITE, R. C.	10th AL Inf.	1839-1904 AL	Lee
WHITE, R. F. M.	33rd MS Inf.	1838-1915 Lawr	Lawr
WHITE, R. P.	13th AL Inf.	1842-1921 AL	Harr
WHITE, Richardson	20th MS Inf.	1824-1862 Wins	Wins
WHITE, Robert L.	32nd AL Inf.	1841-1923 Laud	Laud
WHITE, Rowlette P.	42nd MS Inf.	1830-1892 Tate	Tate
WHITE, S.C.	26th MS Inf.	1841-1909 GA	Tipp
WHITE, T. C.	28th AL Inf.	1841-1862 AL	Chic
WHITE, T. W.	38th MS Cav.	1824-1889 GA	DeSo
WHITE, Thomas	38th MS Cav.	1836-1913 Wilk	Wilk
WHITE, Thomas	9th MS Inf.	1835-1905 Pano	Bent
WHITE, Thomas	1st MS Inf.	1844-1909	DeSo
WHITE, Thomas C.	22nd MS Inf.	Hind	Carr
WHITE, Thomas E.	1st MS Lt. Art.	1824-1880 Yazo	Yazo
WHITE, Thomas Rutherford	TN Lt. Art.	1847-1918 AL	Pear
WHITE, Thomas S.	6th MS Inf.	1813-1874	Rank
WHITE, Thomas W.	36th AL Inf.	1841-1924 FL	Gree
WHITE, Tom	11th MS Cav.	____-1902 AL	Noxu
WHITE, Uzzey	34th MS Inf.	1830-1904 Tipp	Bent
WHITE, W. A.	42nd MS Inf.	184_-1926 MS	Harr
WHITE, W. B.	5th MS Inf.	1836-1912 MS	Noxu
WHITE, W. E.	1st AL Cav.	1817-1909 GA	Harr
WHITE, W. H.	42nd MS Inf.	1848-1893	Rank
WHITE, W. H.	42nd MS Inf.	1845-1926 Tate	Harr
WHITE, W. H.	7th MS Inf.	1844-1897 Clar	Laud
WHITE, W. L.	5th AL Inf.	1835-189_ Laud	Laud
WHITE, W. P.	20th MS Inf.	1843-1918 MS	Leak
WHITE, W. R.	30th MS Inf.	1836-1917 Atta	Atta
WHITE, W. T.	11th MS Inf.	1839-1907 AL	Noxu

170

Name	Unit	Dates	Col1	Col2
WHITE, W. T.	22nd MS Inf.	1847-1925 MS	Fran
WHITE, W. T.	3rd MS Inf.	1838-1927 Pike	Pike
WHITE, Wesley	15th MS Inf.	1832-1895 Webs	Webs
WHITE, William	20th MS Inf.	1811-1871 SC	Wins
WHITE, William Benson	1_th MS Inf.	1837-1921 TN	Holm
WHITE, William G.	36th MS Inf.		Copi
WHITE, William George	1st MS Cav.	1843-1932 MS	Clay
WHITE, William J.	31st MS Inf.	1831-1899 NC	Ston
WHITE, William L.	43rd MS Inf.	1842-1919 AL	Pren
WHITE, William M.	38th MS Cav.	1832-1903 GA	Perr
WHITE, William N.	16th MS Inf.	1844-1900 Wilk	Wilk
WHITE, William W.	9th MS Inf.	1849-1893	Rank
WHITE, Z. J.	36th MS Inf.	1838-1907 MS	Newt
WHITEHEAD, A. J.	MS Bat. S. S.	1843-1886 Holm	Holm
WHITEHEAD, Amazire	4th MS Inf.	1830-1919	Lafa
WHITEHEAD, _. F.	1st MS Inf.	1847-1923 Noxu	Noxu
WHITEHEAD, G. M.	14th MS Inf.	1841-1924 MS	Harr
WHITEHEAD, Henry C.	54th or 64th AL	1842-1923 AL	Sunf
WHITEHEAD, J. Flavins	44th MS Inf.	1834-1895 Amit	Amit
WHITEHEAD, N. E. (Dr.)	18th MS Inf.	1840-1905 Madi	Lefl
WHITEHEAD, Peter F.	Lorings Div. Surgeon	1838-1878 KY	Warr
WHITEHEAD, Richard C.	14th MS Inf.	1841-1924 Fran	Harr
WHITEHEAD, R. Jack	5th MS Cav.	1838-1921 Holm	Holm
WHITEHEAD, T. B.	38th MS Inf.	1835-1898 Fran	Fran
WHITEHEAD, Thomas	3rd MS Inf.	1845-1924	Tipp
WHITEHEAD, Thomas J.	Harveys Scouts	1847-1920 Carr	Mont
WHITEHEAD, W. L.	5th MS Cav.	1840-1922 Monr	Itaw
WHITEHEAD, Wm. Henry	39th MS Inf.	1837-1912 Copi	Fran
WHITEHURST, James (Rev.)	6th MS Cav.	1848-1914 Alco	Alco
WHITEHURST, W. _.	1st AR Inf.	1844-1862 AR	Lafa
WHITES, William	20th MS Inf.	1833-1898 Wins	Wins
WHITESIDE, S. A. H.	32nd MS Inf.	1831-1902 Pont	Unio
WHITESIDE, William H.	41st MS Inf.	1833-1882 Pont	Pont
WHITESIDES, R. J. R.	10th MS Cav.	1847-1926 NC	Lee
WHITFIELD, Albert H. Sr	6th MS Regt.	1849-1918 MS	Hind
WHITFIELD, Anthony Dyer	6th MS Cav.	1842-1916 Lown	Lown
WHITFIELD, Isadore B.	17th MS Batt.	1847-1920 NC	Hind
WHITFIELD, James H.	28th MS Cav.	1834-1912	Rank
WHITFIELD, John J.	32nd MS Inf.	1844-1912 Tish	Tish
WHITFIELD, John W.	2nd MS Inf.	1843-1923 MS	Tish
WHITFIELD, Joseph	6th KY Inf.	1841-1931	Lefl
WHITEIELD, Needham H.	14th MS Inf.	1822-1897 NC	Monr
WHITFIELD, Robert Allen	39th MS Inf.	1839-1923	Rank
WHITFIELD, W. C.	4th MS Cav.	1831-1903 Tish	Tish
WHITFIELD, W. W.	MS Cav.	1823-1903 NC	Lown
WHITFIELD, William S.	7th AL Cav.	1822-1870 Tish	Tish
WHITING, W. A.	1st MS Lt. Art.	1846-___ Hind	Hind
WHITLEY, N. M.	18th MS Cav.	1834-1910	DeSo
WHITLEY, Philip J.	6th LA Cav.	1828-1902 LA	Linc
WHITLEY, Robert	2nd MS Inf.	18_6-1916 MS	Harr
WHITMAN, Ulysses L.	46th MS Inf.	1846-1925 Yazo	Yazo

WHITMIRE, Mitchiel	33rd GA Cav.	1846-1933	AL	Nesh
WHITMORE, J. W.(Dr.)	41st MS Inf.	1825-1878	Chic	Alco
WHITMORE, S. C.	1st MS Inf.	1840-1873	Adam	Adam
WHITMORE, Thomas J.	3rd MS Inf.	1825-___	Sunf	Choc
WHITNEY, C. W.	Jeff. Flying Art.	1829-1917	Jeff	Jeff
WHITNEY, J. J.	4th MS Cav.	1834-1896	Jeff	Jeff
WHITNEY, J. Mort	24th MS Cav.	1846-1923	MS	Wayn
WHITT, M.	3rd MS Inf.		Copi	Calh
WHITT, Richard	19th AL Inf.	1830-19_	AL	Chic
WHITTAKER, A. _.	3rd MS Inf.	1844-1929	Itaw	Harr
WHITTEN, J. J.	31st MS Inf.	1842-1929	Holm	Harr
WHITTEN, J. M.	15th LA Coast Art.	1845-1924	LA	Tall
WHITTEN, J. _.	31st MS Inf.	1842-192_	Tish	Harr
WHITTEN, John H. L.	31st MS Inf.	1844-1922	Pont	Lee
WHITTEN, P. W.	13th MS Inf.	1824-1880	AL	Wins
WHITTEN, Ransom E.	2nd MS Inf.	1817-1885	SC	Tipp
WHITTINGTON, A. J.	36th MS Inf.			Copi
WHITTINGTON, Andrew J.	33rd MS Inf.	1833-1886	Amit	Amit
WHITTINGTON, Daniel L.	14th MS Inf.	1830-1915		Copi
WHITTINGTON, Dempsey	7th MS Regt.	1836-1923	Amit	Amit
WHITTINGTON, G. W.	2nd MS Inf.	1837-1911	Tipp	Unio
WHITTINGTON, Garnet B.	7th & 33rd MS Inf.	1828-1909	MS	Fran
WHITTINGTON, Garnet B.	7th MS Inf.	1839-1909	Amit	Amit
WHITTINGTON, George B.	7th & 33rd MS Inf.	1829-1908	Fran	Amit
WHITTINGTON, J. J.	40th MS Inf.	1821-1910		Copi
WHITTINGTON, J. M.	24th MS Cav.	1846-1925	MS	Amit
WHITTINGTON, Jackson L.	7th MS Inf.	1825-1896	MS	Fran
WHITTINGTON, James M.	22nd MS Inf.	184_-1931	Amit	Amit
WHITTINGTON, John	_8th MS Cav.	18_-1922	Holm	Holm
WHITTINGTON, Jordon	44th MS Inf.	1838-1906	Amit	Amit
WHITTINGTON, Noah	4th MS Cav.	1835-1901	Amit	Amit
WHITTINGTON, Napoleon	7th MS Inf.	1841-1922	Amit	Amit
WHITTINGTON, Robert W.	33rd MS Inf.	1829-___	Amit	Amit
WHITTINGTON, Thomas H.	44th MS Inf.	1828-1912	Amit	Amit
WHITTINGTON, W. D.	25th MS Inf.	1833-1919	MS	Lefl
WHITTINGTON, W. M. L.	22nd MS Inf.	1844-1917	MS	Amit
WHITTLE, H. J.	1st MS Cav.	1836-1914	Carr	Mont
WHITTOM, Thomas	7th MS Inf.	1839-1888		Mari
WHITWORTH, F. M.	1st MS Cav.	1838-1923	Monr	Monr
WHITWORTH, James E.	17th MS Inf.	1832-1918	Choc	Choc
WHITWORTH, John S. (Dr.)	Adams MS Cav.	1829-1868	Madi	Madi
WHITWORTH, Milton Jacob	Brookhaven Lt. Art.	1811-1870	TN	Linc
WHITWORTH, Samuel H.	12th MS Inf.	1843-1889	Lawr	Linc
WHYTE, R. P.	13th TN Inf.	1842-1921	TN	Harr
WICKER, Caswell	17th MS Inf.	182_-19	Mars	Bent
WICKER, Henry	16th MS Inf.	1836-1916	Smit	Smit
WICKER, Henry B.	11th MS Cav.	1843-1899	SC	Wins
WICKER, John Uriah	10th MS Inf.	1842-1912	MS	Tipp

172

Name	Unit	Dates	Col1	Col2
WICKS, David	2nd MS Cav.	1836-1929 Alco	Alco
WIER, Thomas Coke	37th MS Inf.	1827-1920 Gree	Okti
WIGGIN, Thomas	16th MS Inf.	1846-1908 Clai	Lown
WIGGINS, Charles H.	45th MS Inf.	1827-1909 Tipp	Laud
WIGGINS, George	33rd MS Inf.	1838-19 GA	Holm
WIGGINS, James	33rd MS Inf.	1845-1903 Leak	Leak
WIGGINS, Jessie W.	45th MS Inf.	1818-1869 Tipp	Laud
WIGGINS, Sebirn	3rd MS Cav.	1843-1918 MS	Shar
WIGGINS, Stephen	Adams MS Cav.	1828-1898 Monr	Leak
WIGGINS, Thomas P.	45th MS Inf.	1829-1873 Tipp	Laud
WIGGINGTON, Isaac	2nd MS Cav.	1842-1929 Monr	Itaw
WIGGINGTON, W. H.	3rd MS Inf.	1840-1892 GA	Tipp
WIGGINTON, J.T. Jr.	Ashcrafts MS Cav.	1847-1929 Itaw	Itaw
WIGGINTON, J.T. Sr.	Ashcrafts MS Cav.	1804-1872 Itaw	Itaw
WIGGINTON, John	11th MS Inf.	1836-1921 Lafa	Alco
WIGGS, James A.	4th TN Inf.	1839-1911 TN	Warr
WIGINGTON, G. W.	45th MS Inf.	1828-1904 Tipp	Unio
WIGLEY, J. R.	43rd MS Inf.	1832-1899 Lown	Atta
WIGLEY, Joseph M.	29th MS Inf.	1832-1910 MS	Holm
WILBANKS, E. W.	23rd MS Inf.	1835-1920 Tipp	Alco
WILBANKS, J. Sanford	10th MS Inf.	1839-1916 Tipp	Alco
WILBANKS, L.	16th MS Cav.	1824-1906 Noxu	Holm
WILBANKS, W. D.	23rd MS Inf.	1832-1916 Bent	Bent
WILBANKS, W. E.	27th MS Inf.	1839-1907	Leak
WILBANKS, Wm. Absolam	7th MS Cav.	1845-1922 SC	Tipp

(also see WILLBANKS located after WILLARD)

Name	Unit	Dates	Col1	Col2
WILBORN, Clayborn B.	Hams MS Cav.	1833-1904 AL	Pren
WILBORN, J.M.	1st MS Cav.	1845-1927	Yalo
WILBOURN, M. W.	Hughes MS Cav.	1836-1908	Pano
WILBOURN, Robert	1st MS Sharpshooters	1842-1919 Yalo	Yalo
WILBURN, _. _.	1st GA Inf.	1839-1914 GA	Leak
WILBURN, George Thomas	11th TX Inf.	1828-1911 Tish	Lafa
WILBURN, R. _.	22nd MS Inf.	1842-1900 Lafa	Lafa
WILBURN, William S.	18th MS Cav.	1849-1934 MS	Tate
WILCHER, John T.	40th MS Inf.	1836-1909 MS	Leak
WILCOX, Charles A.	Jefferson Flying Art.	1839-1903 Jeff	Jone
WILCOX, W. C.	1st MS Cav.	1832-1880 Pont	Tall
WILDER, L. R.	41st MS Inf.	1839-1913	Pont
WILDER, S. B.	41st MS Inf.	1834-1891 Pont	Pont
WILDER, T. F.	40th MS Inf.	1832-1896 Leak	Leak
WILDER, Talbert	Poagues MS Art.	1828-1891 GA	Madi
WILDER, V. T.	22nd LA Inf.	1846-1928 LA	Laud
WILDS, Oliver A.	10th MS Inf.	1839-1928 Adam	Adam
WILEMON, J. Anderson	26th MS Inf.	1833-1909 MS	Pren
WILES, John H.	8th MS Inf.	1822-1897 Newt	Newt
WILES, W. W.	46th MS Inf.	1825-1894 Yazo	Yazo
WILEY, James	5th MS Inf.	1819-1895 Calh	Unio
WILKERSON, Jack	2nd MS Inf.	1837-1883 MS	Bent

173

WILKERSON, S. J.	Berrys Home Guards	1824-1897 Leak	Yazo
WILKERSON, W. B.	34th MS Inf.	1827-1910 Bent	Bent
WILKERSON, Wiley Wash.	34th MS Inf.	1833-1907	Bent
WILEY, William H.	11th MS Inf.	1844-1927 Lafa	Lafa
WILKES, Abner James	46th MS Inf.	1835-1908 MS	JEDA
WILKIE, John Thomas	Ashcrafts MS Cav.	1847-1925 Pano	Pano
WILKINGS, J. R. (Dr.)	15th MS Inf.	1841-1878 Gren	Gren
WILKINS, Giles	39th AL Inf.	1843-1917 AL	Newt
WILKINS, H. C.	6th MS Inf.	1840-1927 Scot	Harr
WILKINS, J. _.	11th MS Inf.	1835-1862 GA	Unio
WILKINS, J. N.	11th MS Inf.	1842-1862 Unio	Unio
WILKINS, John M.	46th MS Inf.	1849-1900	Scot
WILKINS, Jones S.	21st MS Inf.	1844-1878 Warr	Warr
WILKINS, Oregon T.	2nd MS	1845-1864 Unio	Unio
WILKINS, S. K.	43rd MS Inf.	1832-1921 GA	Unio
WILKINS, Thomas Jeff.	11th MS Inf.	1838-1920 Noxu	Noxu
WILKINS, W. J. (William)	43rd MS Inf.	1837-1864 GA	Unio
WILKINS, Washington P.	29th MS Inf.	1832-1906 Lafa	Lafa
WILKINS, William	18th MS Inf.	1845-1879 Yazo	Yazo
WILKINS, William Henry	LA Art.	1840-1882 LA	Adam
WILKINSON, Angus	16th MS Inf.	1846-1867 Copi	Kemp
WILKINSON, _. _.	7th MS Inf.	18_-1861 Amit	Amit
WILKINSON, B. F.	46th MS Inf.	1830-1878 Pike	Amit
WILKINSON, B. Franklin	7th MS Inf.	1844-___ Amit	Amit
WILKINSON, Hugh	4th MS Cav.	184_-1905 MS	Harr
WILKINSON, I. J.	Lamars Art.	1849-1914 Leak	Leak
WILKINSON, J. A.	5th Conf. Cav.	1837-189_ Chic	Chic
WILKINSON, John C.	33rd MS Inf.	1824-1900	Jeff
WILKINSON, John C.	33rd MS Inf.	1823-1911 Amit	Amit
WILKINSON, Joseph B.	7th MS Inf.	1821-1905 Fran	Fran
WILKINSON, Leonard H.	24th MS Cav.	1846-1920	Clai
WILKINSON, Smylie	1st MS Art.	1839-1873 NY	Hind
WILKINSON, W. A.	38th MS Cav.	1844-1921 Wilk	Wilk
WILKINSON, William C.	1st LA Vol. Art.	1836-1908 IR	Copi
WILKINSON, William H.	33rd MS Vol.	1846-1928 MS	Pike
WILKINSON, Wm. Harrison	33rd MS Inf.	1835-1902	Hind
WILKINSON, William J.	3rd MS Inf.	1821-1895 Newt	Newt
WILKINSON, Winston	44th MS Inf.	1818-1881 Amit	Amit
WILKS, S. _. P.	38th MS Cav.	1837-1898 Covi	JEDA
WILLARD, R. B.	18th MS Inf.	1827-1904	Linc
WILLBANKS, D. P.	1st MS Lt. Art.	1828-1862 Choc	Mont
WILLBANKS, D. T.	1st MS Lt. Art.	1827-1862 Carr	Mont
WILLEY, Thomas	Davenports MS Cav.	1835-1900	Rank
WILLIAM, Benn H.	12th LA Inf.	1839-1917 LA	Laud
WILLIAM, George (Dr.)	16th Cav.	182_-1885 ME	Holm
WILLIAMS, A. B.	Q. M. Transport	1827-1867 Carr	Carr
WILLIAMS, A. G. M.	38th MS Cav.	1842-1918 Pike	Pike
WILLIAMS, A. J.	4th MS Cav.	1832-1886 Lown	Alco
WILLIAMS, Anderson	2nd MS Cav.	1821-1891 Newt	Newt

WILLIAMS, Andrew J.	33rd MS Inf.	1843-___	Amit	Pike
WILLIAMS, Andrew Jackson	36th AL Inf.	1845-___	Clar	Gree
WILLIAMS, Amos	32nd MS Inf.	1841-1890		Ston
WILLIAMS, Asbury	40th MS Inf.	1846-1935	Kemp	Kemp
WILLIAMS, Axem	9th MS Inf.	1832-1912	Gree	Gree
WILLIAMS, B.	4th & 30th MS Inf.	1840-1877	Atta	Atta
WILLIAMS, B. C.	8th MS Inf.	1825-1889	Webs	Webs
WILLIAMS, B. F. (Dr.)	14th MS Inf.	183_-1910	NC	Monr
WILLIAMS, B. F.	26th MS Inf.	1837-1887	Tish	Alco
WILLIAMS, B. _.	46th MS Reg.	18_4-1921	Laud	Laud
WILLIAMS, Benjamin	2nd MS Inf.	1843-1900		Hind
WILLIAMS, Benjamin	18th MS Inf.	1836-1896	Yazo	Yazo
WILLIAMS, Benjamin	8th MS Cav.	1812-1877		Webs
WILLIAMS, Benjamin C.	8th MS Inf.	1835-1914	Clar	Webs
WILLIAMS, Ben Pope	21st MS Inf.	1839-1933		Okti
WILLIAMS, Berry T.	13th MS Inf.	1819-1884	Wins	Tall
WILLIAMS, Bright	12th MS Inf.	1838-1909		Hind
WILLIAMS, Bryant	3rd MS Regt.			
WILLIAMS, C. O.	12th MS Inf.	1826-1906	Jeff	Laud
WILLIAMS, Charles Jr.	2nd MS Inf.	1843-1906	MS	Alco
WILLIAMS, Charles _.	43rd MS Inf.	1836-1903	Lown	Lown
WILLIAMS, Church L.	14th MS Inf.	___-1911	AL	Boli
WILLIAMS, Cleon H.	12th MS Inf.	1821-1883	Jeff	Laud
WILLIAMS, Coleman	24th AL Inf.	1844-1925	AL	Clay
WILLIAMS, D.	24th MS Inf.	1834-1902		Harr
WILLIAMS, D. E.	12th MS Inf.	1837-1923	LA	Laud
WILLIAMS, D. R.	38th MS Cav.	1830-1905	GA	Monr
WILLIAMS, Dan C.	18th MS Inf.			Hind
WILLIAMS, Dan _.	4th MS Cav.	1820-1887		Boli
WILLIAMS, Daniel	16th MS Inf.	1832-1902	Wilk	Wash
WILLIAMS, Daniel J.	22nd & 30th MS Inf.	1842-1882	Carr	Mont
WILLIAMS, David	17th MS Cav.	1833-1899	Gree	Gree
WILLIAMS, David A.	11th MS Inf.	1841-1905	MS	Noxu
WILLIAMS, Deavers D.	46th MS Inf.	1846-1921	Laud	Laud
WILLIAMS, Dee	43rd MS Inf.			Monr
WILLIAMS, Edward G.	6th MS Inf.	1834-1869	VA	Rank
WILLIAMS, Eli	40th AL Inf.	1825-1876	AL	Kemp
WILLIAMS, Eugene F.	19th MS Inf.	1845-1895		Pano
WILLIAMS, F. _.	24th MS Inf.	1841-1862	MS	Lown
WILLIAMS, F. M.	13th MS Inf.	1824-1912	Wayn	Wayn
WILLIAMS, F. M.	5th MS Inf.	1845-1929		Mont
WILLIAMS, Francis M.	3rd MS Inf.	1841-1909	Simp	Simp
WILLIAMS, George A.	2nd MS Cav.	1845-1915		Jone
WILLIAMS, George B.	2nd MS Inf.	1832-1896	AL	Clar
WILLIAMS, George W.	25th TN Inf.	1845-1906		Okti
WILLIAMS, George W.	48th MS Inf.	1849-1914		Hind
WILLIAMS, George W.	4th MS Cav.	1819-1877	MS	Simp
WILLIAMS, Giles	3rd MS Batt.	1838-1900		Hind
WILLIAMS, Giles _.	NC Inf.	1844-1925	NC	Holm
WILLIAMS, H. O.	14th AL Cav.	1845-1922	MS	Harr

175

WILLIAMS, Harvey W.	2nd MS Inf.	1830-1918 Tipp	Newt
WILLIAMS, Henry	1st MS Cav.	1824-1889 Noxu	Noxu
WILLIAMS, Henry	9th MS Inf.	1833-1921 Tate	Tate
WILLIAMS, Henry J.	16th MS Inf.	1846-1918 Pike	Laud
WILLIAMS, Henry J.	9th MS Inf.	1831-1926 TN	Tish
WILLIAMS, Henry P.	39th MS Inf.	1844-1919 MS	Walt
WILLIAMS, Hester	12th MS Inf.	1838-1907 MS	Fran
WILLIAMS, Hood	3rd MS Inf.	1835-1884 Newt	Newt
WILLIAMS, Ira	24th MS Inf.	1837-1900 Gree	Gree
WILLIAMS, J.	1st MS Lt. Art.	1847-1924	Mont
WILLIAMS, J. A.	2nd MS Cav.	1844-1923 Itaw	Lee
WILLIAMS, J. A.	6th MS Cav.	1845-1917 Clay	Itaw
WILLIAMS, J. A.	1st MS Lt. Art.	1839-1921 Holm	Holm
WILLIAMS, J. B.	7th & 24th MS Inf.	1846-1914 Pike	Linc
WILLIAMS, J. C.	43rd MS Inf.	1824-1890 Okti	Okti
WILLIAMS, J. C.	4th MS Cav.	1829-1909 Jeff	Fran
WILLIAMS, J. D.	3rd MS Inf.	1846-1910	Rank
WILLIAMS, J. F.	45th MS Inf.	1824-1908 Pike	Amit
WILLIAMS, J. G.	12th MS Cav.	182_-___ Noxu	Noxu
WILLIAMS, J. H.	6th MS Inf.	1835-1919 Leak	Leak
WILLIAMS, J. H.	13th MS Inf.	1837-1913 AL	Wins
WILLIAMS, J. _.	4th GA Inf.	1847-1923 GA	Pano
WILLIAMS, J. I.(Rev.)	16th AL Inf.	1818-1891 AL	Laud
WILLIAMS, J. J.	3rd MS Inf.	1833-1917 AL	Linc
WILLIAMS, J. J.	28th MS Cav.	1846-1919 Carr	Carr
WILLIAMS, J. M.	46th MS Inf.	1845-1926 Scot	Scot
WILLIAMS, J. M.	11th MS Cav.	1830-1907 Itaw	Lee
WILLIAMS, J. M.	2nd MS Inf.	1839-1891 Pont	Laud
WILLIAMS, J. O.	13th MS Inf.	1841-1929 GA	Wins
WILLIAMS, J. _.	28th MS Cav.	1834-1924 Yalo	Gren
WILLIAMS, J. R.	1st MS Inf.	1844-1925 Itaw	Harr
WILLIAMS, J. R.	45th MS Inf.	1808-1881 Pike	Amit
WILLIAMS, J. T.	11th AL Inf.	1835-1864 AL	Tish
WILLIAMS, J. T. J.	26th MS Inf.	1829-1903	Hind
WILLIAMS, J. W.	1st MS Inf.	184_-1861 AL	Lafa
WILLIAMS, J. W.	45th MS Inf.	1835-1883 Itaw	Lee
WILLIAMS, J. W.	24th MS Cav.	1833-1915 Lown	Harr
WILLIAMS, J. W.	1st MS Lt. Art.	1847-1924 Webs	
WILLIAMS, J. W.	1st MS Lt. Art.	1829-1897 Webs	
WILLIAMS, J. Y.	34th MS Inf.	1822-1895 Mars	Mars
WILLIAMS, Jackson	45th MS Inf.	1843-1925 Pike	Amit
WILLIAMS, Jackson Robt.	35th MS Inf.	1842-1904 Okti	Okti
WILLIAMS, James	11th MS Inf.	18_7-1891	Unio
WILLIAMS, James	27th MS Inf.	1835-1894 Jack	Geor
WILLIAMS, James Alex.	MS Inf.	1846-1909 MS	Scot
WILLIAMS, James Boyd	27th LA Inf.	1845-1862 LA	Warr
WILLIAMS, James H.	2nd MS Inf.	1833-1891 Pont	Pont
WILLIAMS, James Laf.	12th MS Cav.	1835-1883 Pren	Pren
WILLIAMS, James M.	11th MS Cav.	1836-1896 TN	Lee
WILLIAMS, James M.	42nd MS Inf.	1836-1905 Tate	Tate

Name	Unit	Dates	
WILLIAMS, James M.	7th & 24th MS Inf.	1844-1906 Mari	Linc
WILLIAMS, James Munro	28th MS Cav.	1838-1910 SC	Gren
WILLIAMS, James P.	24th MS Inf.	1838-19__ MS	Gree
WILLIAMS, James T.	15th AL Inf.	1837-1887 AL	Simp
WILLIAMS, James W.	29th MS Inf.	1834-1900 MS	Tall
WILLIAMS, J. Ed.	8th AL Inf.	____-1906 AL	Jone
WILLIAMS, Jeff W.	1st MS Lt. Art.	1828-1897 Holm	Holm
WILLIAMS, Jesse M.	16th LA Inf.	18__-1870 LA	Wilk
WILLIAMS, Jim M.	34th MS Inf.	1841-1913 Tipp	Unio
WILLIAMS, Jim M.	Woods Regt.	1846-1936	Rank
WILLIAMS, Joel	16th Conf. Cav.	1827-1901 AL	Laud
WILLIAMS, John	21st MS Inf.	1833-1911 Warr	Warr
WILLIAMS, John A.	41st MS Inf.	1820-1902 Choc	Choc
WILLIAMS, John B.	2nd MS Cav.	1847-1873 Clar	Gren
WILLIAMS, John Burton	25th TN Inf.	1842-1904	Okti
WILLIAMS, John Calvin	Powers Cav.	1847-1878 Hind	Hind
WILLIAMS, John D.	5th MS Inf.	1838-1893 Nesh	Nesh
WILLIAMS, John F.	14th MS Inf.	1838-1862	Lown
WILLIAMS, John F.	40th Inf.	1818-1904 Atta	Atta
WILLIAMS, John G.	18th MS Inf.	1839-1929 Yazo	Yazo
WILLIAMS, John Hamilton	7th MS Inf.	1844-1906 AL	Shar
WILLIAMS, John I.	Stubbs Inf.	1847-1917 MS	JeDa
WILLIAMS, John L.	48th MS Inf.	1839-1901 MS	Okti
WILLIAMS, John Leroy	13th MS Inf.	1845-1910 Kemp	Kemp
WILLIAMS, John R.	24th MS Inf.	1831-1910	Harr
WILLIAMS, John W.	10th LA Inf.	1845-1930 LA	Pike
WILLIAMS, John W.	4th Cav.	1837-1925 AL	Tish
WILLIAMS, John W.	4th MS Inf.	1846-1920	Covi
WILLIAMS, John Wesley	10th LA Cav.	1846-1930	Pike
WILLIAMS, Jones	43rd MS Inf.	1832-1920 Lown	Lown
WILLIAMS, Joseph F.	5th MS Inf.	1845-1908 Nesh	Nesh
WILLIAMS, Joseph J.	21st MS Inf.	1843-1910 Tall	Atta
WILLIAMS, Joseph W.	MS Inf.	1843-1863 Scot	Lafa
WILLIAMS, Josephus	22nd MS Inf.	1830-1861	DeSo
WILLIAMS, Joshua	3rd MS Inf.	1845-1905 Rank	Rank
WILLIAMS, Judson H.	1st MS Inf.	1847-1912 Itaw	Laud
WILLIAMS, L. D.	24th MS Inf.	1844-1925 Gree	Gree
WILLIAMS, L. W.	5th MS Inf.	1844-1909 Nesh	Nesh
WILLIAMS, M. J.	4th MS Inf.	1846-1920 SC	Choc
WILLIAMS, M. L.	39th MS Inf.	1843-1914 Newt	Newt
WILLIAMS, M. L.	5th MS Inf.	1846-1934 Kemp	Unio
WILLIAMS, Merritt	20th GA Cav.	1840-1937 KY	Wash
WILLIAMS, N. A.	16th Conf. Cav.	1815-1902 AL	Laud
WILLIAMS, N. M. (Dr.)	Hospital	1833-1880 TN	Tate
WILLIAMS, Nathaniel	1st MS Lt. Art.	1826-1907 Choc	Mont
WILLIAMS, Newton	Brookhaven Lt. Art.	1822-1877 SC	Unio
WILLIAMS, Newman C.	14th MS Inf.	1843-1864	Monr
WILLIAMS, Nick	3rd MS Batt.	1840-1898	Hind
WILLIAMS, Oliver H.	11th MS Inf.	1833-1907 Pont	Pont
WILLIAMS, R.	MS Cav.	1840-1927 AL	Jone

WILLIAMS, R. A.	18th MS Inf.	1842-1925	Nesh
WILLIAMS, R. B.	37th MS Inf.	1830-19_3 Smit	Smit
WILLIAMS, R. J.	12th LA Inf.	1845-186_ LA	Lafa
WILLIAMS, R. J.	16th Conf. Cav.	1840-1903 AL	Laud
WILLIAMS, R. M.	4th MS Inf.	1840-1928 Holm	Holm
WILLIAMS, R. M.	4th MS Inf.		Carr
WILLIAMS, R. M.	4th MS Inf.	1845-1914 MS	Calh
WILLIAMS, R. M.	15th MS Inf.	1839-1922 Atta	Atta
WILLIAMS, Raleigh J.	39th MS Inf.	1833-1900 MS	Copi
WILLIAMS, Richard	8th MS Cav.	1828-1887 Chic	Chic
WILLIAMS, Richard A.	18th Inf.	1843-1925	Hind
WILLIAMS, Robert Anthony	30th MS Inf.	1838-1916 NC	Mont
WILLIAMS, Robert S.	23rd MS Inf.	1839-1910	Lee
WILLIAMS, Roleigh J.	39th MS Inf.	1833-1900 MS	Copi
WILLIAMS, S. B.	10th MS Inf.	1841-1903	Pike
WILLIAMS, S. F.	6th & 15th MS Inf.	1832-1903 Rank	Linc
WILLIAMS, S. _.	1st MS Art.	1839-1866 Yazo	Yazo
WILLIAMS, Sam	6th MS Inf.	1841-189_ Ston	Ston
WILLIAMS, Samuel	6th MS Inf.	1820-1900	Rank
WILLIAMS, Samuel B.	Adams MS Cav.	1838-1929 Madi	Madi
WILLIAMS, Samuel C.	31st MS Inf.	1819-1888 Chic	Chic
WILLIAMS, Samuel S.	46th MS Reg.	1841-1913 Laud	Laud
WILLIAMS, Samuel S.	46th AR Reg.	1836-1921 AR	Laud
WILLIAMS, Singleton M.	4th MS Inf.	1819-1904 MS	Gren
WILLIAMS, Soloman	28th MS Cav.	1812-1866 MS	Gren
WILLIAMS, Stephen H.	3rd GA Regt.	1849-1934 GA	Rank
WILLIAMS, Steve	26th MS Inf.	1840-1901 AL	Pren
WILLIAMS, Sylvester	18th MS Cav.	1838-1904	Atta
WILLIAMS, T. J.	17th MS Inf.	1839-1914 MS	Quit
WILLIAMS, T. J.	LA Inf.	1839-1862 LA	Chic
WILLIAMS, T. R.	5th MS Inf.	1840-1863 Wins	Clar
WILLIAMS, Thomas D.	15th MS Inf.	1841-1921 MS	Mont
WILLIAMS, Thomas G.	25th MS Inf.	1844-1908 Holm	Holm
WILLIAMS, Thomas H.	11th MS Inf.	1836-1894 Pont	Pont
WILLIAMS, Thomas J.	10th MS Inf.	1847-1918	Warr
WILLIAMS, W. B.	1st MS Lt. Art.	18_6-___ VA	Holm
WILLIAMS, W. B. P.	3rd MS Cav.	1830-1867	Rank
WILLIAMS, W. E.	Wessons MS Art.	1832-1892 GA	Copi
WILLIAMS, W. H.	8th MS Inf.	1834-1900 Jasp	Jone
WILLIAMS, W. H.	1st MS Cav.	1823-1900	Rank
WILLIAMS, W. H.	16th LA Inf.	1840-1921 LA	Copi
WILLIAMS, W. _.	39th MS Inf.	1832-18_6 Newt	Newt
WILLIAMS, W. J.	39th MS Inf.	1836-1921 Hind	Rank
WILLIAMS, W. O.	19th MS Inf.	1848-1925 MS	Pano
WILLIAMS, W. P.	12th MS Cav.	1843-1895	Coah
WILLIAMS, W. R.	38th MS Inf.	1830-1909	Mari
WILLIAMS, W. W.	5th MS Cav.	1820-1895 Carr	Carr
WILLIAMS, Wiley T. (Dr.)	18th MS Inf.	1832-1880 MS	Yazo
WILLIAMS, William	11th MS Cav.	1821-1904 Wins	Linc
WILLIAMS, William	54th GA Inf.	1828-1913	Copi
WILLIAMS, William F.	3rd MS Inf.	1847-1926 KY	Coah

Name	Unit	Dates		
WILLIAMS, William H.	17th MS Inf.	1838-1921 Mars	Adam
WILLIAMS, William J.	9th MS Cav.	1846-1906 Pike	Linc
WILLIAMS, William J.	39th MS Inf.	1841-1885	Rank
WILLIAMS, William M.	46th Inf.	1831-1911 Yazo	Yazo
WILLIAMS, William W.	24th MS Inf.	1836-1909 Gree	Gree
WILLIAMS, William W.	9th MS Cav.	1839-1914 Laud	Laud
WILLIAMS, Wyatt S.	18th MS Inf.	1832-1869 Yazo	Yazo
WILLIAMSON, A.	46th MS Inf.	1839-1910 Scot	Scot
WILLIAMSON, Charles C.	3rd MS Inf.	1842-1917	Newt
WILLIAMSON, D. W.	4th MS Cav.	1843-1912 Simp	Simp
WILLIAMSON, F. H.	4th MS Cav.	1830-1903 Copi	Simp
WILLIAMSON, Elum C.	1st MS Lt. Art.	1841-1929 Perr	Perr
WILLIAMSON, Emanuel	29th MS Inf.	1838-1914 Lawr	Lawr
WILLIAMSON, G. W.	3rd MS Cav.	1830-1904 Simp	Simp
WILLIAMSON, G. W.	15th Conf. Cav.	1839-1895 AL	Wayn
WILLIAMSON, George W.	43rd MS Inf.	1836-18_7 Kemp	Kemp
WILLIAMSON, Henry C.	11th MS Inf.	1841-1913	Nesh
WILLIAMSON, J. E.	14th MS Inf.	1846-1929 AL	Jone
WILLIAMSON, J. J.	1st MS Inf.	1846-1932	Pano
WILLIAMSON, J. J.	3rd MS Cav.	1846-1932	Yalo
WILLIAMSON, J. R.	1st MS Inf.	1849-1923 Tish	Scot
WILLIAMSON, J. S.	7th MS Inf.	1843-1911 Lawr	Lawr
WILLIAMSON, James	4th MS Inf.	1840-1910 Covi	Covi
WILLIAMSON, James C.	12th MS Inf.	1841-1898 Pano	Pano
WILLIAMSON, James S.	37th MS Inf.	1839-1923 Smit	Smit
WILLIAMSON, J. Henry	3rd MS Inf.	1847-1904 Yazo	Yazo
WILLIAMSON, John A.	20th MS Inf.	1840-1921 GA	Holm
WILLIAMSON, John _.	_9th MS Inf.	1842-1863 Newt	Lafa
WILLIAMSON, Julius	14th MS Inf.	1839-1916 AL	Jone
WILLIAMSON, Leander (Dr.)	14th MS Lt. Art.	1837-1900	Pano
WILLIAMSON, N. H.	14th & 43rd MS Inf.	1833-1873 Monr	Monr
WILLIAMSON, Richard	4th MS Cav.	1829-1901 Copi	Covi
WILLIAMSON, Robert _.	3rd MS Cav.	1841-1926 Madi	Madi
WILLIAMSON, Robert F.	31st LA Inf.	1824-1902 LA	Yalo
WILLIAMSON, Robert Jack.	35th MS Inf.	1832-1892 Lown	Okti
WILLIAMSON, Robert White	30th MS Inf.	1832-1908 Lefl	Lefl
WILLIAMSON, S. F.	39th MS Inf.	1830-1906 Newt	Leak
WILLIAMSON, S. _.	18th MS Cav.	1824-1913	Pano
WILLIAMSON, Samuel	39th MS Inf.	1833-1914 Simp	Simp
WILLIAMSON, Sol.	20th MS Inf.	1848-19__ Smit	Smit
WILLIAMSON, W. B.	5th MS Inf.	1820-1913 Kemp	Kemp
WILLIAMSON, W. H.	40th MS Inf.	1830-1897 Nesh	Nesh
WILLIAMSON, William _.	14th MS Inf.	1842-192_ Monr	Monr
WILLIAMSON, William W.	6th MS Inf.	1830-1906 Hind	Harr
WILLIFORD, J. V.	17th NC Inf.	1836-1924 NC	Carr
WILLING, R. P.	12th MS Inf.	1836-1905	Copi
WILLING, W. J.	36th MS Inf.	1842-1909	Copi
WILLIS, Andrew J.	3rd MS Inf.	1829-1901	Hind
WILLIS, B. F.	18th MS Cav.	1831-1913 Mars	Laud
WILLIS, J. R.	18th MS Cav.	1847-1930 Leak	Leak
WILLIS, James M.	8th MS Inf.	1831-1904 Newt	Newt

WILLIS, James Plummer	20th MS Inf.	1839-1910 Monr	Monr
WILLIS, John R.	2nd MS Inf.	1841-1905 Monr	Monr
WILLIS, John S.	18th MS Inf.	1845-1879 Madi	Madi
WILLIS, Josiah B.	1st MS Lt. Art.	Choc	Adam
WILLIS, Lafayette	3rd MS Inf.	1823-1905 Itaw	Monr
WILLIS, R. B.	42nd MS Inf.	1836-1911 Gren	Gren
WILLIS, Richard S.	14th MS Inf.	1838-1872	Nesh
WILLIS, Robert	3rd MS Cav.	1822-1867 IR	Rank
WILLOUGHBY, W. T.	38th MS Inf.	1845-1918 Clai	Mari
WILLOUGHBY, William	38th MS Cav.	1834-1908	Walt
WILROY, Thomas J.	9th MS Inf.	1839-1929	DeSo
WILLROY, Thomas J.	18th MS Cav.	1839-1929	Tate
WILLS, J. U.	5th MS Inf.	1836-1914 Choc	Choc
WILSON, A. J.	43rd MS Inf.	1842-19_3 AL	Chic
WILSON, A. R.	19th MS Inf.	1836-1924 Lafa	Lafa
WILSON, Alex R.	37th MS Inf.	1837-1903 Laud	Laud
WILSON, Alexander	7th MS Inf.	1838-1909 MS	Fran
WILSON, Alonzo E.	15th AL Cav.	____-1912 AL	Clai
WILSON, Andrew Jackson	5th MS Cav.	1845-1926 Choc	Mont
WILSON, B. F. (Dr.)	Harris MO Inf.	1836-____ MO	Lefl
WILSON, Baxter	28th MS Cav.	1846-1933 Yalo	Holm
WILSON, Berry	3rd MS Inf.	1845-1916	Rank
WILSON, D. C.	33rd MS Inf.	1846-____	Amit
WILSON, D. G.	38th MS Cav.	1843-1896 Atta	Atta
WILSON, D. J.	40th MS Inf.	1842-1915 Newt	Newt
WILSON, G. _.	Quitmans Lt.Art.	1832-1913	Rank
WILSON, Edward Alvah	38th MS Cav.	1829-1875 GA	Holm
WILSON, F. A.	4th MS Cav.	1848-1919 Lawr	Lawr
WILSON, G. M. Sr.	24th MS Inf.	1812-1900	Webs
WILSON, George	12th MS Inf.		Rank
WILSON, George _. Jr.	2nd MS Batt.	1844-1925	Webs
WILSON, George W.	41st MS Inf.	1847-1925 MS	Laud
WILSON, George W.	1st MS Inf.	1841-1911 Itaw	Pont
WILSON, H. A.	29th MS Inf.	1834-1921 Tall	Tall
WILSON, H. H.	7th KY Inf.	1841-1862 KY	Lown
WILSON, H. T.	22nd MS Inf.	1844-1909 Lawr	Lawr
WILSON, Henry M.	9th MS Inf.	1847-1924 Mars	Harr
WILSON, Hugh Reid	3rd SC Inf.	1848-1922	Hind
WILSON, Hugh White	41st MS Inf.	1845-1905 Laud	Laud
WILSON, I. W.	3rd MS Inf.	1828-1919	Atta
WILSON, J. C.	33rd MS Inf.	1842-1927 Amit	Harr
WILSON, J. C.	11th MS Inf.	1837-1878 Copi	Nesh
WILSON, J. D.	8th MS Cav.	1831-____ Lown	Chic
WILSON, J. G.	28th MS Cav.	1835-1888 Yalo	Carr
WILSON, J. F.	4th LA Cav.	1839-1924 LA	Amit
WILSON, J. L.	6th & 15th MS Inf.	1847-1914	Copi
WILSON, J. M.	24th MS Cav.	1837-1917	Clai
WILSON, J. P.	43rd MS Inf.	1848-____	Monr
WILSON, J. _.	26th MS Inf.	1843-1907 Tish	Tish
WILSON, J. R.	26th MS Regt.	1843-1918	Hind
WILSON, J. W.	1st MS Cav.	181_-1890 Carr	Webs

Name	Unit	Dates	Col1	Col2
WILSON, W. P.	33rd MS Inf.	1847-1917 Amit	Amit
WILSON, W. _.	22nd MS Inf.	1835-1910 Lawr	Lawr
WILSON, Wiley W.	1st MS Lt. Art.	1820-1901	Mont
WILSON, William	43rd MS Inf.	1821-1911 SC	Wins
WILSON, William H.	3rd MS Cav.	1818-1903 Carr	Carr
WILSON, William J.	AL Reserves	1821-1892 AL	Laud
WILSON, Wister	5th MS Inf.	183_-1917	Webs
WILSON, Wm. Thos.	23rd MS Inf.	1837-1908 AL	Tipp
WILTSHIRE, S. F.	3rd State Troops	184_-1919	Copi
WIMBERLY, I. O.	6th MS Inf.	1824-1902	Rank
WIMBERLY, J. W.	40th AL Inf.	1826-1914 AL	Clar
WIMBISH, J. A.	22nd MS Inf.	1840-1914 Jone	Jone
WIMINGHAM, James S.	2nd MS Cav.	1840-1923 Simp	Simp
WINBON, Samuel W.	34th MS Inf.	1843-1908 Tipp	Atta
WINBORN, J. M.	2nd MS Inf.	1836-1918 AL	Tipp
WINBORN, J. W.	34th MS Inf.	1840-1902 Bent	Bent
WINBORN, W. V.	Ballentines Cav.	1827-1898 Carr	Carr
WINBURN, M. H.	24th MS Inf.	1820-1880 Gree	Gree
WINDAM, Mac	40th MS Inf.	1837-1898 Jasp	Covi
WINDERS, George	10th MS Inf.	1842-1924	DeSo
WINDHAM, A. H. (Dr.)	40th MS Inf.	1843-1910 MS	Jasp
WINDHAM, Albert C.	8th MS Inf.	1826-1920 Jasp	Smit
WINDHAM, Andrew Jackson	23rd MS Inf.	1842-1924 AL	Pren
WINDHAM, D. J.	13th MS Inf.	1840-1924 Laud	Calh
WINDHAM, G. G.	15th MS Inf.	1846-1924 Gren	Mont
WINDHAM, G. U.	17th TX Inf.	1847-1934 TX	Jone
WINDHAM, J. A.	20th & 40th MS Inf.	1840-1909 Jasp	Covi
WINDHAM, J. C.	4th MS Inf.	1837-___ Carr	Wash
WINDHAM, J. H.	5th MS Inf.	1847-1919 Jasp	Jone
WINDHAM, Jared C.	10th MS Inf.	1838-19_3 Jasp	Jasp
WINDHAM, Jeremiah M.	44th AL Inf.	1833-___ AL	Calh
WINDHAM, P. W.	46th MS Inf.	1832-1912 Smit	Scot
WINDHAM, R. C.	6th MS Inf.	1845-1937 Jone	Jone
WINDHAM, S. A.	43rd MS Inf.	1841-1913 MS	Lafa
WINDHAM, Sims M.	23rd MS Inf.	1840-1920 AL	Pren
WINDHAM, T. W.	7th MS Inf.	1848-1914 Newt	Jone
WINDHAM, W. T.	7th MS Inf.	1840-1911 Jone	Jone
WINDHAM, Wesley Wiley	40th MS Inf.	1847-1940 Jasp	Jone
WINDHAM, Willis	3rd MS Cav.	1847-1934 Jone	Jone
WINFIELD, George T.	6th MS Cav.	1827-1909 Lown	
WINFIELD, J. _.	41st MS Inf.	1839-1916 AL	Noxu
WINFREY, A. F.	1st MS Lt. Art.	1817-1903	Mont
WINGATE, Francis M.	12th LA Inf.	1841-1934 Covi	Mont
WINGATE, R. H.	6th MS Cav.	1825-1911	Shar
WINGO, E. S.	4th AL Inf.	1827-1919 AL	Tipp
WINGO, Pink O.	7th AL Cav.	1840-1882 AL	Tish
WINGO, Ransom	1st MS Cav.	1834-1897 Pont	Pont
WINKLER, Alexander	LA Cav.	1838-1914 LA	Adam
WINKLER, Ben	38th MS Cav.	1841-1862 Clai	Clai
WINKLER, Jacob	22nd MS Inf.	1843-1863 Jeff	Lafa
WINN, R. G.	1st MS Cav.	1821-1897 Carr	Carr

Name	Unit	Dates	State	County
WINNER, Mark	3rd LA Inf.	1838-1910 LA		Laud
WINSTEAD, Alford A.	35th MS Inf.	1825-1906 Nesh		Nesh
WINSTEAD, Chas.	18th MS Inf.	1849-1936 Madi		Yazo
WINSTEAD, Dempsey	39th MS Inf.	1836-1899		Scot
WINSTEAD, Henry H.	11th MS Inf.	1846-1864 Nesh		Nesh
WINSTEAD, J. J.	6th MS Inf.	1826-1871 MS		Scot
WINSTEAD, John	18th MS Inf.	1842-1939 MS		Yazo
WINSTON, G. D.	2nd MS Inf.	1833-1910 Pont		Alco
WINSTON, Patrick F.	11th MS Inf.	1834-1879		Pont
WINSTON, Samuel G.	28th MS Cav.	1822-___		Adam
WINSTON, William	2nd MS Inf.	1832-1893 Pont		Pont
WINSTON, William	8th KY Cav.	1840-1917 KY		Lown
WINTER, A. H.	44th MS Inf.	1849-1928 MS		Calh
WINTER, J. W.	10th Cav.	1846-1923 Chic		Chic
WINTER, John M.	42nd MS Inf.	1810-1897 MS		Calh
WINTER, Joshia A.	42nd MS Inf.	1808-1877 MS		Calh
WINTER, Rice H.	31st MS Inf.	1830-1897 AL		Hind
WINTER, William B.	18th MS Cav.	1847-1929 Mars		Gren
WINTERS, W. W.	Bradfords Scouts	1847-1917		Jeff
WINTER, William Jack.	5th MS Inf.	1829-1912 GA		Ston
WINTERTON, John George	1st MS Inf.	___-1863		Rank
WISE, Archibald	3rd MS Inf.	1818-1867		Monr
WISE, J. P. (Dr.)	38th MS Cav.	1836-1901		Copi
WISE, John C.	14th MS Inf.	___-1879		Monr
WISE, Joseph Sr.	17th MS Cav.	1830-1910		Pear
WISE, Thomas J.	30th GA Inf.	1843-191_ NC		Newt
WISE, W. F.	1st NC Inf.	1834-1912 NC		Pano
WISNER, Andrew Jackson	4th MS Cav.	1828-1890 Wilk		Wilk
WISNER, John A.	21st MS Inf.	1839-1911 Wilk		Wilk
WITHERS, E. Q.	3rd MS Cav.	1845-1926		Mars
WITHERSPOON, E. M.	14th MS Inf.	1840-1911 AL		Lee
WITT, _. _.	41st MS Inf.	1844-1925 MS		Pont
WITT, _ington	15th SC Inf.	1846-1933		Newt
WITT, William A.	31st MS Inf.	1835-1932 Pont		Pont
WITTER, John W.	44th MS Inf.	1840-1919 Coah		Tate
WITTY, Calvin T.	15th MS Inf.	1842-1924 NC		Mont
WITTY, Pinkney D.	15th MS Inf.	1836-1890 NC		Mont
WITTY, William H.	30th MS Inf.	1829-1885 NC		Mont
WIYGUL, A. M.	2nd MS Inf.	1841-19_ MS		Itaw
WOFFORD, Absolum R.	31st MS Inf.	1828-1881 Chic		Webs
WOFFORD, Albert A.	24th MS Inf.	1829-1908 Monr		Lown
WOFFORD, Jesse	5th MS Inf.	1843-1913 Chic		Chic
WOFFORD, Thomas G.	7th MS Inf.	1841-1917 Mari		Bent
WOHILEBEN, Hermin	1st MS Inf.	1837-1904 Lafa		Lafa
WOLBRECHT, Fred	33rd MS Inf.	1822-1900 GE		Pike
WOLF, M.	12th MS Inf.	1838-1918 Warr		Warr
WOLFE, Andrew T.	16th MS Inf.			Copi
WOLFE, Charles E.	Powers MS Cav.	1830-1875		Copi
WOLFE, David D.	44th MS Inf.	1845-1924 AL		Sunf
WOLFE, Fred A.	1st MS Lt. Art.	1835-1906		Hind
WOLFE, J. S.	9th KY Inf.	1835-1905 KY		Harr
WOLFE, James F.	20th MS Inf.	1834-1904 Harr		

183

WOLFE, Mitchell Benj.	18th MS Inf.	1804-1863 VA	Yazo
WOMACH, Charity Bufkin	31st MS Reg.	1847-1919	Hind
WOMACK, H. H.	31st MS Inf.	1845-191_ Choc	Webs
WOMACK, Jim _.	9th MS Sharpshooters	1842-1921 DeSo	Tate
WOMACK, John A.	42nd MS Inf.	1834-1927 Yalo	Yalo
WOMACK, Jos. F.	4th MS Cav.	1825-1905 Wilk	Wilk
WOMACK, Levi B.	33rd MS Inf.	1834-1927 Pano	Yalo
WOMACK, V. D.	3rd MS Inf.	1837-1862 Yazo	Warr
WOMACK, W. F/P.	3rd MS Inf.	1831-1898 MS	Pren
WOOD, A. B.	2nd MS Cav.	1847-1923 Monr	Monr
WOOD, A. J.	4th MS Cav.	1817-1878 Tish	Tish
WOOD, Albert Galliton	19th Cav.	1834-1921 Yalo	Yalo
WOOD, Andrew	11th MS Inf.	1837-188_ Monr	Monr
WOOD, Andrew Jackson	3rd GA Cav.	1836-1925 GA	Pano
WOOD, Charles H.	21st MS Inf.	1838-1926 Wilk	Wilk
WOOD, D. M.	46th Inf.	1831-1892 SC	Smit
WOOD, J. L.	43rd MS Inf.	1842-1906 MS	Monr
WOOD, J. _.	10th MS Inf.	1846-1875	Copi
WOOD, J. M.	2nd MS Inf.	1837-1909 Pont	Unio
WOOD, J. M.	26th MS Inf.	1841-1911 Tish	Alco
WOOD, J. R.	15th MS Inf.	1842-191_	Mont
WOOD, J. W.	5th MS Inf.	1838-1905 Choc	Choc
WOOD, James	5th MS Inf.	1845-___	Monr
WOOD, James A.	1st MS Lt. Art.	1827-1898	Copi
WOOD, James A.	24th MS Cav.	1835-1905 Covi	Covi
WOOD, James B.	33rd MS Inf.	1822-190_	Webs
WOOD, James L.	43rd MS Inf.	1842-1906 Monr	Monr
WOOD, James Newton	2nd MS Inf.	1831-1900 Tish	Tish
WOOD, James O. (Dr.)	40th MS Inf.	1847-1920 Leak	Kemp
WOOD, Joel W.	43rd MS Inf.	1843-1923 MS	Monr
WOOD, John W.	43rd MS Inf.	1844-1926 MS	Monr
WOOD, John W.	2nd MS Cav.	1840-1909 Laud	Laud
WOOD, Joseph	43rd MS Inf.	1808-1877 Monr	Monr
WOOD, Joseph A.	McNairs MS Cav.	1818-1889	Copi
WOOD, L. H.	11th MS Cav.	1838-1916 Lown	Lown
WOOD, Mark I.	28th MS Cav.	1841-1863 Adam	Adam
WOOD, Morgan E.	9th LA Inf.	1835-1908 LA	Walt
WOOD, Oliver	16th MS Inf.	1828-1908 NC	Jack
WOOD, R. _.	19th MS Inf.	1846-1926	Lafa
WOOD, Samuel Jesse	Yergers MS Cav.	1848-1883	Copi
WOOD, Silas H.	1st MS Cav.	1830-1905 Pont	Pont
WOOD, W. A.	27th MS Inf.	1835-1917 Leak	Harr
WOOD, W. E.	24th MS Cav.	1825-1895 Covi	Covi
WOOD, W. H.	1st MS Reserves	1846-1923 TN	Mont
WOOD, W. Henry _.	8th MS Cav.	1838-1919 Lown	Lown
WOOD, William	7th MS Inf.	1824-1891 MS	Linc
WOOD, William	22nd MS Inf.	1836-1911 MS	Amit
WOOD, William	24th AL Cav.	1842-1912 AL	Wash
WOOD, William W.	44th MS Inf.	1834-1872 Adam	Adam
WOODALL, J. C.	Blythes MS Inf.	1835-1868 Clay	Clay
WOODALL, J. M.	62nd AL Inf.	1838-1893 AL	Kemp

WOODARD, John James	22nd MS Inf.	1837-1916	Lafa	Lafa
WOODCOCK, Andrew J.	3rd MS Inf.	1842-1915	Jack	Jack
WOODCOCK, Charlie N.	3rd MS Inf.	1829-1917	SC	Harr
WOODELL, W. J.	4th MS Inf.	1832-1921	Carr	Carr
WOODHAM, J. _.	15th AL Inf.	1842-1923	AL	Jack
WOODLEY, J. H.	7th AL Cav.	1833-1908	Tish	Tish
WOODLEY, S. W.	4th AL Cav.	1846-1908	Tish	Tish
WOODRUFF, _. T.	4th MS Cav.	1835-1832	Wins	Wins
WOODRUFF, J. G.	10th MS Regt.	1848-1926		Hind
WOODRUFF, James A.	SC Legion	1843-1919	SC	Pano
WOODRUFF, John D.	SC Legion	1846-1920	SC	Pano
WOODRUFF, John H.	26th MS Inf.	1823-1896	Tish	Tish
WOODRUFF, Milton H.	21st MS Inf.	1843-18_9	Wilk	Wilk
WOODRUFF, T. J.	1st & 43rd MS Inf.	1846-___		Monr
WOODRUFF, W. N.	31st MS Inf.	1840-1900	Pano	Tate
WOODS, Clark M.	4th MS Cav.	1843-___		Jeff
WOODS, Daniel C/O.	12th MS Inf.	1842-1921	MS	Copi
WOODS, Henry Hardaman	34th MS Inf.	1844-1914	KY	Mars
WOODS, J. M.	10th TN Inf.	1844-1928	TN	Pren
WOODS, J. M.	28th MS Cav.	1831-1910	Carr	Yalo
WOODS, J. Q.	2nd MS Cav.	1846-1904	Laud	Laud
WOODS, J. T.	Oteys Art.	1845-1916	AL	Harr
WOODS, Jackson D.	11th MS Cav.	1842-1923	Laud	Laud
WOODS, James Thomas	1st MS Lt. Art.	1838-1895	Warr	Yazo
WOODS, Joe	15th MS Inf.	1820-1901	Atta	Atta
WOODS, McDonald C/G.	14th TN Inf.	1843-1874	TN	Yalo
WOODS, _. _.	15th or 16th MS Inf.	1834-1909		Webs
WOODS, _. M.	15th MS Inf.	1834-1898		Webs
WOODS, Peter K.	4th MS Inf.	1833-1877	Carr	Carr
WOODS, R. G.	15th MS Inf.	1845-1915	Atta	Harr
WOODS, R. M.	8th MS Cav.	1844-1927	Yalo	Yalo
WOODS, Robert J.	15th MS Inf.	1843-1902	Atta	Atta
WOODS, Ruff	15th MS Inf.	1833-1898	Atta	Atta
WOODS, Thomas H.	13th MS Inf.	1836-1910	KY	Laud
WOODS, W. L.	12th MS Cav.	1843-___	Holm	Lefl
WOODS, W. _.	3rd MS Cav.	1825-1895	Yalo	Yalo
WOODSON, Green	15th MS Inf.	1835-1911		Okti
WOODSON, Marshal Fredric	3rd VA Art.	1833-1905	VA	Unio
WOODSON, Robert	4th MS Inf.	1825-1907	Okti	Okti
WOODWARD, Benjamin T.	13th TN Inf.	1830-1905	NC	Mars
WOODWARD, Edward H.	22nd MS Inf.	1840-1904	Lafa	Lafa
WOODWARD, I. C.	35th MS Inf.	1834-1900	Wins	Wins
WOODWARD, James H/R.	44th MS Inf.	1844-1907	Pano	Calh
WOODWARD, John	13th MS Inf.	182_-1912	SC	Wins
WOOLDRIDGE, John Henry	2nd MS Cav.	1846-1937	Chic	Chic
WOOLEY, Wiley C.	26th AL Inf.	1835-1911	AL	Alco
WOOLFOLK, John H.	MS Home Guards	1818-1902	KY	Warr
WOOLLARD, George B.	Adams MS Cav.	1825-1876	Tate	Tate
WOOLLARD, Leander Guy	42nd MS Inf.	1834-1874	Tate	Tate

Name	Unit	Dates	State	County
WOOTEN, Andrew J.	4th MS Cav.	1830-1886	MS	Copi
WOOTEN, J. J.	22nd MS Inf.	1842-1862	Lafa	Lafa
WOOTEN, John	5th MS Inf.	1843-1914	MS	Webs
WOOTON, John	Peytons Cav.	183_-1919	Hind	Harr
WOOTEN, Marion	33rd MS Inf.	1824-1908	Leak	Leak
WOOTEN, Marion	33rd MS Inf.	1832-1908	Leak	Leak
WOOTEN, M.	25th AL Inf.	1849-1921	CN	Webs
WOOTEN, R. W.	3rd MS Inf.	1837-1910	Copi	Linc
WOOTEN, T. J.	33rd MS Inf.	1838-1910	Leak	Leak
WOOTEN, William	3rd MS Inf.			Copi
WOOTEN, William S.	22nd MS Inf.	1840-1920		Lafa
WOOTEN, William W.	4th MS Inf.	1836-1886	Carr	Carr
WORD, Charles	14th MS Inf.	1844-1925	Monr	Monr
WORD, J. W.	9th MS Inf.	1833-1913	MS	Lafa
WORK, Charles	14th MS Inf.			Hind
WORK, George A.	Terrills MS Cav.	1838-1892		Hind
WORK, H. _.	2nd NC Inf.	1830-1918	NC	Bent
WORKS, T. F.	12th MS Inf.	1825-1896	MS	Itaw
WORLEY, J. M.	21st MS Inf.	1834-1862	Tall	Tall
WORLEY, M. R.	21st MS Inf.	1832-1907	Tall	Tall
WORRELL, John W.	14th MS Inf.	1841-1901	Lown	Lown
WORRELL, W. O.	14th MS Inf.	1831-1905	Lown	Warr
WORSHAM, B. F. (Dr.)	7th MS Cav.	1823-1897	SC	Tipp
WORSHAM, L. W.	1st VA Art.	1847-1936	VA	Alco
WORSHAM, W. W.	18th GA Cav.	1821-1895	GA	Alco
WORSHAM, William A.	2nd MS Cav.	1816-1906		Tall
WORSHANN, J. G.	4th GA Inf.	1833-1921	GA	Harr
WORTHAN, William Tyler	3rd MS Cav.	1841-1926	Yalo	Yalo
WORTHINGTON, Albert D.	1st MS Cav.	1839-1863	MS	Wash
WORTHINGTON, Wm. Mason	1st MS Cav.	1835-1897	MS	Wash
WORTHY, L. W.	1st MS Cav.	1832-1912	SC	Wins
WORTHY, W. E.	31st MS Inf.	1839-1904	Kemp	Unio
WORTHY, William	6th & 46th MS Inf.	1828-1909	Covi	JEDA
WOULARD, James	36th Inf.	1837-1909	AL	Gree
WRAY, A. W.	54th AL Inf.	1821-1905	AL	Harr
WRAY, Dock	30th MS Inf.	1844-1916	Mont	Mont
WRAY, J. F.	2nd MS Inf.	1832-1893	Pont	Pont
WRAY, J. Keith	1st MS Cav.	1837-1891	Pont	Unio
WREN, Jeremiah H. A.	12th SC Inf.	1844-1909	SC	Tish
WREN, W. P. (Dr.)	10th MS Cav.	1842-1877	Itaw	Lee
WRENN, John A.	33rd MS Inf.	1838-1912	Pano	Tall
WRIGHT, A. B.	7th KY Cav.	1825-1905	KY	Bent
WRIGHT, Benjamin F.	13th MS Inf.	1834-1915	Laud	Laud
WRIGHT, Charles Edwin	28th MS Cav.	1841-1923	Warr	Warr
WRIGHT, Charles O.	Bradfords Scouts	1847-1933	AL	Warr
WRIGHT, Daniel _.	34th MS Inf.	1829-1888	Bent	Bent
WRIGHT, David C.	4th MS Cav.	1833-1897	Pike	Pike
WRIGHT, David L.	7th KY Cav.	1842-1935	KY	Bent
WRIGHT, Ed L.	VA Lt. Art.	1840-1911	VA	Pano
WRIGHT, Frank Allison W.	34th MS Inf.	1847-1887	GA	Mars

186

WRIGHT, George W.	23rd MS Inf.	1830-1899 NC	Tipp
WRIGHT, George W.	2nd MS Inf.	1841-1866 Tipp	Tipp
WRIGHT, H. C.	4th GA Inf.	1839-1900 GA	Lawr
WRIGHT, Harvey	37th MS Inf.	1841-1917 Laud	Laud
WRIGHT, Jacob	18th MS Cav.	1839-1910	Hind
WRIGHT, James B.	40th MS Inf.	1832-1914 Laud	Kemp
WRIGHT, James F.	33rd MS Inf.	1841-1899 MS	Fran
WRIGHT, James H.	10th MS Inf.	1844-1910 Adam	Adam
WRIGHT, James L.	29th MS Inf.	Yalo	Calh
WRIGHT, James R.	10th MS Inf.	1836-1901 Itaw	Itaw
WRIGHT, James W.	46th MS Inf.	1833-1914 Laud	Laud
WRIGHT, J. Brad	18th MS Cav.	1831-1881	DeSo
WRIGHT, John (Dr.)	15th MS Inf.	1833-1911 Pano	Pano
WRIGHT, John A.	26th MS Inf.	1845-1870 MS	Pren
WRIGHT, John B.	18th MS Cav.	1833-1922	Hind
WRIGHT, John R.	24th & 40th MS Inf.	1830-1897 Leak	Leak
WRIGHT, John W.	28th MS Cav.	1837-1915 Gren	Gren
WRIGHT, Josiah	4th MS Inf.	1838-1895	Lafa
WRIGHT, K. E.	24th Cav.		Copi
WRIGHT, L. B.	28th MS Cav.	1835-1903 Gren	Gren
WRIGHT, M. T.	18th MS Cav.	1827-1923 MS	Pano
WRIGHT, O. P.	23rd MS Inf.	1814-1876	Hind
WRIGHT, Patrick Henry	34th MS Inf.	1837-1916 AL	Lafa
WRIGHT, R. F.	26th AL Inf.	1842-1919 AL	Monr
WRIGHT, R. J.(Dr.)	4th MS Cav.	1834-1894 Fran	Fran
WRIGHT, T. _.	2nd KY Inf.	1838-1916 KY	Harr
WRIGHT, Thomas (Dr.)	26th MS Inf.	1826-1872 Tish	Alco
WRIGHT, Thomas A.	7th MS Inf.	1843-1925 MS	Harr
WRIGHT, Thomas Shepherd	Holm Co. Ind. Cav.	1826-1893 VA	Holm
WRIGHT, Tom Walton (Dr)	Featherstones Brigade	1849-1901 Holm	Holm
WRIGHT, W. S.	19th MS Cav.	1845-1861 MS	Calh
WRIGHT, W. W.	28th GA Inf.	1845-1926 AL	Pren
WRIGHT, William	32nd MS Inf.	1832-1907 MS	Tish
WRIGHT, William A.	3rd GA Cav.	1845-1912 GA	Jone
WROTEN, Earl Carrel	26th MS Inf.	1833-1901 TN	Pren
WROTEN, Thomas Loyd	26th MS Inf.	1843-1862 MS	Pren
WROTEN, Wm. Monroe (Dr.)	4th MS Cav.	1847-1927 Pike	Pike
WYATT, Elijah	6th MS Inf.	1821-1901 Rank	Newt
WYATT, Francis A.	28th MS Cav.	1841-1899 Holm	Holm
WYATT, Ira Byrd	9th & 15th MS Inf.	____-1905	Jack
WYATT, T. J.	28th MS Cav.	1849-1923 Holm	Holm
WYATTS, T. C.	8th MS Inf.	1845-1910 Laud	Laud
WYLIE, D. C.	1_th TN Inf.	1836-1913 TN	Harr
WYLIE, G. A.	Perrins MS Cav.	1845-1921 Wins	Wins
WYLIE, W. M.	56th AL Inf.	1842-1921 AL	Itaw
WYMAN, George	28th MS Cav.	1820-1888 Atlantic Ocean	Warr
WYNN, Francis M.	23rd MS Inf.	1842-1923 Pont	Unio

WYNN, R. W.	19th MS Inf.	1825-1887 MS	Bent
WYNN, Robert Edward	29th MS Inf.	1845-1929 Tall	Tall
WYNN, W. C.	20th MS Inf.	1818-1892 Atta	Atta
WYNN, W. L.	15th MS Inf.	1845-1878 Atta	Holm
WYNNE, Solomon L.	32nd MS Inf.	1823-1913 NC	Tate
WYSE, J.W.	Adams MS Cav.	1844-1912 Madi	Atta
YANCE, Jacob	46th MS Inf.	1829-1889 Smit	Scot
YANCY, G. L.	2nd MS Inf.	1845-1922 VA	Tipp
YANCY, John S.	7th MS Cav.	1823-1928 VA	Tipp
YANCY, Robert L.	2nd MS Inf.	1845-1925 VA	Tipp
YANCY, Samuel N.	2nd & 32nd MS Inf.	1846-1928 Itaw	Tipp
YARBROUGH, A. S.	1st MS Inf.	1840-1914 Pano	Pano
YARBROUGH, C. A.	2nd TN Inf.	1840-1862 TN	Lown
YARBROUGH, D. H.	40th AL Inf.	1839-1917 AL	Laud
YARBROUGH, Edward Riley	4th MS Inf.	1844-1899 Carr	Carr
YARBROUGH, George W.	1st MS Inf.	1842-1911 Mars	Mars
YARBROUGH, J. L.	13th MS Inf.	1848-1930 AL	Jone
YARBROUGH, James L.	13th MS Inf.	1830-1864 Wins	Wins
YARBROUGH, Louis	26th MS Inf.	1826-1905 Tish	Tish
YARBROUGH, R. E.	13th MS Inf.	1841-1917 Wins	Wins
YARBROUGH, Richard	1st MS State Troops	1848-1936 Laud	Laud
YARBROUGH, W. M.	16th AL Cav.	1847-___	Newt
YARBROUGH, William Davis	28th MS Cav.	1840-1907	Boli
YARBROUGH, William M.	2nd MS Cav.	1832-1902 MS	Calh
YATES, D. T.	12th Ms, Inf.	1838-1894	Hind
YATES, Daniel	7th MS Inf.	1839-1863 Jone	Jone
YATES, Frank	14th MS Inf.	1845-1925 TN	Pren
YATES, Hardin H.	23rd MS Inf.	1841-1895 Mars	Pren
YATES, Hiram I.	35th MS Inf.	1841-1915 Simp	Simp
YATES, Jerome B.	16th MS Inf.		Hind
YATES, Lawrence Timothy	1st MS Cav.	1844-1884 Noxu	Noxu
YATES, Luke D.	Adams Cav.		Hind
YATES, R. G.	36th MS Inf.	1827-1886 Copi	Hind
YATES, Robert E. V.	41st MS Inf.	1836-1876 SC	Noxu
YATES, Samuel	3rd MS Cav.	1815-1892	Covi
YATES, William M.	2nd MS Cav.	1831-1871 Newt	Newt
YAWN, C. J.	46th MS Inf.	1844-1908	Jone
YAWN, G. B.	4th MS Cav.	1824-1903 Copi	Covi
YAWN, J. Richard	27th MS Inf.	1843-1913 Covi	Covi
YEAGER, Daniel Wayne	31st MS Inf.	1835-1910 MS	Covi
YEAGER, John	4th MS Inf.	1841-1902 Atta	Holm
YEAGER, R. M.	1st MS Lt. Art.	1832-1890 Carr	Carr
YEAGER, S. Barton	3rd LA Cav.	1834-1910 TN	Adam
YEAGER, W. C.	3rd LA Cav.	1831-1899 TN	Adam
YEAGLEY, David	39th MS Inf.	1844-1912	Hind
YEAEGER, L. P.	28th MS Cav.	1847-1928	Lefl
YEATES, Edward Devilon	11th MS Cav.	1838-1897	Okti
YEATES, Jesse Augustus	6th MS Cav.	1830-1897	Okti
YEATES, John Alexander	6th MS Cav.	1847-1921	Okti

YEATES, Joseph Sr.	30th AL Inf.	1815-1893 NC	Okti
YEATES, Joseph J. Jr.	30th AL Inf.	1838-1905	Okti
YEATMAN, J. W.	11th AL Inf.	1835-1902 AL	Okti
YELVERTON, E. H.	27th MS Inf.	1833-1912 MS	Harr
YELVINGTON, Isaac S.	4th MS Inf.	1846-1927 Carr	Mont
YERGAIN, John W.	Poagues Art.	1831-1894 Madi	Madi
YELVINGTON, J. _	4th MS Inf.	1806-1886 SC	Mont
YERGER, James R.	Yergers Regt.	1840-1891	Hind
YERGER, L. P.	28th MS Cav.	1846-1928 Wash	Lefl
YERGER, W. A.	28th MS Cav.	1843-1900	Boli
YERGER, William	Adams Cav.	1816-1872 TN	Hind
YERGER, William	Armisteads Cav.	1842-1914 Hind	Wash
YERGER, William Gwin	28th MS Cav.	1840-1899 Warr	Wash
YERGER, William Swan	Adams Cav.	1833-1868	Hind
YEWELL, Norman M.	30th MS Inf.	183_-1925 Carr	Carr
YORK, J. A.	16th MS Cav.	1839-1895 Okti	Okti
YORK, J. R.	1st AL Cav.	1838-1911	Lafa
YORK, John B.	3rd NC Inf.	1826-1873 NC	Carr
YORK, Zeb	14th LA Inf.	1819-1900 ME	Adam
YOSTE, George W.	1st MS Lt. Art.	1842-1928 Warr	Warr
YOSTE, Henry	21st MS Inf.	1839-1905 Warr	Warr
YOUNG, A. A.	5th MS Cav.	1850-1925 MS	Pano
YOUNG, A. F.	28th MS Cav.	1836-1901 NC	Leak
YOUNG, A. F.	5th MS Cav.	1845-1901 Pano	Pano
YOUNG, Abraham	28th MS Cav.	1836-1905 Warr	Alco
YOUNG, B. _.	19th MS Inf.	1843-1919 Lee	Unio
YOUNG, Benjamin Franklin	3rd MS Inf.	1823-1912 Jack	Alco
YOUNG, D. S.	13th MS Inf.	1843-1929 MS	Leak
YOUNG, David	9th MS Inf.	1832-1905 MS	Gree
YOUNG, E. D.	1st MS Cav.	1829-1919 Pano	Pano
YOUNG, G. W.	3rd MS Inf.	1845-1929 Scot	Pear
YOUNG, George C.	29th MS Inf.	1834-1882 MS	Tall
YOUNG, George W.	3rd MS Inf.	1840-19_3 MS	Geor
YOUNG, Henry C.	17th MS Inf.	1847-1905	Webs
YOUNG, J. A.	17th & 31st MS Inf.	1839-1891 MS	Chic
YOUNG, J. C.	1st MS Lt. Art.	1821-1891 Yazo	Yazo
YOUNG, J. E.	17th MS Inf.	1833-1923 MS	Harr
YOUNG, J. E.	4th MS Inf.	1813-1895 VA	Holm
YOUNG, J. G.	Gamblins Cav.	1830-1916 Kemp	Kemp
YOUNG, J. M.	1st MS Lt. Art.	1835-1917 Choc	Mont
YOUNG, J. S.	1st MS Lt. Art.	____-1863	Mont
YOUNG, J. W.	1st MS Cav.	1846-1933 Carr	Carr
YOUNG, J. W.	1st MS Lt. Art.	1839-1910 Carr	Atta
YOUNG, James M.	40th MS Inf.	1843-1915 Leak	Leak
YOUNG, Jimmie	12th MS Cav.	1845-1918	Lee
YOUNG, John (Dr.)	15th MS Inf.	1810-1896 Yalo	Yalo
YOUNG, John	14th MS Inf.	1840-1928 SC	Pren
YOUNG, John	2nd MS Cav.	1842-1863 Choc	Mont
YOUNG, John Alford	39th MS Inf.	1845-1914 Newt	Leak
YOUNG, John Alfred	39th MS Inf.	Newt	Atta
YOUNG, John B.	1st MS Inf.	1833-1895	Hind

YOUNG, John Ellis	17th MS Inf.	1840-1916 MS	Alco
YOUNG, John H.	43rd MS Inf.	1842-1928 GA	Wins
YOUNG, John N.	24th MS Inf.	1840-1897 SC	Monr
YOUNG, John S.	12th MS Cav.	1839-19_7 Monr	Lee
YOUNG, John W.	13th MS Inf.	1833-1880	Laud
YOUNG, P. J.	4th MS Cav.	1836-1926	Copi
YOUNG, Robert	12th MS Cav.	1841-1913 Lee	Lee
YOUNG, S. R. (Rev.)	Army of VA	1846-1936 NC	Hind
YOUNG, Sam L.	16th MS Inf.	1837-1929	Copi
YOUNG, T. W.	44th MS Inf.	1838-1911 Calh	Calh
YOUNG, Tandy Key	18th MS Cav.	1846-1933 Pren	Alco
YOUNG, Thomas	41st MS Inf.	1843-1913 AL	Monr
YOUNG, Thomas B.	43rd MS Inf.	1844-1916 AL	Itaw
YOUNG, Thomas H.	7th AL Cav.	1837-1907 AL	Tish
YOUNG, Thomas H.	11th MS Cav.	1819-18_6 Noxu	Noxu
YOUNG, W. H.	2nd MS Cav.	1826-1900 Laud	Kemp
YOUNG, W. L.	11th MS Inf.	1842-1911 Holm	Holm
YOUNG, W. T.	40th MS Inf.	1841-1900 SC	Leak
YOUNG, W. W.	39th MS Inf.	1847-1912 Rank	Pike
YOUNG, Wade Ross	Jeff Davis Legion	1841-1911 Adam	Adam
YOUNG, William	39th MS Inf.	1833-1903 NC	Newt
YOUNG, William H.	1st Cav.	1849-1928 Covi	Covi
YOUNG, Wm. Humphreys	5th MS Cav.	1821-1865 Lefl	Lefl
YOUNG, William T.	31st MS Inf.	1837-___ Clay	Clay
YOUNG, William Walter	3rd MS Art.	1818-1884 Carr	Carr
YOUNGBLOOD, A. W.	31st MS Inf.	1842-1906 Pont	Quit
YOUNGBLOOD, B. F.	4th MS Cav.	1845-1927 Copi	Copi
YOUNGBLOOD, J. A.	46th MS Inf.	1825-1904 MS	Scot
YOUNGBLOOD, J. A.	46th MS Inf.	1841-1914	Scot
YOUNGBLOOD, J. M.	4th MS Inf.	1837-1907 Choc	Choc
YOUNGBLOOD, J. R.	Powers MS Cav.	1821-1906	Copi
YOUNGBLOOD, T. F.	11th MS Cav.	1846-1932 Tall Tate	
YOUNGBLOOD, T. J.	Powers Cav.	1847-1929 Copi	Harr
YOUNGBLOOD, William A.	31st MS Inf.	1845-1916 Wash	
YOUNGBLOOD, William T.	46th MS Inf.	1823-1912 Scot	Scot
YOW, George	7th AL Cav.	1828-1897 AL	Tish
ZACHARY, Robert R.	MS Conscripts	____-1909	Linc
ZACHARY, Theolphis	1st MS Inf.	1826-1928 Itaw	Pont
ZACHARY, Thomas P.	41st MS Inf.	1844-1928 Laud	Laud
ZIMMERMAN, Joseph	36th MS Inf.	1833-1862 FR	Copi
ZUMBRO, John A.	7th MS Inf.	1841-1897 Fran	Fran